INTERNATIONAL PERSPECTIVES ON ENTREPRENEURSHIP RESEARCH

Advanced Series in Management   Volume 18

Series Editors: A. BENSOUSSAN   and   P. A. NAERT

University of Paris-Dauphine
and INRIA
Paris, France

INSEAD
Fontainebleau, France

Previous Volumes in the series:

VOLUME 3:	*Mathematical Theory of Production Planning* A. Bensoussan, M. Crouhy and J.-M. Proth
VOLUME 4:	*Intra-Industry Trade: Empirical and Methodological Aspects* P. K. M. Tharakan (ed.)
VOLUME 5:	*EEC Accounting Harmonisation: Implementation and Impact of the Fourth Directive* S. J. Gray and A. G. Coenenberg (eds.)
VOLUME 6:	*Replacement Costs for Managerial Purposes* J. Klaassen and P. Verburg (eds.)
VOLUME 7:	*Designing Efficient Organizations: Modelling and Experimentation* R. M. Burton and B. Obel
VOLUME 8:	*Data Analysis in Real Life Environment: Ins and Outs of Solving Problems* J.-F. Marcotorchino, J.-M. Proth and J. Janssen (eds.)
VOLUME 9:	*New Challenges for Management Research* A. H. G. Rinnooy Kan (ed.)
VOLUME 10:	*Strategic vs. Evolutionary Management: A U.S.-Japan Comparison of Strategy and Organization* T. Kagono, I. Nonaka, K. Sakakibara and A. Okumura
VOLUME 11:	*Product Standardization and Competitive Strategy* H. Landis Gabel (ed.)
VOLUME 12:	*Applied Stochastic Models and Control in Management* C. S. Tapiero
VOLUME 13:	*Managing International Manufacturing* K. Ferdows (ed.)
VOLUME 14:	*Policy Implications of Antidumping Measures* P. K. M. Tharakan (ed.)
VOLUME 15:	*Corporate and Industry Strategies for Europe* L.-G. Mattsson and B. Stymne (eds.)
VOLUME 16:	*Microeconomic Contributions to Strategic Management* J. Thépot and R.-A. Thiétart (eds.)
VOLUME 17:	*The Prescription Drug Market* C. Huttin and N. Bosanquet (eds.)

NORTH-HOLLAND
AMSTERDAM · LONDON · NEW YORK · TOKYO

INTERNATIONAL PERSPECTIVES ON ENTREPRENEURSHIP RESEARCH

Proceedings of the First Annual Global Conference on Entrepreneurship Research
London, UK, 18–20 February 1991

Edited by

Sue BIRLEY
The Management School
Imperial College, London, UK

Ian C. MACMILLAN
The Wharton School
University of Pennsylvania
Philadelphia, PA, USA

Technical Editor
Sarasa SUBRAMONY
The Wharton School
University of Pennsylvania
Philadelphia, PA, USA

Sponsored by
Ernst and Young (UK)
and

Organised by
The Management School
Imperial College, London, UK

and
The Wharton School
University of Pennsylvania
Philadelphia, PA, USA

1992
NORTH-HOLLAND
AMSTERDAM · LONDON · NEW YORK · TOKYO

ELSEVIER SCIENCE PUBLISHERS B.V.
Sara Burgerhartstraat 25
P.O. Box 211, 1000 AE Amsterdam, The Netherlands

ISBN: 0-444-89526-4

© 1992 Elsevier Science Publishers B.V. All rights reserved.

No part of this publication may be reproduced, stored in a retrieval system or transmitted in any form or by any means, electronic, mechanical, photocopying, recording or otherwise, without the prior written permission of the publisher, Elsevier Science Publishers B.V., Copyright & Permissions Department, P.O. Box 521, 1000 AM Amsterdam, The Netherlands.

Special regulations for readers in the U.S.A. - This publication has been registered with the Copyright Clearance Center Inc. (CCC), Salem, Massachusetts. Information can be obtained from the CCC about conditions under which photocopies of parts of this publication may be made in the U.S.A., should be referred to the copyright owner, Elsevier Science Publishers B.V., unless otherwise specified.

No responsibility is assumed by the publisher for any injury and/or damage to persons or property as a matter of products liability, negligence or otherwise, or from any use or operation of any methods, products, instructions or ideas contained in the material herein.

This book is printed on acid-free paper.

Printed in The Netherlands

INTRODUCTION

This book is a compilation of papers and critiques which were presented at the first annual Global Conference on Entrepreneurship Research held at Imperial College, London, February 1991.

The objective of this conference and of this book is to begin the process of building a global network of young scholars steeped in, and appreciative of, other countries' approaches to research in the area of entrepreneurship. The origins of the conference stemmed from the editors increasing disquiet with the intolerance by one particular research style towards alternative ways of doing research. We therefore decided that what was needed was the creation of a forum in which many styles of research from many different cultures could be presented and discussed in a collegial environment.

The concept which emerged from our discussions was to identify key researchers from a wide variety of countries: people recognized for a particular approach to research or a particular expertise, and invite them to come to a conference where their research would be examined by a wide variety of scholars. We therefore approached a number of senior professors and invited them to submit a paper in "final draft form"-- that is to say a paper which had been developed to the stage that it was about ready to go out for peer review. This paper was required to be one which they had prepared with a junior professor and or doctoral students/researchers. The key idea here was that these senior professors would bring with them a junior partner who would become a core member of the global network of young scholars we were starting to build. The admission ticket to this conference was a completed paper which had to arrive weeks ahead of the conference date. Anyone who failed to satisfy this criteria would be disqualified from attending.

The reason for this admission price was that each paper was distributed to a researcher from another university who was asked to prepare a written critique. The expectation was that the junior professor partner of the team would be allocated this task with the emphasis only on constructive criticism, and upon ways to improve the paper. Timing was tight. Written critiques were due on the day before the conference in order that we could give the critique to the presenters in enough time for them to prepare a rebuttal. Failure to comply would also result in disqualification from the program. In the event, only one colleague who originally accepted our challenge was disqualified.

During the conference each paper was presented for twenty minutes, followed by the critique of twenty minutes from a junior partner from another university, followed by a ten minute rebuttal of the critique, after which the floor was open to an in depth forty-minute discussion by the entire assembled group. This book presents the papers and the critiques.

We wrestled with the idea of publishing the original paper, the critique, and the revised paper and came to the conclusion that this would be too voluminous. In the interest of saving space, we elected to publish the revised paper accompanied by the critique which preceded it. Therefore, every paper is preceded by the relevant critique and the reader is asked to bear with us in those cases where the authors, in preparing their final revision, have substantively addressed the suggestions which were made in the critique. To our regret, in two instances, the critiques did not reach the editors in time to meet the publication deadline and could not be included.

The book falls naturally into four parts. Starting at a very high level of generality, it becomes increasingly focused.

The first part comprises a group of papers which we have headed: *Frameworks for Comprehending Entrepreneurship*. This set of papers presents a number of novel and insightful ways of looking at the phenomenon of entrepreneurship from a perspective that is substantively different from the more traditional U.S. view. The papers are very broad in scope and concept, and show very clearly that there are very different ways of viewing the phenomenon.

Second are a subset of papers which we have headed: *Cultural Perspectives on Entrepreneurship*. This set of papers, also distinctively conceptual and theoretical, gives us some insights and glimpses into the profound differences in culture of the participants and the way that the various representatives' social, political, and religious platforms influence the way they see the evolution of entrepreneurship in their particular countries.

The third subset of papers are studies which address the entrepreneurial environment and the way in which this environment shapes entrepreneurial endeavor. These studies are generally empirical in nature, ranging from multi-case analyses through to detailed statistical analyses of survey data.

The final set we have headed: *Entrepreneurial Strategy and Behavior*. This group looks at different countries' perspectives on how entrepreneurs go about forging and managing their enterprise.

This is the first book in a series we expect to see published after each global conference which will be held annually.

Introduction

We have learned much from this first effort and see many ways of improving what has been done here, but none the less feel that what we learned and the insights which we have gained from assembling, however briefly, this global college is worth sharing with others who were not able to join us.

Sue Birley
Ian C. MacMillan
Editors

ACKNOWLEDGEMENTS

SPONSORS

We are indebted to Ernst and Young (UK) who had both the foresight and generosity to sponsor the conference.

EDITING AND SUPPORT

We are grateful to Imperial College, London, and the Snider Entrepreneurial Center of the Wharton School of the University of Pennsylvania, for their support in this undertaking. We wish to thank Patricia Adams for helping with the production of the manuscript. Thanks also to Oliver Boulind, Aaron Dolgoff, and Elisa Randall for their varied and valuable input into the project.

CONTENTS

	INTRODUCTION	V
	ACKNOWLEDGEMENTS	VIII
	CONTRIBUTORS	XII
I	FRAMEWORKS FOR UNDERSTANDING ENTREPRENEURSHIP	

Critique
Igor Touline   3
Schumpeterian Learning Versus Neoclassical Learning:
Development Options for Post Communist Societies
Max H. Boisot   6

Critique
Daniel F. Muzyka   32
Entrepreneurship in an Economy in Transition:
Perspectives of the Situation in the Ex GDR
Thomas Köllermeier   37

Critique
Svenn Jenssen and Lars Kolvereid   58
The Nature of Entrepreneurial Decision-Making: Inside the Black Box
Daniel F. Muzyka   61

A Vision-Driven Entrepreneurial Study
Akihiro Okumura   76

II	CULTURAL PERSPECTIVES ON ENTREPRENEURSHIP	

Critique
Monserrat Olle   87
Entrepreneurship Development Among Malays in Singapore:
A Community Development Approach
Chong Li Choy and Abdul Jalil Ismail   89

Critique
Timothy M. Stearns 104
Soviet State Firms Facing Transition: Towards a New
Entrepreneurial System
Paola Dubini 106

Critique
Juan Roure 116
The Entrepreneurs' Reasons Leading to Start-Up as
Determinants of Survival and Failure Among Norwegian
New Ventures
Svenn Jenssen and Lars Kolvereid 120

Entrepreneurship and Privatization in the Soviet Union
Andrei Sterlin and Igor Touline 134

III ENVIRONMENT AND ENTREPRENEURSHIP

Critique
Luc Vallée 149
New Venture Strategies: Generic or Industry Specific
Nancy M. Carter, Timothy M. Stearns, Paul D. Reynolds
and Brenda A. Miller 151

Critique
Ian C. MacMillan and Rita Gunther McGrath 169
A Venture Capital Price Index
Robert H. Keeley and Lassaad A. Turki 173

Critique
Tone Ostgaard 199
Interplay Among Strategy, Environment, Competitive Behavior
and Performance on Entering Industrial Markets
M.H. Tsai, Ian C. MacMillan and Rita Gunther McGrath 203

IV ENTREPRENEURIAL STRATEGY AND BEHAVIOR

Critique
Abdul Jalil Ismail and Chong Li Choy 230

Business Start-Ups: The HRM Imperative *Howard E. Aldrich and Mary Ann von Glinow*	233
Critique *Yves-Frédéric Livian and Stéphane Marion*	254
Planning Meeting Intensity in Small Firms *Sue Birley and Paul Westhead*	256
Critique *Nancy M. Carter*	290
From Evaluation of Business Ventures to Prognosis of Success: Results of a Longitudinal Study of 11 French Cases *Yves-Frédéric Livian and Stéphane Marion*	292
Critique *Paola Dubini*	317
New Business Strategies: An Exploratory Examination *John W. Mullins, Richard N. Cardozo, Paul D. Reynolds and Brenda Miller*	320
Critique *Robert H. Keeley and Lassaad A. Turki*	336
The Second Time Around: The Outcomes, Assets and Liabilities of Prior Start-Up Experience *Jennifer A. Starr and William D. Bygrave*	340
Critique *John W. Mullins and Richard N. Cardozo*	364
Critique *Paul D. Reynolds*	366
Business Creations by Quebec's Engineers: Stability of Entry from 1970 to 1987 *Jean-Marie Toulouse and Luc Vallée*	368

CONTRIBUTORS

Howard E. Aldrich, Professor
Department of Sociology
University of North Carolina
U.S.A.

Sue Birley, Professor
The Management School
Imperial College, London, U.K.

Max H. Boisot, Professor
E.S.A.D.E., Barcelona, Spain

William D. Bygrave, Professor
Babson College, Massachusetts, U.S.A.

Richard N. Cardozo, Professor
Curtis L. Carlson School of Management
University of Minnesota, U.S.A.

Nancy M. Carter
Marquette University, Wisconsin, U.S.A.

Chong Li Choy, Professor
Department of Business Policy
National University of Singapore

Paola Dubini
Luigi Bocconi University
Milan, Italy

Mary Ann von Glinow
School of Business Administration
University of Southern California, U.S.A.

Abdul Jalil bin Ismail
Department of Business Policy
National University of Singapore

Svenn Jenssen
Norland College, Bodo, Norway

Robert H. Keeley, Professor
Industrial Engineering Management
Stanford University, California, U.S.A.

Thomas Köllermeier
IESE, Barcelona, Spain

Lars Kolvereid
Norland College, Bodo, Norway

Yves-Frédéric Livian, Dr.
Groupe ESC, Lyon, France

Ian C. MacMillan, Professor
The Wharton School
University of Pennsylvannia, U.S.A.

Stéphane Marion
Groupe ESC Lyon, France

Rita Gunther McGrath
Research Fellow
The Wharton School
University of Pennsylvannia, U.S.A.

Brenda Miller
Curtis L. Carlson School of Management
University of Minnesota, U.S.A.

John W. Mullins
Curtis L. Carlson School of Management
University of Minnesota, U.S.A.

Daniel F. Muzyka, Professor
INSEAD, France

Akihiro Okumura, Professor
Keio University, Yokohama, Japan

Monserrat Olle
ESADE, Barcelona, Spain

Tone Ostgaard
The Management School
Imperial College, London, U.K.

Paul D. Reynolds, Professor
Marquette University, Wisconsin, U.S.A.

Juan Roure, Professor
IESE, Barcelona, Spain

Jennifer A. Starr
Babson College, Massachusetts, U.S.A.

Andrei Sterlin
Institute of World Economy, Moscow, USSR

Timothy M. Stearns
Marquette University, Wisconsin, U.S.A.

Igor Touline
Institute of World Economy, Moscow, USSR

Jean-Marie Toulouse, Professor
École des Hautes Études Commerciales
Montreal, Canada

M.H. Tsai
National Central University, Taiwan

Lassaad A. Turki
Industrial Engineering Management
Stanford University, California, U.S.A.

Luc Vallée
École des Hautes Études Commerciales
Montreal, Canada

Paul Westhead
The Management School
Imperial College, London, U.K.

FRAMEWORKS FOR UNDERSTANDING ENTREPRENEURSHIP

Schumpeterian Learning versus Neoclassical Learning: Development Options for Post Communist Societies

Critique
by
Igor Touline, *IMEMO*

1. The paper "Schumpeterian learning versus Neoclassical Learning: Development Options for Post Communist Societies" is a very interesting, well-grounded attempt to apply methods of dynamic analysis to processes of social development in post communist countries. It successfully combines two conceptual instruments of such an analysis: theories of economic development of a market society, and the basic ideas of theories of social systems and social conduct (behavior).

2. In the sphere of economic analysis the author proceeds from the following: a) the neoclassical model of economic development is inadequate for the present level of problems of transition from communism (totalitarianism) to capitalism (market society); b) the Schumpeterian model of the capitalist process provides a more convincing alternative for countries that have embarked on reforms; c) entrepreneurship as a process of "creative destruction" is the motive force of economic development of the society.

3. The process of entrepreneurship in the framework of the culture-space (C-space) becomes the motor" of a continuous social learning cycle of the society and activates its institutional structures, necessary for maintaining the cycle. The author adheres to the tradition stemming from Hayek, that goes beyond interpreting the role destination of social institutions by their functional characteristics. It is based on the interpretation of social institutions (organizations) as a certain mechanism (mean) of generating information, diffusing it, absorbing and reinterpreting it. From this point of view the attempt (in Weber's style) to classify ideal types of social organizations seems very interesting.

4. The most widely-known attempt to move in this direction, outlined and substantiated to a great extent by Hayek, was made by O. Williamson in his opposition of the market to hierarchy; his strict dichotomy was supplemented by W.Ouchi, who defined a special clan form of organization in the Japanese social system. Max Boisot introduces a new category -- fiefs, which along with bureaucracies (hierarchies), markets and clans represents the most important institutions in the social learning cycle. As a result we have enriched our understanding of social organizations that influence the social learning cycle.

5. In the author's model of the social learning cycle, real societies and the processes of transition occurring in them go beyond the framework of ideal types of socio-economic models. In Boisot's conception the market is such a metasystem or framework, where different cultural traditions, different types of social organizations coexist and cooperate, their specific advantages and merits allowing them to find their place in the general social learning cycle. Such an approach gives the opportunity to combine the SLC instrument with the specific features of each social order, while modeling processes of their modernization or other types of transition. This opportunity is clearly demonstrated in the section dealing with Chinese reforms.

6. In Boisot's conception the transfer from individual learning to social (group) learning and the further diffusion of codified information to the market level leaves open the question of the mechanism of such a transfer and diffusion. Market price information is a codified and completely diffuse information, which, according to Hayek, must be generated in the market as a result of people's interaction. According to Boisot, bureaucracy deals only with codified information, the diffusion of which is limited and is under central control. In this case, the problem of the type of information and impulses of its movement from bureaucratic institutions towards the market remains in the shadow. Most probably, the author lays emphasis on scientific and technological knowledge, which find their way into market structures already codified. In this case, hierarchies providing economy of information costs (according to H. Demsetz) may codify information, coming in the course of individual learning and promote its diffusion. In the course of the SLC, a counter-flow of information (information on prices) from market institutions should occur.

7. The experience of China and of the Soviet Union itself show that when the central power in a totalitarian society delegates authority to local organs of power, anarchy, feudalism, and natural exchange emerge. The society begins moving, not in the direction of the market, but in the direction of institutional relations of a feudal order. In our opinion, this is linked, in the first place, with the fact that authorities on all levels continue to consider organizations and not individuals as the main characters (actors) in the society. The latter are not granted legal and economic freedom to engage in entrepreneurial activity. Thus, conditions for realizing the entrepreneurial phase, i.e. acquiring knowledge on the individual level in the social learning cycle are complicated. At the same time, bureaucratic institutions, without changing the general rules of a social system's functioning, actually impede, both the codification of individual information (in cases, where individual independent learning nevertheless occurs) and its diffusion to the social level.

Besides, the quasi-market in these countries cannot provide bureaucratic structures with realistic information on prices which would force the hierarchy to stimulate codification and diffusion of objective individual information. As a result, the social learning cycle operates with a very low efficiency.

8. While modeling processes of transition from communism to a market society in such a country as the Soviet Union, it is important to take into account a number

of factors which significantly influence the quality and effectiveness of the social learning cycles.

One should take into account distortions in the mentality and learning capacities of vast masses of the population brought about by many years of imposing monotonous and false knowledge. Under conditions when institutional memory is practically completely extinguished, mere pluralism of social institutions, including market ones, will hardly help. In order to launch an effective social learning cycle an outsystem impulse is necessary. We consider that the diffusion and absorption stages of the existing social learning cycle should be accompanied by a mass promarket enlightenment campaign based on the information and knowledge accumulated by well-developed market societies. This campaign should be aimed at teaching people to structure and codify various kinds of information logically and naturally. It should direct their intuitive search and choice towards creative private interest.

9. The existing social institutions, including bureaucratic ones, should be enlivened by new (for our society, but common to these institutions in a market order) knowledge. This process, naturally, is very painful and laborious. The inertia of old knowledge will be supported to a great extent by bureaucratic structures in their attempt, if not to maintain the status-quo of the totalitarian socio-economic order, then at least to reduce the process of modernization to a limited linear transition from one state of equilibrium to another -- in strict conformity with the neoclassical paradigm. Therefore, any information will be structured by the Soviet semi-feudal bureaucratic system in conformity with old ideas and diffused on the markets.

It is therefore exceptionally important that in the process of initiating learning, the transformation of existing bureaucratic institutions according to Weber's ideal "rational-legal" principles, should go side by side with the creation of relevant institutional structures, which make possible not only creative reinterpretation (canning) and diffusion but problem solving and information and knowledge structuring (coding) as well, beyond the framework of bureaucratic institutions.

10. Thus, it is necessary to begin with the entrepreneurial phase of the social learning cycle. Only its active triggering can provoke accelerated movement in the cycle, changing learning paradigms and clearing the space for market institutions. This is true for European countries as well. Methods of initiating and points of influence may vary depending on the power of the market's institutional memory of the population and the extent of rationality of national bureaucratic institutions.

Nevertheless one factor is common for countries transferring to a market order from totalitarianism and it is clearly emphasized by the author of he paper: such a transition is impossible on the basis of "straight-forward" social learning and one type of social institution alone. Economic development depends on constantly renewing the social learning cycle with a sound "creatively destructive" entrepreneurial phase for a motive force.

SCHUMPETERIAN LEARNING VERSUS NEOCLASSICAL LEARNING: DEVELOPMENT OPTIONS FOR POST COMMUNIST SOCIETIES

MAX H. BOISOT, *E.S.A.D.E.*

ABSTRACT

The transition from a centrally planned to a market economy tends to be described as a process of decentralization of decision-making within the neoclassical economic paradigm. Drawing on the experience of the Chinese economic reforms and using the theoretical apparatus of the Culture-Space framework (Boisot 1986), the paper argues that the neoclassical paradigm makes no allowance for "Schumpeterian Learning" and that it is this kind of learning that will be most required by the East European post communist economies as they seek to make up for lost time.

INTRODUCTION

The transition from communism to capitalism in Eastern Europe has sometimes been framed as a move from a hierarchical to a market order. Such a formulation is not new: the leadership in the People's Republic of China from 1979 until 1989 used a similar metaphor to characterize its own programme (Tidrick and Chen, 1987; Perkins, 1988). Of course, there is a difference between then and now. In the case of Eastern Europe the move is perceived as a transformation in which one order is replaced by another; in the PRC the process was thought of more in evolutionary terms, with institutional options available along a continuum believed to exist between hierarchy and markets. (Williamson, 1985; Francis et al.1983).

In spite of the well-established differences in institutional culture between a bureaucratic and a market order that would have to be overcome, the move from the former to the latter, whether incremental or sudden, is justified largely on grounds of efficiency. If Marxist-Leninism has failed in Eastern Europe, it is first and foremost because it has not delivered the goods it had originally promised. Capitalism's superiority is not claimed -- except by a few -- to be of a moral kind but is seen to reside in its ability to allocate scarce social resources more efficiently. The debate that has been simmering quietly since the 1930's on the economic possibilities of socialism (Lange and Taylor, 1948; Lerner 1934; Barone, 1935) has thus been brought to a close by bureaucratic failure on a massive scale, and the continued search for a middle way by a conservative and increasingly beleaguered Chinese leadership now appears doomed to failure.

Socialist thinkers have not been the only ones to locate their institutional choices along a continuum registering varying degrees of decentralization between a bureaucratic and a market order. Libertarians and New Institutionalists both present "the economic problem of society" in much the same terms (Hayek 1945; Williamson 1975). The reform process in the PRC, however, began to run out of steam when it was discovered, not only that intermediate positions along the continuum can be pretty unstable, but also that they give rise to forms of behaviour such as bounded rationality and strategic behaviour opportunism that cannot adequately be conceptualized solely with reference to a decentralization dimension. A copious literature now exists in economics that explores such behaviour patterns, but it remains fragmentary and serves more to qualify the dominant neoclassical paradigm than to seriously challenge it (Putterman,1986; Leibenstein, 1987). The message to those seeking to escape Marxist-Leninist bureaucracies thus still seems to be that the road to efficient markets is full of pitfalls and that it is best not to stop until one has reached the final destination. Only total decentralization, taken here as the freeing up of prices, will effectively achieve post communism's reform objectives.

Indoctrinated by free market messages such as these, would-be reformers in China and Eastern Europe could be forgiven for thinking that a neoclassical market order and a capitalist order are pretty much equivalent and that the main challenge before them therefore is to determine the speed at which they will travel along the continuum from bureaucracies to markets.

I shall argue in this paper that the neoclassical model seriously misrepresents the nature of the challenge and the policy options that confront reformers, that a Schumpeterian model of the capitalist process, with its emphasis on the entrepreneur as an agent of creative destruction, offers an alternative and more convincing interpretation of the issues they face, and that a failure to adopt such a model or some suitably adapted variant thereof will work against the profound cultural and value changes necessary for successful reform.

I proceed as follows:

In the next section, I develop a conceptual representation of the entrepreneurial process drawing on the framework of the Culture Space (C-Space) described in Boisot (1986). In section 3, I outline and discuss the Chinese enterprise reforms embarked upon after October 1984. Since I have described these in more detail elsewhere (Boisot 1987, Boisot and Child 1988), I will confine myself to highlighting those features of the reforms relevant to our analysis. In section 4, I interpret the reform process using the conceptual framework presented. Section 5 then assesses the implications of our analysis for the economic reform process now underway in Eastern Europe. A conclusion follows.

THE C-SPACE

The C-Space builds on the proposition that the structuring and sharing of information is related, and that the more codified knowledge becomes the more easily it diffuses within a target population. The converse of the proposition should also be noted, namely, that knowledge that cannot be structured, put into words, set down on paper, etc., cannot be easily shared other than in face to face situations, and even then, often only over long periods of time. Thus, in Figure 1, while the top right-hand corner of the space is populated by stockbrokers engaged in screen-based trading sharing well-codified prices instantaneously on a global basis, the lower left-hand corner is populated by Zen Buddhists, living in an intimate relationship with small groups of trusting and loyal disciples, each trying to figure out, by means of direct observation, extending sometimes over years, what his master's message might possibly be.

The codification of one's knowledge, as Polanyi well understood, is purchased at a price (Polanyi,1958): the process of cognitive structuring is equivalent to an act of selection in which much uncodified knowledge gets left behind, inhabiting the inner recesses of one's mind, and placed increasingly beyond the reach of unaided memory. The trick, then, is to shed experiential data without at the same time losing useful information. Only when this can be achieved does codification become knowledge preservation. For this reason, therefore, codification has an irreducibly hypothetical character (Gregory,1981); it is subject to testing, and in many circumstances must also be considered a risky business (Popper, 1959).

Figure 1 presents a static picture of knowledge creation. The C-Space however can also be used more dynamically to analyze the way new knowledge is acquired and internalized by a given population -- be it a firm, a village or city, an industry, or a nation state or, put another way, it can used to analyse how social learning occurs. Boisot (1986) hypothesizes that social learning is cyclical and can be schematized as a four-step process in the C-Space (Figure 2).

Step 1: Scanning. Weak signals (Ansoff, 1976) are extracted from uncodified data generally available to a large population, shown on the right-hand section of the figure. These signals are "impacted", as seen on the left-hand side of the figure, in a few minds that interpret them -- often idiosyncratically -- as expressing threats or opportunities in their environment. Such insights tend to escape the larger population even though it is also in possession of the requisite data.

Step 2: Problem Solving. Where the threats or opportunities registered on the left are experienced as sufficiently pressing, they trigger a problem-solving activity in which vague intuitions and perceptions are given structure, uncertainty is reduced, and choices are made. As suggested above, this process of codification is a risky business since the weak signals might have been misinterpreted or structured in distorted ways, i.e. a false hypothesis has been established.

Step 3: Diffusion.   As new knowledge emerges from efforts at codification, it becomes diffusible, and the more it has been codified, the greater the reduction in uncertainty concerning its use and the greater its appeal to potential users of such

codified

STOCKBROKERS

uncodified

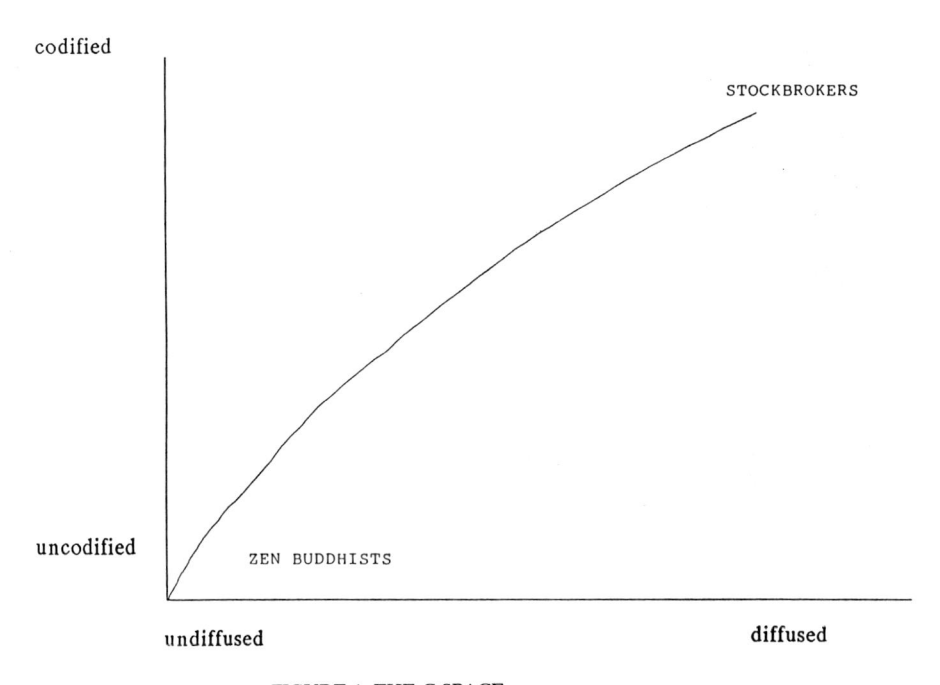

ZEN BUDDHISTS

undiffused   diffused

FIGURE 1: THE C-SPACE

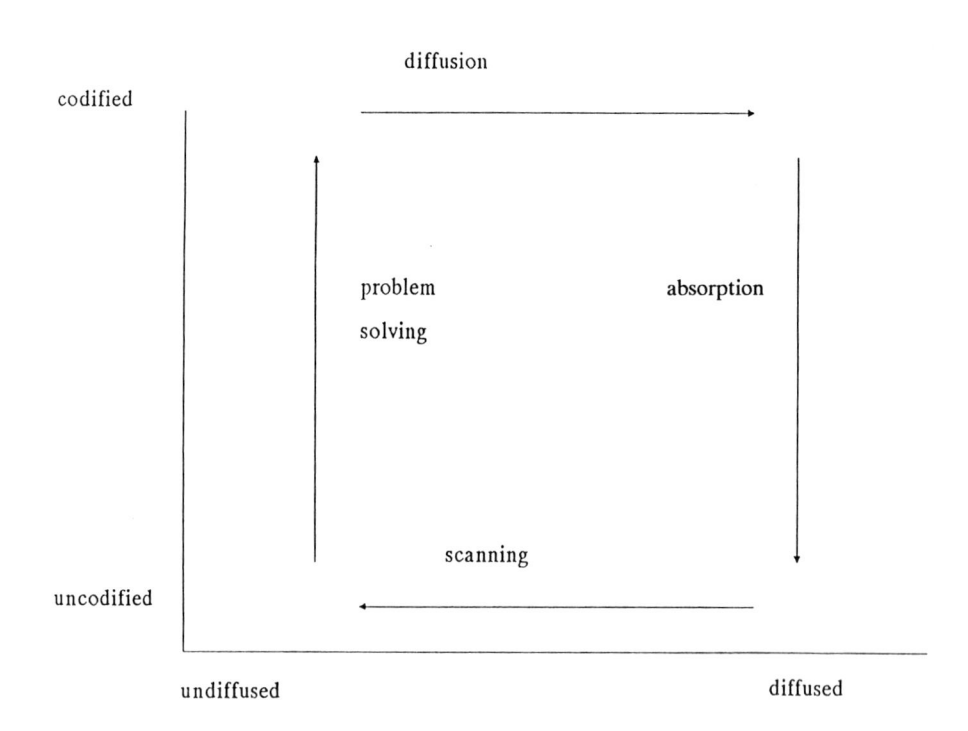

FIGURE 2: THE SOCIAL LEARNING CYCLE (SLC)

knowledge. Codification thus progressively extends the market for knowledge.

Step 4: Absorption. The diffusion of newly codified knowledge in a given population may provide opportunities for testing it in a variety of different circumstances. Domains of applicability are identified and explored in a process of "learning by doing" in which the relevant structures or codes are gradually internalized by users over time. Internalization is accompanied by a growing intuitive "feel" for the possibilities and limitations of the new knowledge, a feeling that is itself uncodified -- hence the downward movement in the C-Space -- and acts as a potential further source of weak signals capable of initiating a new cycle where adjustments to what has been learnt are called for.

The social learning cycle (SLC) just described is a feedback loop subject to many types of blockage that either bring it to a halt or confine it to certain regions of the C-Space (Figure 3). A major influence on the path it will actually follow is the distribution of existing knowledge in the space, knowledge that may exist either in a collaborative or a competitive relationship with what is emerging from the cycle itself. Existing knowledge is given a certain inertia in the C-Space by institutional structures in which it gets embedded, structures whose own internal operations in turn reflect the nature of the information environment in the region of the C-Space where such knowledge is located. Figure 4 identifies a number of such institutions and locates them at different points on the SLC; Table 1 briefly outlines the key information-related characteristics of such institutions.

Our conceptual scheme now allows us to pinpoint the radically different orientations to social learning espoused respectively by the Neoclassical and the Schumpeterian economic paradigms. They can be briefly summarized thus: the Neoclassical model takes the market as an "absorbing" state so that following the codification and diffusion of new knowledge, equilibrium is achieved and the SLC effectively comes to a halt; the Schumpeterian model, by contrast, sees the cycle as continuing beyond market equilibrium with opportunities for learning being generated by the equilibrating process itself (Grossman and Stiglitz, 1980). If such learning occurs, however, it gradually moves one *away* from equilibrium as publicly available knowledge is absorbed and, following a scanning phase, becomes once more impacted by individuals in idiosyncratic ways (Shackle, 1958).

Thus Neoclassical learning is an equilibrating process that terminates with the attainment of market equilibrium -- i.e. with the complete diffusion of new knowledge fully codified through the price mechanism -- whereas Schumpeterian learning is alternately an equilibrating and a disequilibrating process in which codification and diffusion are followed by absorption and scanning, both together constituting the entrepreneurial phase of the SLC and the ultimate source of Schumpeter's "creative destruction" (Schumpeter, 1934). The new knowledge emerging from the entrepreneurial phase of the SLC now threatens to dislodge existing knowledge

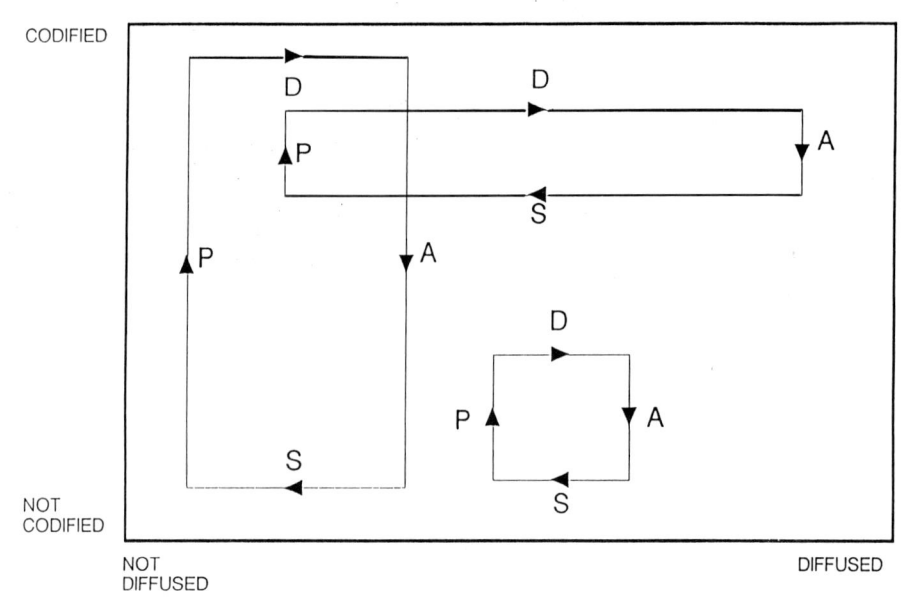

FIGURE 3: DIFFERENT SLC'S

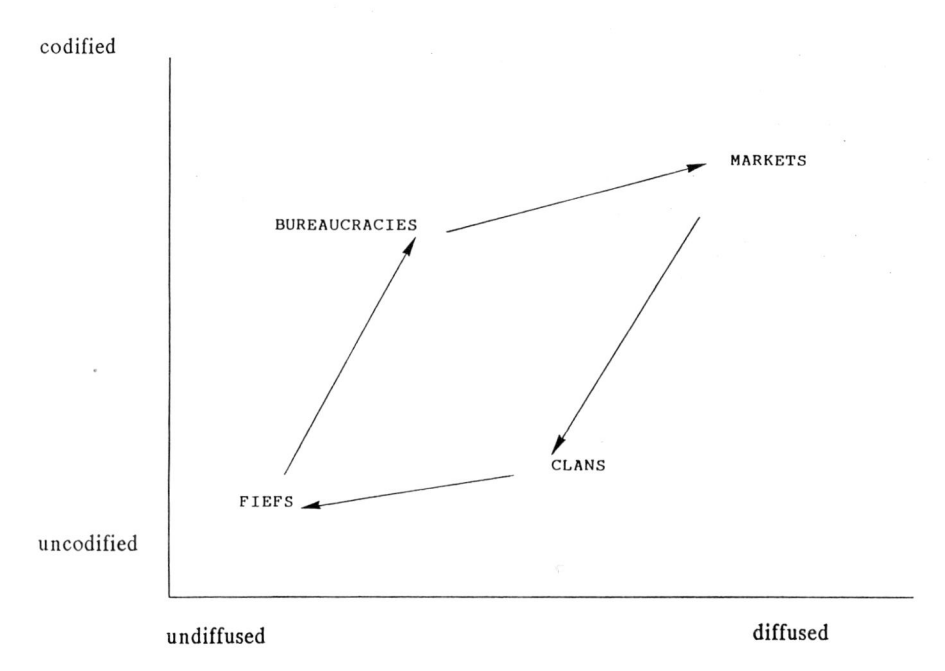

FIGURE 4: INSTITUTIONS IN THE SLC

	UNDIFFUSED INFORMATION	DIFFUSED INFORMATION
INFORMATION	**2 BUREAUCRACIES** ■ Information diffusion limited and under central control ■ Relationships impersonal and hierarchical ■ Submission to superordinate goals ■ Hierarchical coordination ■ No necessity to share values and beliefs	**3 MARKETS** ■ Information widely diffused, no control ■ Relationships impersonal and competitive ■ No superordinate goals - each one for himself ■ Horizontal coordination through self-regulation ■ No necessity to share values and beliefs
INFORMATION	**1 FIEFS** ■ Information diffusion limited by lack of codification to face-to-face relationships ■ Relationships personal and hierarchical (feudal / charismatic) ■ Submission to superordinate goals ■ Hierarchical coordination ■ Necessity to share values and beliefs	**4 CLANS** ■ Information is diffused but still limited by lack of codification to face-to-face relationships ■ Relationships personal but nonhierarchical ■ Goals are shared through a process of negotiation ■ Horizontal coordination through negotiation ■ Necessity to share values and beliefs

TABLE 1: INSTITUTIONAL PROFILES

together with the specific institutions in which it is embedded.[1]

To conclude: Schumpeterian learning, unlike Neoclassical learning, requires a complete SLC operating continuously, which has market equilibrium as but one of its phases. It thus accepts disequilibrium as an essential complement to equilibrium processes and since disequilibrium originates in the lower-left hand corner of the C-Space following the entrepreneurial phase, it will be characterized by an information environment suffused with bounded rationality, opportunism, and strategic behaviour (Williamson 1985). Schumpeterian learning, then, not only accommodates forms of economic behaviour that remain a problem for the Neoclassical paradigm, but it also activates institutional structures -- clans, fiefs, bureaucracies -- that are deemed to be at least as necessary to the smooth and continuing functioning of the SLC as market institutions themselves. The Neoclassical orthodoxy is not such a broad church, institutionally speaking, and for that reason is led to view movements through the SLC as inefficiencies to be temporarily endured on the way to the market rather than as inherently beneficial. Such was the perspective that informed Chinese reform policies in the 1980s.[2]

MARKETS AND HIERARCHIES WITH CHINESE CHARACTERISTICS

The economic reforms initiated in the PRC in 1979 -- first in selected rural areas and later in urban ones (Xue, 1981) -- and pursued energetically until 1989, drew much of their inspiration from the Hungarian reforms of 1968. These in turn looked to Lenin's New Economic Policy (NEP) of the 1920's as a model that would give some legitimacy to Hungary's quest for economic elbow room in the shadow of the country's ever watchful mentor, the Soviet Union (Granick,1976). The term "market socialism" then, far from standing for a coherent economic doctrine, reflected an intellectual compromise imposed by the harsh necessity of good neighbourliness, a compromise in which the market would be allowed to coexist with a planned economy but in a subordinate position from which it could at best correct the latter's worst excesses. The idea, then, in China as in Hungary, was to allow some market signalling to improve the overall allocative efficiency of the existing system and at the same time to raise the X-efficiency of firms (Child and Lu, 1990). The ambiguous status of such an attempt at decentralization was reflected in the slogan popularized at the time by the Chinese press: "The market controls the enterprise and the government

---

[1] For a view of Schumpeterian learning as an equilibrating process see Kirzner. The interpretation of learning presented here is quite at odds with Kirzner's (Kirzner, 1973; 1979).

[2] Schumpeter, in Capitalism, Socialism, and Democracy, viewed bureaucracy as an absorbing state brought about by the codification and stabilization of innovation by the large corporation. He underestimated the powers of creative destruction. See Schumpeter, 1942.

controls the market".[3]

In the PRC, reform consisted both of a delegation of state control over industrial enterprises from central government down to provincial and municipal government[4] and, at the same time, of a decentralization of decision-making powers to industrial enterprises themselves. In May 1984, the State Council issued "Temporary Provisions Further Expanding the Autonomy of State Owned Enterprises", giving firms a measure of autonomy in ten areas. The most notable development was that they would be allowed to retain some funds (the so called "enterprise-fund") for their own investments. The following year firms were authorized to formulate their own plans for technological developments and to design products in response to market demand, provided they also met their obligations under the plan (Child and Lu, 1990).

Meanwhile, in an attempt to put some distance between industrial enterprises and their supervisory authorities, a "Contract responsibility System" (CRS) closely modelled on western notions of management by objectives (MBO) was devised and implemented piecemeal, finally getting incorporated in the Enterprise Law of April 1988 (Child and Lu 1990). Under the CRS, enterprise managers would negotiate a set of annual input and output targets with the bureaus that they reported to at city, provincial, or national level, but would be left largely free to meet these targets as they saw fit, and, once these were met, to pursue other profitable activities that might then present themselves.

In an important sense, the delegation of administrative control over firms to lower level territorial units and the economic decentralization of control over firms worked against each other. Local authorities interpreted the delegation as a property transfer and in most cases quickly moved to assert control over their newly acquired possession. The very irrationality of the economic system facilitated the process: in the absence of a rational-legal order or a workable price system, arm's length accountability of the kind envisaged by the CRS is impossible to maintain and rapidly gives way to the kind of interpersonal accommodation and renegotiation that Kornai (1986), in the East European context, has labelled the "soft budget constraint". The scope offered to state bodies to "protect" the firms in their care from the irrationalities of the system in return for their "loyalty" and compliance was thus maintained, only now, with the delegation of administrative responsibility to lower levels, the nature of the relationship became more intimate and hidden from view. Boisot (1987) has labelled the resulting arrangements "industrial feudalism".

They frequently proved to be arrangements much sought after by enterprise managers disinclined to compete (Montias 1988). A study carried out by Child and Lu

---

[3] The term "regulates the market" does not effectively convey the Chinese government proprietary attitude to this new institution.

[4] The term "municipality" in China is normally only used to refer to the cities of Beijing, Shanghai, Tianjin. Our own use of the term here is more conventional.

(1990) on decision-making patterns in six industrial enterprises in the Beijing area between 1985 and 1988, in fact, found little evidence of any increase in enterprise autonomy. Each enterprise had signed a contract with its local supervisory bureau under the provisions of the CRS, but, as noted by the authors, the inflexible nature of the targets written into the enterprise contracts constrained the freedom of managers to adapt to changing circumstances without returning to the bureau for a renegotiation, a situation that played into the latter's hands. Moreover, CRS targets had a strongly bureaucratic character -- last year's figure plus 7% -- and rarely expressed an adapted entrepreneurial or even a managerial response to a rapidly changing external environment. The lack of any economic rationality of the targets contracted by enterprise managers thus further eroded their autonomy when they subsequently proved to be beyond reach.

Another problem noted by Child and Lu in their study is that with the reforms, decision making became more complex. Many of the regulations promulgating delegation and decentralization were kept deliberately vague in order to ensure that powers of interpretation were retained at the centre. This however did not prevent a proliferation of demarcation disputes between local administrative agencies eagerly competing with each other for control over the enterprise's resources. Some medium sized industrial enterprises had to contend with up to 22 of these "mothers-in-law" -- as such agencies were known -- empowered to issue arbitrary and often contradictory instructions and to levy a variety of charges or fees on local firms for "services rendered" (Boisot and Xing 1991). The result was a slowing down of decision making and a further loss of efficiency as enterprise managers sought to navigate these new constraints. Paradoxically, then, the economic reforms, if anything, increased rather than decreased the external dependency of industrial enterprises in China.

Faced with increasing complexity, the managers of firms in the Child and Lu study appeared to rely on market data even less than they had before. For them, the information that mattered was government policy and its interpretation by the bureaus. Whatever market data they felt they needed -- and where they were serving local markets this was modest indeed -- was in the hands of their supervising bureau and they continued to rely on the bureau for whatever information they needed to orient their activities. The local administration, however, usually only had figures for sales conducted within its own jurisdiction, and firms were often "encouraged" to make the local market their strategic priority. Exports to neighbouring cities or provinces were then only attempted when local producers there could not satisfy local demand. The local shortfall was made known through local biannual trade fairs known as "order meetings" which rarely allowed national demand patterns for a given product to emerge with any clarity. Such a distribution structure, designed to maximize local self-sufficiency, was a source of rampant protectionism at the provincial and municipal level, of non competitive interregional trade kept at levels well below what a market system would justify, and consequently of a low level of specialization by Chinese industrial enterprises frequently condemned to enjoy monopolistic positions in very modest local market segments.

As the reforms progressed, in many parts of the country the original intentions of Chinese policy makers were turned on their head: what had started as a delegation of state power to local authorities turned into a de facto decentralization in which the latter increasingly felt free to pursue their own objectives opportunistically; what had originally been conceived of as a decentralization of decision-making power to firms designed to enhance their autonomy was by degrees converted into delegated powers in which the goals of local authorities, acting through their industrial bureaus, were substituted for those which firms might reasonably have pursued had they been free to do so. The result was a very limited manifestation of horizontal market relationships -- strongest in consumer goods where consumers were given more scope for "exit" -- and a maintenance of hierarchy, to be sure, much weakened at the apex where central control had been lost, but strengthened at the base where "loyalty" would henceforth count for more than "voice" had done in the past (Hirschman, 1970).

The central government's reform problems were further compounded by the fact that it had never put in place the macroeconomic control tools necessary for an effective decentralization of markets. The country's level of investment, for example, was regulated microeconomically through direct intervention by the central authorities, and the fiscal system in force was somewhat reminiscent of tax farming in eighteenth century France (Boisot and Child, 1988). The Chinese leadership thus faced an age-old dilemma which confronts all imperial forms of governance: centralize and stagnate; decentralize and face chaos. In the autumn of 1988, faced with an economy that was by then rapidly spinning out of control, the central government ordered a halt to all construction projects; the process of recentralization had begun. That intermediate point on the continuum between markets and hierarchies so eagerly sought by the Chinese leaders had certainly proved elusive.

INTERPRETING THE CHINESE REFORMS

There is a broad consensus among Chinese reformers and foreign observers that the modernization of the Chinese economy will require the development of viable institutions culturally located in or near the market region of the C-Space. Although the challenge has been framed in terms of a decentralization of economic power from a centralizing bureaucratic order -- i.e. a move from left to right in the C-Space -- an earlier development tradition going back to Durkheim and Tonnies would stress the need to move *up* the C-Space, towards a more differentiated and structured -- or codified -- set of social institutions as a precondition for the move to the right (Durkheim, 1964; Tonnies, 1955). In the European case, for example, the move in the late middle ages from a feudal society located primarily in fiefs to a market society was not -- *pace* Marx -- a direct one but was mediated by the rational-legal bureaucracies of the absolutist state and a mercantile economic order explicitly serving its interests. First there was a codification, an increase in the potential for rationality within the system, concentrated monopolistically in a few all-powerful state structures, and then secondly, a gradual diffusion of their power as the newly created

codified

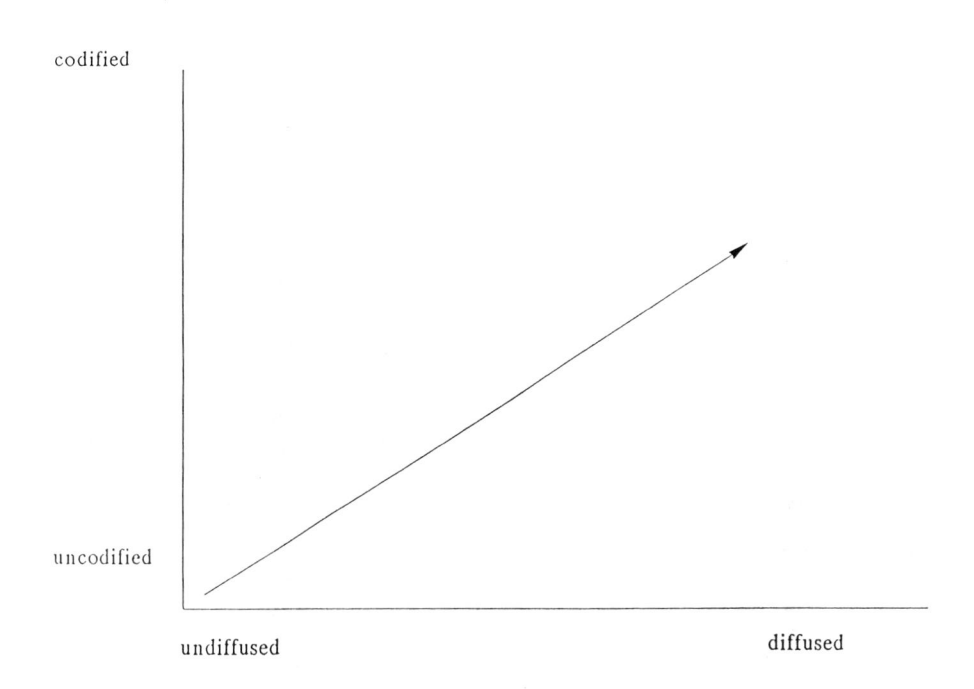

uncodified

undiffused   diffused

FIGURE 5 a): MODERNIZATION AS A LINEAR PROCESS

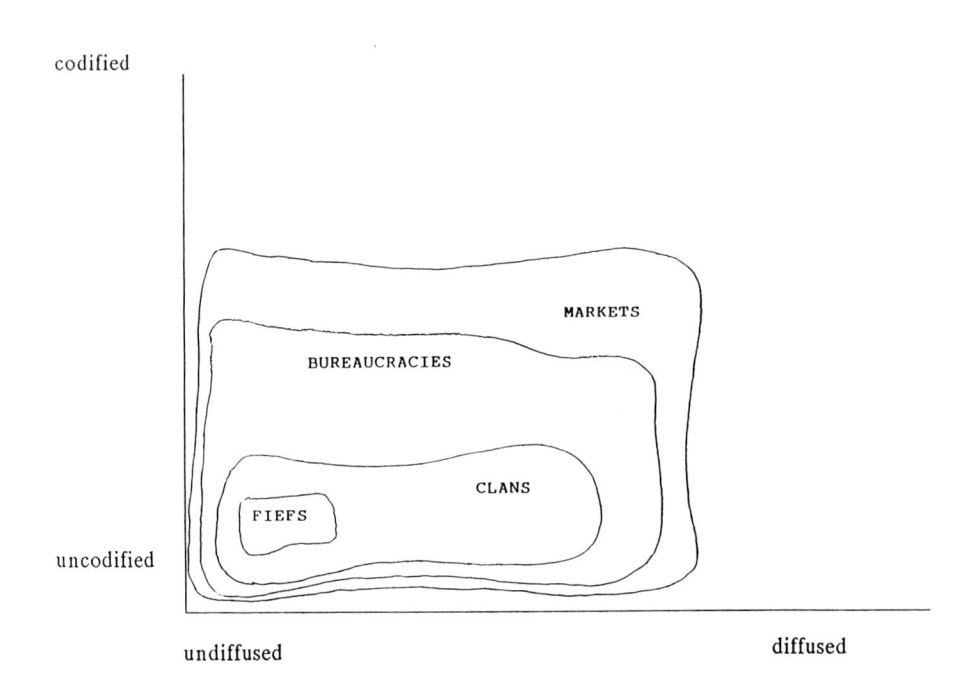

FIGURE 5 b): MODERNIZATION AS INSTITUTIONAL CRYSTALLIZATION

rationality spread to the system as a whole. The codification and diffusion of knowledge might then be viewed as the two phases of a modernization process which sooner or later lands the social system in the market quadrant. Some theoreticians have stressed the first phase -- Tonnies described it as the move from <u>Gemeinschaft</u> to <u>Gesellschaft</u> -- others the second, e.g. Rostow (1960).

Both phases together amount to a theory of convergence in which the cultural particularism of earlier stages of development are gradually metabolized out of the evolving system as it moves towards an impersonal and universally shared socio-economic order (Boisot 1983). From a convergence perspective, market society is an absorbing state located in a given region of the C-Space, and progress towards this state moves a society through a succession of other regions in the space -- feudalism, (fiefs), absolutism (bureaucracies), etc.-- now described as stages of development. Marxist-Leninism is also a theory of convergence, albeit a truncated one, with a bureaucratic order acting as an absorbing state -- a case of codification without diffusion, of knowledge being monopolistically hoarded by planners.

The fundamental problem of a Marxist-Leninist bureaucratic order, however, is precisely that it cannot act as an absorbing state. It lacks the rational-legal framework that has been a source of stability for western-style state bureaucracies (Hayek, 1945; Von Mises, 1981). The knowledge that goes into central plans is never complete and gets rapidly out of date. Quotas have constantly to be renegotiated with enterprise managers, and adjustments in one part of the plan rapidly propagate and trigger adjustments throughout the plan as a whole. Such a process always lags behind events and increasingly saps the capacity for a rational response to them: it is quite common in the PRC, for example, for enterprise managers to receive their "official" quotas under a given five-year plan two to three years <u>after</u> the plan was supposed to go into effect!

The consequence of this "bureaucratic failure" is a continued inability to establish stable codifications according to universalistic criteria, and a constant return to particularistic "accommodations" based on favours and the deployment of personal power -- in short, a constant regression from the bureaucratic region of the C-Space back into the fief region (Boisot and Child, 1988). In China this "iron law of fiefs" is further compounded by a strong cultural preference for personalized rather than impersonal relations. The Confucian tradition, which has hardly been dented by the past forty years of communism, continues to prize a personalized hierarchy held together by reciprocal bonds of loyalty and benevolence.

The image of Chinese society mired down in quasi-feudal relations from which it is repeatedly striving to escape in order to move up the C-Space is broadly consistent both with the various theories of modernization held by western observers and with the interpretation put forward by many Chinese reformers themselves. The latter, like Marx before them, credit capitalism with an ability to sweep away the "cobwebs of feudalism," thus preparing the ground for the administration of things rather than people -- i.e., for an impersonal codified order.

Such a "stages" interpretation of China's development problems, however, plausible as it might be, comes up against new ways of thinking brought about by Japan's own modernization experience. Although the Meiji reformers borrowed heavily from western institutional practices and thus facilitated selective moves up the C-Space (Hirshmeier and Yui, 1975; Lockwood, 1968), Japanese culture remained heavily invested in the lower regions of the C-Space (Boisot 1983), but possibly more so in the clan region where knowledge-based power is diffused among small elite groups, than in fiefs where it gives rise to opportunistic behaviour by individuals competing for personal dominance. (Van Wolferen, 1989).

A stages model of development however, finds it hard to account for the continued coexistence of institutional forms located in different parts of the C-Space in a fully industrialized society such as Japan. At best some of these forms are viewed as vestigial, and thus set to disappear when the modernization process has run its course. From a convergence perspective the enduring cultural strength of the clan region in Japan has slowed down the country's adaptation to outgroup expectations -- in this case the countries that Japan trades with -- and hence also to a market order, but with the globalization of the world economy and the gradual deregulation of the country's financial markets and distribution system, it is held that Japan's progress towards a full-fledged market society will once more be resumed.

Others are more sceptical and some even anticipate a further strengthening of the country's clan-like institutional practices over time (Van Wolferen 1989). It certainly seems odd to think of them as vestigial when so many students of the Japanese enterprise have come to acknowledge them as a major source of its competitiveness. Clan forms of governance, then, may not facilitate collaboration with outgroups, but almost as if by way of compensation, they certainly help to compete with them (Ouchi, 1981; Clark, 1974; Abbeglen, 1985) -- a case of "if you can't join them, beat them".

If we grant clan forms of organization -- both within and between firms -- the degree of stability that they appear to enjoy in the Japanese institutional landscape, then we may have to abandon a development model that moves us in linear fashion from one region of the C-Space to another, and begin to think of development as a cumulative process in which older institutional forms are retained and used in conjunction with new ones. Moves up the C-Space towards bureaucracies and markets are certainly to be expected, but since with institutional coexistence these cease to be viewed of necessity as absorbing states, the case for convergence loses much of its force. Markets may be part of the picture, but market society not necessarily so.

Apart from a certain loss of innocence with respect to the prospects for a universal market society, what is gained by complicating the development picture in this way?

Simply this: by switching from a view of development as a linear progression up the C-Space to one where institutions crystallize in different regions of the Space (see figure 5), we create the conditions for Schumpeterian learning to take place, conditions that now allow the SLC to move <u>down</u> the C-Space as well as up. One of the key strengths of the Japanese firms has resided in their ability to absorb and reinterpret (scan) readily available and well-codified knowledge. The effectiveness of such "entrepreneurial" learning, however, would be much diminished without institutional structures in the lower regions of the C-Space that can keep the SLC going. Within the firm in Japan those structures are located in clans: a move further to the left into fiefs would be considered opportunistic. Codification, the move up the C-Space that follows scanning, is for the most part internalized by large firms and there it is broadly consensual: creative destruction is thus a managed process which in the Japanese firm offers little scope for individual entrepreneurs (Van Wolferen 1989; Martin and Irving 1989) and outside it receives little or no institutional support (Chalmers-Johnson, 1982).

Western industrial culture, in contrast, on account of its tradition of individualism, is willing to tolerate opportunistic leftward moves into the fief region of the C-Space, but since it has little by way of institutional investment in this region[5], these are sporadic and do not occur on a large scale.

To summarize: a Neoclassical view of economic development emphasizes the growth of institutional structures in the market region of the C-Space and their atrophy elsewhere as market processes progressively take over; a Schumpeterian view, on the other hand, associates development with institutional investments in all regions of the space in ways that make continuous learning possible. Earlier structures therefore, providing they actively contribute to the maintenance of a SLC, not only retain their full vigour but may well justify further investment.

A clear understanding of Schumpeterian learning would lead to some important changes in current thinking on China's modernisation problems. For the challenge is not to escape from fiefs into an equally absorbing bureaucratic or market order -- or some subtle mix of the two -- but to devise an institutional pluralism that makes existing fief-like relations synergistic with structures that are allowed to emerge in other parts of the C-Space. This was the trick that Japan successfully pulled off with respect to clans, thus opening the door to Schumpeterian learning. It is a trick, however, that continues to elude Chinese policy makers. The reasons for this failure are instructive.

In the Chinese context, access to the fief region of the C-Space is, as far as possible, restricted to existing power holders trying to resolve, by recourse to the use of interpersonal power, issues that cannot be dealt with bureaucratically. They have entered fiefs from senior positions in the administrative hierarchy, whether at the

---

[5] Venture capital and intrapreneurship minimize investment risk by encouraging rapid codification and hence move away from fiefs often prematurely, before these have been able to deliver.

enterprise level or above it, and since they are there for want of viable codified solutions to the problems they face, their incumbency has little perceived legitimacy and is consequently vigorously denied. The administration of "things" rather than people in a socialist order -- in theory at least -- has no need for the personalized power of fiefs: everything has a codified solution embodied in a plan or a budget that essentially does away with arbitrary decisions.

The lack of economic rationality that these plans and budgets suffer from, however, serves to create a "mock bureaucracy" (Gouldner, 1954) in which a ritual response to codified but essentially false signals emanating from the top right of the C-Space i.e, the figures collected by the planners from lower level units, most of which are "laundered" on the way up to create the "right" impression, are given priority over more promising but less codified "entrepreneurial" signals emanating from a deeper SLC. Why?.

The reason lies in the possibility that the genuine problem solving to which such uncodified signals might then give rise would become a source of creative destruction, a threat to existing institutional structures and to the distribution of power that they legitimize. To codify in China is to invite a level of conflict which the system is institutionally and culturally ill-equipped to manage. For this reason, problems addressed in the fief region have to be resolved in the fief region, discreetly hidden from public view so as not to destabilize the fragile structures already in place. We are dealing here with uncertainty <u>absorption</u> rather than uncertainty <u>reduction</u>, a strategy for living with problems rather than solving them, a strategy in which Schumpeterian learning effectively comes to a halt: in China it does so in the fief region, a persistenty absorbing state created by the interplay of history, culture, and institutions.

China and Japan both sought to modernize by borrowing institutional forms from the west that would move them further up the C-Space towards a more codified social order. Each was equally concerned to do so while preserving its cultural identity (Moulder, 1977). But whereas Japan, in a revolution from above, drew its inspiration from a tested liberal model that happened to be the dominant paradigm at the time it was starting to modernize in the 1870s, China, starting more than half a century later, looked to the new but as yet untested Marxist-Leninist paradigm to drive a revolution from below (Moore, 1966)

Foreign borrowing in each case led to very different results. Although both cultures were very heavily invested in the lower regions of the C-Space, only Japan was able to spread out from there through institutions that promised stable codifications. Moves up the C-Space did not westernize Japan, and many observers (Dore, 1987; Vogel, 1979) have noted that the rational-legal perspective in Japan to this day remains comparatively underdeveloped.

What we hypothesize here is that in spite of current criticism of Japan's "vestigial feudalism" -- and many of these criticisms stem from an implicit assumption that a modern Japan <u>should</u> be a market society -- the country has spread itself sufficiently far up the C-Space to be driven, economically if not politically, by what we have called Schumpeterian learning, a social feedback process that activates earlier and new institutional forms in an integrated way. China, by contrast, having failed to stabilize a viable set of rational-legal institutions further up the space is, for the time being, unable to harness the power of Schumpeterian learning to developmental ends.

What implication, if any, does the analysis presented here hold for the post communist economies of Eastern Europe?.

THE IMPLICATIONS FOR EASTERN EUROPE

In contrast with China -- or for that matter with the USSR (Carr, 1966) -- Eastern Europe shares with the rest of the Old Continent a bureaucratic tradition that Weber has termed "rational-legal": behaviour is regulated through the rational application of universal principles, impersonally applied by role incumbents selected on grounds of merit and performance (Weber, 1947). The Chinese bureaucratic tradition, on the other hand, is described by Weber as "patrimonial" and builds on a hierarchy of personal loyalty and protection (Levinson, 1958; Weber, 1978).

Weber, of course, was describing an ideal type: what European bureaucracies aspire to, rather than what they actually are. Yet insofar as the type finds its organizational counterparts in the real world -- today, given its recent past, probably less so in Eastern than in Western Europe -- these will have spread further up the C-Space than Chinese organizations and institutions and hence will be much less heavily invested in fiefs than the latter. For this reason when a Marxist-Leninist ideology and practice was imposed on East European institutions after the Second World War, its tendency to drag the system into fiefs on account of its lack of economic rationality was somewhat counterbalanced by a rational legal tradition pulling in the opposite direction. The administrative structures inherited by the new Marxist-Leninist order amounted to an institutional memory of practices that had earlier stabilized in the C-Space around bureaucracies and markets working in tandem.

Forty years of communism never succeeded in wholly erasing such memories and they provide important building blocks for the post communist reforms. To simplify somewhat, if the challenge in China is one of moving up the C-Space in order to secure the level of codification and rationality required to modernize, in Eastern Europe it might be considered one of moving from left to right in the C-Space, but in the upper regions, from bureaucracies to markets -- the very goal that the Chinese reformers had originally set themselves, under the illusion that they already effectively inhabited a bureaucratic order. There is indeed a broad consensus emerging in Eastern Europe among reformers and broad sections of the population that the task before them now is to prepare for market society.

Market society, however, as we have seen, is an ambiguous term: taken in a narrow Neoclassical sense, it refers to a set of structures and institutions -- a central bank , a stock exchange , a securities and exchange commission, a law of contracts, etc -- designed to steer economic transactions towards the market region of the C-space and to keep them there. Yet taken in the broader Schumpeterian sense, it refers to a process (Langlois, 1986; Kirzner, 1979) of learning, of visioning, of risk taking, of competing, etc. designed to keep one moving through a SLC that activates all regions of the C-space.

The second interpretation of market society incorporates the first and thus acknowledges a need for the kind of institutions it seeks to promote. It moves beyond that interpretation, though, in also advocating institution building in clans and fiefs of the kind that promote and maintain Schumpeterian learning.

Eastern Europe is embarking on its reforms at a time when Schumpeterian learning is coming to be recognized by managers and policy makers alike as a major source of competitive advantage. Ever shorter product life cycles and the role models provided by Japanese firms have rekindled an interest in entrepreneurship, internal venturing, and organizational learning (Pinchot, 1985; Garratt 1989) that had all but been extinguished by Neoclassical concerns with allocative and X efficiency.

The evolution of organization design away from large monolithic multidivisional structures towards lighter, more personalized networks is symptomatic of the change in thinking. In the language of the C-Space it represents a move down the space, away from markets -- this time internal markets -- and towards clans.

The Neoclassical paradigm can neither accommodate institutional investments further down the C-Space nor respond to them. The reason for this is that they are microeconomic and hence relate to institutional change at the enterprise level. Since in neoclassical thinking the firm is little more than a point on a production function, policy prescriptions from this perspective remain essentially macroeconomic -- necessary, to be sure, but in the light of our analysis, hardly sufficient.

The difference between the Neoclassical and the Schumpeterian perspective on economic reform in Eastern Europe can be brought out by considering the privatization of state-owned firms. The first focuses the attention of policy makers almost exclusively on the creation of an efficient market for enterprise shares, on accurate asset valuation, the avoidance of monopolistic market structures, etc., with a view to getting the firm as quickly as possible into the market region of the C-space. The second perspective, without in any way rejecting such measures, broadens the focus to include considerations of internal organization such as attitudes to risk taking, management developent, culture change, and so on.

While there is plenty of evidence that, with western help, the macroeconomic issues are being addressed, the microeconomic ones do not appear to be receiving anything like the same attention. On the day that the protective mantle of the state is removed from state-owned firms, enterprise managers will be left to fend for themselves, unprepared, in what promises to be a highly turbulent environment.

It might be objected that this is, after all, what management and entrepreneurship is all about, and that it is not for policy makers to intervene once more in what are now internal organization matters. Henceforth, managers must manage. Such an objection overlooks the fact that East European firms, like Soviet and Chinese firms, are little more than branch plants with little or no organization autonomy of their own. To privatize them without a careful preparation of the internal organization for such a momentous transformation is comparable to the Spartan practice of exposing newborns to the elements in the belief that only the strong deserve to survive. The predictable outcome of such an approach will be an unnecessarily high mortality rate among privatized firms that have found no foreign partner to rescue them, and a consequent souring of popular affection for a market society cast in such an unforgiving -- should I say "unlearning"? -- Darwinian mould.

CONCLUSIONS

A Schumpeterian perspective allows a clear distinction to be drawn between China's reform problems and those faced by Eastern Europe. The challenge in China is how to initiate a Schumpeterian learning cycle; in Eastern Europe it is how to complete it. The first requires the development of institutions that, by promoting the codification and diffusion of information within the economic system, enhances its capacity for rational action. The second focuses on the absorption and scanning capacities of the system in order to improve its ability to respond to new problems and opportunities in a timely fashion. All of these diverse information processing skills are essential components of the learning process. Concentrate on one to the exclusion of the others and social learning comes to a halt. This became the critical problem for the Soviet Union and Eastern Europe when an imposed bureaucratic order was intentionally converted into an absorbing state; it continues to be a problem for China whose traditional culture even today helps to maintain fiefs as an absorbing state. And it now conceivably threatens the reform process in Eastern Europe, where a belief that the Neoclassical economic paradigm has provided the institutional underpinnings of western industrial performance promises ill-conceived attempts to convert the market region of the C-space into an absorbing state. The world is Schumpeterian and East European policy makers urgently need to be made aware of this fact.

REFERENCES

Abbeglen, J., and G. Stock, Kaisha, The Japanese Corporation New York: Basic Books, 1985.

Ansoff, I. et. al. (Eds.) From Strategic Planning to Strategic Management, New York: Wiley, 1976.

Barone, E., "The Ministry of Production in the Collectivist State" in F.A. von Hyek (Ed) Collectivist Economic Planning, London: Routledge and Kegan Paul, 1935.

Blum, Lord and Peasant in Russia: From the Ninth to the Nineteenth Century, Princeton, New Jersey: Princeton University Press, 1961.

Boisot, M., "Markets and Hierarchies in Cultural Perspective" Organization Studies, Spring, 1986.

Boisot, M., Information and Organization: The Manager as Anthropologist, London: Collins (Fontana), 1987.

Boisot, M., and J. Child., "The Iron Law of Fiefs: Bureaucratic Failure and the Problem of Governance in the Chinese Economic Reforms" Administrative Science Quarterly, December, 1988.

Boisot, M., "Industrial Feudalism and Enterprise Reform -- Could the Chinese Use Some More Bureaucracy" in M. Warner (Ed.) Management Reforms in China, London: Frances Printer, 1987.

Boisot, M., and G. Xing (Forthcoming) "Managerial Work in the Chinese Enterprise" Organization Studies.

Boisot, M., "Convergence Revisited" Journal of Management Studies, 1983.

Boisot, M., "Markets and Hierarchies in Cultural Perspective" Organization Studies, Spring 1986.

Carr, E.H., The Bolshevick Revolution: 1917-1923, Middlesex: Penguin Books, 1966.

Chalmers-Johnson, MITI and the Japanese Miracle, Stanford, California: Princeton University Press, 1982.

Child, J. and Y. Lu "Vertical Dependencies in Decision Making: Investment Decisions in China and a Comparison with Hungary" November 1990.

Clarke, R., The Japanese Company, New Haven: Yale University Press, 1979.

Dore, R., British Factory -- Japanese Factory, Berkeley: University of California Press, 1973.

Dore, R., Taking Japan Seriously: A Confucian Perspective on Leading Economic Issues, London: The Athlone Press, 1987.

Durkheim, E., The Division of Labour in Society, New York: The Free Press, 1933.

Francis, A., J. Turk,, P. Williams (Eds.), Power, Efficiency, and Institutions: A Critical Appraisal of the Markets and Hierarchies Paradigm, London: Heinemann, 1983.

Garrat, R., The Learning Organization, London: Fontana, 1987.

Gouldner, A., Patterns of Industrial Bureaucracy, New York: The Free Press, 1954.

Granick, D., Enterprise Guidance in Eastern Europe, Princeton, New Jersy: Princeton University Press, 1976.

Gregory, R., Mind in Science, Middlesex, England: Penguin Books, 1981.

Hayek, F., "The Uses of Knowledge in Society" American Economic Review Vol. 35, September, 1945.

Hirschmann, A.O., Exit, Voice, and Loyalty: Responses to Decline in Firms, Organizations and States, Cambridge, Mass: Harvard University Press, 1970.

Hirschmeier, J., and T. Yui, The Development of Japanese Business, London: George Allen and Unwin, 1975.

Kirzner, I., Perception, Opportunity and Profit: Studies in the Theory of Entrepreneurhip, Chicago: The University of Chicago Press, 1979.

Kirzner, I., Competition and Entrepreneurship, Chicago: The University Press, 1986.

Kornai, J., "The Hungarian Reform Process: Visions, Hopes and Reality" Journal of Economic Literature, 24: 1687-1737, 1986.

Langlois, R., (Ed.) Economics as a Process: Essays in the New Institutional Economics, Cambridge: Cambridge University Press, 1986.

Lange, O., and F. Taylor, On the Economic Theory of Socialism, Minneapolis: University of Minnesota Press, 1958.

Leibenstein, H., Inside the Firm: The Inefficiencies of Hierarchy, Cambridge, Mass.:

Harvard University Press, 1987.

Lerner, A.P., "Economic Theory and Socialist Economy" Review of Economic Studies, Vol. 2, October 1934.

Levinson, J., Confucian China and its Modern Fate: A Trilogy, Berkeley: University of California Press, 1958.

Lockwood, W., The Economic Development of Japan, Princeton, New Jersey: Princeton University Press, 1968.

Martin, B., and Irving, J., Research Foresight: Priority in Science, London: Pinter Publishers, 1989.

Montias, "On Hierarchies and Economic Reforms" Journal of Institutional and Theoretical Economics, 144: 832-838, 1988.

Moulder, Japan, China and the Modern World Economy, Cambridge: Cambridge University Press, 1977.

Ouchi, W., Theory Z: How American Business Can Meet the Japanese Challenger, Reading, Mass: Addison-Wesley, 1981.

Perkins, D., "Reforming China's Economic System" Journal of Economic Literature, 26: 601-645, 1988.

Pinchot, G., Intrapreneuring. New York: Harper and Row, 1985.

Polanyi, M., Personal Knowledge: Towards a Post-Critical Philosophy. RKP., 1958.

Polanyi, K., The Great Transformation. Boston: Beacon Press, 1944.

Popper, K., The Logic of Scientific Discovery. London: Hutchinson and Co., 1959.

Putterman, L., (Ed.) The Economic Nature of the Firm: A Reader. Cambridge: Cambridge University Press, 1986.

Rostow, W., The Stages of Economic Growth. London: Cambridge University Press, 1960.

Schumpeter, J., The Theory of Economic Development. Cambridge, Mass: Harvard University Press, 1934.

Schumpeter, J., Capitalism, Socialism and Democracy. New York: Harper and Row, 1942.

Shackle, G., Time in Economics. Amsterdam: North-Holland, 1958.

Tidryck, G., and Chen, (Eds.) China's Industrial Reforms. Oxford: Oxford University Press, 1987.

Tonnies, F., Community and Association. London: Routledge and Kegan Paul, 1955.

Vogel, E., Japan as N° 1. Tokyo: Charles E. Tuttle and Co., 1979.

Von Mise, L., Socialism. Indianapolis: Liberty Classics, 1981.

Warner, M.,(Ed.) Management Reforms in China. London: Frances Pinter, 1987.

Weber, M., The Theory of Social and Economic Organization. New York: The Free Press, 1947.

Weber, M., Economy and Society. Berkeley: University of California Press, 1978.

Williamson, O., Markets and Hierarchies. New York: The Free Press, 1975.

Williamson, O., The Economic Institutions of Capitalism. New York: The Free Press, 1985.

Xue M., China's Socialist Economy. Beijing: Foreign Language Press, 1981.

Zhou Taihe, (Ed.), "Economic System Reform in Contemporary China". Beijing, Zhongguo Shehui Kexue Chubanshe, 1984.

Entrepreneurship in an Economy in Transition:
Perspectives of the Situation in the EX GDR

Critique
by
Daniel F. Muzyka, *INSEAD*

This paper addresses an interesting topic -- the development of entrepreneurial phenomena in Eastern Europe. The paper identifies some of the issues related to studying entrepreneurial phenomena in formally centralized economies. In addition, it also serves to identify some of the general weaknesses in the existing models of entrepreneurial phenomena.

DISCUSSION OF EXISTING LITERATURE

There are several characteristics of the existing body of knowledge on entrepreneurship which the author discusses. The first is with regard to the characteristics of entrepreneurs (and the definition of entrepreneurship), the second is what characterizes entrepreneurship vs. "small business" and the third deals with certain weaknesses of existing models of entrepreneurship that relate to the environment in which these models were constructed.

Characteristics. The author has touched on one of many weaknesses in entrepreneurship literature -- the definition of an "entrepreneur". There are, as the author suggests, many models currently in existence. We should not, however, unduly criticize our efforts to-date too harshly, since, in many ways, we are addressing a phenomenon whereby individuals act in ways that are out of the ordinary and may have many and varied characteristics. However, this paper does point to the need for a potential reintegration of frameworks of entrepreneurial behavior. As the author suggests, there are many models with common factors.

The author, however, has not necessarily summarized all existing major behavioral models of entrepreneurship -- not that summarizing all models should be the focus of the author's work in life. The paper does not include, for instance, any discussion of Stevenson's model. The "Harvard School" of models (i.e., those proposed by Howard Stevenson and Jeffrey Timmons) are frequently referred to. He may wish to at least mention these in future drafts.

In the end, the author has done justice to the many definitions of entrepreneurship. Individuals may argue about the existence of other definitions, but the most important addition the author could make to his existing article is to more clearly summarize his perception of the differences among the various definitions rather than to spend too much space summarizing them. This would serve as a strong prelude to readers as they attempt to understand the initial orientation of this research concerning entrepreneurship in the Eastern Europe.

Entrepreneurship vs. Small Business. This problem of definition has been with us for some time. What is the borderline between the two? Unfortunately, this is a difficult question, as the author has noted -- particularly in situations where an entrepreneur may grow his/her business as a network of smaller enterprises that appear to be small businesses. As the author has noted, this is an important dimension to monitor, especially in the context of restructuring economies.

Cross-Cultural Aspects. Another weakness that is discussed as part of the paper (but should probably be more forcefully expressed) is the cultural biases inherent in existing research. The concepts about authority and relationships inherent in many of the existing models generally contain a U.S. or North American bias. This has caused difficulties in interpreting the results from questionnaires from such studies applied in other cultures, especially the third or developing world. Clearly, the culturally sensitive aspects of existing models, as the author suggests, need to be understood before applying them to behavior in another culture.

Economic Context of Existing Models. Another weakness of existing models of entrepreneurship discussed by the author involves the nature of the economic context in which the entrepreneurial behavior was observed. The author describes this as a limitation of existing models of entrepreneurship. This is a legitimate criticism, especially when it comes to notions of "resource scarcity". The economies of the East do not have the same levels of resource slack, the same funding mechanisms or the same flows of capital that exist in the relatively resource rich Western economies.

Summary. The only major suggestion with regard to the existing literature is to be more forceful in recognizing the weaknesses of these models vis-a-vis the situation in Eastern Europe. The results of the on-going research presented in this paper will be interesting to compare to existing Western models of entrepreneurship. In the end, the author should not feel bound to spend much energy defending their model of entrepreneurial behavior vis-a-vis existing models given the differences in context.

DISCUSSION OF EASTERN GERMANY

The article contains a reasonable discussion of a difficult environment. The economies of the East are generally problematic when it comes to general classification and description. It demonstrates a clear and necessary understanding of the development of the existing situation. The author appears to understand the need to capture the context in a reasonably complete way.

The description of the current situation also suggests certain challenges for research. First, it is important to understand the evolution of the economic context. It would appear that the existence of a single bureaucratic agency to dispose of assets will have a large impact on what opportunities are available to entrepreneurs. Second, the fact that assets are so centralized also creates opportunities for large scale enterprises from Western Germany to play a major role in shaping opportunities. Third, given the role that large enterprises will play, it is important that researchers should also be dedicated to the question of how financial institutions from Western Germany will affect the nature of entrepreneurial activity.

Clearly, the situation in Eastern Germany is evolving and is impacted by rules and traditions imported and adapted from Western Germany. Throughout the research, as in this initial paper, the evolution of this context will be a critically important element to clarify for fellow researchers.

RESEARCH METHODS

The research methods suggested would appear to be generally appropriate to the task at hand. There are no magic econometric methods applicable to this situation. Qualitative and quantitative techniques would appear to be requisite, especially in sorting out the complex interrelationships.

CONCEPTUAL MODEL

The performance model that is presented as the initial basis for the work would appear to have the basic "structure-conduct performance" framework underlying it. While providing a simple, clear description of the factors affecting performance, it would appear that this model might require further adaptation in this situation. The complexity of the environment in these transitioning economies and the nature of the existing beliefs concerning economic performance suggest that elements of what is currently described as "environment" may affect all of the primary elements of the model presented. It may be necessary, given the complexity of the existing situation, to desegregate the elements of the model and to draw a more robust set of interrelationships.

In summary, while conceptual models predicated on recognized relationships are certainly helpful in organizing the variables identified by the research, the complexity of the environment in transitioning economies may require a more specific definition of terms. "Environment", especially in this context covers a plethora of factors.

Furthermore, the complexity of the existing "environment" may create the need for an entirely new model. The author may wish to question whether he should feel constrained by existing extensions of the 'structure-conduct-performance' of industrial organization economics and strategic management. The evolution of the economy in East Germany may provide fascinating new insights into the organization of various factors that affect organizational performance.

CONCERNS

There would appear to be several concerns with regard to this research.

<u>Definitions.</u> With regard to concerns raised in the discussion by the author of ambiguities in existing models of entrepreneurship, the authors may wish to be sensitive to the definition of "entrepreneurial business" and "small business". What many may term the "entrepreneurial business" sector and others term the "small business sector" will both develop extensively in what was the GDR. It is important that some operational definition be arrived at -- even if existing researchers are somewhat vague on the topic. For reasons noted earlier, existing definitions should not be used to condition the definition used as part of research into entrepreneurial phenomena in the "East".

<u>Language.</u> As the author has noted in his discussion of research methodology, it is important to use the language of the entrepreneurs under study and to understand the factors that drive them through <u>their</u> logic -- not the observers'. One of the criticisms I have frequently heard in cross-cultural research of entrepreneurship is that the questions are written in the business-academic language of industrialized, first-world academics -- not in the language or conceptual framework of the local entrepreneur. The author's efforts, in this case, appear to be intent upon seeking the variables and their definitions in a local context. This is important, especially given the economic, political and social models that have prevailed for over thirty years and have conditioned an entire generation of entrepreneurs.

<u>Generalizability.</u> One of my concerns in reviewing this research is just how generalizable the findings will be outside of the context of the development of the former GDR. Germany does represent a special case in Eastern Europe, just as Hungary does. East Germany is being rebuilt through the generous efforts of an economically powerful brother that is not only funding development but is also extending its own institutions to this new territory. Just as in the case of Hungary, the starting point for Eastern Germany is not the same as for Poland and other countries. This would suggest that the "transition behavior" is dramatically different in the case of the former GDR. The impact of the long-standing and powerful institutions of Western Germany on the development of entrepreneurship must be clearly recognized and recorded.

<u>Research Methodology.</u> Another concern is that the "definition" or "exploratory" phase of the research may be prematurely terminated. There is a tendency in our profession to jump on the bandwagon of "statistical significance" and "generally accepted techniques" in order to publish "rigorous" research. Hence, we strive for

early definition. Based on this paper and those of others, the development problems of the East defy simple categorization. Patience will be required as we continue to explore what variables are important, how the variables should be defined and how the variables interact. Anthropological research techniques may be in order in this context. The use of qualitative and quantitative methods would appear to be appropriate and necessary under the circumstances -- do not apologize for having to use them.

SUMMARY

This appears to fundamentally be a good paper, but more importantly, addresses an interesting topic. It is clearly an early paper defining a new research program. Further evolution of the paper is requisite.

The primary suggestion to the author is to not be bound to developing somewhat weak entrepreneurship paradigms developed through observation of the phenomena in a different economic context. This research represents a unique opportunity to observe how individual entrepreneurs who are not steeped in the rituals, traditions and constraints of "free enterprise" economics develop their entrepreneurial models. They may, in fact, teach us something that we do not recognize about entrepreneurs and entrepreneurship. In the end we are flawed observers who bring to our observations many biases -- layers of models presented by economics, strategic management, and organizational behavior which can not only serve as tools to improve our understanding but as blinders preventing us from seeing fundamental new truths. Be entrepreneurial in your continued research endeavors!

ENTREPRENEURSHIP IN AN ECONOMY IN TRANSITION: PERSPECTIVES OF THE SITUATION IN THE EX GDR

THOMAS KÖLLERMEIER, *IESE, UNIVERSITY OF NAVARRA*[1]

ABSTRACT

This paper develops some thoughts about the context and appropriate methodology of a research project which aims at understanding the phenomenon of entrepreneurship in an economy in transition.

Early in 1990, the political system in the ex GDR started to change. When both parts of Germany were united in October, 1990, the economic system also radically changed. The huge differences, but also some surprising similarities between both parts of Germany will be described in this paper.

The current research in entrepreneurship is reviewed with regard to its applicability to and usefulness for the study of the greening entrepreneurship in the ex GDR. An initial, modified framework is proposed, which reflects the impact of the specific phenomena of an economy in transition, such as resource scarcity, rapidly changing values in the population, and a highly volatile economic environment.

INTRODUCTION

One of the major problems facing the field of entrepreneurship research is the lack of a common set of agreed-upon frameworks and definitions. A review of the literature suggests that there is not much agreement beyond the basic definition of entrepreneurship as the creation of organizations, and that resource scarcity is one of the most important problems of new and growing ventures. The major differences in opinion concern the selection of a behavioral, psychological, or social approach and the differentiation between new ventures, entrepreneurial ventures, and small businesses. What characterizes most studies is that they were performed in a relatively stable economic environment where, in addition, the necessary infrastructure for finance and professional advice was abundantly available. Furthermore, the majority of studies used qualitative methods and were based on personal or expert

---

[1] The research leading to this paper was partly supported by the "Fundacion Bertran" Chair of Entrepreneurship and the Research Department of IESE, Universidad de Navarra.
This paper forms part of the author's dissertation research.

experience or case research. Quantitative approaches utilized mostly traditional statistical methods, such as univariate analysis of variance for the analysis of relationships (Duchesneau and Gartner, 1990; McDougall and Robinson, 1990).

This paper argues that the majority of earlier approaches will only be of limited usefulness for the attempt to deeply understand the development of entrepreneurship in the ex GDR. In the former centrally planned economy (CPE), the ruling party system had systematically nationalized private companies. In the last decade, only about 100,000 small businesses continued to operate privately. But a restrictive legislation, such as the limitation of the number of employees to ten and an income tax with a progression up to 96%, prohibited any aspiration for growth. This economic environment with a hostile climate for any kind of entrepreneurship prevailed until early in 1990. In such a context, implicit assumptions of most traditional frameworks of economics, strategy, and entrepreneurship will not hold true.

Gartner (1985) proposed a multi-dimensional framework for studying the creation of new ventures. He combined four dimensions - individual, process, environment, and organization. Furthermore, he claimed that the complexity of new venture creation can only be adequately investigated if the researcher attempts to discover how variables from each dimension interact with variables from other dimensions.

In the ex GDR, probably all variables from these four dimensions are subject to change of a magnitude which has hardly been experienced in previous studies. The situation in 1990 had many characteristics similar to those of developing countries. The reunification of East and West Germany is expected to lead to an increase in the number of private enterprises in the eastern part to reach the levels in West Germany. This goal can only be achieved through an extended number of new venture creations in the area of the ex GDR during the next few years. As a result, there will occur an adaptation to those characteristics which prevail in the highly industrialized western countries much faster than observed in studies of developing countries.

This paper forms part of a larger research project which aims at understanding the dynamic development process of entrepreneurship in the ex GDR. The research design which will be presented argues for the application of a hybrid approach in order to develop a deep understanding of this dynamic phenomenon. It suggests utilizing a mix of qualitative and quantitative methods in consecutive steps. The objective of this study is to generate insights which will help understanding of how the development of entrepreneurship can be supported during the transition of a CPE into a free market economy. Those findings which do not stem from the characteristics of West German institutions might also be extended to the other East European countries, which follow at a slower pace in converting their economies to the western model.

THEORETICAL CONTEXT

The literature on entrepreneurship and the management of small businesses seems to have increased in recent years. The knowledge in this field, however, remains fragmented. An agreed-upon set of definitions and a general framework is missing. Instead, partly contradictory concepts are utilized, such as trait versus behavioral, uni- versus multi-dimensional, or static versus process approaches. In addition, rigorously defining and contrasting small businesses and entrepreneurial ventures has proven to be very difficult. Many authors use the terms rather loosely because they include a large variety of companies, from the mom-and pop store to the Apple-in-the-garage experiment with extremely high growth potential (d'Amboise and Muldowney, 1988). The objective of this section is to comment on those recent developments in the field which seem to be most relevant for the development of an adequate framework for studying entrepreneurship in the ex GDR.

Trait Approaches

One of the dominant objectives of entrepreneurship research has been the identification of individuals who might found and grow successful new firms. Numerous researchers have worked on studies which seek to prove that entrepreneurs are different from non-entrepreneurs. Others followed a similar line of investigation and compared entrepreneurial and non-entrepreneurial firms. Their research was based on the assumption that entrepreneurs and their firms have similar characteristics. A detailed discussion of previous research concerning these characteristics can be found in, among others, Bird, 1989; Brockhaus, 1982; Carland, Hoy, Boulton, and Carland, 1984; d'Amboise and Muldowney, 1988; Duchesneau, 1987; Gartner, 1989; Wortman, 1987. The prevailing uni-dimensional search for those clearly distinguishing characteristics has been criticized. Brockhaus (1982), Gartner (1985 and 1989), Glueck and Mascon (1980) and McCain and Smith (1981) argue that these distinguishing variables frequently do not bear to closer examination.

Yet, the search for these elusive, personality based predictors of new venture success is continued. Stanworth, Stanworth, Granger, and Blyth (1990) claim that previous research, which is based on questionnaires with socially acceptable motives like becoming one's own boss, will not help to identify those individuals who actually become entrepreneurs. They contrast the psychological models of Brockhaus (1982) and McClelland (1961) with the psycho-dynamic approaches (Collins, More, and Unwalla, 1964; Kets de Vries, 1977) and the social marginality model (Chell, 1986; Schumpeter, 1934; Stanworth and Curran, 1973). They identify individual socialization patterns, existing incongruence between personal attributes and role, and the composition of the available economic roles as the key factors. Their conclusion is that sociological models seem to have a higher explanatory power than psychological models.

Miner (1990) has identified two sets of motivational patterns which should allow a clearer distinction between managers and entrepreneurs. With their help he wants to identify those individuals who seem most likely to start a new venture and nurture it to a significant size. Six motive patterns are derived from hierarchic theory and related to the requirements for successful performance of managers in hierarchical organizations. The second set of five motivation patterns reflects an entrepreneurial role model. They are based on task theory and demonstrate some marked parallelisms to McClelland's (1961) theory of the achievement situation. The use of a single trait approach and also the measurement of n-ach with the help of the Thematic Apperception Test (TAT) has been criticized on the grounds of subjectivity and lack of consistency. Miner (1990) instead measures various traits with the Miner Sentence Completion Scale-Form Hierarchy or Task (MSCS-H/T), on which he reports high scale reliability for earlier applications.

Behavioral Approaches

In a much cited piece of work, Gartner (1989) contrasted the characteristics of the trait approaches, which focus on the personality of the entrepreneur, with the characteristics of the behavioral approach, which focuses on the activities of the entrepreneur. The objective of his paper was to initiate a paradigm shift in the field of entrepreneurship research. He claims that trait approaches do not have predictive power because they concentrate their analysis on a fixed state of existence. He instead advocates the use of the behavioral approach which views the phenomenon of entrepreneurship as the process by which new organizations come into being (Vesper, 1982). The creation of an organization is seen as the outcome of a complex process and as a contextual event, which depends on many influencing variables. Here, the organization is the primary level of analysis and the entrepreneur is studied with respect to the activities which he performs in order to enable the creation of this organization (Gartner, 1985).

Another type of behavioral model of the entrepreneurial process is proposed by researchers from the Harvard Business School (e.g. Kao, 1989; Stevenson, Roberts, and Grousbeck, 1989; Timmons, 1990). They basically view entrepreneurship as a managerial behavioral phenomenon. The attempt to create value through the recognition and pursuit of business opportunities is conducted while disregarding the limited amount of resources currently controlled. The domains of entrepreneurial versus administrative behavior are here defined as having a significant overlap, although they are distinct.

Recently, several studies have focused their attention on the activities of the entrepreneur. (Bird and Jelinek, 1988; Brytting, 1990; Diomande, 1990; Mitton, 1989). Duchesneau and Gartner (1990) use a process approach, which concentrates mainly on the activities of the entrepreneur. But the three dimensions of their framework -- lead entrepreneur, start-up behavior, and firm's behavior and strategy -- contain variables from the behavioral and the trait approaches. Venkatraman, Van de Ven, Buckeye, and Hudson (1990) also present a process model. They try to explain the new small firm failure process. But their framework is restricted mostly to the dimension of the firm's behavior and strategy.

Other authors do not employ a process point-of-view. Instead, they extend the dimension of firm's behavior and strategy to also include environmental variables, such as industry structure, governmental agencies, and availability of venture capital (Goto, Yoshimura, Keeley, and Roure, 1990; Keeley and Roure, 1990; Roure and Keeley, 1990; Smallbone, 1990).

In the above two sections, the major approaches to the analysis of entrepreneurship have been summarized. This was not done in order to judge them but rather to prepare the reader for the description of the context of entrepreneurship in the ex GDR in part 2 of this paper. He should consider how far the "ceteris paribus" assumption of static, uni-dimensional approaches support or limit the analysis of decision making under extreme uncertainty and environmental volatility in the context under study.

Small Businesses Versus Entrepreneurial Ventures

Another item, which is characterized by a lack of agreement in the field of entrepreneurship research, is the question of whether, and how, to distinguish between small businesses and entrepreneurial ventures. The selection of a behavioral approach implies the view that the entrepreneurial behavior ceases once the creation of the organization is over (Gartner, 1989). The new venture will continue its life cycle through consecutive stages of growth, maturity, or decline (Chandler, 1962). The entrepreneur will either take on other roles at these stages, or he will turn over control of the established venture to professional management. This, in turn, will then have to ensure further growth, while the entrepreneur will continue to create new organizations (Miner, 1990).

The idea that the entrepreneurial founder of an organization is a different type of person from the manager, who is required at subsequent stages of growth, had already been developed early (Chandler, 1962; Clifford, 1973; Greiner, 1972; Smith and Miner, 1983; Steinmetz, 1969; Thain, 1969). Some researchers explicitly quantify this point, for example describing the cutoff as around thirty employees and $750,000 in assets (Steinmetz, 1969). Other authors see this shift from one stage of growth and style of management to another as marked by the installation of professional management.

Miner (1990) focuses his attention on the rather small group of highly ambitious entrepreneurs. He claims that the specific point in time and size when control shifts depends on the level of task motivation of the entrepreneurial founder. The ability of the entrepreneur to control the venture by face-to-face means is seen as equally important and interrelated with the level of task motivation. If this point is surpassed, new leadership with a higher task motivation will be required for further growth, and a hierarchy has to be introduced. He admits, however, that it only makes sense to apply the concepts of task motivation theory to those entrepreneurs who found ventures which seem to be predestined for fast growth. It would not be of any help to apply these concepts to the vast majority of organization founders who never intended to achieve substantial growth, such as mom-and-pop stores, small professional practices, or craft workshops. He concludes that the inclusion of large members of low-growth firms in research samples has been responsible for the lack of clarity of the results of personality dynamics research (Begley and Boyd, 1987; Brockhaus and Horwitz, 1986).

A contrary position is taken by Brytting (1990) who implicitly sees all small business founders as objects of his research. He claims that traditional theories and concepts of small business management fail because they have a rationalistic bias and separate the organizational phenomena from the cognitive sphere of the entrepreneur. Stage-of-growth-models, for example, are dominantly used in the field of small business and entrepreneurship research although the vast majority of venture founders lack any significant growth willingness (Davidsson, 1989).

Carland, Hoy, Boulton, and Carland (1984) also build their argument on the idea that entrepreneurs exist as entities which are distinct from non-entrepreneurial managers and small business owners. The inconsistency of their conceptual distinction between small business and entrepreneurial venture owner has already been indicated in a brilliant review by Gartner (1989).

The Small Business Administration (USA) uses a conceptual definition for small businesses which is widely accepted by researchers: A small business is one which is independently owned and operated, and which is not dominant in its field of operation. D'Amboise and Muldowney (1988) report that this construct is operationalized by a growing number of researchers in terms of no more than 500 employees and less than $20 million sales. Roure and Keeley (1990) recently introduced the term "high potential new venture". This refers to those start-ups which aim at achieveing well over $10 million sales within a few years after their foundation as an objective of their initial strategy.

In this first part of the paper, the theoretical context of entrepreneurship has been briefly reviewed. This should provide the reader with an idea of some of the weaknesses of the existing models of the entrepreneurial phenomenon. Before any conclusions are drawn with regard to the described research project, the special characteristics of the economic environment in the ex GDR will first be described.

THE SITUATION OF VENTURES IN THE EX GDR

The important contribution of small businesses to the prosperous development of a free market economy has frequently been acknowledged (Carland, Hoy, Boulton, and Carland, 1984; Vesper, 1984). Their major advantages are seen in, among others, higher efficiency in the use of R&D expenditures, faster new product introduction, more flexibility reacting to changes in the economic environment, creation of new jobs at a time when most large scale enterprises are reducing their workforce, and a general increase of competitiveness at home and abroad. The following section will describe the impact which nationalization and merging of firms, the two dominant trends of economic policy during the last 45 years in the ex GDR, had on the structure of its economy. The resulting picture will then be compared with the situation in the western part of Germany in order to illustrate the magnitude of new business creation which will have to occur in the eastern part within the next few years.

The Historic Development

After the end of the Second World War, the new government in the Soviet zone of Germany soon started to nationalize private firms in accordance with the communist ideology of the ruling party. This conversion into "Volks-Eigene Betriebe"-VEB (state owned companies) continued parallel to the development of political cadre staff who were assigned as "management" to these firms in order to secure the accomplishment of the central plans. The inherent inefficiency of a CPE, however, resulted in constantly scarce supply of most types of goods.

As a countermeasure, the government started to merge several VEBs and thereby formed "Kombinate", large-scale enterprises with characteristics similar to those of diversified holdings. The objective of this concentration was to create large autonomous units. On the one side they should obtain significant economies of scale. On the other side it was expected that the implementation of the central five-year-plans would be facilitated. But whereas the core businesses achieved impressive dimensions, and also an extremely high degree of vertical integration, the supportive and complementary companies operated at minimum scale. This even increased the level of administration, which had already been elevated.

A typical Kombinat could, for example, be composed of a small construction company, a nursery, a clinic, restaurants, a recreation center, and a multitude of craft workshops, which all joined a large number of medium-size hard- and soft-ware companies in order to form a computer Kombinat, such as VEB ROBOTRON.

Both trends, nationalization and merging of companies, led to a strong concentration of the structure of the economy. In 1950, 23,440 companies[2] had been reported in the industrial sector. At that time, the nationalization efforts had been concentrated on large scale companies first. Significantly later, in 1972, about 12,000 small businesses were nationalized in an additional effort, and were either merged or discontinued. As a result, only 3408 companies figured in the official statistics in 1988. They formed part of 173 Kombinate which constituted 72.8% of the industrial sector, 12.1% of construction, 8.8% of agriculture, 1.7% of transportation, and 4.6% of other sectors. This concentration led to the result that several industries were allocated to just a few cities. The Kombinat Baumwolle

---

[2]Source: Statistisches Jahrbuch 1989, Statistisches Amt der DDR

(cotton), for example, was located in Chemnitz (formerly Karl-Marx-Stadt). With 70,000 employees, it was one of the largest Kombinate and produced 52.5% of the output of the entire textile industry of the ex GDR. The second highest degree of concentration could be observed in the chemical industry. The Kombinat "Leuna", close to the city of Halle, produced 41.3% of the output of the whole chemical industry, amounting to 5.6% of the GNP of the ex GDR.

Since 1972, private companies were only granted permission to employ up to ten workers. This restricted their activity to mostly small trade and craft workshops, while small professional practices and speciality manufacturers could only be found in very exceptional situations. (These small businesses had experienced a reduction in business of 89%, a rate similar to that of medium and large companies in the industrial sector during the last 40 years.) In 1989, about 100,000 private small businesses with an average size of 3.2 employees were registered. The initial fieldwork suggests that the dominant motivation of these individuals to continue operating their firm despite severe repression from the official system had been their determination to continue their family's business. The second reason was stated less openly. It was their desire to escape from the overwhelming dominance of the official bureaucracy and realize their own objectives and ideas.

Profit and growth, however, figured at the end of a possible ranking of motivators. This was basically due to the limited number of employees and a marginal income tax rate which resulted in a higher net income after tax with a smaller fraction of the otherwise possible profits before tax. Another important limitation of growth was the fact that it was practically impossible for private companies to obtain new machinery. The ex GDR had focused its efforts on strengthening the machine tool industry. It was the eighth largest producer of machine tools in the world and the fourth largest exporter. However, only 20% of the whole production remained in the country, and these machines were entirely reserved for the state-owned companies.

The other major obstacles for a growth- and profit-oriented management of private small businesses were:

* Managerial decisions concerning employment and product-mix required local or central permission.

* Government authorities arbitrarily added taxes on the price calculations of private firms in order to eliminate their competitive advantage.

* Special export agencies held the monopoly for exporting whole product lines and excluded private firms from exporting.

* Depreciation of assets was not allowed.

* Private companies did not obtain government credits.

*   Family members did not receive a salary. Instead, a 2,000 Mark annual tax allowance was granted.

Forty-five years of a policy which aimed at the concentration of the whole economic environment had resulted in marked differences between the ex GDR and the western economies. The resulting industry structure represents a difficult starting position for catching up with the western part of Germany. The differences will now be illustrated in more detail. Several selected ratios of small, medium, and large firms in the eastern and western part will be compared in order to allow for a tentative estimation of the required amount of change. The data are mostly drawn from publications of the "Statistisches Bundesamt" and the "Statistisches Amt der DDR" (statistics institutions of East and West Germany). The number of employees is the only available dimension which allows the classification of size of businesses. However, it was not used in a consistent manner. Therefore the specific numbers will be indicated wherever possible because their use differs significantly from the prevailing unofficial standard of 500 employees for small businesses.

A Problematic Starting Point

About twenty years ago, the concentration in the industrial sector had not yet advanced too far. The percentages of small businesses with up to twenty employees within the total number of firms were about similar in both parts of Germany. The ratio of percentages "east-to-west" of small businesses with up to one hundred employees was 1:2, and those with more than one hundred employees was 3:2. In 1989, the continuous effort of the former government to concentrate the structure of the economy had led to a ratio of 1:5 for small trades, craft workshops, or small professional practices. Larger firms, with more than one hundred employees, were, on the contrary, represented at a ratio of 8:1. The most striking ratio, however, could be observed in the service sector. Here, the number of reported firms in West Germany was thirty times higher in relative terms than in East Germany.

After the reunification of both parts of Germany, the level of small businesses in the area of the ex GDR will have to develop to a level similar to the western part of Germany. The number of medium and large size firms, at the same time, will drastically be reduced by ungrouping the Kombinate. "Treuhand" is a federal institution which basically has the task of selling the resulting 8,200 companies to private investors. In addition, it has the objective of settling the transfer of those companies which were nationalized in 1972 back to their former owners. Official estimates however claim that this will occur only in less than a third of all cases. There are two main explanations for this limited amount of interest. On the one side, these companies are uncompetitive, have too many employees, a mostly outdated product line, outmoded facilities, and high expected costs due to earlier environmental pollution. On the other side, the new owners will not be allowed to sell their companies within the next couple of years. Instead, they are expected to restructure them personally for survival and manage them for future growth.

The differences in company size between east and west causes only one set of problems. Others will result from the extreme concentration of the industrial sector in the southern counties. Half of the population of about 16 million people live in the south of the ex GDR, close to the border of the CSFR. They produced about half of the GNP in the four counties of Chemnitz, Dresden, Halle, and Leipzig, which account for only 24% of the territory. In the western part of Germany this phenomenon of regional concentration can be observed to a lesser degree. About a third of its population as well as the GNP are allocated each to the central part -- the state of North-Rhein Westfalia -- and to the southern part -- the states of Bavaria and Baden-Wurtemberg.

Such a strong concentration in the ex GDR represents both a threat and a challenge. The former Kombinate are uncompetitive due to factors such as the low efficiency of labor, the low marketability of their former product line, and the lack of up-to-date process technology. Estimates of Treuhand state that only about a third of the firms on sale are expected to be competitive and another 27% might possibly be put on solid ground (Seifert, 1990). Their weak competitive position makes these firms especially susceptible to any downturns in the economic environment. Several authors have stated the expectation of an aggregate unemployment rate of 40% during 1991 with regional structural peaks of up to 70%.

In 1989, exports of the ex GDR amounted to $17.3 billion or an equivalent of about 9% of its GNP. Roughly a quarter were each exported to the Soviet Union, the other communist countries, the ex FRG, and to the other western countries. But when the West German currency was introduced in July 1990, this was accompanied by several unfavorable side effects for industry in the eastern part of Germany. Half of all exports had been executed either in Transfer-Mark or in Transfer-Rubel, which are synthetic, non-convertible currencies. An interim solution allowed the settlement of payment of ongoing transactions with these currencies until the end of 1990. But from January 1991 on, all exports have to be paid in a convertible currency. As a consequence, more than 80% of all export contracts to the former East Bloc countries were cancelled.

The export volume to the western countries also experienced a significant reduction, since the former practice of export subsidies was discontinued gradually after the reunification. The most influential reduction of sales occured, however, in the home market. The long years of repression, the shortages of merchandise, and the perceived inferiority compared to western standards has resulted in a strong aversion on the part of much of the population to everything which seems to represent the former system. This also holds true for "Made-in-GDR"-merchandise. As a consequence, even some commodities and basic groceries from the western countries were preferred to products from local producers. In addition, the majority of distribution channels has been acquired by West German corporations. They now permit only 10% of East German merchandise to be traded through these channels. This has led de facto to an almost complete exclusion of East German companies from the existing distribution channels in their home area.

The challenge of the inherited situation can be seen in the concentration of expert knowledge and skills. The proportion of East German managers who hold a masters or doctoral degree is generally higher than in most other western countries. Furthermore, students automatically participate in an apprenticeship before they enter university, and some deliberately enter a second or even a third one. This kind of expert knowledge combined with broad practical skills is extremely scarce in West Germany and has been for many years. The creation of technology centers in the new federal states of Germany with numerous high-tech start-ups and spin-offs is seen as an alternative for highly qualified employees who are now moving to the western states. For example, an Optic Valley at Jena, similar to the Silicon Valley in California, could be created during the restructuring of the former Optic Kombinat "Carl Zeiss" in Jena with its 60,000 employees. The core business will probably have to be reduced to an estimated 20,000 employees. Some of the experts from the remaining workforce might hopefully be kept in the region by encouraging them to create a multitude of technology-based new ventures or joint ventures in the same industry or related services (Seifert, 1990).

In this section, huge differences in the economic environments of East and West Germany have been reported, and the same applies to the standards of living. This situation offers extensive opportunities for entrepreneurs who will have to create an increased number of new ventures in the coming years. Beyer et.al. (1990) estimate that about 15,000 new ventures with twenty to one hundred employees are needed to bring the eastern areas in balance with the western industry structure. Furthermore, about 50,000 craft workshops and 190,000 small professional practices and service businesses with less than twenty employees will be necessary to provide the supply of population in the area of the ex GDR with a level of services that is comparable to that in the west. These estimates refer to surviving ventures. The actual number of creations thus has to be much higher.

Some Surprising Similarities between East and West Germans

A frequently raised argument is that this adjustment process will be hindered by factors such as the low mobility of West German executives, the lack of business experience of East German managers, and the low efficiency of the workforce which is described in derogatory terms such as "indifferent" and "easy-going".

However, Noelle-Neumann (1990) has conducted several inquiries which reveal surprising similarities between traits and perceptions of the eastern and western population of Germany. With an association test she analyzed the understanding of economic terms like capitalism. She found that the rank order of associations was almost identical, with the top three items being profit, scoring 96% in the east and 92% in the west; entrepreneurial spirit, scoring 95% in the east and 83% in the west; and excellence, scoring 93% in the east and 81% in the west.

Tables 1 and 2 are based on 1,500 interviews which Noelle-Neumann (1990) conducted in both parts of Germany in August 1990. For the information shown in

Table 1, -- Self-Portrait of German Strengths -- the interviewers asked which descriptors would best characterize the personality of each respondent. For Table 2, -- Self-Portrait of German Virtues -- the questions aimed at those goals which the respondents would regard as very important in their life. Both tables reveal that the perceptions of both parts of the German population are surprisingly similar after 45 years of separation.

Table 1: Self-Portrait of German Strengths

Characteristics	East %	West %
I normally expect to be successful	65	68
I give advice to others frequently	62	57
I enjoy assuming responsibility	50	50
I am able to have my way easily	45	52
I enjoy exercising leadership	23	30
I posses something for which I am envied	19	26
I am usually ahead of others	11	17

Source: Institut f_r Demoskopie, Allensbach, Germany

Table 2: Self-Portrait of German Virtues

Characteristics	East %	West %
Cleanliness and Neatness	73	63
Law and Order, Security, Social Justice	73	69
Peace and Independence	62	66
Thriftiness	54	41
Willingness to Succeed	51	47
Financial Well-being	41	28
Political Activities	17	16

Source: Institut f_r Demoskopie, Allensbach, Germany

The reported research of this section has been included to enlarge the richness of the provided data about the situation in Germany in order to allow for the development of a better understanding of the context of the studied phenomenon beyond its economic aspects. Psychological and sociological concepts like values, beliefs, self-esteem and their impact on the evolution of the transition process of the East European economies deserve more attention than they have received in current research.

IMPLICATIONS FOR THEORY BUILDING

In the preceding section, evidence has been provided that any attempt to understand the developing entrepreneurship in the ex GDR will have to overcome a large number of problems which, in addition, constantly change their characteristics. One major problem is estimating the number of potential entrepreneurs. In the theoretical section, the ongoing debate between researchers who advocate the trait, behavioral, or situational approach has been reviewed extensively. Goto, Yoshimura, Keeley, and Roure (1990) view the outcome of this discussion as rather unclear and not very useful for their purpose. They therefore include all managers in the pool of potential entrepreneurs. Smallbone (1990) observed a parallel trend between self-employment or business start-ups and unemployment. Stanworth, Stanworth, Granger, and Blyth (1990) comment on the importance of role models, such as entrepreneurial parents or previous work experience in small businesses, for the decision to actually start a business as an entrepreneur.

In the ex GDR, only about 100,000 small private businesses were reported in 1989. Beyond this limited number, previous experience from private businesses had mostly been acquired before 1972, and therefore, has to be included with scepticism. In addition, the level of unemployment has been predicted to exceed even 70% in selected counties in the south of the ex GDR in the first half of 1991. Finally, Beier et al. (1990) estimate that between five and ten percent of the working population will have to create their own business in the next few years in order to adjust the structure of the economy in the eastern and western part of Germany. This suggests that it might be very useful to include the whole working population of the ex GDR in the pool of potential entrepreneurs until the characteristics of the economy in that area have adjusted to those which prevail in the western countries.

Another important problem concerns the possible distinction between entrepreneurial ventures and small businesses. The main distinguishing dimension for this problem has been the growth of the venture, either in achieved or in proposed quantities. The majority of researchers apply these terms in non-specific usage or use metaphors like "mom-and-pop store". Roure and Keeley (1990), on the contrary, concentrate their research on those ventures which state the initial objective of achieving more than $10 million sales soon after their creation.

The present conditions in the ex GDR, as described two paragraphs above, also determine the answer to this question. In addition, Beier et al. (1990) state that small practices, trades, and craft workshops in West Germany have, on the average, 2.5 times the number of employees as compared to their eastern counterparts. Furthermore, private chains of stores, restaurants, or other service facilities did not exist in the ex GDR. Consequently, almost all private businesses will experience a phase of strong growth in the next few years. Role models of high growth ventures, which might help to shape the initial expectations of organization founders, have, however, not existed. Therefore it seems useful to make no distinction between small businesses and entrepreneurial ventures. This will probably hold true for the first few years which might best be described by the metaphor of the "Gold Digger Age".

The question of an adequate approach has already been answered implicitly in the previous paragraphs. Personality traits like n-ach, locus-of-control, or risk-lover could be expected to have been significantly influenced by the communist ideology. It is unclear however, whether this influence has been more than superficial. The study of Noelle-Neumann (1990) suggests that the personalities of Germans in the East and West are much more similar than has been expected.

Socialization patterns and role models were also severely limited under the former regime. The economic situation in 1991 will additionally contribute to render explanations based on social marginality theory (Stanworth et al. 1989) of little use. The effects of restructuring the economy and the resulting high level of structural unemployment will create a dominant bias. First, alternative economic role models were almost not available. Even moving to the western part of Germany or to other countries will only represent a temporary solution for a limited number of people. In 1990, about 500,000 people selected this alternative, about 100,000 per month in spring and about 15,000 per month at the end of the year. Second, the ongoing change will create high levels of incongruence between personal attributes and role for major parts of the working population.

The behavioral approach therefore seems to be the most appropriate alternative for studying the process of venture creation in the transition phase of the ex GDR. It is obviously a very extreme point of view to pretend to study the creation of each organization and, in addition, base the analysis on a pool of more than eight million people. The argument is made however, that the whole population of the ex GDR is unlearning the concepts which served under the former system. Instead, everybody gathers as many "rules" of the free market economy as possible. Some will learn very fast because of their higher ability or increased exposure to the new model, others might "click" later or never. The search for the "ideal" entrepreneur will therefore not be too fruitful in the present time. This paper argues that it is better to focus on the <u>activities</u> of those entrepreneurs and ventures who successfully survive the time of reconstruction and start to grow.

RESEARCH DESIGN

The preceding parts have presented rather general perspectives of the situation of entrepreneurship in the ex GDR. The purpose was to set the groundwork and specify the focus for future research. The objective of the proposed project is to develop a profile of successful entrepreneurship in an economy in transition. This will be accomplished based on a sample of small businesses which have either been handed back to their former owners, bought out by some or all of their former employees or created new by East Germans. In twelve case studies sponsored either by the European Foundation for Entrepreneurship Research (EFER) or by IESE, special attention will be given to the formation and adjustment process of entrepreneurial strategies under the chaotic circumstances of extreme uncertainty, resource scarcity, and volatility of the whole environment.

The initial framework includes concepts from Duchesneau and Gartner (1990), Gartner (1985), and Keeley and Roure (1990). It comprises four dimensions -- the entrepreneur, the transition behavior, the firm and its strategy, and the environment -- and it is represented in Figure 1. The size of the arrows indicates the expected strength of influence between the dimensions. Each dimension contains a number of variables, which have been selected after a review of several comprehensive discussions of research on factors which influence new venture performance. The variables have, in addition, been found to be very useful during the initial fieldwork. The measures focus predominantly on activities, but also refer to historic facts. They stem in the majority of cases from the behavioral approach but also represent a few concepts from trait approaches.

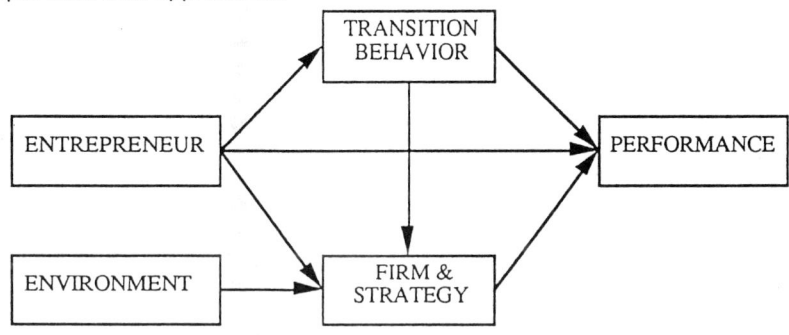

Figure 1: Interrelation of Venture Dimensions and Performance

The successful entrepreneur is expected to have had ample entrepreneurial role models and managerial experience. He is likely to actively engage in the transition process of the community and intensively search for the rules of the new free market economy. Furthermore, he will seek to reduce risk and see firm success as being within the sphere of his influence.

The transition behavior of the successful entrepreneur will be influenced predominantly by the high volatility of the economic environment. This is determined by factors such as the rapidly changing price system, the unknown competitive situation due to an elevated number of new market entrants, which either come from the west or are start-ups or reprivatizations, and the extreme scarcity of resources with regard to capital and management know-how. The entrepreneur will most likely spend more time in an intuitive, but comprehensive planning process which considers all functional areas. He will probably have needed less refocusing and planning iterations in order to refine a clear and broad business idea with ambitious objectives. He will use his political activities in order to keep track of the changing economic environment and build a spiderweb of firms in order to make best use of different support programs. Finally he is likely to seek professional advice and search for partners from the west, and he will actively support his employees in their effort to develop a better understanding of the "new rules of the game".

Successful firms are expected to have an entrepreneur who is solely in command; a philosophy which supports the interfunctional cross-training of the management; multi-skilled employees; and encourage participative decision making at the strategic and the operational level. The limited resources will be used more flexibly, alternative marketing channels will be employed as a reaction to the lack of access to traditional distribution channels, and the strategy will be more aggressive and global.

Variables from the environmental dimension have normally been used as rather static descriptors of the situation. This paper has shown, however, that the economic environment of the ex GDR is experiencing a period of rapid change. Some factors of this environment are expected to influence all ventures alike and have little impact on their performance, such as regional concentration, or the transient phenomenon of high, structural unemployment. Other variables, like up-to-date facilities, easy flow of material and information, or accessibility of suppliers and services, will have a major influence and can be moderated significantly by the firms. In many cases, the core assets of a firm will be mostly intangible, because the existing facilities and process technology call for immediate replacement. It is expected that successful ventures actively search for better communication, infrastructure and facilities. They will have higher availability of suppliers, services and of technology. They are also likely to have managed survival based on their initial competitiveness, and use the existing support programs in order to increase their capitalization for planned expansion.

The question of the appropriate measure of performance is rather difficult to answer. Some authors see the internal rate of return as the true measure of value (Keeley and Roure, 1990). In studies of new venture creation, it seems very reasonable to apply this measure, because the value of the new investment can clearly be identified. When the performance of reprivatized or bought-out ventures in the ex GDR is studied, a common starting point is difficult to identify. The different amounts of new investment which are required from the prospective owners are not standardized, and are instead determined in individual negotiations with Treuhand. Beyond the problem of the exact evaluation, each company will require a different degree of restructuring, and of product and process innovation. It can be expected that the aversion of the population to merchandise from their own territory will soon fade away. Additionally, it will probably be feasible to revitalize some traditional brand names. Other alternatives include the creation of a pro-forma company in the western part of Germany.

All these arguments suggest that a single measurement of performance for a comparative evaluation of firms will be at least an elusive phenomenon, if not an illusion. Furthermore, additional field work carried out since the original presentation of this paper led to the suspicion that the performance of ventures depends on more than just the traditional dimensions of industry boom, institutions, infrastructure, and conduct. Possibly, a larger part of the new venture's success depends on the stage of the lead entrepreneur in a sequential "transition pattern". This pattern seems to start with the recognition of the impact of those business functions which have been neglected in the ex GDR, like design, market research, sales, distribution, and strategic planning. Hopefully, this then leads to a widening of the horizon concerning the recognition of opportunities and consecutively to an enlargement of the growth aspiration. Consequently, time is a critical dimension in an environment with highly volatile windows of opportunity. Due to the purely speculative character of this paragraph, future research will dedicate special effort to further exploring this indicated pattern.

In the introduction to this paper it has been claimed that the study of entrepreneurship in an economy in transition, such as that of the ex GDR, requires a hybrid approach. The uniqueness of this transient situation requires the use of qualitative and quantitative methods. Initially, this research project will have an exploratory character which requires the utilization of qualitative methods. The aim is to generate a level of understanding which will allow the development and formulation of knowledge in the form of an empirically rooted theory. Therefore, the first part of this project will follow the grounded theory approach of Glaser and Strauss (1967). A small number of case-studies will describe the activities and characteristics of entrepreneurs and their ventures. These "thick" descriptions serve to develop a level of understanding which will allow us to better evaluate the applicability of the current models. Furthermore, special emphasis will be put on the readjustment of entrepreneurial strategy and the suspected transition pattern.

Parallel to this, the initial literature review will be continued. The complexity of the analyzed phenomenon calls for an additional review of related streams of literature, such as chaos theory, decision science, or organizational learning. A third course of action is the use of delphi rounds. Experts from East and West German universities,institutions, associations, and companies will assess the relevance of variables as key success factors for new ventures. The use of multiple approaches will help to minimize the introduction of errors during the first phase. The resulting variables will be compared for consistency and comprised into a final set. Based on this, the initial framework and model will be refined. The subsequent application of quantitative methods for the confirmation of the findings will depend on the outcome of this first phase of the project.

CONCLUSION

Traditional theories of entrepreneurship and small business management are predominantly based on relatively stable environments with abundant resources and role models. They fail to capture specific aspects of the situation of entrepreneurs who create organizations in an economic environment in transition and with minimal resources. The entrepreneurs in the ex GDR had primarily been motivated by non-material factors such as family tradition or their desire for independence. Since the change in the political and economic system, they are also able and eager to make a profit by capitalizing on resources, and they now represent one of the major driving forces for economic and social change in their environment.

This paper has illustrated the many differences but also some surprising similarities between the eastern and the western parts of Germany. It is stated that many of the current approaches to the study of entrepreneurship will not capture those specific phenomena which characterize it in this highly volatile environment. Resources like capital and management experience are extremely scarce. The established order system becomes gradually replaced. The population rapidly changes its values and beliefs. And the working population, although gifted with a high level of skills and ingenuity, experiences a phase of high structural unemployment. This makes flexibility and speed of learning much more important factors for new venture performance in the present period than, for example, procedural planning.

This study suggests the need to identify a modified framework for an analysis of entrepreneurship in an economy in transition. More research is required to confirm and elaborate the indicated changes. Other researchers should be encouraged to continue in this direction because the reconstruction of the economies of the other countries in Eastern Europe will represent challenging tasks for entrepreneurs who will welcome any kind of support or help through research.

REFERENCES

Begley, T.M. and Boyd, D.P. 1987 "Psychological Characteristics Associated with Performance in Entrepreneurial Firms and Smaller Businesses". Journal of Business Venturing, 2, 79-83.

Beyer, H.J., Fischer, M., K_sling, F., Kranhold, H., Richter, A., and Schmidt, W. 1990-July "Zur Entwicklung von Klein- und Mittel-Betrieben in der DDR". (On the Development of Small and Medium Businesses in the GDR) Stiftung Gesellschafts-Analyse e.V., Berlin, Germany.

Bird, B.J. and Jelinek, M. Winter-1988. "The Operation of Entrepreneurial Intention" Entrepreneurship Theory and Practice , 21-29.

Bird, B.J. 1989 Entrepreneurial Behavior Scott, Foresman, Glenview, USA.

Brockhaus, R.H. 1980 "Risk Taking Propensity of Entrepreneurs" Academy of Management Journal, Vol 23(3), 509-520.

Brockhaus, R.H. 1982 "The Psychology of the Entrepreneur" in C.A.Kent, D.L.Sexton, and K.H. Vesper, eds. Encyclopedia of Entrepreneurship Prentice-Hall, USA.

Brockhaus, R.H. and Horwitz, P.S. 1986 "The Psychology of the Entrepreneur" in D.L.Sexton and R.W.Smilor eds The Art and Science of Entrepreneurship, Ballinger, USA.

Brytting, T. 1990 "Spontaneity and Systematic Planning in Small Firms - a Grounded Theory Approach" International Small Business Journal, Vol 9(1), 45-62.

Carland, J.W., Hoy, F., Boulton, W.R., and Carland, J.C. 1984 "Differentiating Entrepreneurs from Small Business Owners: A Conceptualization" Academy of Management Review, Vol 9(2), 354-359.

Chandler, A.D. 1962 Strategy and Structure: Chapters in the History of the American Industrial Enterprise MIT Press, USA.

Chell, E. 1986 "The Entrepreneurial Personality: A Review and Some Theoretical Developments" in C.Curran, J.Stanworth, and D.Watkins eds The Survival of the Small Firm Vol 1, Gower Press, USA.

Clifford, D.K. 1973 "Growth Pains of the Threshold Company" Harvard Business Review, Vol 51(5), 143-154.

Collins, O., Moore, D. and Unwalla, D. 1964 The Enterprising Man Michigan State University, USA.

d'Amboise, G. and Muldowney, M. 1988 "Management Theory for Small Business: Attempts and Requirements" Academy of Management Review, Vol 13(2), 226-240.

Davidsson, P. 1989 Continued Entrepreneurship and Small Firm Growth, EFI,Sweden

Diomande, M. 1990 "Business Creation with Minimal Resources: Some Lessons from the African Experience" Journal of Business Venturing, Vol 5, 191-200.

Duchesneau, D.A. 1987 New Venture Success in an Emerging Industry, Nova University, USA.

Duchesneau, D.A. and Gartner, W.B. 1990 "A Profile of New Venture Success and Failure in an Emerging Industry" Journal of Business Venturing, Vol 5, 297-312.

Gartner, W.B. 1985 "A Framework for Describing the Phenomenon of New Venture Creation" American Journal of Small Business, Vol 11, 12-22.

Gartner, W.B. 1989-Summer " "Who is an Entrepreneur?" Is the Wrong Question" Entrepreneurship Theory and Practice, 47-68.

Glaser, B. and Strauss, A. 1967 The Discovery of Grounded Theory: Strategies for Qualitative Research, Aldine, USA.

Glueck, W. and Mescon, T. 1980 "Entrepreneurship: A Literature Analysis of Concepts" Paper presented at the Annual Conference of the Academy of Management, USA.

Goto, M., Yoshimura, K., Keeley, R.H., and Roure, J.B. 1990, Entrepreneurship is Risky! Should it also be Costly?, Science University of Tokyo, Japan.

Greiner, L.E. 1972 "Evolution and Revolution as Organizations Grow" Harvard Business Review, Vol 50(4), 37-46.

Kao, J.J. 1989, Entreprenurship, Creativity, and Organization, Prentice Hall, USA.

Keeley, R.H. and Roure, J.B. 1990 "Management, Strategy, and Industry Structure as Influences on the Success of New Firms: A Structural Model" Management Science, Vol 36(10), 1256-1267.

Kets de Vries, M. 1977 "The Entrepreneurial Personality: A Person at the Crossroad" Journal of Management Studies, Vol 14(1).

McCain, G. and Smith, N. 1981-Summer "A Contemporary Model of Entrepreneurial Style" Small Business Institute Review, 40-45.

Mitton, D.G. 1989-Spring "The Compleat Entrepreneur" Entrepreneurship Theory and Practice, 9-19.

Noelle-Neumann, E. 1990 "Die Deutschen: _berraschende Gemeinsamkeiten nach 45 Jahren Trennung" (The Germans: Surprising Similarities after 45 Years of Separation) Capital, Vol 29(11), 254-259.

McDougall, P. and Robinson, R.B. 1990 "New Venture Strategies: An Empirical Identification of Eight 'Archetypes_ of Competitive Strategies for Entry" Strategic Management Journal, Vol 11, 447-467.

Miner, J.B. 1990 "Entrepreneurs, High Growth Entrepreneurs, and Managers: Contrasting and Overlapping Motivational Patterns" Journal of Business Venturing, Vol 5, 221-234.

Mitton, D.G. 1990-Spring "The Complete Entrepreneur" Entrepreneurship Theory and Practice, 9-19.

Romano, C.A. 1988 "Research Strategies for Small Business: A Case Study Approach" International Small Business Journal, Vol 7(4), 35-43.

Roure, J.B. and Keeley, R.H. 1990 "Predictors of Success in New Technology Based Ventures" Journal of Business Venturing, Vol 5, 201-220.

Schumpeter, J.A. 1934 <u>The Theory of Economic Development</u>. Translated by R.Opie. Cambridge: Harvard University Press, USA.

Seifert, B. 1990 "_berlebensstrategien Ostdeutscher Firmen" (Survival Strategies of East German Companies) <u>Capital</u>, Vol 29(11), 186-207.

Smallbone, D. 1990-Spring "Success and Failure in New Business Start-ups" <u>International Small Business Journal</u>, Vol 8(2), 34-47.

Smith, N.R. and Miner, J.B. 1983 "Type of Entrepreneur, Type of Firm, and Managerial Motivation: Implications for Organizational Life Cycle Theory" <u>Strategic Management Journal</u>, Vol 4, 325-340.

Stanworth, J. and Curran, J. 1973 <u>Management Motivation in the Smaller Business</u> Gower Press, USA.

Stanworth, J., Stanworth, C., Granger, B., and Blyth, S. 1989 "Who Becomes an Entrepreneur?" <u>International Small Business Journal</u>, Vol 8(1), 11-22.

Steinmetz, L.L. 1969 "Critical Stages of Small Business Growth: When They Occur and How to Survive" <u>Business Horizons</u>, Vl 12(1), 29-36.

Stevenson, H.H., Roberts, M.J., and Grousbeck, H.J. 1989 <u>New Business Ventures and the Entrepreneur</u> 3rd edt Irwin, USA.

Timmons, J.A. 1990 <u>New Venture Creation</u> 3rd edt Irwin, USA.

Venkatraman, S., Van de Ven, A.H., Buckeye, J. and Hudson, R. 1990 "Starting up in a Turbulent Environment: A Process Model of Failure among Firms with High Customer Dependence" <u>Journal of Business Venturing</u>, Vol 5, 277-295.

Vesper, K.H. 1982 "Introduction and Summary of Entrepreneurship Research" in C.A.Kent, D.L.Sexton and K.H.Vesper eds <u>Encyclopedia of Entrepreneurship,</u> Prentice-Hall, USA.

Vesper, K.H. 1984 <u>Entrepreneurship and National Policy</u> Heller Institute, Chicago, USA.

Wortman, M.S. 1987 "Entrepreneurship: An Integrating Typology and Evaluation of the Empirical Research in the Field" <u>Journal of Management</u>, Vol 13(2) 259-279.

The Nature of Entrepreneurial Decision-making:
Inside the Black Box

Critique
by
Svenn Jenssen, *Bodo Graduate School of Business*
Lars Kolvereid, *Bodo Graduate School of Business*

The introduction of the paper raises at least two important issues. First, it identifies an aspect of entreprenuership that may have been neglected in previous studies within the field (i.e. the creative decision process). Second it gives an opinion of the research approach used in the ongoing research, well known to the different "schools" present in the field of entrepreneurial and small business research. In general both issues are interesting and important in relation to the development of entrepreneurship research.

The focus of the article is on the implications for research of the "creative" decision model. The introduction outlines two concepts: entepreneurs, and decision processes. The paper defines the entrepreneur as one who specializes in making judgmental decisions about the coordination of scarce resources. This is a very wide definition. The paper focuses mainly on decision processes, but is not clear what type of decision processes it deals with. Decision processes may be psychological or organizational, and the paper does not distinguish between these different levels of analysis while terms such as "teams", "managers" and "entrepreneurs" are used interchangeably.

The paper builds on a well documented assumption that the entrepreneur makes the difference to the success of the firm. It is the individual that represents the basic unit of analysis in entrepreneurship research, and the author argues that entrepreneurial behavior involves decisions, and points out a need for a fuller description of the decision process, or, as he states, of "what is going on within the black box".

The paper looks at some of the previous research within the field of entrepreneurship and focuses on the methodology and research approach used in these studies, making this an issue for discussion, which in turn introduces the need for more detailed information about the decision making that entrepreneurial behavior involves . It would have been useful to have a clearer understanding of what part of the entrepreneurial field this specific aspect is relevant to. The paper suggests that it would be relevant to answering fundamental questions such as "how do I get more entrepreneurial behavior from my manager, from my organizations or in a socioeconomic group?" Some may argue that this fundamental question may be answered by using the "black box" technique which sometimes is very helpful, while others may reply that the important question is, "what makes individuals or even organizations take the step into starting a new business or launching a new product?", thus focusing more on the entrepreneurial event rather than the process.

Muzyka argues that the black box technique is the heart of the scientific method. This can hardly be correct since most philosophers of science agree that all science has the scientific method in common. The methodology of science is the logic of justification, while the techniques of a discipline are the specific tools and apparatus that researchers in a discipline have found useful, such as the choice of measurement instruments and data collection techniques. Muzyka is also concerned that the development of a theory "becomes an activity working within an artificially defined world". This may be the case for the topic under investigation, but hardly for theory development, since all theories are simplified descriptions of real phenomena.

The paper covers relevant theory, in respect to the areas discussed, though it sometimes seems to use literature and previous work primarily focusing on large organizations with a managerial structure and a strong management function which entrepreneurs and small businesses, in general, lack. This is especially the case in relation to the literature on decision making under uncertainty, and this may present a problem in discussing small entrepreneurial organizations, teams and individuals.

The paper ends with the suggestion that changes may be required in several areas of our research plan, including the research methods used, environment for research and time horizon. The conclusions and implications are general and do reflect one opinion about method, research focus etc. but seem to be independent of the literature study.

The paper introduces the Creative/Inductive decision process as an approach to a better understanding of the entrepreneurial behavior and entrepreneurs as managers. The paper focuses on the need for what other research efforts and disciplines have to offer researchers in entrepreneurship. The paper however deals with these suggestions in a very general manner, and does not indicate ways of taking a closer look at the black box using theories on decision processes, of which there are many.

The study of entrepreneurial decision models created a need for new research approaches as the paper suggests. The paper does not point out specific areas of improvement in research approach other than emphasizing the need for a new mix between quantitative and qualitative approaches.

The paper starts out with a very limited description of what part of the entrepreneurial field the emphasis is on. The theory reviewed is no doubt worth looking into for new exciting studies in entrepreneurship and small businees. The subsequent discussion is more concerned with the general field of entrepreneurship and how this should be developed, and the need for new methods and encouragement of speciflc types of studies. This sometimes seems to be at the expense of the theory used, and in our opinion, the question of theory needs to be explored further.

THE NATURE OF ENTREPRENEURIAL DECISION-MAKING: INSIDE THE BLACK BOX

DANIEL F. MUZYKA, *INSEAD*

ABSTRACT

One of the central and critical elements in entrepreneurship remains the behavior of, and, more specifically, decisions made by entrepreneurs. Currently we have only limited understanding of the nature and flow of the entrepreneurial decision-making processes. Clearly, we have made strong contributions to our understanding of some of the factors that influence or are involved in the process, but we still have little clear, formal understanding of the actual decision processes. In addition, the characteristics we attribute to the entrepreneurial decision process suggest that it is "inductive" in nature and must cope with high levels of uncertainty. Research into induction and decision-making under uncertainty (DMUU), which have both developed significantly in the last decade, suggest that special care must be taken in researching the nature and outcome of such decision processes. Furthermore, this research also suggests that if we are to really understand an inductive decision process operating in an environment characterized by high levels of uncertainty, we must take great care to follow the process and not simply rely on time independent analytical techniques to assess factors associated with the decision process. This research into induction and DMUU poses some challenges, conditions and constraints on the nature of research we do conduct and suggests some challenges in the nature of research we should conduct.

INTRODUCTION

The last decade has seen significant strides in the development of both macro and micro models of the entrepreneurial process and its impact (e.g., Kirchoff and Phillips (1988); Birley (1987)), entrepreneurial management (e.g., Miner (1990) and entrepreneurial behavior (e.g., Ginn and Sexton (1990); Scheinberg and MacMillan (1988)). At the "micro" or individual level, there has been a long history of studying the characteristics of entrepreneurs (see, for instance Carland, et. al. (1984) a discussion of the lineage of studies). In addition, there have been a number of studies dedicated to understanding the "factors" that influence entrepreneurship within a given environmental context (e.g., Dubini (1988)) and across socioeconomic contexts (e.g., Scheinberg and MacMillan (1988)). Finally, at the "micro" level there have been studies (e.g., Sexton and Bowman (1986)) that have dealt with issues concerning the psychological characteristics of entrepreneurs, though some argue (e.g., Timmons (1990)) that this research is inconclusive.

One of the underlying and/or stated assumptions of most of the research is, however, that the entrepreneurs themselves make the difference. It is the actions of an individual or individuals in identifying and exploiting opportunities through the marshaling of scarce resources that is at the heart of the entrepreneurial process (e.g., see Stevenson, et.al. (1985); Timmons (1990); Vesper (1980); Gartner (1990)). It is the individual (or entrepreneurial team) versus the entrepreneurial enterprise that represents the basic unit of analysis in entrepreneurship research. It is individuals or groups of individuals who collectively perceive economic opportunities, assemble resources, overcome obstacles and realize value.

Research has generally shown that entrepreneurial actions on the part of the individual are not somehow genetically motivated nor motivated solely through some set of psychological traits developed at an early age. Rather, research has suggested, through many "behavioral" models of entrepreneurship (e.g., Stevenson, et. al. (1985)), that there may be some common behaviors exhibited by those we refer to as entrepreneurs. These "behaviors" are the result of a series of conscious and unconscious decisions made by individuals. In fact, Casson (1982) describes an entrepreneur as one who specializes in making "judgmental decisions about the coordination of scarce resources".

If we accept that the behavior is composed of a stream of decisions, we are led to ask ourselves "what type of decision making are we dealing with?" and "what is the nature of the environment in which these decisions are composed?" Both of these have been addressed in one of the more recent and popular textbooks in entrepreneurship (Timmons (1990)) in two lists. The first question is addressed by summarizing some of the attitudes and behaviors this text lists as being associated with entrepreneurship (see Timmons (1990), chapters 5 and 6 or Gartner (1990)): creativity, innovativeness, intelligence, flexibility, "counterintuitiveness", and perceptiveness. The second question, regarding the environment, can similarly be summarized from concepts introduced in the same text: uncertainty, ambiguity, risk, nonlinear and nonparametric events, and rapid change. These concepts characterizing entrepreneurial behavior and attitudes and the entrepreneurial environment are echoed throughout the presentations of our research (e.g., Vesper (1980); Gartner (1990); Stevenson, et.al. (1985)). Both creativity and the ability to contend with uncertainty appear to be dominant themes in a discussion of entrepreneurial decision making.

Current writing on entrepreneurship, while describing the general nature of entrepreneurial decision making and factors affecting it, does not contain a formal or complete description of this decision process that is so important to the entrepreneurial process. Despite the fact that a more complete understanding of the process aids both theory and practice, we do not have a more complete description for many reasons, but especially because it is difficult to fully describe and classify the decision behavior. However, it is clear that if we are to answer such fundamental questions as "how do I get more entrepreneurial behaviour in my managers, in my organization, or in a socioeconomic group?", we will need a fuller description of the decision process.

We continue to rectify this lack of a complete model through incremental research, much of which attempts, in classical research form, to dismember the problem and to test incrementally the impact of various factors in order to uncover the nature of the underlying decision process (Kuhn, et.al. (1988), chapters 1 and 2; Raiffa (1970), chapter 10). This work naturally raises the question of whether the "creative," entrepreneurial decision-making in uncertain environments is most appropriately (and successfully) studied by researching it as a "black box" subject to stimulus-response measurement. Is there a deterministic (or relatively deterministic), replicable process that can be discerned through isolated, comparatively simple testing of the impact of a given stimulus or groups of stimuli?

We may raise a simpler question with regard to the lack of a formal definition of the "creative", "counterintuitive" decision making process that is at the heart of entrepreneurship. The question is whether we may, given the nature of the decision process, really be able to investigate "creative" decision making?

The implications for research of the "creative" decision model is the primary focus of the article. Given the lack of a formal definition of the decision model, we are obligated to investigate the nature of "creative" decision models by looking at other fields of research including artificial intelligence, psychology and decision theory where the nature of human decision processes are central to the work of the field. A summary of what these fields currently have to offer us in order to address the above questions is included in the next section. This is followed by a discussion of the implications for entrepreneurship research.

ISSUE

Simon (1984) and others involved in the field of artificial intelligence (e.g., Holland, et.al. (1986)) study behavior similar to that attributed to entrepreneurs and similarly refer to the nature of such decision making as "creative" or "intuitive," often referring to it formally as "induction"). Researchers in the decision sciences (e.g., Keeney (1982); Hogarth (1982); Raiffa (1970); Luce, et.al. (1957)) characterize the nature of entrepreneurial decision making as decision making under uncertainty. Both streams focused on creating models of rational decision behavior during the early years of work (e.g. Von Neumann and Morgenstern (1947); Simon (1955)) in an attempt to structure and formalize the work. (A summary of the common assumptions of the model of decision analysis that resulted from some of this work are shown in Exhibit 1.) The current state of research in these fields suggests that the early models of rational decision behavior, which drive many of our research assumptions, do not hold when it comes to creative processes or high levels of uncertainty.

In the following sections we will discuss current research on decision making under uncertainty as well as what we know about creative/inductive decision making. In addition, we will discuss what psychologists have learned about the nature of humans as decision makers. Work in this field has yielded quite a number of surprises about the extent of systematic biases in decision making. These summary discussions of some of the findings of current work in these areas is followed by a discussion of the broad requirements this imposes on the nature of our research.

<u>Assumptions of Rational Decision Model</u>. The first, and probably most fundamental issue with regard to decision making is that the model of rational decision making (e.g., where individual decision makers specify the problem, identify the alternatives, analyze which alternative is appropriate and then act) does not hold, especially under uncertainty. Researchers from Cyert and March (1963) through Cohen, et.al. (1972) to those studying the model more recently (e.g., Winkler (1982)) have noted the systematic weakness in the notions that date from Von Neumann and Morgenstern (1947) that decision making is a relatively clear, standardized process. Though the literature in economics and finance still discusses the notion of a rational decision maker (e.g., Jensen and Meckling (1976)), many researchers who systematically study decision making, especially under conditions of uncertainty, suggest that there are major flaws in the traditional, rational, deterministic model of decision making.

For instance, the limitations of the traditional rational model of decision making are evident in such work as that of Cohen, March and Olsen (1972). They developed an explicit model to deal with uncertain environments -- where the problems and choices are uncoupled. Their "garbage can model" attempts to bring order out of the chaos they observed in decision making in environments characterized by a high level of uncertainty. What they demonstrated in their model was that decision making was context sensitive: the matching of problems, choices and decision makers was subject to problem content, relevance and the competence of those involved. It was also sensitive to the timing of problems, the nature of other problems being considered and the decision load and availability of slack and attention (described as "energy") in the system. The conclusions of this and other related work in organizational decision making is echoed in the findings of the work by those engaged in work on artificial intelligence.

The literature in this area suggests that some part of the differences between the observed and prescribed models of decision making may not be entirely a result of problems with the state of information or high levels of uncertainty. Rather, this research suggests that some of the differences may be attributed to the fact that there are a number of inherent limitations in the prescribed model itself which must be overcome in practice, especially in environments of high uncertainty[1]. Hogarth (1982), Morris (1982), Keeney (1982) and others have argued that current theory, and its applicability in high uncertainty environments requires some rethinking. Dreze (1978) makes a similar observation with reference to the theory of information economics by noting that it has doubtful descriptive realism due to the spontaneous behavior of rational actors and difficulties in formalizing even simple decision problems so that the theory may be applied in a prescriptive fashion.

Literature from those involved with researching the model of "rational decision analysis" or DMUU has also noted the limitations with regard to the calibration of probabilities. Dreze (1978) notes the difficulties with calibrating probabilities as a major weakness in the theory of information economics. Morris (1982) argues that the tools of rational decision making and analysis do not recognize the context dependency of probability assessments of particular data. Winkler (1982) notes that modeling uncertainty is a particularly difficult problem, especially because the assessments of probability are "contaminated" by the subjective judgments of humans who may desire specific outcomes.[2] Therefore, the problems related to developing and utilizing probabilistically expressed risk measures may have been related to weaknesses in the available tools.

Discussion of the weaknesses of the classic model of decision making under uncertainty notes that the notion of the "simple" selection of an "optimal" is relatively flawed.[3] The determination of desirability was compounded by another difficulty: often in the face of uncertainty, individuals do not realize what it is they want (i.e., they do not have a good calibration of their utility function[4] or what they would find most desirable under the circumstances). All of this indecision concerning the desirability of individual alternatives is even further compounded by the normal difficulties involved in modeling group judgments.[5]

In the end, we would suggest that we should emulate the practitioners we are studying in several ways. First, we would suggest that it is important not to be trapped by the definitions, frameworks and attitudes of others. The definition of "rigor" for purposes of research in the physical sciences and in the more abstract regions of economics may not be entirely applicable when it comes to the entrepreneurial phenomena we are interested in studying. For, indeed, many entrepreneurial phenomenon fall outside the predictions of research in economics -- entrepreneurs appear to "feed" on imperfections in theory and market. In the end, by adopting the definitions of rigor produced to satisfy the needs of other disciplines, we may not only be capturing the strengths of the disciplines but also their weaknesses. We submit that we do not want to fall victim to what John Tukey (see Raiffa (1970), page 264) refers to as a Type III error -- solving the wrong problem -- simply because we wish to apply methods which our own prior training suggests are "accepted." Besides, research has shown that research orientation can significantly impact the interpretation of events (e.g., see Allison {1971}).

<u>Change in Academic Environment.</u> In order to support acceptance of alternative methods and approaches (or even to emphasize those which do not fit the current definitive model) we need to provide the environment for such "risky" behavior, especially on the part of junior faculty. Changes in the research environment which we may have to accept, and indeed encourage, include publication of partial work (to permit publication and dissemination of long-term longitudinal research), and the support, acceptance and encouragement of researchers who undertake such longitudinal research or who attempt to apply new methods. Furthermore, encouragement of those who adapt methods and knowledge from other fields would seem appropriate -- the history of science is strewn with "disciplines" that fell after

insulating themselves from knowledge gained in other disciplines (see Lakatos and Musgrave (1970); Kuhn (1962)).

Tenured, senior faculty can be most helpful by providing encouragement to fellow professors to undertake such research. This encouragement could come in the form of positive role models -- undertaking such research themselves -- and being open-minded about the acceptance of articles in refereed journals which exhibit such behavior. In addition, senior faculty, in their role as reviewers, could enforce certain norms in order to encourage research that recognizes the reality of entrepreneurial decision behavior. For instance, reviewers should require that authors be quite clear about the comparability of those included in their research samples. In the case of those studying entrepreneurial behavior, the experience(s) and stage of development of those included in the sample should be well stated. In addition, reviewers should require that authors demonstrate a practical understanding of the entrepreneurial behaviors they are studying.

Another "environmental" change that would permit entrepreneurship research to more accurately reflect the nature of entrepreneurial thinking and remain dynamic would be an ongoing acceptance of alternative research styles and methods.

Unfortunately, as Kuhn and others have chronicled, a group of relatively successful studies may define the field and attitudes around what is "acceptable research" thereby limiting the ability of contradictory or novel new research to be communicated through existing channels for academic research. The acceptance and/or maintenance of the attitude that large database studies may be as rigorous as more limited, long-term studies of entrepreneurial behavior would be a welcome step in this direction.

SUMMARY

In summary, this paper does not purport, in any way, to fully address the topic of entrepreneurial decision making or its impact on the research agenda or practices for entrepreneurship.

However, it does suggest that while we have not been entirely successful in understanding entrepreneurial decision making, we must be careful to not abandon our search for a better understanding of the decision model, which is central to entrepreneurial phenomena. Research in related fields such as artificial intelligence suggests that an understanding can be achieved, but such an understanding may require extensive time and effort and involve the definition of new frameworks and research methods.

Research in related fields also suggests that a multi-disciplinary approach may be required. All of this suggests that we in entrepreneurship research may wish to emulate our "subjects" through flexible and creative thinking. This does not suggest that we should abandon a scientific approach to understanding phenomenon, but that we may wish to be more open to changes in frameworks and methods than has typically been evidenced in scientific research.

EXHIBIT 1

KEENEY'S AXIOMS OF DECISION ANALYSIS

Axiom 1a: (generation of alternatives) at least two alternatives can be specified.

Axiom 1b: (identification of consequences) possible consequences of each alternative can be identified.

Axiom 2: (quantification of judgment) the relative likelihoods (i.e., Probabilities) of each possible consequence that could result from each alternative can be specified.

Axiom 3: (quantification of preference) the relative desirability (i.e., Utility) for the possible consequences of any alternative can be specified.

Axiom 4a: (comparison of alternatives) if two alternatives would each result in the same two possible consequences, the alternative yielding the higher chance of the preferred consequence is preferred.

Axiom 4b: (transitivity of preferences) if one alternative is preferred to a second alternative and if the second alternative is preferred to a third alternative, then the first alternative is preferred to the third alternative.

Axiom 4c: (substitution of consequences) if an alternative is modified by replacing one of its consequences with a set of consequences and associated probabilities (i.e., A lottery) that is indifferent to the consequence being replaced, then the original and the modified alternatives should be indifferent.

EXHIBIT 2

CHARACTERISTICS OF INDUCTIVE SYSTEMS

(1) general knowledge can be represented by condition-action rules.

(2) Rules can represent both diachronic relationships (for instance between current and expected future states) and synchronic rules (associations and re-categorizations of categories), and the two types of rules act together to generate inferences and solutions to problems.

(3) Higher-order knowledge structures such as categories correspond to implicit or explicit clusters of rules with similar conditions. This implies that larger structures of rules are composed of more elementary building blocks.

(4) Superordinate relations among categories and rules yield an emergent default hierarchy.

(5) A set of synchronic and diachronic rules, organized in a default hierarchy, gives rise to an emergent mental model.

(6) Rules act in accord with a principle of limited parallelism. In effect, multiple rules may be triggered which may guide thinking and action and may compete to represent the current state of affairs. The inductive system may use multiple sources of weak support to arrive at a confident conclusion.

(7) Induction involves (1) mechanisms for revising parameters such as the strength of existing rules (or determining how relevant they are to the situation at hand); and (2) mechanisms for generating plausibly useful new rules (ways to modify and/or add new rules).

(8) Mechanisms for generating new rules are constrained or guided by mechanisms which ensure that new rules will be useful and generated in response to weaknesses in the current state of knowledge.

(9) Induction is guided not only by the static or deterministic set of rules concerning conditions and actions and the organization of these rules but by knowledge of the variability of the environment.

REFERENCES

Allison, Graham T., Essence of Decision, Little Brown and Company, Boston, 1971.

Arrow, Kenneth J., Social Choice and Individual Values, Wiley, New York, 1951.

Arrow, Kenneth J., The Economics of Information, Belknap Press, Cambridge, Massachusetts, 1984.

Bailey, John E., "Learning Styles of Successful Entrepreneurs", Frontiers of Entrepreneurship Research, Center for Entrepreneurial Studies, Babson College, Wellesley, MA, 1986.

Baty, Gordon B., Entrepreneurship for the Eighties, Reston Publishing, Reston, Virginia, 1981.

Bell, David E., "Regret in Decision Making Under Uncertainty", Operations Research, Volume 30, No. 5, September-October, 1982.

Bell, David E., "Potential Contributions to Decision Analysis", Decision Sciences, Volume 13, Number 4, October, 1982.

Birley, Sue, "New Ventures and Employment Growth", Journal of Business Venturing,

Volume 2, Number 2, Spring, 1987.

Bourne, Lyle F., Roger L. Dominowski, Elizabeth F. Loftus, Alice F. Healy, Cognitive Processes, Prentice-Hall, Englewood Cliffs, New Jersey, 1986.

Budnick, Frank S., Richard Mojena, and Thomas Vollmann, Principles of Operations Research for Management, Richard D. Irwin, Inc. Homewood, Illinois, 1977.

Carland, James W., Frank Hoy, William R. Boulton, and Jo Ann C. Carland, "Differentiating Entrepreneurs From Small Business Owners: A Conceptualization", Academy of Management Review, Volume 9, Number 2, 1984.

Casson, M.C., The Entrepreneur: An Economic Theory, Martin Robertson, Oxford, 1982.

Chase, A. Editor, Visual Information Processing, Academic Press, New York, 1973.

Churchman, C. West, Russel L. Ackoff and E. Leonard Arnoff, Introduction to Operations Research, Wiley, New York, New York, 1957.

Cohen, M.D., J.G. March, and J.P. Olsen, "A Garbage Can Model of Organizational Choice", Volume 17, Administrative Science Quarterly, 1972.

Cyert, Richard M., and James G. March, A Behavioral Theory of the Firm, Prentice Hall, Englewood Cliffs, NJ, 1963.

Diamond, Peter and Michael Rothschild, ed. Uncertainty in Economics, Academic Press, Orlando, Florida, 1978.

Dickson, John W., "Subjective Risk and Choice as Related to The Transitivity Condition", Psychological Reports, pp. 723-726, June 1978.

Dreze, J.H., "Axiomatic Theories of Choice, Cardinal Utility, and Subjective Probability", Uncertainty in Economics (edited by Peter Diamond and Michael Rothschild), Academic Press, Inc., Orlando, Florida, 1978.

Dubini, Paola, "Motivational and Environmental Influences On Business Start-Ups", Frontiers of Entrepreneurship Research, Center for Entrepreneurial Studies, Babson College, Wellesley, MA, 1988.

Feller, William, An Introduction to Probability Theory and its Applications, Volume 2, John Wiley and Sons, New York, New York, 1971.

Ferber, Robert, Editor, Readings in Survey Research, American Marketing Association, Chicago, 1978.

Fishburn, P.C., "Comments on 'Research Directions in Decision Making Under Uncertainty'", Decision Sciences, Volume 13, Number 4, October, 1982.

Forsyth, Richard, Expert Systems, Chapman and Hall, New York, New York, 1984.

Gartner, William B., "What Are We Talking About When We Talk About Entrepreneurship?", Journal of Business Venturing, Volume 5, Number 1, January, 1990.

Gilmore, Thomas N. and Robert K. Kazanjian, "Clarifying Decision Making in High-Growth Ventures: The Use of Responsibility Charting", Journal of Business Venturing, Volume 4, Number 1, January, 1989.

Gimpl, Martin L., "Decision Making Under Ambiguity: Western vs. Japanese Managers", Journal of Business Forecasting, Summer 1986.

Ginn, Charles W. and Donald L. Sexton, "A Comparison of the Personality Type Dimensions of 1987 Inc. 500 Company Founder/CEOs With Those of Slower Growth Firms", Journal of Business Venturing, Volume 5, Number 5, September, 1990.

Gleick, James, Chaos, Penguin Books, New York, New York, 1987.

Hadley, G., Introduction to Probability and Statistical Decision Theory, Holden-Day, New York, New York, 1967.

Hillier, Frederick S., and Gerald J. Lieberman, Introduction to Operations Research, Holden-Day, San Francisco, California, 1967.

Hofstadter, Douglas, Godel, Escher, Bach: An Eternal Golden Braid, Basic Books, New York, New York, 1979.

Hofstadter, Douglas, The Mind's I: A New Science Explores the Human Mind, Basic Books, New York, New York, 1981.

Hofstadter, Douglas, Metamagical Themas: Questioning of the Essence of Mind and Pattern, Basic Books, New York, New York, 1984.

Hogarth, Robin M., "From Romanticism to Precision to . . .", Decision Sciences, Volume 13, Number 4, October, 1982.

Holland, John H., Keith J. Holyoak, Richard E. Nisbett, and Paul R. Thagard, Induction: Process of Inference, Learning and Discovery, MIT Press, Cambridge, MA, 1986.

Jackson, Barbara Bund, Multivariate Data Analysis, Richard D. Irwin, Homewood, Illinois, 1983.

Jensen, Michael C. and William H. Meckling, "Theory of the Firm: Managerial Behavior, Agency Costs and Ownership Structure", Volume 3, Journal of Financial Economics, 1976.

Johnson, George, Machinery of the Mind, Time Books, New York, New York, 1986.

Johnston, James M. and H.S. Pennypacker, Strategies and Tactics of Human Behavioral Research, Lawrence Erlbaum Associates, 1980.

Joyce, Edward J. and Gary C. Biddle, "Anchoring and Adjustment in Probabilistic Inference in Auditing", Journal of Accounting Research, Volume 19, No. 1, Spring 1981.

Kahneman, Daniel and Amos Tversky, "Choices, Values and Frames", American Psychologist, Volume 39, No. 4, April 1984.

Kahneman, Daniel and Amos Tversky, "The Psychology of Preference, Scientific American, Volume 246, No. 1, 1982.

Kahneman, Daniel, Jack L. Knetsch, and Richard H. Thaler, "Fairness and the Assumptions of Economics", Journal of Business, Volume 59, No. 4, 1986.

Keeney, Ralph L., "Potential Research Topics in Decision Analysis", Decision Analysis, Volume 13, Number 4, October, 1982.

Keeney, Ralph L., and Howard Raiffa, Decisions with Multiple Objectives: Preferences and Value Trade-Offs, Wiley, New York, 1976.

Kirchoff, Bruce A. and Bruce D. Phillips, "The Effect of Firm Formation and Growth on Job Creation in the United States", Journal of Business Venturing, Volume 3, Number 4, Fall, 1988.

Kirk, Roger E., Experimental Design: Procedures for the Behavioral Sciences, Brooks/Cole Publishing, Belmont, California, 1968.

Knorr-Cetina, Karin D., The Manufacture of Knowledge Pergamon Press, Oxford, 1981.

Kuhn, Thomas S., The Structure of Scientific Revolutions, University of Chicago Press, Chicago, Illinois, 1962.

Kuhn, Deanna, Eric Amsel and Michael O'Loughlin, The Development of Scientific Thinking Skills, Academic Press, San Diego, 1988.

Lakatos, Imre and Alan Musgrave, Editors, Criticism and the Growth of Knowledge, Cambridge University Press, London, 1970.

Langer, E.J., "The Illusion of Control", Journal of Personality and Social Psychology, Volume 32, pages 311-328, 1975.

Leinhardt, Samuel, Editor, Sociological Methodology 1983-1984, Jossey-Bass Publishers, San Francisco, 1983.

Luce, R. Duncan and Howard Raiffa, Games and Decisions, Wiley, New York, New York, 1957.

Luria, A. R., Higher Cortical Functions in Man, Basic Books, New York, 1980.

Martin, Linda J., "Uncertain? How Do You Spell Relief?", The Journal of Portfolio Management, Volume 11, No. 3, Spring, 1985.

McNeil, B., S. Pauker, H. Sox and A. Tversky, "On The Elicitation of Preferences for Alternative Therapies", New England Journal of Medicine, Volume 306, 1982.

Miner, John B., "Entrepreneurs, High Growth Entrepreneurs, and Managers: Contrasting and Overlapping Motivational Patterns", Journal of Business Venturing, Volume 5, Number 4, July, 1990.

Morlock, Henry, "The Effect of Outcome Desirability on Information Required for Decisions", Behavioral Science, pp. 296-300, July 1967.

Morris, Peter A., "Thoughts on Decision Analysis Research", Decision Sciences, Volume 13, Number 4, October, 1982.

Newell, A and H.A. Simon, Human Problem Solving, Prentice-Hall, Englewood Cliffs, NJ, 1972.

Perrin, E.C. and H.C. Goodman, "Telephone Management of Acute Pediatric Illnesses", The New England Journal of Medicine, Volume 298, No. 3, January 19, 1978.

Pratt, J.W., H. Raiffa, and R.D. Schlaifer, Introduction to Statistical Decision Theory, McGrawHill, New York, New York, 1965.

Raiffa, Howard, Decision Analysis: Introductory Lectures On Choices Under Uncertainty, Addison-Wesley, Reading, Massachusetts, 1970.

Ronen, Joshua, "Effect of Some Probability Displays on Choices", Organizational Behavior and Human Performance, pp. 1-14, February 1973.

Scheinberg, Sari and Ian C. MacMillan, "An 11 Country Study of Motivations to Start a Business", Frontiers of Entrepreneurship Research, Center for Entrepreneurial Studies, Babson College, Wellesley, MA, 1988.

Schwenk, Charles R., "Cognitive Simplification Processes in Strategic Decision-Making", Volume 5, Strategic Management Journal, 1984.

Sexton, Donald L. and Nancy B. Bowman, "Validation of a Personality Index: Comparative Psychological Characteristics Analysis of Female Entrepreneurs, Managers, Entrepreneurship Students, and Business Students", Frontiers of Entrepreneurship Research, Center for Entrepreneurial Studies, Babson College, Wellesley, MA, 1986.

Simon, Herbert, "A Behavioral Model of Rational Choice", Quarterly Journal of Economics, February, 1955.

Simon, Herbert A., "What We Know About the Creative Process", Working Paper, Department of Psychology, Carnegie-Mellon University, 1984.

Slovic, P. and S. Lichtenstein. "Comparison of Bayesian and Regression Approaches to the Study of Information Processing Judgment", Organizational Behavior and Human Performance, pp. 649-744, 1971.

Smith, Ken G., Martin J. Gannon, Curtis Grimm, and Terence R. Mitchell, "Decision Making Behavior in Smaller Entrepreneurial and Larger Professionally Managed Firms", Journal of Business Venturing, Volume 3, Number 3, Summer, 1988.

Staw, B.M., "The Escalation of Commitment to a Course of Action", Academy of Management Review, Volume 6, 1981.

Stevenson, Howard H., Michael J. Roberts, and H. Irving Grousbeck, New Business Ventures and the Entrepreneur, Richard D. Irwin, Homewood, Illinois, 1985.

Taylor, Frederick W., Principles of Scientific Management, Harpers, New York, New York, 1919.

Taylor, Frederick W., Scientific Management, Harpers, New York, New York, 1947.

Timmons, Jeffry A., New Venture Creation, Irwin, Homewood, Illinois, 1990.

Tully, Donald S. and Gerald S. Albaum, Survey Research: A Decisional Approach, Intext Educational Publishers, New York, New York, 1973.

Tversky, Amos and Daniel Kahneman, "Judgment Under Uncertainty: Heuristics and Biases", Science, Volume 185, 1974.

Vesper, Karl H., New Venture Strategies, Prentice-Hall, Englewood Cliffs, NJ, 1980.

Von Neumann, J. and O. Morgenstern, Theory of Games and Economic Behavior, John Wiley and Sons, New York, New York, 1947.

Whitley, Richard, The Intellectual and Social Organization of the Sciences, Clarendon Press, Oxford, 1984.

Winkler, Robert L., "Research Directions in Decision Making Under Uncertainty", Decision Sciences, Volume 13, Number 4, October, 1982.

Zeleny, Milan, "Intuition--Its Failures and Merits", in Surviving Failures edited by Bo Persson, Humanities Press, Atlantic Highlands, N.J., 1979.

ENDNOTES

(1) As Hogarth (1982) noted: "...many good guides and check lists do exist. Nonetheless, theory is weak. Furthermore, when one looks at the creativity literature, one notes that it is replete with examples of creative problem definitions and solutions in the areas of hard sciences and technology but not in the messier realm of decision-making in social contexts to which DMUU is typically applied."

(2) Winkler (1982) argues explicitly for more systematic and extensive work into understanding how individuals understand uncertainty and process information in an uncertain environment.

Among the questions to be addressed are: (1) "How can information from different sources be combined?" and (2) "How can information from different sources be valued, especially in a noisy environment?" Morris (1982) also argues for further research in this area and believes that further research into the axioms of decision theory are required. He calls into question the idea that subjective probabilities are a sufficient descriptor of the uncertainty surrounding decisions. Morris argues that the numerous apparent deviations from the basic axioms of DMUU indicate that there may be some basic logical flaws in the existing theory, especially as it categorizes and deals with uncertainty. Current decision theory, he argues, fails to address uncertainty "in the degree to which the underlying decision model represents the real world."

(3) See Dreze (1978).

(4) Dreze (1978) also lists this as a limitation in the theory of information economics.

(5) See Arrow's (1951) "Impossibility Theorem" which outlines the difficulties

inherent in modeling group decisions -- they do not necessarily have a unique solution.

A VISION-DRIVEN ENTREPRENEURIAL STUDY

AKIHIRO OKUMURA, *KELO UNIVERSITY*

INTRODUCTION

The environment in which firms operate is becoming increasingly uncertain. On a macro basis, the world economy is becoming more turbulent, and competition among firms, as well as nations, is becoming more fierce. Furthermore, the world's political situation is becoming problematic. These environmental threats are creating higher risks for firms attempting to take adaptive measures.

At the same time, a creeping bureaucratization has advanced the dilution of firms' capacities for organizational adaptability. Organizations rely on the experience of past success for future activity, and this paradigm is difficult to alter. Although a rigid organizational structure works well in stable environments, it does not adapt to changing ones. Since its stresses are on efficiency rather than innovation, a culture of organization usually works against a corporate venturing climate.

However, firms are required to make bold and innovative decisions to cope with these uncertainties. This means that firms have to act entrepreneurially. Although several studies concerning entrepreneurial decisions have been written, virtually all of them have focused on individual traits and personality. Admittedly, many entrepreneurial decisions are made through intuition and risk-taking. Yet it is also true that entrepreneurial decisions are determined by organizational structure. Many large organizations are therefore seeking a framework of entrepreneurial decision making. Faced with dynamic environmental changes, these organizations are often forced to make equally dynamic organizational changes in order to adapt.

It is the intention of this article, then, to discuss the manner in which an organization exhibits entrepreneurial behaviors, the types of entrepreneurial strategy that may be most effective, and how these strategies appear to emerge from within these organizations. In this context, the article focuses on the issue of "vision," which seems to play a significant role in entrepreneurial decision making. Thus, several empirical cases relating to this vision-driven entrepreneurial strategy are also analyzed. Through this analysis, theoretical implications for entrepreneurial strategy are also briefly discussed.

ENTREPRENEURIAL STRATEGY

An entrepreneurial strategy is defined as one in which a firm, faced with high uncertainty, makes a dynamic change in its strategy, transforming its alignment to the environment as well as its overall arrangement. Usually this kind of decision takes place once or twice in the history of the firm. This may be called a critical (Selznick 1957) or non-routine decision (March and Simon, 1958). Thus, entrepreneurial strategy requires discontinuous behavior of a firm, and demands the unlearning of past experience.

Entrepreneurial strategy is regarded, on one hand, as a result of certain decisions, and on the other, as a process of organizational decision making. In the initial stage, top management intends and conceives a broad corporate vision of the future. Several responses will then emerge from within the organization in the form of actions or proposals. There may be an interactive relationship between top and middle management, and strategy may evolve through this organizational arrangement, gradually becoming concrete. It is rather difficult to locate the individual entrepreneur within a large, complex organization. Even top management may find it difficult to act in the manner of the classical-type entrepreneur, as organizations tend to be characterized by persistent inertia and resistance to change. As a result, entrepreneurial strategy demands using the perspective of organizational behavior in constructing a theory.

There are, in general, three types of entrepreneurial strategy. One is the so-called analytical model, which we label here, Mode-1. This model assumes that individuals take a rational approach to decision making. Environmental opportunities and threats are identified, and then internal resource capabilities are measured. After an appraisal of these data has been undertaken, an organization will make the most rational decision. Professionals, such as one finds in a corporate planning staff, would play a major role in formulating strategy. The implementation of this strategy is assumed to be automatically executed by other members of the organization, the success or failure of the strategy being dependent upon the quality of the plans. Even in turbulent periods, most large organizations tend to make this kind of decision.

The so-called process model, the one used by most Japanese firms, we label Mode-2. Major decisions are made through organizational processes, particularly on a bottom-to-top basis, demonstrating an incremental approach toward even strategic decisions. Quinn (1980) identifies this model as a kind of logical incrementalism. Organizations adapt to the changing environment on an incremental basis, although the direction of the organization is already well-determined. Consequently, while long-term goals are being pursued, organizational processes appear to be determined on an ad hoc basis.

The third model, Mode-3, is a vision-driven one. An organization is driven by shared values and beliefs, and as Selznick (1957) argues, it becomes an institution as values are infused by top management. Without values, the organization is merely an instrument for achieving goals. Only value transforms it into a living social system. Furthermore, this model assumes that an organization can actually enact its environment through its intended strategy. There are two perspectives on the relationship between organizations and environment. The first is a natural selection model, in which organizations follow environmental selection rules. The second is an enactment in which organizations can select, and in some cases change, given conditions through the activity of a subjective will. Mode-3 follows the second perspective.

It is common to find advantages and disadvantages with each type of entrepreneurial strategy. Mode-1 is a typical bureaucratic model. It may function well under conditions of certainty or when problems are readily identifiable. In other words, when data relating to the issues are all clear, organizations can pursue a rational approach. Unfortunately, almost all entrepreneurial decisions are made in conditions of complete uncertainty, and on some occasions, organizations cannot even determine what the problems are.

In Mode-2, the process-oriented model, the organization has a long-term goal without having a short-term plan. Usually, short-term planning systems play a major role in coping with environmental uncertainty. However, one of the strengths of this model may be its flexibility. Since it is very difficult to predict environmental changes with certainty, organizational flexibility is an essential quality in coping with contingencies. What becomes important here is shared direction; that is, members need a common understanding of what direction the organization intends to take. Otherwise, we find the appearance of chaos.

The strengths of Mode-3 lie in its ability to handle discontinuity. Since past learning may not be reliable under these circumstances, innovative and bold behavior becomes necessary. However, there is a likelihood of resistance to change, coming from within the organization. Furthermore, this kind of decision-making behavior opens the organization to higher risk, resulting in reluctance on the part of the organization's members. As such, this mode is most frequently applied to individual, rather than organizational, behavior. In an interesting book concerning the essence of decision making, Allison (1971) treats the case of the Cuban Missile Crisis with no less than three analytical models: Rational, Organizational, and Political, each with its own strengths and weaknesses. The point in mentioning this is only to note that there is no consensus on the decision-making process, and furthermore that there are very few analyses of corporate strategic decision making - with almost nothing on entrepreneurial decisions. We find many case studies and success stories, but little has been done to identify what strategic entrepreneurial behaviors are.

Therefore, because it includes typical elements of entrepreneurial strategic decision making, we take up, here, for analysis, Honda's creation of a new market of small motorcycles in the United States. Though the case is an old one, it provides a good example of the elements that determine entrepreneurial decision making.

HONDA

Established in 1948 in rural Japan, Honda is well-recognized as a successful company in the motorcycle and automobile industries. After launching its small engines for bicycles, it was only a short time before Honda had overwhelmed the Japanese motorcycle industry, becoming the world's foremost producer by the early 1950s. Even with such rapid success, Honda had ambitions to do even better. Although the company had intentions of entering the automobile industry in the future, its technological competence at the time was inadequate. Honda's management, Mr. Soichiro Honda and Mr. Takeo Fujisawa determined that the company had to develop a new market, as the Japanese small motorcycle market would soon be more or less matured.

Mr. Fujisawa then ordered Mr. Kawashima, who would become Honda's second president twenty years later, to undertake extensive market research to determine where Honda should next enter into a domestic market. His initial report suggested that the European market would be a promising one, but he then concluded that they should enter the South East Asian market. Despite the recommendations, Mr. Fujisawa preferred the idea of entering the U.S. market. As such, they had three alternatives before them to consider. Mr. Kawashima felt that the U.S. market would be too risky, while Mr. Fujisawa saw it as the most strategic. As it is well known, Honda did finally choose and succeed in the U.S. market.

The process by which Honda made its decisions provides for a worthwhile subject of study. We can consider each element in the process and compare the risks and expected outcomes of the various alternatives the organization faced.

Several components are going to be considered in any decision that is made: market volume, income level, size of the potential market, the level of traffic infrastructure, the attitudes of consumers, market needs, channel accessibility, freight cost, service station location, commonality of the market, and so on.

Mr. Kawashima, as a planner, surveyed market possibilities. He concluded that while the European market had the largest volume of small motorcycles (approximately 3 million), higher competition should be expected. Furthermore, the long geographic distance between Europe and Japan would mean higher freight costs than they would have delivering to the South East Asian market. As for the U.S. market, although it provided the highest economic potential, its market volume appeared to be limited to the 50,000s, most of which were larger than 500cc products. However, the most serious problem appeared in the form of customer attitude and need towards small motorcycles. American consumers maintained a negative attitude toward motorcycles, due to the image of Hell's Angels riding on Harley Davidsons.

This short, but well-known, case will be analyzed using the strategic decision-making model. Following the Mode-1 model, the decision will be analyzed in terms of rational thinking.

In a model representing product life cycle, with diffusion rate set on the vertical axis and time horizon set on the horizontal axis, we can illustrate the transition undergone by transportation vehicles. The bicycle takes its position at the first stage - beginning to grow, maturing, and finally declining. Next to the bicycle, we have the motorcycle, which takes its place at the second stage; it, too, follows the same product life cycle. After a full diffusion of the motorcycle, the automobile stage begins. After WWII, the product life cycle of the Japanese transportation industry had just traced this transition.

Honda had marvelous success, in its early history, transforming the product life cycle from bicycle to motorcycle. Yet the Japanese motorcycle market had become saturated in the 1960s. Facing serious growth problems at that moment, Mr. Kawashima demonstrated the typical rational approach in dealing with the problem. In 1960, South East Asia might be located on the early phase of the bicycle, Japan on the later stage of the motorcycle, Europe on the early stage of the automobile, and the U.S. on the maturity stage of the automobile.

If Honda was to follow this product life cycle model, it should have gone into the South East Asian market, the unknown U.S. market appearing to be too risky. Honda was also following the strategically logical theory of the experience curve, which says that the more one accumulates in terms of manufactured products, the less likely one is to achieve total cost. Honda's basic philosophy involved the pursuit of providing cheaper motorcycles to the public. It was therefore important to reduce costs by developing a mass market. According to the initial research, Europe showed a visible market of approximately three million small motorcycles; however the U.S. and South East Asian markets also showed great potential. The problem, then, was in how to evaluate the potency of each market.

Mr. Kawashima decided to follow the logical approach, selecting the least-risky market, South East Asia; but contrary to the proposal, Mr. Fujisawa decided upon the most-risky market, the U.S. We can identify this as a Mode-3 type of decision.

The company's supreme philosophy, "to be Honda of the world," was strongly shared by both of the its founders, Mr. Fujisawa and Mr. Honda, as much as it is today. While Mr. Honda took responsibility for technological issues facing the company, Mr. Fujisawa took charge of the company's general management.

A real market man, Mr. Fujisawa confessed himself to be a rationalist. However, at the critical moment he appears to have chosen vision over logic. Although the South East Asian market seemed to be safer for the company to develop, inadequate economic conditions meant that much time would be needed in order to cultivate the market. On the other hand, while the U.S. consumers appeared unfriendly toward motorcycles, the market was a huge one. If Honda succeeded in developing the market, the company would have achieved its vision, and both the S.E. Asia and American alternatives appeared to provide the same opportunity for becoming first in the world.

We can talk about two basic types of risk. One is of the calculated type, usually derived from a rational thinking process. The other is perceived risk. It may be that what the company faced was a worthwhile risk. If the company felt that the risk should be taken, though calculations made it appear to be a high risk, the risk of entering into the U.S. market would have appeared worthwhile, for the purpose of achieving the status of first in the world. This alternative, furthermore, appeared to coincide with the corporation's vision. If Honda could succeed in the U.S. market, its global aim of dominating the world market would be promoted in a rational manner.

This case can be interpreted in other ways. Mr. Kawashima had spent two years in surveying markets, and after deliberate research he concluded that the company should go to South East Asia. He played the role of corporate staff. Mr. Fujisawa probably made good use of the intensive research, but with opposite results. Without any assurance of success, he was forced to utilize organizational processes and procedures to realize his aims. Otherwise, he could hardly have achieved consensus with Mr. Kawashima and other members of the organization. We may call this a Mode-2 style decision.

Designated as the first president of U.S. Honda, Mr. Kawashima intended to sell the product to students and other less wealthy Americans; however, his first intention proved to be misconceived. Honda's success was brought about by changing the target and product concept itself, from lower-end users and transportation vehicle buyers to second car owners and sports vehicle buyers. After initial miserable performances Mr. Kawashima was able to create a new market. This example demonstrates the interaction between entrepreneurial decision making and implementation. The implementation of strategy is a responsibility of the organization, while the entrepreneur provides only direction and vision. It will be up to the organizational members to create the content of the strategy through the process of formation and implementation stages.

This case exemplifies the interaction of entrepreneur and organization, with an effective use of vision, particularly in terms of its contribution to the making of strategic choice.

A VISION-DRIVEN ENTREPRENEURIAL STRATEGY

As we have seen in the case of Honda's entry into the U.S. market almost thirty years ago, entrepreneurial decision making tends to involve a mixture of styles. However, we know that large organizations tend to lose this ability to mix styles in making decisions. Therefore, it is important to look at the problem of how to keep the various entrepreneurial decision styles available to the large organization.

As we know, Jack Welch, CEO of GE, has recently been trying to introduce this decision-making mode into the company as a means of effecting a restructuring. GE had so long been dominated by business-school-type planners that the company eventually became mired in bureaucracy. Feeling strong threats from this organizational pathology, Mr. Welch decided to construct an entrepreneurial style in the organization that would allow it to survive in a turbulent environment. Envisioning GE as a number one company, even in the 1990s, he led the organization through a total transformation.

NEC, a world leader in the production of IC chips, is another case of vision allowing for transformation of a company. Formerly, the company was totally dependent for its business on NTT, Nippon Telephone and Telegram - to the extent that people called the company "Bureau of NTT." In the 1980s, Mr. Kobayashi, former CEO, introduced a vision he called "C&C"(Computer and Communication technology). This involved a complete restructuring of the composition of the business, from telecommunications to general electronics. Although this vision, "C&C", appears to specify the domain of the company, it really also works as a philosophy. Mr. Kobayashi had always said that the company would create the new world through the development of computer and communication technology. In order to achieve this new world, NEC underwent a major dynamic shift, from the traditional arena to the challenging.

Sony provides yet another example of choosing an entrepreneurial strategy. The company was defeated tremendously by Matsushita in the VCR wars. Whereas Matsushita adopted the VHS method, Sony adopted Beta. And because Sony's strength lay in its technological competence, the company was quite restrictive in releasing the technology. In contrast, Matsushita and its subsidiary, JVC, were completely open and aggressive in forming allies. Consequently, Sony's strategy was unsuccessful.

Sony did, however, seek a means of turning the situation around. The company changed its focus from the home appliance arena to "audio visual and computer, communications and components," known as "AV&CCC" at Sony. They, too, chose to follow a vision, most recently demonstrated by the decision to purchase the American company, Columbia Pictures. Probably envisioning movie software as a strategic weapon in the future world of AV, the company may be aiming at domination of this software business, and eventually, at a reversal of today's VCR situation.

Vision may play a significant role in entrepreneurial strategy. It provides the driving force of strategy. It also provides a premise for value decisions. Entrepreneurial strategy pursues much more stylistic ends, containing personal achievement and self-actualization, sometimes also enacting its chosen environment. There is much evidence of vision transforming and enlarging the boundaries of an organization. These functions are strongly related to creative activities, creativity being one of the key sources of excellent strategy.

There are several impacts that vision has on strategy. First, it creates a visionary sphere in the company. While the company feels anxiety in the face of higher uncertainty, vision allows organizational members to recognize, more or less, a likely next step. Vision also provides a map for the company. As in the cases of Sony and NEC, the company can determine direction and then make an allocation of the limited resources required.

Second, vision has the ability to stimulate human cognitive limits. In other words, it facilitates the knowledge creation of organizational members. Despite the limits of cognition (H.A. Simon 1957), these limits are expandable when people have the ability to change their perspectives. People's cognitions are constantly evolving through learning. With an entrepreneur providing a well-defined vision, people's attitudes and ways of thinking are open to dramatic change. Vision itself is an intellectual construct, sometimes including the dream of an entrepreneur, inspiring the imagination and motivation of others.

Third, vision provides a base of value judgement in the organization. Because strategic decisions usually involve higher uncertainty, rational decisions are only reached with difficulty in these situations. When the organization does have a vision, people can rely on it at the ultimate stage, just as we have seen in the case of Honda. This implies that an organization's members need to share a strong sense of value.

Vision also relates to organizational learning. An organization tends to gain knowledge through the experience of past successes, gradually developing a rigidity in its confidence. We find this to be true in the case of Honda, where Mr. Kawashima allowed himself to rely on the company's existing knowledge base. In opposition, Mr. Fujisawa chose to return to the company's original vision, then trying even to revise past knowledge. Argyris and Schon (1974) call this a kind of double-loop learning. Under the lead of a strong vision, an organization can restructure its strategic contents through constant dialogue between the entrepreneur and the organization's members.

Vision also relates to innovation. Higher goals force people toward distinction. Driven by clear and ambitious visions, NEC and Sony made great technological breakthroughs. Without the thrust of vision, only the threat of crisis could arouse these companies into such action. Vision allowed positive thinking toward such crises. While constructive thinking is useful in bringing innovation, it takes vision to provide a climate for organization.

Finally, vision provides for an integrative force within the organization, with the power to integrate differentiated activities. In general, a creative and active organization has the tendency to achieve higher differentiation and integration at once. Honda's people currently enjoy an atmosphere of greater freedom within the organization, while they maintain the vision that says, "Honda of the world." Although there are numerous tools of integration, vision provides the subtle underlying control that works so well in a creative organization.

As Nonaka (1989) informs us, information or knowledge creation is the key to organizational creativity. It is an organization's creativity that assures its survival, particularly in an age of information. The creation of knowledge is brought about through the introduction of a clear but heterogeneous vision. This vision will have several meanings among the members of an organization, but active discussion will lead them towards a common understanding. Through this process, the contents of a strategy will emerge from within the organization.

REFERENCES

Allison, G. T. 1971. Essence of Decision: Explaining the Cuban Missile Crisis. Little, Brown and Co.:Boston.

Argyris, C. and Schon, D. 1974. Theory in Practice. San Francisco: Jossey Bass.

Nonaka, Ikujiro. Spring 1988. Toward middle-up-down management: Accelerating information creation. Sloan Management Review. 3-20.

Quinn, J.B. Summer 1980. Managing strategic change. Sloan Management Review. 3-20.

Simon, H.A. 1957, Models of Man. NY:Wiley.

Simon, H.A. and March, J.G., 1958. Organizations. NY:Wiley.

Selznick, P. 1957. Leadership in Administration. NY:Harper & Row

CULTURAL PERSPECTIVES ON ENTREPRENEURSHIP

Entrepreneurship Development Among Malays in
Singapore: a Community Development Approach

Critique
by
Monserrat Olle, *E.S.A.D.E*

The paper compares entrepreneurship among members of the Malay community with that of other ethnic communities in the Republic of Singapore.

The working hypothesis is that the lack of entrepreneurship among the Malay community is due to lack of appropriate values coupled with sociocultural barriers that serve as obstacles to entrepreneurial endeavors.

The paper proposes that a community of mutually supportive businesses be built in order to foster the entrepreneurial spirit and make the Malays as competitive and enterprising as the other communities in Singapore.

The aforementioned working hypothesis is well-developed. The paper provides relevant background information on, the traditional Malay social system; relevant historical references that illustrate the dominant scale of values: hierarchy, loyalty, importance of the family unit, disinterest in the rational accumulation of wealth and economic power; government policy towards the Malays; a comparison of jobs available to the Malay and Chinese communities over the years; the percentage of those who are employees or employers in both communities, and the influence of Islam.

The paper gives a clear picture of the characteristics of the Malay community and these characteristics are almost the exact opposite of those qualities that mark an entrepreneur, i.e. the need for achievement, perception of opportunities, orientation to the future, and skill in organizing.

Shapero's studies show that one important personality dimension of entrepreneurs is the degree to which they think they can affect the world around them. People who are external believe that the rewards in life come from forces outside themselves. People labelled "internal" believe they can influence events to their own good or detriment.

The gap between the cultural values of the Malay community and the characteristics of entrepreneurs goes a long way towards explaining the lack of enterprise among the Malays. However, it is interesting to note that when surveyed by the authors of this paper, Malay entrepreneurs gave the following reasons for their community's lack of motivation: lack of social status for entrepreneurs; lack of capital, lack of expertise, lack of opportunity (perception of discriminatory practices towards the Malays in Singapore).

In view of the situation of the Malay community in Singapore, the authors propose a community-based entrepreneurial development approach aimed at removing the obstacles which currently stand in the way of developing the spirit of entrepreneurship among the Malays.

The core of this program would be:

- to build a community of mutually supportive businesses.

As far as I can see, these proposals do not include any plans for action in the very fields that the researchers have identified as fertile ground for planting the seeds of entrepreneurship. It would be useful to review these areas and explore what policies may be implemented to encourage entrepreneurship:

Education. Generally speaking, the educational system tends to stifle creativity and it is precisely creativity that future entrepreneurs need. Schools need programs designed to develop a spirit of enterprise.

The family. It is within the family that the need for achievement is developed. Individuals raised in an authoritarian atmosphere usually need to be told what to do. The individual is not accustomed to making his or her own choices and this hampers the development of independence.

The social status of entrepreneurs. The degree of social status varies from one country to another and also varies within a single country, depending upon the particular moment in history. It is easier to develop the spirit of enterprise in countries where businessmen are given high status.

Role models. It can happen that a particular community has no role model with which entrepreneurs can identify. Instead they are often perceived as exceptions or oddities.

Financial and material aid alone is not enough to foster a spirit of enterprise. The results of programmes designed to develop or awaken this spirit have been highly uneven. Any success they might have in contributing to the development of local entrepreneurs is due more to the commitment and enthusiasm of the people responsible for the programs than to the application of any specific techniques.

ENTREPRENEURSHIP DEVELOPMENT AMONG MALAYS IN SINGAPORE: A COMMUNITY DEVELOPMENT APPROACH

CHONG LI CHOY, *NATIONAL UNIVERSITY OF SINGAPORE*
ABDUL JALIL ISMAIL, *NATIONAL UNIVERSITY OF SINGAPORE*

ABSTRACT

The Malay community in Singapore is one ethnic community which is lagging behind other groups, particularly the Chinese and Indians, in economic development in Singapore today. Business entrepreneurships among Malays, particularly successful ones, are rare. This paper attempts to understand the problem of entrepreneurship among Malays in Singapore and to propose an appropriate approach for entrepreneurship development for the Malay community. It seeks understanding of the problem by examining the value orientation of the Malays based on their culture and social system and by interviewing selected Malay entrepreneurs and business leaders. It advocates a community development approach to entrepreneurship development.

INTRODUCTION

Since becoming an independent republic in 1965, Singapore has made such great strides in economic development that her economic attainment is often referred to as a miracle. Although the Malays, like other ethnic communities in Singapore, did benefit from the economic progress, they are nevertheless lagging behind the Chinese and Indian communities in Singapore in terms of integration into the modern economy. The absence of economic institutions to help Malays has often been cited as the reason for their economic backwardness and lack of entrepreneurship. The setting up of new economic institutions, such as development banks for the explicit purpose of helping Malays, has been advocated. However, the problem is really deeply rooted in the Malay culture and social system, which new economic institutions can certainly overcome to some extent.

This paper points out that the lack of entrepreneurship among Malays is more the result of a lack of appropriate values for entrepreneurship as well as the presence of socio-cultural barriers which obstruct entrepreneurship and entrepreneurial behaviour within the Malay community. A community development approach can do much to overcome these as well as other practical problems.

Efforts in entrepreneurship development are often aimed at correcting certain weaknesses in enterprises or strengthening entrepreneurs in certain areas of business activity. Comprehensive efforts have attempted to help the development of the total enterprise and often include networking with other businesses, and community development, where dying towns are revitalised through entrepreneurship development (Chong and MacMillan, 1990). However, it is seldom that the culture and social system of a community is studied for the purpose of entrepreneurship promotion and development.

Understanding the culture and social system of a community for the purposes of entrepreneurship promotion and development is extremely important. This is because the lack of entrepreneurial ventures among community members is often the result of socio-cultural barriers rather than the non-availability of mere economic opportunities. Whereas the lack of appropriate economic institutions, such as development banks, to help a specific community in business undertakings may have made business venturing more difficult, their presence will not necessarily produce the desired results, particularly if certain socio-cultural barriers were to remain.

We understand that the setting up of an enterprise must inevitably involve the entrepreneur making certain decisions to change the direction of his life and to start a business (Shapero, 1984). We also know that it involves the perception of and alertness to business opportunity as well as seizing the opportunity (Kirzner, 1979). Where the socio-cultural underpinnings of a community are such that the entrepreneurial career is unacceptable for whatever reasons, or the carrying out of certain business functions are considered immoral or wrong, or where the perception of opportunities or the seizing of opportunities are not possible or not readily undertaken, entrepreneurship is unlikely to take place. The Malay community in Singapore is one community with such socio-cultural barriers and obstacles to entrepreneurship. However, like any other community, there are also values, though less universal, which could enable the community members to overcome the negative socio-cultural connotations and justify, and even encourage, entrepreneurship among them. Such values could be identified and used to promote entrepreneurship in the community.

BETWEEN MODERNITY AND TRADITIONS

The Malays in Singapore can be said to be caught between the modernity of present day Singapore and their traditional socio-cultural system. While all communities in Singapore can be said to have been caught in the same predicament, and the contrast between modernity and traditions are not less stark for other communities, the Malays remain very much rooted in their past traditions long after the other ethnic groups, like Chinese and Indians in Singapore, have adapted to modern urban, industrial and commercial society.

1. The Traditional Malay Social System

To understand the value orientation of Malays in modern Singapore, it may be useful to look back at the social system of traditional Malay society and see how it affects the modern Malay Singaporean. Consistent with Li (1989), Malays for this paper are defined as the broad category of people originating from Malaysia, Indonesia and Singapore. Census of Population of Singapore (1980) further added that Malays can be ".....subdivided into specific community groups, namely, Malays, Javanese, Boyanese, Bugis and other Malays" (p 5).

The traditional Malay social system was hierarchically structured along customs and practices between two groups, the aristocracy and the subjects (Ahmad, 1960). The relationships between these two groups were defined in terms of wisdom, character, correctness and procedure: a set of social expectations called "adat".

The dominant norm circumscribing this relationship was loyalty. The ruler was seen as the representative of God and the submissiveness and obeisance of his subjects were seen as natural and necessary. This emphasis on status and exclusiveness among the aristocracy extended to the utilization of wealth and deterred the involvement of the commoners in economic activities (Tham, 1983). The usage of land by the commoners, who had no proprietary rights to it, was subject to rent determined by the rulers, a practice similar to that under a feudal system. Thus the motivation to acquire wealth to enhance the status of the rulers led to the lack of incentives to conserve or improve the land on the part of the subjects. Furthermore, the rulers would forcefully take away or borrow any assets of the commoners without any intentions of repayment.

Gullick (1956) pointed out that another obstructing factor to the accumulation of wealth among the commoners was the institution of debt-bondage. It was a system whereby the creditor (usually a ruler) had rights over the future labour of his debtor (usually a commoner) should the latter fail to repay the loan. The relative advantage of this to the debtor was that it facilitated the opportunity to be a member of the ruler's retinue and carried with it some prestige. This helped to instill the notion that indebtedness was socially appropriate, and more damagingly, it did not encourage the habit of frugality.

For the commoners, the value orientaion within such a hierarchical and agrarian society was thus expressed in the importance of the collective unit of the family, clan and village. Life was kin-centred and the integrity of the family was crucial. Primogeniture was an instrument of status determination and age and generational seniority was associated with wisdom and knowledge.

A social conception of the ideal personality in the form of "budi" became central to the development of the individual. "Budi" emphasises the nobility of character, not social ascent or material wealth. To give, to compromise and to pity are distinctive traits embodying "budi". Even in the realm of competition, defeat is honourable (Tham, 1983).

The conception of natural justice is thus determined by observation of one's status and the social expectations associated with that status. This has a profound effect on the perception of human limitations in terms of effort. Natural justice determined the fortunes of each individual. No man is a master of his fate. Worldly existence was transitory and a more permanent and happy existence awaited one in another world.

The salient factor in the description above is that the central theme in traditional Malay society is not the achievement of socio-economic mobility nor the rational accumulation of wealth and economic power. The individual's locus of control was external and wealth was transient and unworthy of serious pursuit. Malay oral and literary traditions did not put great emphasis on human aspiration, achievement in education and success in economic activities. The exclusiveness of the aristocracy and the passivity of the commoners perpetuated this value orientation.

Such value orientations would obviously make entrepreneurship an extremely difficult undertaking for members of the community. However, there are also other traditions which could be drawn upon to support entrepreneurship.

It is not true that entrepreneurial activity was totally lacking in Malay society. The migration of the Arabs and Indians, and together with them Islam, as well as the emergence of the spice trade, coincided with the presence of the Malacca Sultanate during the fifteenth and sixteenth centuries. There emerged then, the trading class among the indigenous people. Alatas (1977) contended that Malays and Javanese dominated inter-regional shipping facilities as Malacca and several other Javanese ports opened their doors to international trade. However, it can be argued that the emergence of this trading class may have permeated only to the aristocracy and was also due to the assimilation of Arabs and Indians into the local community. Whether such activities filtered throughout the society is debatable. Alatas (1977) argued that the coming of the Dutch and the Portuguese systematically eliminated the indigenous trading class through the signing of treaties with local rulers prohibiting indigines from undertaking international trade, or from selling local produce to the Europeans unless they were appointed agents of the rulers. By the time the British arrived they found no indigenous trading class.

This period of Malay history could be useful for justifying Malay entrepreneurship, even if it were limited to the aristocracy and the Arabs and Indian Muslims. It demonstrates very clearly that entrepreneurship and business undertakings are neither anti-Malay nor anti-Islam. Getting into the mainstream of economic activities in Singapore is as much the right of the Malays as it is the right of every other ethnic group and community in Singapore.

2. The Emergence of the Malay Singaporean

In the 1980 Singapore Census, Malays formed 14.7 % of the population. When Raffles landed on Singapore in 1819, he found it to be a fishing village inhabited by Malays. Li (1989), however, contended that a large number of Malays migrated from the Malay Peninsula and Indonesia during the 1945-70 period. This implies that the settlement pattern and values of Malays could reflect an urban orientation.

The Singapore Malay culture has thus developed out of the varied traditions of the migrants and out of the conditions of life in Singapore. The interface with other migrant races such as Chinese, Indians and the Eurasians, as well as the experiences under the leaderships of the colonists and the PAP government, added another dimension to the socialisation process of the Singapore Malays. However, the features that positively characterise Singaporean Malays are the Malay language and Islam. Furthermore, the Constitution of Singapore recognises the special position of the Malays as the indigenous people of the island.

With reference to modern Singapore, it may be useful first to look at the impact on social integration and mobility as a consequence of structural policies and education, and see how these affect the Malays in Singapore. The basic premise of the Singapore government's economic planning is that rapid growth must exist prior to equality of distribution of rewards. High wage differentials which provide the incentive for effort is considered functional for economic growth.

The government policy on rehousing the population into government-built flats has resulted in the breaking up of the Malay settlements and with it, the importance of kinship for the Malays. Through resettlement, they have been forced to interact with members of the other ethnic groups. The family planning policy has also made the Malay family smaller. However, within the confines of housing estates, the Malays have tried to reestablish relationships with other Malays through social and religious activities. This is fundamental to the image of Malays within contemporary Singapore. The smaller family size has made the nuclear family tighter and more akin to that of the other races.

The influence of education has an even greater impact on the participation of the Malays in economic activities. Prior to 1959, opportunities for Malays to obtain an English education were limited. Colonial policy reserved English education and government positions for Malay royalty and restricted the access of the Malay masses. Roff (1967) argued that colonial policy was intended "to educate the rural (Malay) population in a suitable rural manner to equip them to continue to live a useful, happy rural life (p 28). The government of PAP, on assuming office in 1959, has adopted the principle of equal opportunity in its education policy. Realising that social mobility can be achieved through education in post-independence Singapore, Malay parents have readily seen education as an investment for their children. However, the educational performance of Malay children have always lagged behind those of other races in Singapore.

TABLE 1
Malays, Chinese and Indians Working Males Aged 10 Years and Over by Occupation, 1957, 1970 and 1980 (%)

	1957			1970			1980		
	M	C	I	M	C	I	M	C	I
P'sional & Tech'cal	2.8	3.6	3.2	4.4	6.7	5.9	4.6	8.3	7.5
Ad'trative & M'gerial	0.3	1.8	1.7	0.3	2.1	1.2	0.8	6.7	4.7
Clerical	15.0	11.5	13.2	13.9	11.2	12.6	13.0	8.5	11.0
Sales	3.0	23.8	20.6	3.7	20.0	22.8	3.1	15.4	15.3
Services	13.7	9.0	14.8	21.6	7.6	19.7	18.0	6.2	16.5
A'culture & Fishing	10.0	7.6	2.8	5.9	4.6	4.6	3.1	2.5	1.3
Prod'n & Transport	42.1	42.3	42.3	45.4	43.2	32.8	53.5	43.2	34.7
Not C'fiable	13.1	0.4	1.4	4.8	4.6	2.7	3.7	9.1	9.2
	100.0	100.0	100.0	100.0	100.0	100.0	100.0	100.0	100.0

Sources: Census 1970:277, 281, 285; Census 1980: IV.66

Table 1 shows the distribution of jobs occupied by males for the three main races in Singapore; Chinese, Malays and Indians. According to the 1980 Census, these three ethnic groups made up 98% of the total population (Chinese: 76.9%; Malays: 14.7%; Indians: 6.4%). The distribution of opportunities and rewards in the economy, as shown by Table 1, clearly indicated that Malay participation lagged behind those of the Chinese and Indians. In 1957, the differences in the percentages between

Malays and Chinese as well as with the Indians in the two higher occupational categories were 2.3% and 1.8% respectively. By 1970, the differences increased to 4.1% for the Chinese and 3.4% for the Indians. In 1980, the figures continued its upward trend to reach 9.6% and 6.8% for the Chinese and Indians respectively. However, this is not to deny that, in absolute terms, the Malays have shown progress in the two higher occupational categories.

Conversely, looking at the differences in percentages of participation for the lower manual category (production and transport) in Table 1, we can see that whilst the three groups had almost the same proportion of their population in that category in 1957, by 1980, there were more Malays in that category than the other two ethnic groups. Specifically, there were 10.3% and 18.8% more Malays than Chinese and Indians respectively.

Table 2 shows that while the percentage of Malays earning less than S$400 per month increased by 1.5% to 64.1% from 1975 to 1980, 25.3% and 21.6% of Chinese and Indian male workers respectively moved out of that category within the same time period. For those earning more than S$1000 a month, the percentages

TABLE 2

Employed Male Malays, Chinese and Indians by Monthly Income, 1975, 1978 and 1980 (%)

	Earning Less Than S$400 Per Month			Earning More Than S$1000 Per Month		
	Malays	Chinese	Indians	Malays	Chinese	Indians
1975	62.6	67.1	74.0	0.8	7.0	6.3
1978	75.8	53.3	63.5	1.8	8.9	9.1
1980	64.1	41.8	52.4	2.7	12.9	10.6

Sources: Report on the Labour Force Survey, 1975:95; 1978:98; 1980:69

for the Chinese and Indians clearly showed a greater leap than the Malays within the

1975-80 period (Chinese: +5.9%; Indians: +4.3%; Malays: +1.9%).

A rough comparison of entrepreneurial activity between the Malays and the other two races is given in Table 3. Generally, it can be discerned that all the three races experienced a gradual slide in the number of people willing to work on their own, either as employers or to have account workers under their charges, from 1957 to 1980. Perhaps, the industrialisation programme and better education over the period concerned had opened opportunities for better earnings by being a wage earner. In 1980, only 4.4% of working Malays were involved in entrepreneurial activities either as employers or self-employed workers compared to 22.5% for the Chinese and 14.6% for the Indians. To put it differently, almost one out of every four male working Chinese and one out of every seven male Indians are involved in entrepreneurial activities compared to one out of every twenty-five for male Malays.

TABLE 3

Malays, Chinese and Indians Working Males Aged 10 Years and Over by Employment Status, 1970 and 1980 (%)

	1957 M	1957 C	1957 I	1970 M	1970 C	1970 I	1980 M	1980 C	1980 I
Employee	93.1	67.4	81.8	93.5	70.2	77.7	95.3	75.2	84.5
Employer	0.2	5.1	4.1	0.7	3.9	3.5	0.5	6.3	4.8
Self-employed	6.2	22.7	12.9	5.9	22.3	17.7	3.9	16.2	9.8
Unpaid family worker	0.5	4.8	1.2	0.3	3.6	1.1	0.4	2.3	0.9
	100.0	100.0	100.0	100.0	100.0	100.0	100.0	100.0	100.0

Sources: Census 1970: 280, 284, 285; Census 1980:IV.34

It is evident here that the Malays, just like the other ethnic groups, have had to reorient their values given the rapidly changing environment in Singapore. Their uprooting from traditional village settlements into an urban and cosmopolitan surroundings has meant that the collective spirit of the Malay village had to be modified into that of a cosmopolitan village. Perhaps, we can extrapolate a shift from a collective spirit to that of individualism given the system of opportunities and rewards that exists in modern Singapore. However, the collective spirit of mutual and self-help within the community ("gotong royong" or "bersatu teguh, bercerai roboh") can be drawn upon to promote community development and entrepreneurship.

It cannot be denied that the Malays, just like other ethnic groups in Singapore, have benefitted from Singapore's economic progress. What is worrying is the fact that the rate at which they are immersing themselves in the economic mainstream is much slower than the other groups. From the figures above, even the Indians, whilst a smaller community in Singapore than the Malays, have been more successful in economic participation. It must be stressed that a weak Malay community will not be helpful for Singapore in its economic endeavours.

Education, certainly, is not the only key to upward social mobility and the narrowing of the economic gap between Malays and the other communities. In this paper, we will argue that the development of entrepreneurship within the Malay community can be yet another key to economic progress for the Malays.

MALAY ENTREPRENEURS AND THEIR COMMUNITY

Through in-depth interviews carried out by one of the authors with selected Malay entrepreneurs and business leaders, the possible reasons as to why the Malays lack the motivation to engage in entrepreneurial activities is identified and discussed here, with reference to the cultural background of the community, and within the context of modern Singapore.

1. The Issue of Acceptance

Achievement, as appreciated by others, is essentially culturally defined (Tham,1983). Certain categories of activities may be highly valued among members of a society and hence carry social prestige and honour. In traditional Malay societies, activities were defined according to one's social standing. During the colonial occupation of Singapore, Malays were mainly involved in the economy as employees of the government or European households. They were employed as gardeners, drivers, servicemen in uniformed groups -- all essentially unskilled jobs. The more succesful ones became teachers, journalists or administrators. Again, these people were employees. They are also the role models in the community even today, although the strata of occupations may have widened to include other categories like lawyers, medical doctors and engineers. The point is that within the Malay community, the notion of being self-employed is not highly valued. Achievement through entrepreneurship is clearly lacking in the Malay ethos.

In Singapore, Malays are often seen as synonymous with Muslims, although there are Malays who have embraced other religions as much as there are other races who have followed Islam as their way of life. As such, the influence of Islam is dominant in the perception of daily activities. Islam favours entrepreneurship as was noted by Geertz (1963), but unlike the Protestant ethic which was crucial in the early development of capitalism in Europe (Weber, 1930), Islam as perceived by Malay Singaporeans does not consider wealth to be essential to salvation nor proof of social or moral worth. Those who participate in entrepreneurial activities are therefore very careful not to breach any of the religious injunctions in their business dealings.

Business is an endeavour in which the motivation to accumulate is central. To operate as an expanding enterprise, further motivation is required. This could be the desire to be very rich, or the desire to establish an estate that could be passed on to descendants. Li (1989) contended that personal honour is deeply involved in business dealings within the Malay community. Malay entrepreneurs found that distrust among traders and between traders and the rest of the community was pervasive. Given the collective attitude of the community, this served as a further deterrent to business enterprise. Gossip or rumours are tangible threats. This has led Malay entrepreneurs to downplay their motivation by claiming that the business is done to help others, that the extent of the business activity is small. They do not set prices in the belief that the buyer is aware of its value and would voluntarily give an appropriate price (Li, 1989).

Added to this is the issue of "riba" (usury or interest). "Riba" technically means any unjustified increase in capital for which no compensation is given. "Riba" is therefore prohibited in Islam, although there are various interpretations of what is considered "riba". The consequence of this is the uncertainty among the Malays in Singapore, given their affiliation to Islam, about the morality of business practices in such areas as insurance, savings and loans.

2. Lack of Capital

An often cited reason for the lack of business enterprise within the Malay community is lack of funds. Malays have always been characterised by their carefree attitude towards life. Monthly salaries are used mainly for daily consumption. As such the orientation towards future uses of money is limited to that of consumption. That is not to say that savings are not seen as a virtue. Personal savings are kept either as a means of maintaining oneself in old age after retirement, or to fulfill the intention of going on pilgrimage to Mecca during old age.

The economic relationship within the Malay household also plays an important part in the expansion of resources. In the traditional Malay society, the transfer of land to children was natural. However, this transfer was seen in the context of a gift. In modern Malay society in Singapore, the gift that parents transfer to their chidren is the upbringing they provide to the children. As Muslims, Malay parents bring up their children in the hope that they will become better Muslims. Parents do not hope for any return for their efforts except through the prayers of their children. Any money which the children give their parents is seen as a gift, and this relationship extends to other siblings as well. There is thus a lack of incentives to garner resources together as a unit. This is further exacerbated by the tendency of Malay children to marry at an earlier age relative to other races in Singapore.

For those aspiring to set up business, difficulties in obtaining funds from financial institutions is a further disadvantage. Financial institutions commonly require collateral for loans. The only tangible property they have which could serve as collateral are their flats. Unfortunately, the government stipulates that public housing cannot serve as collateral. The lack of suitable persons to act as guarantors for loans is also an obstacle to business financing.

3. Lack of Expertise

The dominance of Malays within the more "primitive" sectors of the economy is a significant factor explaining the lack of knowledge of modern business activities. As explained in the preceding section, whilst the Chinese were moving out of the unskilled sector, the Malays appeared to remain stagnant, or even increased their involvement in this sector of the economy.

Education has an important role here. The poor educational performance of the Malays relative to other races has also contributed significantly towards the low level of Malay participation in the tertiary sectors of the economy. Given such a scenario, Malay traders continue to focus on crafts, pilgrim brokerage, and the publication of Malay and Muslim texts and food production specifically for the Malay market.

Related to this low level of business expertise is the lack of entrepreneurial tradition within the family unit. As discussed earlier, wealth was seen in terms of consumption. Children were not brought up in the spirit of accumulating wealth as a means of ensuring one's livelihood in the future. Attitudes such as the willingness to take risks were not an important virtue. Even those who have the opportunity to work under employers of other races do not take the opportunity to learn the trade. Instead they were content to be employees. Therefore the contention that they do not possess the expertise could be due to their unwillingness to take the opportunity to learn from other races, particularly the Chinese.

4. Lack of opportunity

During the colonial era, the Malays were positively favoured in the uniformed services. By 1957, almost 20% of Malay working men were employed in the uniformed services. The withdrawal of the British defence establishment by the early 1970s dealt a great blow to the Malays. Many of these people had risen through the ranks with little formal education. The government of Singapore in taking over the defence of the country has emphasized paper qualifications considerably. This, coupled with an unspoken policy then of excluding the Malays from the armed forces and particularly from certain key appointments, which has been gradually changed since then, has caused many young Malays to feel that they have fewer opportunities and advantages compared to other races. Most job descriptions stipulate that male applicants must have completed military service, and even if the Malay applicant gets the job he will be at a disadvantage in terms of salary. In the Singapore context, it is not illegal to specify the race of the employee required in a job advertisement. Advertisements such as "Malay driver" or "Chinese secretary" are common. This practice is still pervasive within the private sector and leads to inequities in terms of recruitment, pay, working conditions and opportunities for training and career advancement.

The Malays have always felt that this lack of opportunity stemmed from the government not doing enough to help the Malay community. In a meritocratic and multi-racial system, the government cannot be seen to favour one group over any other. The Malays feel that campaigns to support the use of Mandarin over dialects and the setting up of Special Assistance Programme schools to nurture the use of Mandarin among the Chinese children have all resulted in discriminatory practices in the economic arena. Furthermore, the dominance of Chinese enterprises run along family lines also meant a deterrence to greater Malay participation in the economy.

However, several Malay entrepreneurs felt that the government factor must not be overemphasised. They felt that the government has provided opportunities for everyone through various programmes organised through its agencies such as the Economic Development Board, the Trade Development Board and the National Productivity Board. What is lacking is the effort of Malay entrepreneurs to seek these opportunities and take advantage of what is available. Furthermore, the existence of the Malay Chamber of Commerce and Industry has not been fully utilised and exploited by the Malay entrepreneurs.

5. A Recapitulation

Four factors which have contributed to the lack of entrepreneurship within the community have been discussed. They are: social acceptance, lack of capital, lack of skills and the perception that discriminatory practices exist towards the Malays in Singapore. The alleged Malay attitude of indolence has been discussed and identified by several writers to also explain their problem (eg. Leong, 1978). However, the authors feel that such an explanation is perhaps unfounded. The Malay culture and value systems are primarily based on an agrarian and feudal society of the past. Indolence as observed among Malays is probably due to their lifestyle based on this agrarian society.

The predominant reason which underlies the problem of Malay participation in entrepreneurial pursuits is the lack of a cultural tradition and value system which supports such activities. The four factors discussed above are mere manifestations of the one real problem: the lack of an entrepreneurial ideology within the Malay social and cultural heritage.

A COMMUNITY-BASED ENTREPRENEURIAL DEVELOPMENT APPROACH

It is evident from the foregoing discussion that to promote entrepreneurship among Malays, the socio-cultural impediments must first be addressed. One convenient way to do so is to promote, through the efforts of community leaders (including religious teachers), Malay writers and educationists, journalists and Malay media personalities like actors, singers, and television programme directors, a mental revolution which helps the Malays to change their mindset, from those of traditional peasants to those of the aristocratic business class. This is essentially an upward social mobility for the mind, a change of perception of the self which is essentially consistent with the economic realities of today -- the standard of living of Malays in Singapore today are certainly more akin to those of the traditional aristocratic class than the traditionally impoverished peasants. This must be an exercise in community self-renewal, something undertaken from within the community rather than imposed from outside, although outside resources could be made available to community leaders to help them. Such assistance could be in the form of expert advice, specialised skills, business networks, as well as the financing of projects. However, the adoption of a community development approach also means that this has essentially to be based primarily on community self-help and the community's own resources.

It is obvious that in promoting changes in values, there will be a minority who will adapt to the new values naturally and quickly. These members of the community should be given every encouragement and assistance to set up their own businesses. This is where entrepreneurship development ought to start. A community approach to entrepreneurship development similar to that of an internationally-linked business community approach proposed by Chong and MacMillan (1990) could be helpful.

The proposal here is to build a community of mutually supportive businesses. These could be built around an established business, irrespective of ethnic origin or ownership, which has an established business network that may even have international connections, or around certain business projects or activities whose viability is ascertained with the help of qualified consultants or experienced and successful business people. Once chosen, the community of entrepreneurs will be given the necessary expert advice and training with the help of the consultants who have helped to map out the community development project. In this manner, the selected entrepreneurs will, through their individual and team efforts, bring about business success for themselves and the successful continuation of the community project.

Such entrepreneurial success by members of the community will encourage others to become entrepreneurs. Over time, and with the successful functioning of a number of community entrepreneurial development projects, the Malay community should be as competitive and entrepreneurial as any other community in Singapore.

REFERENCES

Ahmad, Kassim (1960), Kesah Pelayaran Abdullah, Oxford University Press, Kuala Lumpur.

Alatas, Syed Hussein (1977), The Myth of the Lazy Native, Frank Cass, London.

Chong, Li Choy and Ian C. MacMillan, (1990), "International Development through Entrepreneurship: A Business Community Development Approach", ENDEC International Entrepreneurship Conference, Singapore.

Chong, Li Choy, (1986), "The Entrepreneur as a Social Person: Implications for Entrepreneurial Promotion and Development in Singapore", Journal of Small Business and Entrepreneurship, Canada.

Geertz, C. (1963), Peddlers and Princes: Social Development and Economic Change in Two Indonesian Towns, University of Chicago Press, Chicago.

Gullick, J.M. (1956), Indigenous Political Systems of Western Malaya, The Athlone Press, London.

Kirzner, I.M. (1979), Opportunities and Profit: Studies in the Theory of Entrepreneurship, University of Chicago Press, Chicago.

Leong Choon Cheong (1978), Youth in the Army, Federal Publications, Singapore.

Li, Tania (1989), Malays in Singapore: Culture, Economy and Ideology, Oxford University Press, Singapore.

Roff, William R. (1967), The Origins of Malay Nationalism, Yale University Press, New Haven.

Tham Seong Chee (1983), Malays and Modernization: A Sociological Interpretation, Singapore University Press (2nd Edn), National University of Singapore.

Weber, Max (1930), The Protestant Ethic and the Spirit of Capitalism, trans. by Talcott Parsons, George Allen & Unwin, London.

Singapore: Censuses and Surveys

Report on the Census of Population 1957, Government Printer, Singapore (Abbreviated in references as "Census 1957").

Census of Population 1970, Government Printing Office, Singapore (Abbreviated in references as "Census 1970").

Report on the Census of Population 1980, Parts 1-9, Government Printing Office, Singapore (Abbreviated in references as "Census 1980").

Report on the Labour Force Survey (1975, 1978 1980), Ministry of Labour, Singapore.

Soviet State Firms Facing Transition: Towards a New Entrepreneurial System

Critique
by
Timothy M. Stearns, *Marquette University*

The paper describes a Soviet publishing firm in transition due to perestroika. In general, it offers insights into the process of de-bureaucratization of the firm. Three important issues of global entrepreneurship are raised in the paper: (1) conceptualization of firms as entrepreneurial, (2) introduction of environmental variations to entrepreneurial firms, and (3) the structure and composition of stakeholders.

(1) Conceptualization of the firm as entrepreneurial:

Most Western views of entrepreneurship assume a model of firm founding and growth that culminates either in failure or maturity. Growth is the stage in the model that leads the firm away from its entrepreneurial character, culminating in a maturity that embodies a non-entrepreneurial firm, sometimes referred to as a bureaucracy. The author, by examining a firm's transition under economic and political change in the Soviet Union, has captured a different model. The publishing firm under study has at founding assumed a bureaucratic form of organisation. The characteristic struggles of solving problems associated with entrepreneurship in the West such as securing supplies, locating customers, etc are relatively absent . Rather, the struggles are more directly tied to moulding the structure of the firm in a manner that will receive state support.

With economic and political change throughout the Soviet Union underway, the firm's existing structure is replaced with one that resembles a firm in its growth stage in the Western view of the firm. That is, a reversal in direction, with regard to the Western model, has taken place, with the firm moving from bureaucracy to an entrepreneurial structure. The significance of this process rests not only in the challenge it makes to the Western view of entrepreneurship, but also to its generalizability to firms throughout the Soviet Union and Eastern Europe where countries are undergoing similar transitions.

This leads to two important research questions: To what extent is the Western model appropriate for understanding entrepreneurship in countries that have moved from centralised economic planning to that of free market economies? With the advent of a free market and the emergence of firms under these conditions, will they replace existing firms or will they offer a competing model of entrepreneurship to the bureaucracies that have transformed into entrepreneurial firms?

(2) Introduction of environmental changes to entrepreneurial firms:

Under planned economies, environmental changes play a lesser role in their impact on the fortunes of the entrepreneurial form. Environmental variations encompass distributions and fluctuations in such critical resource areas as labour, capital, materials, and information. The author describes a publishing firm that was largely shielded from environmental changes by state agencies. However, with the shift to a market that introduces more freedom in the acquisition and distribution of its products, the firm receives greater exposure to environmental turbulence.

Western views of entrepreneurship envision a firm at its founding to be most susceptible to environmental changes. They present problems that must be solved to owners and managers. Efficiency in the solving of these problems is believed to be one critical route to survival and growth of the firm. As the firm grows, so does its ability to shield its activities from problems caused by environmental changes. Hence, those firms that grow and flourish tend to be those that are most efficient under existing environmental conditions. Clearly, this view is challenged by the author in the analysis of the Soviet publishing firm. The firm is operating under conditions that guarantee a flow of resources as well as access to buyers. Problems that entrepreneurs in the West must solve are not embedded in the structures of the publishing firm. Under conditions of change, however, the author describes a transition of the firm's structure that is characteristic of Western entrepreneurial firms. What unique problems are associated with this transition? What advantages or disadvantages does a firm have in going from a bureaucratic form of organisation to an entrepreneurial form? Can Western models of entrepreneurship provide blueprints for reorganisation of the firm to meet the challenges of a new environment?

(3) The structure and composition of stakeholders:

Stakeholders play an important role for all types of firms. Stakeholders represent bases of power in the environment of a firm that can influence internal firm activities. Managers seek understanding of stakeholders in efforts to adapt firm activities in a way that will enable the firm to grow and prosper.

Under the former Soviet system, the author describes a set of stakeholders that are stable and similar in composition (eg. state agencies, suppliers, and buyers of the firm). Stability and similarity of stakeholders enables management to readily identify products that can be produced and products that will be received in the market. However, the shift to a freer market also means a shift to a set of stakeholders that are more likely to be unstable (no guarantee of access to supplies or the purchase of a product) and dissimilar (different wants and needs of suppliers and purchasers).

What impact will this shift have on the fortunes of the publishing firm? How will this change its product portfolio? To what extent will the firm be forced into increasing stakeholder instability by seeking greater access to foreign markets as a means of survival? All these questions raise important issues in the study of the firms as it moves from a bureaucratic firm to that of an entrepreneurial firm.

SOVIET STATE FIRMS FACING TRANSITION: TOWARDS A NEW ENTREPRENEURIAL SYSTEM

PAOLA DUBINI, *LUIGI BOCCONI UNIVERSITY*

ABSTRACT

The paper presents a case study on the management of transition by a Soviet State firm in the publishing industry that can be viewed as typical of the Soviet situation. The management of the firm has been interviewed in order to understand the characteristics and the relations between the key elements of a company structure in the USSR before and during transition. The key elements are:
- institutional aspects
- economic processes
- organizational structure and procedures
- cost structure

Results describe how the management has insisted in interpreting environmental pressures towards change using traditional tools.

INTRODUCTION

The turmoil affecting all aspects of Soviet society has been in the recent past examined quite thoroughly by academics and practitioners. The interest raised by Soviet events is not only due to their historical importance, but also to the lack of theoretical models that could be applied to analyze the transition. " The kind of society that is now taking shape in Eastern Europe will bear no resemblance to previous Stalinist or neo-Stalinist societies, nor will it be the perfect copy of Western societies. It is already apparent that the changes which have taken place cannot be accounted for by dual thinking -- socialism vs. capitalism" (Bogomolov 1990). In a recent interview [1], J. Kornai stressed how unique the transition is and how important it is for Eastern and Western "specialists" to work together, as each of them brings some of the know-how necessary to interpret the transition phase. Eastern specialists know the "rules of the game" under the old regime which still affect present behaviour and which westerners are unlikely to understand. Westerners, on the other hand, know the "rules of the game" of a possible "target situation" that Eastern counterparts sometimes are not willing to accept. Each of the Eastern economies has its own story; although some of the problems faced tend to be the same, each country can leverage on different variables to face transition. For example, Bulgaria still remembers what a free enterprise is, while in the Soviet Union people tend to avoid risk and responsibility; Soviet Union has a huge reserve of raw materials, Romania has virtually no State deficit.

In this paper, the case of a well know publishing firm -- whose name is disguised, since a formal authorization to publish data was not obtained -- is presented, in order to show how Soviet State firms are dealing with transition trying to use models and practices consistent with past "rules of the game" [2]. In particular, pressures towards a decentralized decision system are analyzed in their implications for entrepreneurial and managerial behaviour; managers operating within State owned companies facing the transition are now beginning to be held responsible for their decisions in running the business; this means that they can no longer justify inefficiency by blaming "somebody" outside their span of control.

METHODOLOGY

In the following paragraphs, the Sunrise case study is first presented referring to the model developed by Airoldi, Brunetti and Coda (1989), which describes the characteristics and the relations between the key elements of a company structure:
- institutional aspects
- organizational structure and procedures
- technical system
- economic processes
- economic and financial structure

The paper focuses on the characteristics of Sunrise's institutional aspects, economic processes, organizational structure and procedures, and cost structure before 1989 and the major changes which occurred until March 1991.

* Institutional aspects are examined in order to determine the confines of the firm, its institutional goals and the institutional stakeholders ultimately responsible for the existence and development of the company. The role of the government in influencing companies' behaviour is also considered.

* Economic processes are analyzed in order to identify the core processes performed by the company and assess which of them are most relevant in value generation, and how purchases, manufacturing and sales are carried out.

* The organizational structure and procedures are examined to define the division of labour within the company, the most common management practices, the operating mechanisms implemented -- if any -- for human resources management.

* Finally, some hints are given on the cost structure of Sunrise, in order to identify the "key figures" in a Soviet State firm.

The firm's evolution is examined by comparing the pre-1989 situation with the reactions of the structure to environmental and institutional pushes. Finally, the Sunrise case peculiarities are discussed and compared to the characteristics of the Illustrated Books Division of an Italian Publishing Group.

THE SUNRISE CASE STUDY

Sunrise was founded in 1969 as a State firm by its first Deputy Director Nicolai Pisdocov, an ex-military representative greatly interested in art. The goal of the firm was to promote Soviet art and Soviet collections through the manufacturing of art books for the international and the domestic market. The quality of the product and a privileged access to the huge photographic file of the Hermitage Museum were the distinctive features of the firm, which gained over time a strong reputation in its segment. In 1985 Sunrise was ranked the top book producer in the Soviet Union and at a high level in the international market.

1) Economic processes

Until 1989, Sunrise enjoyed a strong "competitive" position, due to the quality of its products and to the interest shown in the firm by the Government and the local community. Apart from the cultural aspects related to the mission of the firm -- to spread Soviet art and culture -- Sunrise was given particular attention because it was oriented to the international market and therefore it provided hard currency to the Government; nearly 50% of the production in volume (art books, posters, art reproductions, postcards and art albums [3]) is aimed at the international market.

In common with every State owned company, the Government covers 100% of raw material needs and gives full directions on which suppliers to use, which customers to sell to, and how much to produce. Sunrise can decide the number of pages of each book, having a set limit on the total number of pages to print every year.

Break-even point is calculated at 20,000 copies; in order to make a profit, Sunrise manufacturers 25,000 to 30,000 copies (depending on paper availability) for each title, in multiples of 3 languages.

Sunrise designs and manufactures 25 art books per year; at least half of them must refer to Soviet masterpieces and collections (according to Gosplan specifications), and the rest to the international collections in the Soviet Union. The State company is responsible for gathering the photographic material, while most of the printing activity is contracted out to different countries, chosen on the basis of the quality of their printing. It has to be noted, though, that the foreign printers are not chosen by Sunrise, but by the Government, through a set of bilateral agreements with the Communist Party in different countries. 60% of the printing is done in Moscow and Leningrad, the rest abroad. All operations prior to printing are performed by Sunrise and coordinated by the Technical Editorial Department (see organizational chart); the firm also gives the printers all the standards related to paper quality, size, cover and so. Moreover, Sunrise personnel are in charge of proof reading; in this way quality control is assured, even if manufacturing is partially decentralized.

Every new title contains approximately 30% brand new photographs; therefore, the company's archives are rich in material and represent one of its main strengths, especially as far as the Soviet art photos are concerned. In order to be able to take pictures and duplicate the images, Sunrise has to pay a royalty to the Museum which owns the masterpiece; however, if the photo is already available in the company's archives, this is not needed.

Although Sunrise was created to serve the international market -- thus granting a flow of hard currency -- it does not have the ability to make direct contact with Western counterparts, or take full advantage of the hard currency. The company is not responsible for book distribution; all the production is sold to two distribution agencies, Soyuz Kniga (which distributes to the national bookstores) and Miezdunarodnaia Kniga (in charge of the international market), both located in Moscow.

2) The Organizational structure

As in most Soviet State firms, Sunrise has a functional structure, except for two "divisions" for the editorial content (Soviet art division/International art in Soviet collections division).

Sunrise employs about 220 people; the editorial staff is, for the most part, composed of people holding a degree in history of art. Each of the divisions has about 20 editors, coordinated by the Chief Editor. The company is given instructions by the Government regarding the number of new titles and the format, but editors are free to choose the topics to cover, Each editor can make a proposal to the editorial Committee. If the proposal is unanimously accepted, a "plan of action" is made, detailing the number of pages, the format, the number and type of photographs to be used and so on. This new proposal is then presented to the Editorial Board (which includes the C.E.O., the Chief Editor, the Vice President for printing, the translator and the Vice President for Sales); if it is approved, the Sales Department prepares an English version of the program which will be included in the catalogue presented at the International Book Fairs. Each catalogue is prepared as early as two years before the exhibition takes place in order to grant the Project Leader (usually the editor who first made the proposal) to gather all the necessary resources.

Basic salary for employees is not high, but bonuses are frequent and common; a member of the technical editorial staff receives 130 rubles per month, a proof reader 120, an editor approximately 100. Authors receive 300 rubles every 24 typed pages, while translators 150; the C.E.O. is paid 430 rubles per month. Bonuses amount to 150% of basic salary, and are distributed every three months.

Working conditions are fairly good, and there is virtually no control over performance; the editors are viewed as "intellectuals" and therefore are by far the group with the highest power in the company. Mild attempts are made to increase productivity and to reduce absenteeism, but with no success. People learn quickly how to bypass the rules, so that no significant improvement is reached; in any case, a stable flow of input and a stable flow of output grant stability and continuity to the firm.

The Gorbachev era has brought some changes to the management of the company; democracy calls for a less hierarchical system and a higher involvement of individuals in the firm's decision making process. A few committees have been created, with the aim of finding ways to increase productivity in a participative way. In this period, the worker collective (something like the unions at factory level) became more and more powerful.

3) Cost structure

70% of the revenues deriving from a contract signed with a Western counterpart go back to Miezdunarodnaia Kniga (the remaining 30% in hard currency is taken by the Government). 10% of this amount is kept by the distributor; the remaining 90% is equally divided among Sunrise and the printers. Sunrise uses its percentage of hard currency to cover operating costs and investments in new equipment and machinery.

B) THE FIRST EFFECTS OF PERESTROIKA: GETTING INTERNATIONAL

By 1988, Sunrise was a well established firm willing to grow in the international market. The domestic market for art books in the USSR is apparently very big and not fully saturated. In order to exploit this opportunity, Sunrise started evaluating the possibility of using high quality Soviet-made paper for books aimed to the domestic market, and imported paper for international production. However, direct access to the international market seems to be the best and most profitable way to grow.

At the end of 1987, a law had been approved in the USSR, offering firms involved in international trading the opportunity to deal directly with foreign counterparts. Sunrise views this law as an opportunity to gain independence from Miezdunaradnaia Kniga and to operate directly on the open market, thus keeping a higher portion of the margin in hard currrency. This would also generate a stock of hard currency necessary for Sunrise to get access to high quality raw materials, particularly to paper and film, which are increasingly hard to find in the domestic market.

In October 1988, the Sunrise Publishing Company spun off the Sunrise Commercial Company; the new firm is funded with 200,000 rubles from a governmental agency and through a loan granted by Sunrise Publishing Company, but is fully independent in its management in that is able to operate on the open market. Through the independent unit -- which is entitled to have a hard currency account -- Sunrise can set up representative offices abroad, and leverage on its international scope. Sunrise Commercial is supposed to receive 10% of the new firm's revenues;

the new firm has to pay 42% of its net income to the local community. The new firm employs 13 people from Sunrise Publishing who are among the brightest of the work force, and are more willing to accept the challenge posed by the uncertainty of the open market.

C) 1989-1991: MANAGING CHANGE

The new-born firm started its activities by visiting international fairs and exhibitions and presenting Sunrise catalogues; the reaction of the market showed that Sunrise's books -- although technically well made -- were not "modern" in their layout and formal characteristics. Moreover, the subjects and the maquettes presented by Sunrise did not acheive the expected appreciation; finally, some foreign counterparts were willing to start working with Sunrise on the condition that deadlines were rigidly met and that all contracts were formalized and renegotiated every time. The rigidity of foreign counterparts is likely to create some problems for Sunrise, in spite of its reputation and its almost exclusive access to photographic archives, as it suffers from chronic shortages of raw materials.

In the meantime, the growing independence accorded to State owned firms with respect to their international activity was accompanied by a loosening of the links between firms and Government in the internal market; in 1989 Goskomisdat still granted 100% of raw materials, but it soon became apparent that by 1990, only 50% of supplies would be provided by the Government, thus enabling Sunrise to print only 14 new books every year.

The problem of finding raw material is not new for Sunrise, but the good relations with the Government and the quality of the product had so far granted stable supplies; unlike some of its competitors, Sunrise Publishing had decided not to integrate backwards, relying instead on the help of the Government, so that now it could not even count on the amount of paper printing facilities managed to gather.

In 1988, the existence of the commercial firm had made Sunrise Publishing believe that it would be able to generate an adequate flow of hard currency to cover its needs for imported goods, thereby solving the problem of supplies with imports, and also allowing some investment. The problem was that most of the raw material needed had now to be bought abroad and paid in hard currency. Sunrise's statute does not allow barter. As a consequence, virtually all the hard currency available was used to cover operating expenses.

Finding the raw materials necessary for production is only one part of the problem; the creation of a market -- although imperfect -- together with chronic scarcity of products and services make prices skyrocket. In 1989 Sunrise Publishing could still count on paper at 1,200 rubles per ton; in 1990, prices for paper on the market -- when raw materials were available in rubles and not hard currency -- ranged from 5,000 to 10,000 rubles per ton. Prices for photographs have increased up to 6 times, and museums now request payment of royalties for photographs already in Sunrise's archives.

The unexpected reactions of Western counterparts to Sunrise's products, together with the more complicated domestic situation, created strong feelings within Sunrise and its publishing spin-off. The editors of the publishing company feel offended in their professional pride by the criticisms made of their work by their colleagues in the commercial firm; in their opinion, it is quite strange that a product appreciated for years is now considered not appropriate. Some resentment was also generated by the fact that the publishing firm did not raise salaries to satisfactory levels because of the difficult economic situation, wheras in the commercial firm, salaries were about double those of other state owned companies.

In 1990 Sunrise was finally allowed to partially transfer the increase in prices to the consumer; in 1987 the average price for an art album aimed at the domestic market was about 18.7 rubles, while in 1990 it could be found for 60-80 rubles in the bookstores and 700-800 rubles on the black market. However, the increase in retail price was not enough to cover the growing needs for funds, as prices for raw materials has increased about 6 times in 2 years.

During the second half of the year, the situation in the country became increasingly tense, while a shortage of raw material became the rule for all of the companies. For the first time, publishers were requested to provide all necessary paper in order to get their books printed; highly integrated competitors -- who had in the meantime learnt how to obtain paper in the domestic as well as the Western market -- managed to manufacture enough to meet Plan specifications. On the contrary, Sunrise, which was not accustomed to getting resources through the market, struggled to meet even 50% of the Plan.

The scarcity of raw materials, together with the bad news from abroad, required a reorganization of the publishing firm in spite of the opposition from the Collective; a few committees were created to study possible solutions and to evaluate how bad the situation was: by August 1990 it was clear to the Deputy Director that Sunrise was in serious danger. One project presented to the Collective advocated using some governmental funds and the money available within Sunrise (approximately 4 million rubles) to create a series of small enterprises and joint ventures to diversify in the publishing business. The "old" Sunrise should keep no more than 50 people, while the others could be given 200,000 to 500,000 rubles each to start the new ventures; this amount would let the new firms survive for about two years. The study concluded that the situation is very delicate, but not desperate; the suggested measures should be implemented before the end of the year, as inflation and a new law for the reconstruction of Leningrad were going to quickly absorb the patrimony of Sunrise in 1991. Due to a growing inflation rate, salaries had increased; authors now received 600 rubles each 24 typed pages, while translators received 175 rubles, thus contributing to worsen the already delicate position of Sunrise.

The proposal for a drastic reorganization was received with mixed feelings by the Sunrise employees, who were for the first time in their lives facing the risk of being fired. The "communication problems" within the firm and the emerging of different cultures (the entrepreneurs versus the nostalgics) became increasingly noticeable. After long internal discussions, the Collective refused to implement the proposed plan of reorganization and asked the Deputy Director to resign.

At the end of 1990, Sunrise Publishing was about to close; no governmental supply was granted for 1991, because of a law approved by the Soviet of USSR that determines that only manuals and schoolbooks may be printed at Government expense and must be sold at a fixed price.

Moreover, for the first time in its history, Sunrise had not met the Plan specifications for 1990; the production for the first quarter of 1991 was granted by the inventories available, but the firm owed about one quarter's worth of salaries to the Government. In the meantime, assets worth 4 million rubles had decreased to two million because the City of Leningrad had absorbed funds for reconstruction.

In November 1990, the Deputy Director resigned; the new Director -- the founder of the company, with a strong personality and charisma -- had to decide the future of the company. As lack of raw materials was probably the single most relevant problem for the firm, Sunrise considered the possibility of expanding the product line to include some items requiring little raw material such as calendars, postcards and so on. However, these alternatives do not yield high margins because they are heavily taxed. A much more interesting opportunity was offered by the leasing of pictures to different counterparts in exchange for a royalty.

CONCLUSIONS

The case of the Sunrise Publishing Firm is quite typical of the difficulties managers from Soviet State firms are facing during transition.

Sunrise has been able to identify the most value-added phases in art book manufacturing and to build up distinctive skills in design and publishing. Access to a large amount of significant photographic material is still one of the major assets Sunrise can leverage in negotiating with foreign counterparts.

In spite of its superior product quality which differentiates Sunrise from the other Soviet publishers, the company is finding it very hard to survive, because it has been unable to capture precise environmental signals for a change in behaviour. In 1988 Sunrise had the typical structure of a State owned Soviet firm, inconsistent with the new rules of the game:
- no control over supplies;
- no opportunity to choose customers;
- no possibility of deciding about investments/diversification and soon:
- no orientation to cost control and to economic behaviour
- a solid economic and financial structure on paper, based on external support and not on internal strengths.

The fact that in the last two years the company has not been able to build competitive advantage out of its distinctive features can be attributed to the characteristics of its corporate culture and to managerial practices which are resistant to change:

- employing too many personnel;
- following managerial patterns successful in the past, based on good political connections,
- low salaries;
- career paths based on seniority and not on merit;
- a competitive advantage based only partially on distinctive core competencies (quality of books, almost exclusive availability of photographic material), and mainly on external advantages (political support);
- little willingness to change, and continuing presence in the firm of people with very low professionalism.

The "old" managerial model lost validity, as a few intervening factors changed the situation:
- the firm was asked to make its own decisions;
- the firm was asked to behave according to economic criteria;
- the Government was no longer taking care of Sunrise's structural inefficiencies.

The environment pushed Sunrise Publishing to become a "firm" in the Western sense, that is, to reach decisional autonomy and to take responsibility for its decisions. The interpretation of the external situation by Sunrise managers shows the difficulties Soviet managers are now facing in accepting a managerial model calling for a high personal involvement.

The initial solution to the pressures of change (the creation of Sunrise Commercial) created more problems over time than opportunities, as Sunrise Commercial became the internal turbulence generator factor, pushing the firm to accelerate internal transition. No wonder, internal conflicts arise when one part of the company is asked to interact with the West, and another sticks to old paradigms.

The traditional economic institutions (the big, inefficient and bureaucratic State firms) are finding it very hard to adapt to transition; new institutional solutions are emerging to grant the few managers/entrepreneurs in the Soviet Union the opportunity to "manage" more flexible and opportunistic organizations: small enterprises and cooperatives. People working in this type of economic institutions are not only able to identify opportunities, but -- more important -- are willing to be held responsible for their behaviour. They are few, their time horizon is short and they are hindered by the powerful bureaucrats of State firms. Their challenge is to build up long lasting entrepreneurial companies able to revitalize the Soviet economic system.

NOTES

(1) Interview on Corriere della Sera, January, 6, 1991.

(2) Data for this paper were drawn during a research project on the management of Soviet firms sponsored by LIMI, a joint venture between Bocconi University - Milan and Leningrad University. The joint venture was founded in 1989 with the aim of creating a business school devoted to the development of managerial skills in the Soviet Union. The help of M. Kolesnikova, E. Cattaneo and C. Filippini during the project is here warmly acknowledged.

(3) An album is much richer in pictures than a book; in an album, in fact, over 50% of pages are pictures.

(4) A maquette is the prototype of an art book, from which it is possible to get an idea of the content of the book, the physical quality of the paper and pictures, the cover, the size and so on. The maquette is generally presented at international book fairs and it represents the basis of discussion between the editor and the foreign counterpart for co-editions or distribution abroad.

BIBLIOGRAPHY

Airoldi G., Brunetti G., Coda V. 1989 Lezioni di Economia Aziendale, Il Mulino.

Bogomolov O. 1990. Revolutions in Eastern Europe: the birth of new political and economic realities. Most, 1.

Cattaneo E., Dubini P., 1991. Understanding management practices in Soviet companies. working paper, SDA Bocconi.

Colombo G. Restructuring the Socialist Economy starting from the Companies. Economia Aziendale, forthcoming.

The Entrepreneurs' Reasons Leading To Start-up As Determinants Of Survival and Failure Among Norwegian New Ventures

Critique
by
Juan Roure, *IESE*

The purpose of the paper is to investigate within the context of Norway the relationship between the reasons entrepreneurs start their business and the future survival or failure of the venture. In this discussion, I will highlight the hypothesis, methodology and key findings and comment on them such that they will complement the arguments of the paper or approach them from another perspective.

The paper begins by referring to the role that small businesses play in the social and economic development of a country. In particular, the authors mention new ventures as a major source of new jobs. It is important to emphasize that "high growth" ventures are really major job creators as Birch has shown lately.

After reporting the contradictory findings of the role that the original motivations of entrepreneurs play in the performance of the firm, the authors suggest two hypotheses:

H.1   Surviving and failing entrepreneurs may be distinguished from each other by their reasons leading to the start-up.

H.2   Certain clusters of entrepreneurs will be over-represented by surviving ventures, while other clusters will be over-represented by failing ventures.

The argument behind the first hypothesis is that the initial motivation of the entrepreneur will influence his behavior, and that behavior will influence firm performance. Except for a few authors that have found some motivaitonal factors related to a firm's performance, most researchers in different countries find no identifiable relationship between initial motivation of the entrepreneur and the subsequent success of the business. As the paper indicates, several authors have found that some positive factors and negative situational factors seem to motivate the start-up of new fims. However, not much influence has been found in the firms' subsequent evolution. It may clarify the arguments of the paper if it is mentioned that several other factors, such as background, experience, personal traits and demographics may also influence the behavior of the entrepreneur. In addition to entrepreneurs' behavior, other variables such as environment characteristics, firm's strategy and management team, may influence venture performance (Keeley and Roure, 1990).

The second hypothesis argues that based on their motivations, it is possible to classify different "types" of entrepreneurs, and these "types" of entrepreneurs may show different rates of failure. Previous research has shown that the motivational factors in starting a business can be classified in different categories which are labeled under different names, depending on the authors. But in any case, these categories have been related to venture performance. Therefore, based on previous research one cannot draw the direct conclusion that entrepreneurs' motivation does affect failure rates.

This study is part of a larger project in which environment and personal background as well as motivations to start a business, are studied. The questionnaire used was translated from the one used by the Society of Associated Researchers of International Entrepreneruship (SARIE) and was distributed in 1986 to 511 random independent entrepreneurs who have created a for-profit organization since 1980 and had at least one employee. Of the 148 entrepreneurs who answered the questionnaire, 35% were in manufacturing and 65% were in service industries. They had an average of 8.5 employees. About four years later the 148 entrepreneurs were approached again and the finding was that 36 of them had not survived.

Given the potential influence of the methodology on the interpretations, two points need to be made. First, the question of reasons leading to starting a business was not answered by the entrepreneur when he actually initiated the company, but between one and six years later. Therefore, his response could have been influenced by the experience that he had had, or by the evolution of the firm's performance. For example, let's imagine an entrepreneur that started a company four years ago, and despite working very hard, the venture did not take off, and is a marginal company or "living dead". If you ask the entrepreneur about reasons that moved him to start the company, his reason at the beginning might have been something like "making a direct contribution to the success of the company", but it is very unlikely that he would mention this reason after the four years experience. The opposite case is also possible. Let us imagine an entrepreneur who five years before found himself unemployed and the only option he had was to start a company to take advantage of certain subsidies that the government was offering. He has done very well growing a profitable business. If you ask this entrepreneur today about reasons that moved him to create his own company, there is a chance that he may answer, "in order to make a direct contribution to the success of a company". I do not mean that the entrepreneur gives a false reponse, but it seems reasonable that personal experience may influence his answer.

The second aspect of the methodology that should be considered is that the performance is measured by contrasting survival and failure. This method of measuring performance has the advantage that failure or discontinuity of operations is normally a good indicator of not being successful. However, it has the disadvantage that survival is not a clear measure of success. Thus, there are many small businesses for whom surviving is more related to the entrepreneur having a low level of needs, and to financial resistance, than to success. Therefore, the conclusions drawn from the results could be stronger in the case of firms not surviving than in surviving ones.

The results of the stepwise discriminant analysis showed that twelve of the thirty-eight items discriminate between surviving and non-surviving firms, and therefore supported H.1. Thus, the reasons leading to start-up were the following:

FOR SURVIVORS
1. To make a direct contribution in the company
2. To follow a role model
3. To achieve a higher position
4. To work in a desirable location
5. To work with certain people
6. To have a better use of his training and skills

FOR FAILURES
7. To contribute to the community welfare
8. To have considerable freedom in the work place
9. To have access to fringe benefits
10. To increase status
11. To have an element of variety and adventure at work.
12. To keep learning

These twelve variables were factor analysed using varimax rotation, resulting in four factors of motivation: Status (3,10,2,7,4), Freedom (11,6,8), Learning (5,7,12,1), and Benefits (9,4). Based on these factor scores, cluster analysis was performed in order to group the entrepreneurs in accordance with their motivation to start the business. Four cluster results were large enough for further analysis. Of these four clusters, surviving companies are overrepresented in clusters 1 and 2, while most failures were found in clusters 3 and 4. Each cluster was characterized by different motivating factors:

SURVIVORS

CLUSTER 1 (30%)	CLUSTER 2 (10%)	CLUSTER 3 (23%)	CLUSTER 4 (37%)
Benefits	Status	Learning	Learning
Status	Freedom	Benefits	Benefits
	Benefits	Freedom	Freedom

These results partially support H.2 and show that entrepreneurs motivated mainly by benefits (to have access to fringe benefits and to work in a preferred location), freedom (to have an element of variety and adventure at work, to have better use of training and skills, and to have freedom at work) and communitarianism, are more likely to fail. I will label this type of entrepreneurs "light" versus the "classic" entrepreneur.

Finally, these results make us think about the real contribution from an economic and social point of view of certain public policies implemented following the rise in popularity of entrepreneurship. Thus, it is clear that a lack of support infrastructure and public policies that facilitate the creation of new ventures result in high entry barriers, and therefore, low start-up rate, and much waste of human potential. On the other hand, public policies based on too many incentives and subsidies may result in an overpromotion of entrepreneurship, and therefore, a high rate of start-up. However, many of these start-ups might be created by "light entrepreneurs" instead of "classic entrepreneurs" that may represent a waste of resources because of the higher failure rate and potential unfair competition. In conclusion, in order to have an optimum administration of economic and social resources, public policies promoting entrepreneurship should be balanced. Otherwise, the pursuit of the opportunity to create value that characterizes entrepreneurship may very easily become the pursuit of a job to survive.

THE ENTREPRENEURS' REASONS LEADING TO START-UP AS DETERMINANTS OF SURVIVAL AND FAILURE AMONG NORWEGIAN NEW VENTURES

SVENN JENSSEN, *BODO GRADUATE SCHOOL OF BUSINESS*
LARS KOLVEREID, *BODO GRADUATE SCHOOL OF BUSINESS*

ABSTRACT

The purpose of the present research was to investigate the relationship between entrepreneurs' reasons to start their business and future survival or failure of the ventures created. Data on motivation was collected from 148 Norwegian entrepreneurs in 1986. In 1990, the same entrepreneurs were aproached again in order to find out which firms had survived and which had failed. The results suggest that it is possible to determine the chances for future survival of a venture by investigating the entrepreneur's motives to start the business.

INTRODUCTION

Most scholars agree that small business formation and small businesses play a major role in the economic and social development of a country. New ventures are considered a major source of new jobs (Hofer and Sandberg, 1987; Armington and Odle, 1982; Birch, 1979; Teitz et al., 1981), technical innovation (Kamien and Schwartz, 1982) and economic flexibility and growth (Swain, 1985).

In Norway, the recognition of the importance of new small ventures combined with increased unemployment rates and major crises in some of the country's traditional industries has resulted in a flow of public policies and support services to promote entrepreneurial activities. In terms of contribution to economic growth and the creation of new jobs, those firms which have the capability of growth and long term survival are of particular interest. High failure rates among new ventures represent sizeable losses in funds and opportunities, and there is an obvious stake and potential profit in understanding why new ventures fail or succeed (Sandberg, 1986).

One may assert that the most valuable "asset" a new small firm holds is the entrepreneur. Understanding the entrepreneur and his reason to start the business in the first place are important inputs in the work of promoting entrepreneurship. The purpose of this paper is to investigate whether the founding entrepreneur's initial motivation to start the business influences the probability of survival.

ENTREPRENEURIAL MOTIVATION

Motivation theory is concerned with why behaviour occurs. Atkinson et al.(1983) define motivation as a general term referring to the regulation of need-satisfying and goal seeking behaviour. Baron (1986) uses a similar definition when he indicates that motivation starts out with a need arousal, which then energises a person's behaviour and directs it toward attaining some goal. The important point made here is that behaviour generated through some kind of need will be directed towards some goal. The individual has a choice between different behaviours. Motivation involves making intentional choices and selecting goals which implies that motivation could be understood as an interaction between stimuli in the environment and a particular psychological state of the organism (Atkinson et al., 1983).

Hofer and Sandberg (1987) argued that the key characteristics of the entrepreneurs that affect new venture performance are individual behaviour patterns. If this assumption is correct, it can be argued that a person's motivation will lead to some need-satisfying and goal-seeking behaviour. The person chooses the kind of behaviour that is most likely to fulfill his needs.

If one accepts that motivation influences the entrepreneur's behaviour, the interesting issue becomes whether the entrepreneur's motivation influences the venture's ability to survive. It is possible that the entrepreneur's objectives are reflected in his motivation, and thereby influence his choice of action and priorities (Atkinson et al., 1983).

Research in entrepreneurship has investigated a number of different psychological factors which are related to entrepreneurial behavior. It has been suggested that individuals characterized with high Need for Achievement are more sensitive to changes in economic opportunities, compared with those who are low in Need for Achievement, which leads them to seize these opportunities and start businesses (McClellan, 1953, 1961). Locus of Control is another characteristic which has been related to entrepreneurship (Rotter, 1966; Brockhaus, 1975). Desire for independence, dissatisfaction with previous employment, role models and risk willingness are other factors often referred to in studies of entrepreneurs (Hornaday and Aboud, 1971; Shapero, 1975; Brockhaus and Nord, 1979; Brockhaus, 1980; Komives, 1972).

One of the most commonly cited reasons for entrepreneurs to leave their previous job and become an entrepreneur is dissatisfaction with previous work experience (Cooper ,1971; Shapero, 1975; Brochaus, 1980). This is explained by the push theory of entrepreneurial motivation which claims that individuals are pushed into entrepreneurship by negative situational factors such as dissatisfaction with existing employment, loss of employment and career setback. The pull theory, on the other hand, suggests that the existence of attractive and potentially profitable business opportunities will attract individuals into entrepreneurial activities.

A person may be primarily motivated either by internal motives or by external rewards; an internally motivated person will direct his behaviour toward achieving the fulfillment of internal needs such as the need for innovation and independence, and be less concerned by external factors such as security and status. He will be less likely to be concerned about monetary outcomes, and therefore less likely to be successful in obtaining them. The externally motivated entrepreneur, on the other hand, will be more concerned about security, status, and monetary rewards.

A large proportion of previous research on the motivation of entrepreneurs has attempted to identify factors that distinguish the entrepreneur from non-entrepreneurs. To a certain extent this research has failed to identify psychological dimensions that helps us distinguish successful entrepreneurs from less successful entrepreneurs (Begley and Boyd, 1987).

Moreover, most previous research on the relationship between entrepreneurial motivation and performance has failed to use a longitudinal design. Another problem is that different researchers have used different indicators of success, and very few have focused on survival versus failure.

In one study, Need for Achievement and Locus of Control have been found to influence performance (Sandberg, 1986). Some findings also suggest that psychological factors such as Locus of Control influence the probability of surviving (Brockhaus, 1980). Brockhaus explained this by suggesting that externally motivated entrepreneurs may have been resigned to accepting rather than reversing unfavourable outcomes to such a degree that they were more likely to slide into failure.

In another study, Brinkman and Rimler (1988) reported significant positive correlation between independence and profitability, and between enjoyable work and profitability. Smith, Bracker and Miner (1987) also found significant positive correlation between entrepreneurs' task motivation and growth both in terms of sales and in number of employees.

Not all research has found support for the relationship between entrepreneurial motivation and performance. Birley (1985) found, when evaluating an enterprise program that expressed the intention of creating new ventures, no identifiable relationship between the initial motivation of the entrepreneur, whether positive or negative, and the subsequent success of the business.

Dunkelberg, Cooper and Woo (1987) also failed to find significant differences between growing and declining firms with regard to the entrepreneurs' most important reasons for starting the business.

Even though some contradictory findings have been reported, the theoretical discussion and some empirical evidence leads us to suggest the first hypothesis:

H1: Surviving and failing entrepreneurs may be distinguished from each other by their reasons leading to the start-up.

Recent research has found that the decision to start a new business is not influenced by the same motivations for all entrepreneurs. Dunkelberg and Cooper (1982) identified three groups of entrepreneurs, those motivated by a craftsman orientation, those motivated by freedom, and another group motivated by growth.

Scheinberg and MacMillan (1988) reported six different factors of motivation from their cross cultural study of entrepreneurial motivation. They are:

*Need for Approval (being related to external approval and input and McClellands theories on need for achievment).

*Perceived Instrumentality of Wealth (a drive for monetary rewards).

*Degree of Communitarianism (related to cultural belonging).

*Need for Personal Development (important in influencing the performance of the business).

*Need for Independence (related to rewards from the work itself).

*Need for Escape (related to negative circumstances referred to in the push theory of motivation).

A similar result is reported from the joint study of Swedish and Italian entrepreneurs (Alenge et al.1988; Dubini, 1988). From this one may draw the conclusion that the entrepreneurs' motivation does affect failure rates. The entrepreneurs' motivation influences the firms' probability of surviving. Different "types" of entrepreneurs are therefore expected to show show different rates of failures. In formal terms:

H2: Certain clusters of entrepreneurs will be overrepresented by surviving ventures, while other clusters will be overrepresented by failing ventures.

METHODOLOGY

This paper is the result of an international study of entrepreneurship initiated by The Society of Associated Researchers of International Entrepreneurship (SARIE). In 1986 the SARIE network collected data from entrepreneurs in 14 different countries. The development of the questionnaire was based on the theoretical contributions of: Aldrich (1986), Baumol (1985), Bruno and Tyebjee (1982), Friberg (1976), Hofstede (1980), Lodge (1986), McClellan and Winter (1969) and Shapero and Sokol (1982).

The questionnaire was translated into Norwegian and back translated to ensure accuracy. The questionnaire is divided into three sections: 1) Motivation to start a business , 2) Environmental influence and 3) Personal background of the founding entrepreneur and information about the business started. A fourth section, which dealt with attitudes towards entrepreneurs, was dropped in the Norwegian version. Only the 38 items which concern motivation to start the business are considered in this paper.

The criteria for selection of entrepreneurs to participate in the survey were as follows: only independent, for-profit organisations with at least one employee in addition to the entrepreneur were to be approached. In addition, the venture should not be more than six years old. The original sample included 600 organisations which were randomly selected from the Norwegian government's database of employees. After eliminating 89 non-profit organisations, the questionnaire was mailed to 511 entrepreneurs. Eleven questionnaires were returned undeliverable. After one reminder we received 148 answers, a response rate of approximately 30%.

The organisations investigated are all relatively small, with an average of 8.5 employees (range 1-130). Thirty-five percent were in manufacturing and 65 percent in services. In January 1990 the 148 entrepreneurs were contacted again through questionnaires, telephone interviews and an updated Government database in order to find out whether the venture had survived or failed. The findings showed 36 bankrupcies or failures, about 25% of the original respondents.

RESULTS

In order to identify motivational items that discriminated between the entrepreneurs that had failed and those that had survived the data were subjected to a stepwise discriminant analysis. The results of this analysis show that twelve of the thirty-eight items discriminate between the two groups. The eigenvalue of 0.74 is acceptable, and the results show that 71.6% of the businesses were classified correctly (106 out of 148). The results are shown in table 1 below:

TABLE 1

Stepwise discriminant analysis on reasons leading to start-up; failures versus survivors.

MOTIVATION VARIABLES	Standard. cannocial function	Structure matrix	Wilks' lambda	Sign. level
To make a direct contribution to the success of a company	-0.76423	-0.34255	0.9619	0.032
To contribute to the welfare of the community I live in	0.56387	0.23590	0.9281	0.012
To have considerable freedom to adapt my own approach to my work	0.54737	0.6786	0.8791	0.001
To have access to fringe benefits	0.42198	0.27594	0.8520	0.001
To follow the example of a person I admire	-0.40332	-0.23702	0.8297	0.000
To increase the status/prestige of my family	0.64205	0.27798	0.8127	0.000
To achieve a higher position for myself in society	-0.43196	-0.14161	0.7974	0.000
To be able to work in a location that is desireable to my family and myself	-0.35540	-0.03708	0.7854	0.000
To be able to work with people I choose	-0.30190	-0.06264	0.7765	0.000
To have an element of variety and adventure in my work	0.34003	0.04824	0.7650	0.000
To have better use of my training or skills	-0.28733	-0.12898	0.7573	0.001
To keep learning	0.27327	0.01100	0.7480	0.001

Function 1: Eigenvalue: 0.73680; Percent of variance: 100; Cann. corr: 0.5494050; Wilks'lamda: 0.7480058; Chi-square: 32.511; DF: 12; Significance: 0.0012; Percentage of cases grouped correctly: 71.62%

Note that the scale is reversed. A negative sign on the coefficient indicates that this item is important for surviving entrepreneurs.

The remaining items after the stepwise discriminant analysis were then factor analysed using varimax rotation. The factor analysis yielded four factors of motivation, explaining 59 percent of the variance. The results are shown in table 2 below:

TABLE 2
Varimax factor analysis of reasons leading to start-up.

	Status	Freedom	Learning	Benefits
Eigenvalue	3.05	1.79	1.19	1.06
Cum.pct.	25.4	40.3	50.2	59.0

	Status	Freedom	Learning	Benefits
To achieve a higher position for myself in society	.76			
To increase the status/ prestige of my family	.79			
To follow the example of a person I admire	.64			
To have an element of variety and adventure in my work		.77		
To better use my training and skills		.65		
To have considerable freedom to adapt my own approach to work		.75		
To be able to work with people I choose			.44	
To contribute to the welfare of the community I live in	.42		.52	
To keep learning			.77	
To make a direct contribution to the success of a company			.76	
To have access to fringe benefits				.77
To be able to work in a location that is				

desirable for my family and myself	.42 .59

Factor loadings under .4 are omitted.

Factor 1 includes items primarily related to status and prestige. The factor includes items concerning external rather than internal reward, and is similar to Scheinbergs and MacMillan's (1988) first factor which they labeled "need for approval". The second factor concerns freedom, adventure and the use of skills. Entrepreneurs with high scores on this factor will tend to be motivated and rewarded by the work itself. This factor is similar to Scheinberg and MacMillan's factor "need for independence". The third factor is related to the need for learning, contribution to the success of a company and sense of communitarianism. Entrepreneurs motivated by this factor will also tend to be more motivated by the content of the work than external factors. This factor is similar to Scheinberg and MacMillan's (1988) "need for personal development" factor. The last factor represents items related to concrete rewards, including access to fringe benefits and the opportunity to choose the place to live.

Based on the factor scores, cluster analysis was performed in order to group the entrepreneurs in accordance with their motivation to start the business. The seven cluster solution which was chosen made it possible to remove several outliers at the same time as four clusters remained which were large enough for further analysis. Table 3 below presents the remaining clusters:

TABLE 3

Cluster analysis of reasons leading to start-up.

	Cluster 1	Cluster 2	Cluster 3	Cluster 4	Sig.
	Sacrificing idealists	Status seeking individualists	Benefit seeking conservatives	Curious speculants	
Status	.40	-1.84	-.16	.29	abdef
Freedom	-.07	-.56	-.32	-.45	ac
Learning	.11	-.09	1.24	-.63	bcdef
Benefits	1.11	.23	-.55	-.52	abcde

a represents significant difference (p < .05) between cluster 1 and 2;
b represents significant difference (p < .05) between cluster 1 and 3;
c represents significant difference (p < .05) between cluster 1 and 4;
d represents significant difference (p < .05) between cluster 2 and 3;

e represents significant difference (p < .05) between cluster 2 and 4,
f represents significant difference (p < .05) between cluster 3 and 4.

Note that the scale is reversed. A negative figure indicates that this factor is an important motivator for entrepreneurs in that cluster.

About 30 percent of the entrepreneurs in the remaining four clusters are classified into the first cluster. Entrepreneurs in this cluster are not concerned about benefits and status, and seem to be willing to sacrifice their freedom when becoming an entrepreneur. We have labeled this cluster "sacrificing idealists".

Approximately 10 pecent of the entrepreneurs are classified into cluster 2. Members of this cluster seem to be primarily motivated by status and the need for freedom. These entrepreneurs have a high need to improve the outside perception of themselves and their families, they also have a need for independence in carrying out their work. We may call these entrepreneurs "status seeking individualists".

The third group of entrepreneurs represented in cluster 3 are motivated by benefits, factors that represent expected indirect consequences of the start-up. They are also characterized with a low score on the desire to learn and are relatively more concerned about freedom and status. About 23 percent of the entrepreneurs are classified in this cluster, which we have labeled "benefit seeking conservatives"

The last cluster includes entrepreneurs motivated by the learning factor, benefits and freedom, but not concerned about status. Cluster four is the largest of the clusters, encompassing about 37 percent of the entrepreneurs investigated. We have labeled this cluster "curious speculants". A cross tabulation between cluster membership and survival versus failure yields significant results as shown in table 4.

TABLE 4

Motivation cluster membership and survival versus failure.

	Cluster 1	Cluster 2	Cluster 3	Cluster 4
	Sacrificing idealists	Status seeking individualists	Benefit seeking conservatives	Curious speculants
Survivers	27 (23.6)	11 (8.1)	16 (18.5)	25 (28.8)
Failures	5 (8.4)	0 (2.9)	9 (6.5)	14 (10.2)

Chi-square = 8.90; significance = .03
The number of observations expected in case of independence among clusters is represented within parentheses.

Table 4 shows that survivers are overrepresented in clusters 1 and 2, while most failures are found in clusters 3 and 4.

CONCLUSIONS

The discriminant analysis illustrated that it is possible to predict future survival of new ventures based upon the entrepreneurs reasons to start the firm in the first place. When the 12 items which remain after the discriminant analysis are factor analyzed, 4 factors emerge. Unfortunately items which load on the same factor do not always have the same sign in the discriminant function. For example, while a desire to contribute to the success of a new venture is positively related to survival, a desire to contribute to the welfare of the community is negatively related with survival. Nevertheless, these two items load together on the same factor. For this reason one cannot expect large differences in the factor scores between surviving and failing entrepreneurs.

The cluster analysis yielded 4 clusters which contained a sufficient number of respondents. The two clusters which were found to be overrepresented by failing ventures, "benefitseeking conservatives" and "curious speculants" both contained entrepreneurs who were significantly more concerned about the indirect benefits of starting a business than entrepreneurs in the other two clusters.

The present research suggests that entrepreneurs who are devoted to their company want to utilize their skills, want to follow the example of a person admired, and are concerned about their own status are more likely to start businesses that survive. On the other hand, entrepreneurs concerned about individualism, freedom, fringe benefits and communitarianism are more likely to fail.

The results give support to the pull theory of entrepreneurship which suggest that successful entrepreneurial activities are a function of attractive opportunities. Moreover, the results may be interpreted as an indication that self-determination, a measure of egoism and willingness to sacrifice monetary benefits and freedom are important prerequisites of entrepreneurial success.

Being able to predict the future of a venture by investigating the entrepreneurs motives to start the business has obvious implications for potential entrepreneurs as well as policy makers and financial institutions. The results presented here highlight the need for future longitudinal studies in entrepreneurship.

ACKNOWLEDGEMENTS

The authors would like to thank Bodø Graduate School of Business and The Royal

Norwegian Ministry of Industrial Affairs for the financial support that made this research possible. We would also like to thank SARIE under whose auspices the data for this study was collected, and Ian C. MacMillan for valuable comments during the research process.

REFERENCES

Aldrich, H. E., Rosen, B. and Woodward, J., 1986. A social role perspective of entrepreneurship: Prelimanary findings from an empirical study. Unpublished working paper, University of North Carolina.

Alenge, S., and Scheinberg, S. 1988. Swedish entrepreneurship in a cross-cultural perspective. In B.A. Kirchoff, W.A. Long, W. ED. McMullan, K.H. Vesper, W.E. Wetzel, jr, (eds.), Frontiers of Entrepreneurship Research, Wellesley, Ma: Babson College, 1-15.

Armington, C., and Odle, M. 1982. Small business - how many jobs? The Brooking Review, Winter 1 (2): 14-17.

Atkinson, R.L. and Hilgard, E.R. 1983. Introduction to Psychology. NY: Harcourt Brace Jovanovich Inc. USA.

Baron, R.A. 1986. Behaviour in Organizations; Understanding and Managing the Human Side of Work. Mass: Allyn and Bacon Inc.

Baumol, W.J. 1985. Entrepreneurship and the long run productivity record. Unpublished Paper, Center for Entrepreneurship Studies, New York University.

Birch, D. L. 1979. The Job Generation Process. Cambridge, MA: MIT Program on Neighborhood and Regional Change, UK

Birley, S. 1985. Encouraging entrepreneurship: Britain's new enterprise program. Journal of Small Business Management, 23(4).

Begley, T.M., and Boyd, D.P. 1987. Psychological characteristics associated with performance in entrepreneural firms and smaller businesses. Journal of Business Venturing, 2(1).

Brinkman, L.H., and Rimler, G.W. 1988. Motivation and values of Virginia entrepreneurs as they relate to demographic and performance charaterististics. In B. Kirchhoff, W.A. Long, W. ED McMullan, K.H. Wesper, and W.E. Wentzel, jr. (eds.), Frontiers of Entrepreneurship Research. Wellesley, Ma: Babson College, 59-60.

Brockhaus, R. 1975. I-E locus of control as predictor of entrepreneurial intentions. Presentation to the the Academy of Management, New Orleans.

Brockhaus, R. 1980. Risk-taking propensity of entrepreneurs. Academy of Management Journal, September.

Brockhaus, R.H., and Nord, W.R. 1979. An exploration of factors affecting the entrepreneurial decision: Personal characteristics vs environmental conditions. Proceedings of the National Academy of Management.

Bruno. A.V. and Tyebjee T.T. 1882. The environment for entrepreneurship. In C.A. Kent, D.L. Sexton and K.H. Vesper (eds.) Encyclopedia of Entrepreneurship. Englewood Cliffs, NJ: Prentice Hall, 288-307.

Cooper,A.C: The founding of technologically based firms. Milwaukee: Center for Venture Management, 1971.

Dubini, P. 1988. Motivational and environmental influences on business start-ups: Some hints for public policies. In B. Kirchhoff, W. Long, W. ED McMullan, K. Wesper, and W. Wetzel (eds.), Frontiers of Entrepreneurship Research. Wellesley, Ma: Babson College, 31-45.

Dunkelberg, W.C., Cooper, A.C., Woo, C., and Dennis, W. 1987. New firm growth and performance. In N. Churchill, J.A. Hornaday, B.A. Kirchhoff, O.J. Krasner, and K.H. Wesper (eds.), Frontiers of Entrepreneurship Research. Wellesley, Ma: Babson College, 337-356.

Friberg, M. 1976. Ar lonen det enda son sporrar oss at arbeta? (Is the salary the only incentive for work?). Sociologisk Forsking, 1:24-42.

Hofstede, G. 1980. Culture's Consequences. London: Sage.

Hofer, C.W., and Sandberg, W.R. 1987. Improving new venture performance: Some guidelines for success. American Journal ofSmall Business, Summer, 11-25.

Hornaday, J.A., and Aboud, J. 1971. Characteristics of successful entrepreneurs. Personnel Psychology, 24, 141-153.

Kamien, M. and Schwartz, N.L. 1982. Market Structure and Innovation. Cambridge, England: Cambridge University Press.

Komives, J. L. 1972. A preliminary study of the personal values of high technology entrepreneurs. In A.C. Cooper and J.L. Komives (eds.), Technical Entrepreneurship: A Symposium Milwaukee WI: Center for Venture Management.

Lodge, C. 1986. The American Ideology. New York, NY: Knopf.

McClelland, D. 1961. Achieving Society. Princeton N.J: D Van Nostrand.

McClelland, D. 1965. Achivement motivation can be developed. Harvard Business Review, November/December.

McClelland, D. and Winter, G.D. 1969. Motivating Economic Achievment, New York: Free Press.

Rotter, J. Generalized expectancies for internal versus external control of reinforcement. Psychological Monograph, 80:1, 1-27.

Sandberg, W.R. 1986. New Venture Performance: The Role of Strategy and Industry Structure. Mass: Lexington Books.

Sandberg, W.R., and Hofer, C.W. 1987. Improving new venture performance: The role of strategy, industry structure and the entrepreneur. Journal of Business Venturing, 2:1.

Scheinberg, S., and MacMillan, I.C. 1988. An 11 country study of motivations to start a business. In B.A. Kirchhoff, W.A. Long, W. ED McMullan, K.H. Wesper, and W. Wetzel (eds.), Frontiers of Entrepreneurship Research. Wellesley, Ma: Babson College, 669-687.

Shapero, A. and Sokol, L. 1982. The social dimensions of entrepreneurship. In C.A. Kent, D.L. Sexton and K.H. Vesper (eds.), Encyclopedia of Entrepreneurship. Englewood Cliffs, N.J.

Shapero, A. 1975. The displaced uncomfortable entrepreneur. Psychology Today, 9:6, 83-88

Smith, N.R., Bracker, J.S., and Miner, J.B. 1987. Correlates of firm and entrepreneurs success in technologically innovative ocmpanies. In N. Churchill, J.A. Hornaday, B.A. Kirchhoff, O.J. Krasner, and K.H. Vesper (eds), Frontiers of Entreprenership Research. Wellesley, MA: Babson College, 337-356

Swain, F.S. 1985. The New Entreperneur - an old answer for todays marketplace. Frontiers of Entrepreneurship Research, Wellesley, MA: Babson College, 400-408.

Teitz, M.B., Glasmeier, A., and Svensson, D. 1981. Small business and employment Growth in Claifornia, Berkeley, CA: Institute of Urban and Regional Development, Working Paper No. 348, March.

ENTREPRENEURSHIP AND PRIVATIZATION IN THE SOVIET UNION

ANDREI STERLIN
IGOR TOULINE
*INSTITUTE OF WORLD ECONOMY AND INTERNATIONAL RELATIONS,
SOVIET ACADEMY OF SCIENCES*

INTRODUCTION

The most profound economic crisis in the USSR is conditioned not only by structural imbalances in the national economy, which developed for decennials under the rule of the centralized planning system which disregarded the natural laws of economic and social development, but also by major errors of the last years.

Moreover, there is every reason to assert that the old bureaucratic command way of managing the economy has suffered considerable changes during the perestroika period. It was in 1990 that a more or less serious discussion of the issues concerning a really radical management reform on a national level began. An introduction of a "500-day program" became a good incentive for this work.

It is common knowledge that this program was rejected and the country's Parliament adopted a presidential reform plan which can be called a declaration of intentions to reform an existing system, rather than a plan for concrete action.

It is clear now that reform, understood as a transition to an economic system with an economic interest, and not an administrative compulsion, being the main driving force, is inconceivable without the enterprises moving away from bureaucratic pressure and undergoing dramatic changes in ownership relations. In tune with this, denationalization is being more talked about, although progress in this area is hampered by substantial difficulties. This paper focuses on the analysis of these obstacles and considers the influence of privatization on entrepreneurship.

1. Sociological and political background.

About one or two years ago, the existence of private property was practically out of the question. However, the policy of glasnost, which has gathered force, submitted an opportunity to openly criticize the communist ideology and concomitantly one of its dominant postulates -- complete prohibition of private ownership.

As it turned out, there was no need to persuade the majority of the population about the advantages of private ownership of the means of production. It was the growing openness that allowed people themselves to compare the "achievements" of the planned economy with those of the so called "capitalist countries".

Polls show people holding generally positive attitudes towards the idea of private enterprise and land ownership. The idea of private ownership of Soviet enterprises by foreign citizens though, got less support (Table 1):

	it is necessary	it can be allowed	it cannot be allowed	no answer
Soviet citizens own:				
-small stores and workshops	28	45	17	10
-large enterprises and factories	6	16	58	20
-plots of land	53	34	7	6
Foreign citizens own:				
-small stores and workshops	20	42	28	10
-large enterprises and factories	7	17	60	16
-plots of land	8	21	56	15

Table 1. Population attitudes towards the possibility of private Soviet and foreign ownership of enterprises and land (% of polled, January, 1990).

73% of those polled consider the emergence of private firms owned by Soviet citizens necessary or permissible; 62% of respondents supported the idea of private ownership of firms by foreign citizens. The difference between those who are against private ownership of firms both by Soviet and foreign citizens is also 11% (27% and 38% respectively). This difference clearly reflects "foreign origin of the entrepreneur or/and the invested capital" factor influence upon public opinion.

Remarkably, this difference almost disappears in attitudes towards large enterprises owned both by Soviet and foreign citizens. In other words, at this time, the population is almost indifferent towards the subject of who may become "a big capitalist" -- a compatriot or a foreigner. The majority of the population is against large private enterprises in general.

Attitudes towards private property differ appreciably in various regions of the country. The most powerful backing given to the idea is in the Baltic republics, where traditions of private business undertaking are fairly strong. In the Ukraine, support is less warm, in the Russian Federation, even less. In spite of this, an overwhelming majority of those polled in these regions speak in favour of the development of small private businesses.

In the political sphere, forces polarized by the attitude of the Communist Party of the Russian Federation take an extremely negative stand on the issue. This is backed by the most reactionary groups of the party, state and management machinery as well as by certain strata of the ideologically blind population (such as elderly people, people with low education levels and low-income groups). The idea of private ownership is not supported by the supreme electoral bodies of the country -- the Supreme Soviet and the Congress of People's Deputies -- a majority of which is drawn from conservatively oriented leaders at all levels.

Political parties and democratically oriented movements, speaking in favour of private property, are organizationally disintegrated and hostile to each other. That is why they have been unable, either to counteract their opponents at the all-union level, or defend the interests of the majority of the population. We are witnessing a paradoxical, but common, for the Soviet Union, state of affairs: supreme bodies of legislation uphold decisions contradicting voters' opinion. And, if, under a totalitarian repressive regime this discrepancy had practically no meaning, now it results in a dramatically growing disrespect for the laws being adopted as well as for the lawmakers (bodies adopting such laws). Hence there appears a paralysis of power and a chaos in the country.

Opposition of the republican parliaments to the central government (excluding Asian republics) aggravates political and social tension. These parliaments definitively advocate the development of private property and entrepreneurship, and alongside with adopting suitable laws, take practical steps in this direction.

Thus, the existing sociological and political privatization scheme can be viewed as follows:

The majority of the population supports private property. Meanwhile the communist party machinery, an almost unique organized political force preserving substantial influence in the army, KGB, economic bureaucracy, and most important, among all representatives of big business and the military-industrial complex, and possessing real political power, opposes this idea in principal (although they implicitly anticipate it in a form of a nomenclatural privatization). Opponents of privatization attack in three directions, each having a distinct ideological and populistic character:

1) legalization and development of private property is a betrayal of socialist principles;
2) it will lead to an increasing economic chaos and
3) it will lead to further cuts in the people's level of life (especially low-income groups).

2. Main objectives and a scale of privatisation.

Some statistical data on the structure of the Soviet economy will help us get an idea of the possible scale of privatization:
16,800 enterprises may be potentially privatized in industry (including 20,000 enterprises with less than 200 employees), and 736,000 in retailing (including 65% with trading space less than 100 sq.m and only 0.1% with more than 3,500 sq.m). 351,000 catering establishments (67 seats on average) may be privatized.

The residual value of fixed capital in the Soviet economy is about 3,000 billion Rb including 2,000 billion -- in manufacturing, transportation and construction (wear and tear is on average 30-40%). The state owns about 90% of fixed capital.
Current capital is 800 billion Rb; stock of commodities is 500 billion Rb.
Balance sheet value of fixed capital in the USSR economy : 1 billion Rb, 1988) (See Table 2)

We consider that taking into account the existing structure of the economy, a smaller part of the state property could be actually privatized in the foreseeable future. The big share of the heavy industry, enterprises of the military-industrial complex, power engineering, transportation and other strategic elements of the economic infrastructure, which apparently will not be subject to privatisation either in the first, or in the second wave, decrease the total value of the potentially privatized property to the amount hardly exceeding 1 trillion rubles.

3. Financing privatization

In the absence of corresponding legislative acts, privatization in the USSR develops spontaneously, acquiring rather distorted forms. Numerous facts provide evidence that the state property is being actually plundered, handed over to cooperatives and private organizations at a minimal (often symbolic) price, or even without compensation. It is absolutely clear that those state functionaries who previously controlled the property thus privatized, benefit from such transactions. Thus, estimates of solvent demand for privatized state property could end up having only academic, if any, value.

3.1 Solvent demand for property. According to official statistics, 99.3% of the population has a per capita income of less than 500 Rb/month and owns 46.2% of savings. Consequently, the remaining 0.7% (2 million) constitutes the most wealthy

INDUSTRIAL SECTOR

manufacturing	-901,9
construction	- 96,6
agriculture and forestry	-395,6
transportation	-356,6
communication	- 28,8
procurement	- 31,2
information services	- 2,6
retailing, catering	- 60,7
subtotal	-1880,3

SERVICES

housing services	-524,8
communal services	-125,2
education	-102,0
science	- 49,6
culture and arts	- 20,3
health care	- 60,7
miscellaneous	- 42,3
subtotal	-924,9
TOTAL CAPITAL	-2805,2

Table 2. Value of Capital in the USSR Economy.

group which owns 53.8% of total savings (estimation made by the ECO business journal, 1990, #3, p.27).

Though total savings are estimated at 450-500 billion Rb (in cash, in the savings banks, in government bonds and certificates), effective demand for privatized property should be rather limited. According to some estimates, in the most favourable conditions, the population should spend in several years not more than 100 billion Rb to buy shares and privatized state property. After sharp retail price increases, this figure could drop dramatically -- to a third of its value or to 30-35 billion Rb.

NOTE. Polls show that only 6-8% of workers want to buy shares or other privatized state property with their money. About one third of top managers want to invest. (Country average is 8.7% [Econ. & Life, #48, 1990). But attitudes may change very rapidly when people see the advantages of such investment and get used to the idea of private ownership. Such mentality shifts may be already seen in some cases of completed privatization of certain enterprises.

Another 20-30 billion Rb could be invested by so called "alternative", i.e. non-governmental, economic structures -- cooperatives, commercial banks, stock companies, various foundations, etc. An additional 10-20 billion Rb from labor force compensation funds of state enterprises may be reallocated for buy-out purposes. Therefore, the total investments in privatization may reach at the first stage 60-140 billion Rb (excluding foreign investments which are very difficult to estimate, government credits and state-owned enterprises' funds).

As a result, at best only 5-7% of the value of state property may be bought out by the population and various legal entities in the near future, even if the process of privatization should be thoroughly designed and coordinated. But if we calculate less directly, but with relevance to the estimated value of the property actually subject to privatization, this figure might rise to 15-20%

In any case, central, republican and local power structures should keep ownership of the great bulk of real estate, service sector assets and industrial funds for at least 5-10 years, if the rights for this property are not be transferred in some way directly to the citizens or to trust funds.

4. Various approaches to privatization.

Numerous proposals for transforming an economy based almost completely on state property into a system with diverse forms of property -- joint-stock, private, collective, mixed -- exist at present. We shall point out the main approaches without discussing them in detail.

4.1. State enterprises' property transfer to the enterprises' personnel free of charge. Establishment of a "collective enterprise" on that basis. Its capital is indivisible property of "the collective", but a part of the property may be allocated among the employees or sold to them on favourable conditions.

4.2. Division of state property among all citizens free of charge. Every citizen is granted a certificate to his (or her) share of a special bank account. The funds at this account can be used only for purchasing the state-owned shares of the newly created stock companies or other property which is going to be denationalized.

To reduce a citizen's risk in such investments, it is necessary to establish special institutes which will act as a sort of trust fund; citizens should own shares of these funds.

If 30% of a state property is privatized each individual's share will make about 3,500 Rb.

4.3. Sale of a state property or a long-term lease with option. Different types of support measures are supposed to stimulate large-scale buy-out: low interest credits, buying by instalment, rebates, etc. It is also supposed that enterprise employees will be granted preferential rights to buy out its assets.

4.4. A mixed approach will probably become the main method of privatization. It will take the form of selling with granting buyers various privileges.

Depending on the size and financial conditions of enterprises, the following alternatives could also be employed:

- sale of shares of medium-sized and large enterprises to provide stock companies or a "collective enterprise" with a division (split) of the total property or of its part (10-15%) among employees;

- direct sale of small enterprises to establish private firms or limited partnerships;

- transfer of ownership rights of unprofitable enterprises from government organizations to individual entrepreneurs or institutional buyers without any compensation to the previous owner.

It is extremely difficult to find correct criteria for distribution of state property. Unfortunately, even among specialists, there is by far no common understanding that privatization is a way to economic efficiency, not to social justice. Any privatization scheme which is designed should be aimed at the instant and just division of property, while at the same time increasing capital utilization efficiency.

5. Process of privatization

With no legal private property, no private means of production, no entrepreneurial culture, and severe opposition to the very idea of privatization from some social groups, the process of privatization in the USSR should be carried out mostly in an administrative way (at least for the first two waves) as a government program directed and controlled from the top. Under such conditions privatization in the USSR may begin from denationalization of large enterprises and their transformation into stock companies. In general, privatization cannot be artificially limited to a certain sector of the economy; in addition to privatizing retailing, one should also privatize wholesale enterprises, agribusiness, transportation, and some other services. Real market behaviour of industrial enterprises is impossible without well developed entrepreneurial surroundings. Therefore, in our opinion, privatization should involve all sectors of the economy from the very beginning. The following points are worth noting:

5.1. Introduction of new economic legislation allowing private property rights and registration of the new ventures, instead of the authorization practice still existing in most republics, are going into effect in Russia and in the Baltic republics, though they contradict the federal law in some cases.

5.2. The federal government has declared privatization without solving the problem of valuation of privatized property.

5.3. The management structure for privatized property will soon be established. It is supposed to establish a <u>State Property Agency</u> (SPA) reporting to the President or to the Parliament, with the full responsibility to manage and control property and ownership.

Funds which control state property in a certain branch or territory on behalf of the state should be established. Their role would depend on the economic situation and the objectives of privatization programs in certain areas.

Investment Funds should own 51-100% shares of the enterprises in some industries at the early stages, though they would have no direct control over their operations. IF share may be even less than 51% but it should be specified that some key, strategic decisions (export of the capital, entry into another industry, participation of the foreign investor, etc.) could be made only with IF approval.

The Funds' main task, however, would not lie in being a shareholder but in forming stock companies and their boards, and organizing public offerings of the companies' stock in various ways (trading, private placement, free distribution, and so on).

Stock transfers also need special institutional support, i.e. the setting up of a central and regional stock exchanges (perhaps in the form of special departments in banks), which could at least record transfers of stock and establish a regulation body similar to Securities and Exchange Commission, etc.

5.4. It is supposed that the revenues the Investment Funds gain in trading stocks will be used for crediting further privatization and development of the economy in general.

6. Valuation of property

6.1. Valuation of property is probably the most complicated issue of privatization in every country but especially in the USSR, with its monopolistic structure of the economy (about 60% of large enterprises are monopolistic manufacturers of certain products), centralised pricing and consequently absolutely distorted prices. An enterprise which is unprofitable today may become extremely profitable if it is given the opportunity for market pricing. And in contrast, the value of the capital of, say, defence contractors equipped with unique, state-of-the-art machinery may become worthless under military production conversion programs and cutting of arms purchases.

In any case, it is recognized that in evaluating an enterprise's worth, its residual value, current prices of its products, current market situation and its future development, etc., should be taken into account.

6.2. There are a number of approaches proposed for evaluation of privatized enterprises.
For fixed capital: using its residual value.
For current capital: cash in hand plus temporarily undisturbed profit.

6.3. It is proposed to put in order an enterprise's financial and other records prior to evaluation to increase its value.

Small businesses may be sold at auctions.

7. Probable scenario.

The established socio-economic climate restricts the privatization process to some extent both in time and in forms. On the one hand, these limitations involve financial cuts which prevent mass participation of population in the process of transforming state-owned enterprises into public corporations and in direct buyout of enterprises, on the other, they entail low profitability of production investments, thus decreasing in the short-run, entrepreneurial revenues and the attractiveness of dividend payouts as a source of personal income.

These limitations are due to the lack of legal participation of social groups possessing large fortunes, to the total impoverishment of population (according to some estimates more than half of the population found itself below the poverty level after the retail price rise), to the drop of the purchasing power of the rouble, to the rupture of economic ties between enterprises and regions, followed by the fall of labor productivity and the GNP.

In this connection one may single out short and long-term perspectives, arising from the character of the finance resources constraints and the scale of the state property being privatized.

Most probably there will be three waves of privatization.

The first one is developing at this time and will gain momentum in the course of the next two years (provided there is no sharp reactionary turn in economic policy, and reform proceeds at rates at least not lower than at present). It will be characterized by the privatization of mainly small industrial enterprises and services in the first place -- small shops and catering, everyday repairs and other services, parts of transportation enterprises. It is evident that at this stage, forms of direct buyout of small businesses in a short time period, namely, collective (by the enterprise employees), cooperative, family and private forms, will prevail. Sales on a competitive basis, auctions and lease with option will constitute basic approaches.

Even now (data as for late 1990) about 17,000 service enterprises in Russia have been transferred into collective property; 7,600 into private property and 7,400 into other forms of property.

At the same time the state will partly denationalize big industrial enterprises by transforming them into joint-stock companies with limited distribution of shares (as has been done at the KAMAZ truck plant). These processes will take the form of distributing ownership rights between two major shareholders: the state (in the face of opposition from ministries or other authorized organs) and employees ("labour collectives"). The latter will buy out their shares partly by paying their own money, partly through instalments (in the form of leases). Under state budget projections announced by the government for 1991, industrial enterprises will be obliged to transfer half of their development funds into a so-called stabilization fund being established by the central government. For this sum the employees of the enterprise receive their shares and formally become co-owners of the enterprise.

A smaller part of the shares will be sold freely to other enterprises. Such mutual ownership of shares will increase the enterprises' interest in stability of their partners' work and contribute to the administrative efforts to stabilize the Soviet economy.

Mutual stocks sales would be primarily practised by involving the share of the state property in such transactions which support government economic stabilization programs. The Investment Funds could become the organizations which would accomplish these financial operations and accumulate realized profits.

An insignificant part of the shares will be sold freely to private citizens, thus absorbing savings of those who prefer the reliability of the state and semi-state structures to the risky operations of new market entities (the most recent example is the rush demand for the shares of the state-cooperative banking association MENATEP).

It is evident that the first stage will be primarily significant, not so much for the scale of privatization as such, as for the psychological shift which privatization might create in the public opinion. As soon as the majority of people get used to the idea of private property (not abstractly, but by coming across this phenomenon in every day life), as it got used to the fact that Stalin was a murderer, and communism an utopia, then mass, explosive privatization could be expected.

It should also be noted, that to a certain extent, privatization in the USSR has already been going on for a long time. The volume of such privatization is unknown, but it clearly is significant. The scale of the shadow economy (i.e. economic activity, evading taxes) is estimated to be 70-150 billion Rb. Under conditions of incredible corruption, a weak taxation system and powerful mafia structures, many enterprises, especially in the southern regions of the country, have already been functioning as private enterprises for a long time. Some of them, using the liberalization of economic legislation, are now coming out of the "shade" and forming a new private entrepreneurial sector.

The second wave will consist of the denationalization and privatization of mainly low profit and unprofitable middle-sized enterprises and companies. It will start against a background of a rising first wave, which, hopefully, will contribute to stabilizing the situation in the economy and regulating the credit and monetary system, the latter clearing the way for privatization "on credit", which may become a mass phenomenon. Employees of low-profit enterprises will get the opportunity to carry out a leverage buyout (using ESOP methodology), and also use a long-term lease with option. A wide-range application of such instruments of privatization will allow continuing employment in this category of enterprises and ease the social problems prevalent in a deep economic crisis. Individual citizens might more and more frequently invest their savings in shares of such enterprises as their financial and production indices improve.

The third wave will be characterized by large-scale denationalization and privatization of big industrial enterprises and macroeconomic infrastructures. Its scale and efficiency will evidently depend greatly on the level of the development of the market economy infrastructure, the credit and monetary system, and especially the securities market. These mechanisms will allow privatization on a larger scale of that part of the property of the denationalized enterprises that still remains in the hands of the state. The result will be the creation of a relatively well-developed market economy structure, where the share of the state property will amount to 25-45%. The state will retain complete ownership only over enterprises and branches of the economy traditionally considered strategic in the USSR.

Investment funds may well play the most critical role on the course of the third wave of privatization. They will have to act not only as holding companies of the stock belonging to the state, but also as reorganizers of big closed stock companies (such as KAMAZ), established during the first wave of privatization, into real public corporations. In the course of the founding of such corporations, the mutual sale of enterprises' stocks by investment funds, which began during the first privatization wave, as well as the sale of securities of different enterprises to individuals and institutions, including commercial and investment banks, will proceed more widely.

It is clear, that under conditions of low savings rates of the population, different institutions, including specialized open and closed trusts along with the state, will become preferential holders of shares of big enterprises in key industries of the Soviet economy. As a result, Investment Funds will act as controllers by the state mechanisms of the flow of capital between various industries of the Soviet economy in periods of structural change and during the period of creation of efficient stock exchanges.

However, organizational specifics of the establishment of Investment Funds and the quasi-market character of their functioning makes it possible to accomplish privatization according to a plan in which institutions and individuals, defending the interests of nomenclature, are given the role of owners or managers of the dramatically important share of the former state (formally public) property.

It is necessary to note, that this or a similar scenario can be realized only if market reforms (however halfway or inconsistent they may be) continue and a complete return to the system of administrative control does not occur.

8. Privatization and nomenclature

Investment Funds, acting as organizations with the delegated rights of management and administration over state property, are actually legal successors of branch ministries and regional agencies of economic management. Naturally, the key position in them will be occupied by the representatives or ministerial nomenclature.

This has already happened in so called Soviet concerns, created to take the place of formally disbanded federal and republican ministries. The ministries were agencies that managed not their own, but the state property. The state as an owner could disband or reorganize them at any time. The concerns, on the contrary, claim to be non-state organizations (in the sense that they no longer report to any state regulatory agency) and to have the right to fully control the property under its management independently (to enjoy quasi-ownership rights).

From the organizational point of view that means that the management came from the government organisations' hierarchy. In other words, former ministries' units seize state ownership rights which no longer belong to the impersonal State, but to a quite concrete concern's top management or the board, i.e. to former ministerial functionaries.

New institutions, and Investment Fund-like concerns, when they become privatized, will most likely be able to nominate representatives of economic and party nomenclature (of newly established organizations under their control) as main holders and administrators of the former state property. This may well be achieved by including these organizations as founding members of new stock companies or through the sale to them of a large number of shares on favourable terms. In other words, using their relations inside the establishment network (what actually forms nomenclature), party and state bureaucrats will start the process of buying out state-owned enterprises at much lower prices than their market and sometimes, even residual price.

The CASU is already becoming one of those privileged members of privatization. The Communist Party owns property worth several millions. Party officials do their best to transfer the organization's money and physical property into legal business structures. A number of commercial banks, "independent" publishing houses and other enterprises have been created recently using Party capital. Former Party functionaries occupy top positions in these firms, thus forming a strong economic network ready to defend the nomenclature's political and economic interests.

All attempts by democratic forces to stop the process and to nationalize the Party's property in the legal way are blocked by the President's decrees.

At this stage nomenclature privatization does not actually handle the ownership rights themselves. However, in the course of concomitant enterprises' reorganization, the property is split and diffusion takes place. To a certain extent, this is not undesirable because it contributes to the development of competitiveness. Property chiefly still belongs to the state. What is different is that in new structures (such as concerns and so forth), its top management can exercise its right to be a quasi-owner by speedy privatization of denationalized property, for example, by transferring enterprises on a leasing basis, or their buying out or going public, and carry all this out, it should be underlined, to their benefit.

Is this develpment good or bad? There is no simple answer to that question. On the one hand, real privatization (a transfer of property directly into private ownership) does not occur. On the other hand, management positions are still being held by a qualified part of the bureaucracy (this situation in itself being a result of a specific natural selection of individuals having entrepreneurial abilities), who gradually become real owners and will evidently, with greater conscientiousness, manage their own property. In the new situation these former functionaries prove to be deeply interested in the economic success of their "own" business. From this point of view the nomenclature's privatization process based on realities of today might be assessed as positive.

Privatization with active nomenclature participation is accompanied by an increase in the professionalism of management. A sharp rise in demand for consulting services is clear evidence of this process. On the whole this will contribute positively to the development of entrepreneurial behaviour in the economy.

ENVIRONMENT AND ENTREPRENEURSHIP

New Venture Strategies:
Generic or Industry Specific

Critique
by
Luc Vallée, *École des Hautes Études Commerciales*

Everyone should welcome a paper which tries to link strategies of young firms to industry characteristics. Such a link is essential to understanding the causes of success and failure of new ventures. It is especially courageous of the authors to have engaged in an empirical study on the subject. However, I feel that the authors do not provide the reader with a sufficiently coherent vision of their findings. One section of the paper which has improved significantly is the introduction which states clearly the paper's goals and objectives. It identifies a very promising avenue of research. Nevertheless, the empirical section of the paper does not live up to its promises.

The main flaw of the paper remains the same as that of the earlier version. This is the lack of interpretation of the results by the authors. It is disconcerting that the authors justify their methodology at great length but avoid the simple exercise of interpreting their results. For instance, the main finding of the paper is that "there was more diversity in strategies among firms further down the supply chain". Not a single interpretation is given for this result whereas we ought to expect a complete discussion of the issue. When the authors offer interpretations for some of their results, it is at best a conjecture backed by no empirical evidence. Such is the trivial explanation offered for the unanticipated "pattern found for the market responsiveness factor dimension" (see the 4th paragraph of the findings section).

The purpose of the paper is to test the proposition often made in the strategic literature "that organisations must fit with their environment to be successful or even to survive". Even if we admit that the authors have shown that different industries give birth to different configurations of strategies, they must deepen their analysis. Why we should care and, more importantly, what might contribute to explain these differences is what we ought to be able to learn from the paper.

A lot more attention should be devoted to identifying industry characteristics. Technologies, the nature of competition, industry concentration, the nature of the product sold, financial constraints, etc. are crucial elements for defining the environment (i.e. the constraints and the resources) into which new firms enter and to understanding the choice of strategy made by an entrepreneur or a manager. In other words, what should be addressed more directly is why and how the constraints and the resources of each industry interact with the strategies to give rise to the type of configuration that we observe.

Finally, the authors allude to the uncertainty surrounding their measure of strategy diversity: "Whether (the Super Achiever strategy) is an artifact of the desire to do all, or failure to recognise the strategy they are emphasising, is unclear". It seems crucial to me that the authors resolve this issue before going any further in order to provide the readers with a coherent paper. I suspect that this confusion is one reason for the authors' inability to interpret their results. Moreover, they offer no explanation for how uncertainty may have resulted from the way they conducted their survey. Even if the authors claim that previous research has recently demonstrated the validity of using perceptual data, any set of perceptual answers will raise suspicions. If you ask people whether they would rather be beautiful or rich and you give them the opportunity to answer "I would like to be both" or "I do not know", you will usually have lots of problems separating the two types. If one has such data, there are serious reasons to doubt any results obtained by them. In such a case, the potential flaws of the data should then be clearly exposed and identified.

NEW VENTURE STRATEGIES: GENERIC OR INDUSTRY SPECIFIC

NANCY M. CARTER, *MARQUETTE UNIVERSITY*
TIMOTHY M. STEARNS, *MARQUETTE UNIVERSITY*
PAUL D. REYNOLDS, *MARQUETTE UNIVERSITY*
BRENDA A. MILLER, *MARQUETTE UNIVERSITY*

ABSTRACT

The founding strategies in representative samples of new firms at three stages in the industry supply chain (manufacturing, distribution, and retail) were examined. There was more diversity in strategies among firms further down the supply chain. While a substantial proportion adopted either a "Price/Service" or a "Differentiation" strategic focus, two other strategies were also significant. A "Super Achiever" emphasis (trying to excel at everything) was the dominant strategy among manufacturing new firms and pursued by a significant minority in distribution and retail. An "Equivocator" strategy (an absence of any clear focus) was found for a significant minority of distribution and retail new firms.

INTRODUCTION

A central argument in the strategic management literature is that organizations must fit with their environment to be successful or even survive. One theoretical perspective that has guided organizational-environmental fit research holds that organizations' managers are responsible for developing strategies that maintain "satisfactory alignments of environmental opportunities and risks on the one hand, and organizational capabilities and resources on the other "(Miles, 1982:14). Attempts to specify appropriate strategies have yielded numerous typologies and spawned a prodigious body of insightful research (e.g., Glueck, 1980; Hofer and Schendel, 1978; Lawrence and Dyer, 1983; Miles, Snow, Meyer and Coleman, 1978; Mintzberg, 1984; Porter, 1980). Despite the contribution of these models, some researchers have questioned the appropriateness of the typologies for explaining strategies of small (Carter, 1990) or new venture firms (Feeser and Willard, 1990).

Many of the extant strategy typologies assume that organizations maintain alignment with the external environment by (a) adapting their strategies or (b) moving to more favorable environmental niches when their success or survival is threatened. Typically, however, small firms are seen as having insufficient resources to navigate the environment and, thus, their strategic choice is highest when considering domain selection i.e., which product markets to compete in. Bourgeois (1980) refers to this as primary strategy; an initial strategic focus that, once established, constrains organizations' subsequent actions. Numerous researchers (Boeker, 1989; Eisenhardt and Schoonhoven, 1990; Miles, Snow, Meyer and Coleman; 1978) support the supposition that founding strategies narrow the range of strategic alternatives available to new firms. Indeed, Boeker (1989) contended that not only may a founding strategy have substantial influence on subsequent success but may even limit future survival. As the founding, primary, or initial strategies of a new firm can have major consequences, they deserve careful study.

Given the shaping power of founding strategy it is not surprising that researchers continue to explore whether previous typologies adequately encompass new venture strategies. One may even question whether new ventures have a "strategy" as the term is utilized in the literature. Are the short-term objectives that new ventures struggle to meet during their early stages of existence reflective of long-term strategies intentionally formulated? We propose to extend the understanding of founding strategies by examining new firms across multiple industries to discern if distinctive types of strategies exist. The identification and elaboration of strategy types would prove especially useful in future research for addressing questions of why some new ventures overcome the "liability of newness" (Stinchcombe, 1965) while others succumb.

THEORETICAL BACKGROUND

Strategic Alternatives

Development of the strategy construct in the literature reflects the supposition that firms share considerable commonalities. This view has led to a number of classification schemes which assume that a limited number of strategic archetypes capture the essence of most competitive postures. These typologies reflect generic strategies often broadly applied across all industries, organization types, or organization sizes. Herbert and Deresky (1987) recently provided an insightful comparison of several widely recognized "grand strategy" typologies.

Conceptually, the typologies of firm strategies are appealing. Typologies provide a method for clustering apparently diverse characteristics across firms into a few common representations. Many researchers in the application of typologies, however, ignore the diversity that can exist within types in an effort to make the data "fit" the typology.

It is our contention that strategy types are most diverse among new ventures and this diversity is a function of the industry in which the new venture was founded. In this respect, we concur with Hambrick's (1983) conclusion following a study of 107 large firms. He suggested that industry conditions will influence the number of strategic types both within and across industries. In addition, we extend this view by incorporating the work of Galbraith (1983) by suggesting that location in the industry supply chain will further influence the range of strategic types among new ventures. Dividing the supply chain into stages, Galbraith demonstrated that strategy varies depending upon whether a firm is "upstream" or "downstream" in the industry. Seemingly, the fundamental or dominant functions associated with each stage leads to differing management processes and competencies. These "learned lessons" are hypothesized to translate into strategies peculiar to each stage in the industry supply chain. The following analysis focuses on the diversity of the initial strategies in three major stages of the supply chain: manufacturing, distribution (wholesale), and retail new firms.

New Venture Strategies

The development of strategic typologies has greatly influenced research on small firms. However, much of the writing about new venture strategies has dealt with the debate over whether new ventures (a) must avoid direct competition with large firms and pursue "niche" strategies or, (b) can risk an aggressive, proactive assault and compete on a broad front. These discussions tend to overlook the distinction between the start-up of an autonomous firm with limited resources, and the entry into a new market by an established firm backed by considerable resources. The assumption underlying the "niche" perspective is that a start-up organization possesses the "liability of newness" (Stinchcombe, 1965) in which limits in both resources and organizational learning constrain its chances for survival and success. Such new ventures have traditionally been encouraged to design specialized, high-quality products targeted to market segments overlooked by larger, more established firms (Broom and Longenecker, 1971; Cohn and Lindberg, 1974; Hosmer, 1957) rather than attempting to compete on the basis of price (Deeks, 1976; Stegall, Steinmetz and Kline, 1976).

More recently, researchers have argued that new ventures should consider a broader range of strategic alternatives, including head-to-head competition with market leaders (MacMillan and Day, 1987; Miller and Camp, 1985). Typifying the logic underlying this challenge, Biggadike (1976) argued that unless new ventures enter markets aggressively, on a large scale, they penalize themselves by lacking the broad appeal of their competitors. Such a strategy would obviously require substantial resources, appropriate for an established firm entering a major market for the first time.

McDougall and Robinson (1990) recently characterized the basic thrusts of these two bodies of literature (niche versus aggressive) as an important foundation, but challenged the 'measurement' of strategy that underlies the work. In an attempt to further differentiate new venture strategies, they examined the strategic actions of firms in the information processing industry. Using cluster analysis they identified eight different competitive strategies. They intentionally restricted their study to one broad industry to control for the impact of industry differences. In this way, they sought to examine new venture strategies across different competitive methods rather than across a variety of industries.

This important body of research raises an important question. How industry specific are the strategy archetypes that evolved in McDougall and Robinson's study? Are these archetypes peculiar to the information processing industry or are there generic strategies among new ventures that can be generalized across industries? If so, are the strategies similar to those depicted in the extant strategy literature that focus on large firms? These questions guided the present study. Following Galbraith's (1983) and Hambrick's (1983) lead, we selected a cross section of industries that represent various stages in the supply chain. Specifically, we wanted to explore the types of strategies that new ventures pursue as a function of their industry and location on the supply chain.

METHODS

Sample

The source of data is a survey of 1,119 autonomous new firms in a midwestern state of the U.S.A. (Minnesota) completed in 1986 (Reynolds and Miller, 1988). All regions of the state and all industry sectors, except for agricultural production, were represented in the sample. The sample was based on firms identified by Dun's Marketing Identifier files as being from one to six years old just prior to the survey. Phone verification excluded all listings that were not new, not autonomous, and not active; about one-half of the listings qualified. During the phone call, a person involved in the startup of the new firm and currently active in management was identified as the respondent for the new firm. Each eligible respondent was sent a mail questionnaire three times, with a reminder post card between the first and second mailings. Phone interviews were completed with about half of those not returning the mail questionnaire. The final response rate was 75%.

The sample was stratified by industry and age (1-6 years old at the time of data collection). For this study we selected only firms from the three industry classifications presented in Table 1. Selecting these industries from the larger data set reduced the number of new ventures considered in this study to 636. These industries were chosen because they represent a cross-section of activities and because they signify three stages of the industry supply chain. All analyses are based on data weighted to represent the total population of new firms in the state. Thus, the values that correspond to number of firms in Table 1 reflects the pattern of new firms across the three industry sectors. For example, for every new firm in manufacturing, three are established downstream, one in distribution and two in retail.

TABLE 1

CLASSIFICATION OF FIRM ECONOMIC EMPHASIS

	S.I.C. Codes	Description of Industry Classification	No. of Firms
Manufacturing	2000-3999	Manufacturing of all kinds	142
Distributive	4000-4999	Transportation, other public utilities	182
Services	5000-5199	Wholesale of all kinds	
Retail	5200-5999	Retail of all kinds	312

Operationalizing Strategy

A central concern in the study of organizations is determining which member of the organization is the most suitable informant. The person may vary depending on the differences in organizational characteristics. In the strategic management literature, researchers have often relied on top managements' assessments of firm strategy, citing the unavailability of archival data. For new ventures in particular, the "self-typing" approach seems appropriate. As architects of the founding strategies, these individuals are uniquely qualified to assess strategic intentions. Indeed, the firm strategies undoubtedly embody the founders' wishes and thus, relying on owners' perceptions as the source of data is justifiable. Further support for using perceptual data is provided by Shortell and Zajac (1990) who recently demonstrated convergent validity using perceptual and archival measures of strategic orientations.

Respondents to the survey questionnaire were asked to indicate the importance of thirteen attributes of competitive strategy to their firms' strategic focus. They replied using a four-point scale: critical (1), important (2), marginal (3), and insignificant (4). The items were chosen for their representation of previously identified strategy attributes (Dess and Davis, 1984; Hambrick, 1983) and their appropriateness to new ventures (Changanti, Changanti, Mahajan, 1989; MacMillan and Day, 1987; McDougall and Robinson, 1990). Because of our interest in founding strategy, items that asked about the importance of firm location were added. The items were reverse coded prior to analysis to aid interpretation of the strategy emphasis.

Principle-components factor analysis of the strategic focus responses was completed on the entire sample of 1,119, weighted to represent the population. This revealed five underlying dimensions with an eigenvalue greater than one. Further analysis using a varimax rotation was used to aid in interpretation of the factors. The results indicated that a sixth factor, representing firm pricing, should also be included. Although this factor did not meet the minimal eigenvalue we established, the strong face validity of price as an important dimension of firm strategy argued for its acceptance. The factor loadings and communalities from the varimax rotation are displayed in Table 2.

TABLE 2

PRINCIPAL-COMPONENTS FACTOR ANALYSIS WITH VARIMAX ROTATION OF STRATEGIC FOCUS

	1	2	3	4	5	6	Communality
Lower prices	.06	-.05	.09	.06	.04	.97	.96
Better service	.01	.07	.12	.85	.13	.13	.77
Quality products/services	.26	.05	.12	.81	.04	-.08	.75
More choices	.70	.01	.22	.02	.07	.14	.57
Effective marketing	.12	-.01	.81	-.01	.16	-.03	.69
Response to market	.08	.19	.80	.14	.05	.08	.71
Serve those missed	.27	.13	.51	.30	.05	.12	.45
Location/convenience	.11	-.11	.11	.10	.85	.02	.77
Distinctive goods/service	.78	.08	.06	.28	.06	-.09	.71
Better facilities	.17	.17	.11	.07	.83	.03	.76
Contemporary products	.70	.25	.10	.03	.21	.01	.61
Utilize new technology	.15	.88	.13	.13	.06	-.05	.83
Develop new technology	.11	.90	.09	.01	-.01	-.01	.83
Eigenvalue	3.62	1.55	1.21	1.15	1.01	.90	
Percentage of variance	27.8	11.9	9.3	8.8	7.7	6.9	
Cumulative percentage of variance	27.8	39.7	49.0	57.8	65.5	72.5	

Reliability of the items loading on each factor was determined by computing the Cronbach Alpha (Cronbach, 1951) across items within each factor (those with factor loadings greater than .60). The Alpha coefficients ranged from .62 to .81 and were all within the range of acceptability recommended by Nunnally (1978). Table 3 displays a description of each factor. Corresponding to the descriptions are the complete questionnaire items used to represent the aspects of competitive strategy. These are ordered by the magnitude of the factor loadings (displayed in parentheses). The Alpha reliability coefficients are included.

Cluster Analysis to Identify Strategy Archetypes

Consistent with the prevailing conceptualization in the literature we assumed that firm strategy is a multidimensional construct which represents a composite or "bundle" of actions. As such, our intent was to identify the "pattern" of strategic attributes emphasized in new ventures. We chose cluster analysis as the analytical tool because it offered two distinct advantages. First, it overcomes a major limitation in the way strategy has often been operationalized in the literature. Venkatraman and Prescott (1990) contended that treating strategy as a vector of scores, which is frequently done, may produce misleading results. Such treatment assumes each dimension of strategy has equal importance. Instead, they argued that the weighing of the dimensions should reflect the differential emphasis that corresponds to the deployment of firms' resources. Cluster analysis, which classifies data on the basis of patterns of observed differences and similarities provides one solution to this concern.

TABLE 3

ASPECTS OF NEW FIRM COMPETITIVE STRATEGY ASSOCIATED WITH FACTOR DIMENSIONS

Competitive aspects emphasized	Descriptive
Factor 1 (Alpha = .66)	Product Distinction
Distinctive goods/services (.78) More contemporary, attractive products (.70) More choices (.70)	Seek to distinguish the firm from others in the market place by providing exceptional or unique products or services. Offering contemporary, attractive products gives consumers greater product choice.
Factor 2 (Alpha = .81)	Technology
Develop new/advanced technology (.90) Utilize new/advanced technology (.88)	Emphasize process or product technology by developing or using new or advanced technology
Factor 3 (Alpha = .62)	Market Responsiveness
More effective marketing/advertising (.81)	Knowledge of the market
Fast response to changes in markets (.80)	Emphasized to reach and respond quickly to key customer needs.
Factor 4 (Alpha = .68)	Service
Better service (.85)	Provide a higher level of service than competitors

Quality products/services (.81)

Factor 5 (Alpha = .66) | Site Appeal

Superior location/customer convenience (.85) | Attractiveness and convenience of facilities and location emphasized

Better, more attractive facilities (.83)

Factor 6 (Alpha not applicable) | Price

Lower prices (.97) | Sell products or services at a lower price than competitors

The second advantage of cluster analysis for the present study is that cluster analysis procedures require no prior assumptions about differences in the population being studied. (This is not true for some other statistical methods for classification, such as discriminant analysis.) Since our intent was not to test the fit of an existing model but rather to explore the patterns of strategy among new ventures, this technique was best suited to the purposes of this study.

The six dimensions of strategy attributes identified in the factor analysis were used as variables in the cluster analysis. We computed these dimensions by summing the items loading above .60 on each factor and dividing by the number of applicable responses. The reliability of these variables is reported in Table 3. Z-scores were computed for each variable and used in clustering the firms.

We adopted the two-step cluster analysis technique recommended by Punj and Stewart (1983). In this technique a hierarchical agglomerative method is first used to produce centroid estimates. These estimates are then used in the second step to set an iterative partitioning method for the final cluster solution. Ward's (1963) minimum variance method was used to determine cluster linkage. Separate cluster analyses were performed for each of the industries. Since we anticipated an industry difference, collapsing the data into one analysis may have produced misleading results.

FINDINGS

The results of the cluster analyses are displayed in Table 4. Only the cluster centroids that were above the mean are shown. These values signify the strategic dimensions, developed from the factor analysis, emphasized in each cluster. Since Z-scores were used in the analyses, the magnitude of the centroids can be compared to a mean of zero (0.0). The industries are ordered from upstream to downstream in the supply chain: manufacturing, distribution, and retail.

Focusing first on a general comparison across the industries, one can see that the number of clusters representing strategy archetypes varies across industries. The "stopping rule" defined by Mojena (1977) was used to determine the optimal number of clusters in each analysis. This rule determines the significance of the "jump' between each stage of the hierarchical agglomeration by calculating and comparing fusion coefficients (see Aldenderfer and Blashfield, 1984 for an example of computations). The fewest strategy archetypes are found among new manufacturing firms (three), while the most are evident among new distribution firms (five), and there is an intermediate number (four) among retail new firms. It is quite clear that compared to other industries in the value change, a narrower range of strategies are adopted by new manufacturing firms.

A comparison of the factor dimensions associated with the clusters that emerged across the supply chain is instructive. Several patterns are consistent with intuitive knowledge of firm strategy. First, as one moves downstream from manufacturing to retail, the importance of the site selection and appeal dimension increases in the strategy clusters. Conversely, the technology dimension is more important in defining strategy clusters upstream.

Unanticipated is the pattern found for the market responsiveness factor dimension. It is expected that the typical retail outlets can rely heavily on advertising to attract customers while managing inventory in such a way that they can react rapidly to changes occurring in the market place. The results in Table 4 suggest that market response is least emphasized downstream at the retail level while more heavily emphasized by distribution firms. It is possible that the very establishment of a new retail firm, with an emphasis on site selection, is a market response. If this "market response" is inappropriate, the new retail firm may disappear. In contrast, new distribution and manufacturing firms--which require more substantial investments--may be more oriented toward responding to shifts in the market.

TABLE 4

STRATEGY CLUSTER MEANS

MANUFACTURING

Strategic Factor Dimensions

Strategy Types

	Price	Appeal	Site Technology	Service	Market Response	Distribution
Super Achievers	0.21	0.14	0.32	--	0.50	0.58
Price/Service	0.19	--	--	0.13	--	--
Differentiation:						
Service	--	--	0.30	1.18	0.20	--

DISTRIBUTION

Strategic Factor Dimensions

Strategy Types

	Price	Appeal	Site Technology	Service	Market Response	Distribution
Super Achievers	1.04	0.78	1.07	--	1.04	0.78
Price/Service	0.71	--	--	--	0.58	--
Differentiation:						
Site/Service	--	0.35	--	0.31	--	0.20
Differentiation:						
Technology	--	--	1.27	--	0.60	0.89
Equivocator	--	--	--	0.43	--	--

RETAIL

Strategic Factor Dimensions

Strategy Types

	Price	Appeal	Site Technology	Service	Market Response	Distribution
Super Achievers	0.71	0.68	1.02	--	0.61	0.65
Price/Service	0.80	0.13	--	0.70	--	--
Differentiation:						
Site/Distribution	0.31	--	--	--	0.38	
Equivocator	--	--	--	0.55	--	--

A comparison of the specific strategy archetypes that evolved from the cluster analyses, presented in Table 4, supports the supposition that generic strategies exist across industries, albeit within an array of alternatives. For example, Porter's (1980) distinction between low cost and differentiation strategies is evident. The price factor dimension is important in defining clusters in all three industries; the other five factor dimensions reflect different aspects of differentiation. A strategy type that emphasized price was developed from the cluster analysis in all three industries, although it was typically associated with aspects of service; these represented variations of Porter's cost leadership strategy.

The essence of cost leadership is that firms develop a competitive advantage by controlling costs to become the low cost producer in the industry. By passing along cost savings to consumers via lower prices, such firms can undercut competitors while still accruing an acceptable return. New firms in both manufacturing and retail adopt a price/service strategy where low prices are combined with a commitment to compete by providing better service to customers. In the distribution industry, firms pursue a classic price strategy where low prices are augmented with marketing and advertising efforts.

The assortment of differentiation strategies listed in Table 4 suggests that although a generic archetype exists, variations of the strategy among new venture firms are specific to industries. In manufacturing, differentiation is based on a service. New firms adopting this strategy demonstrate an overriding concern for the customer. The use and/or development of new technology and marketing activities are assigned supporting roles. We speculate that these firms may be those manufacturing firms linking with customers in providing just-in-time delivery. In distribution, new firms seem to differentiate either by emphasizing technology and market responsiveness or by accentuating the combination of site appeal and service. Both strategies emphasize product or service distinctiveness. In retail, new firms rely on product distinction and their site appeal to differentiate them from others.

Finally, there are two strategy archetypes common across the industries that seem to fall outside the recognized strategy archetypes. The first we labeled "Super Achievers." Firms adopting this strategy strive to emphasize multiple strategy dimensions simultaneously. The only dimension these firms do not stress is service. Apparently, they want to "be all things to all people." The second strategy is more difficult to interpret. Labeled "Equivocators" in Table 4, this strategy is the reverse of Super Achievers. Firms adopting this strategy focus on only one strategy dimension: service. Either these firms are highly focused on satisfying customer demand for service or they are uncertain about which strategy dimensions to accentuate. Their ambivalence may result in falling back on the service dimension as a "socially acceptable" response to inquiries regarding firm strategy. Further research will be needed to determine if these strategies, despite their differences, epitomize Porter's (1980) description of firms "stuck in the middle."

A comparison of the strategy types across the value chain is presented in Table 5. It presents the percentage of new firms found to adopt each strategy for the three industries.

TABLE 5

STRATEGY CLUSTERS BY INDUSTRY

	Manufacturing	Distribution	Retail
No. of firms	138	176	311
Super Achievers	54 %	18 %	25 %
Price/Service	32	22	22
Differentiation-Service	14	--	--
Differentiation-Site/Service	--	27	--
Differentiation-Technology	--	14	--
Differentiation-Site/Distribution	--	--	27
Equivocator	--	19	26
Total %	100 %	100 %	100 %

NOTE: Chi-square value is 803, statistically significant at 0.00001 level. If all four differentiation categories are consolidated, Chi-square is 666, significant at 0.00001 level.

The differences are substantial, with over half the new manufacturing firms (54%) adopting a single strategy (Super Achievers) and two in five (41%) of the distribution new firms reflecting a differentiation strategy. Retail new firms are almost evenly divided among the four strategies. Hence, there is more strategy diversity the further one moves down the value added chain.

DISCUSSION

This paper showed that strategies of new ventures vary across and within industry sectors. Specifically, the numbers and types of strategies deployed by new ventures vary by the location of the firm in the supply chain. Manufacturing new ventures, located upstream in the supply chain, have the least number of strategic archetypes and most closely resemble the strategic typology identified by Porter (1980): cost leadership and differentiation. However, the largest number of new ventures in manufacturing pursue a super achiever strategy representing a firm that attempts to excel in all aspects of strategic performance.

These three strategies represent "core" strategies throughout the supply chain. A pricing strategy, whether based on service or market response, provides new ventures with opportunities to compete with larger firms. Larger firms may be bound to a larger cost structure and lack the ability to respond to buyers through service and quickness because of poor information. Differentiation, a strategy promoting products to buyers based on their unique package of method of distribution, varies greatly by industry sector. Downstream, product distinction takes on greatest importance for new ventures pursuing differentiation. This is also true with site appeal. Clearly, visibility in location and packaging is an important strategic effort for new ventures residing further down the supply chain stream.

Super Achievers represent perhaps the most unique strategy of the clusters. Whether this is an outcome of the desire to do it all, or failure to recognize the strategy they are emphasizing, is unclear. However, it may represent a third strategy overlooked by many theorists in the field: the combination of low price and high quality may be a formidable strategy deserving of additional research. As a starting point, it may be fruitful to investigate the cross-national presence of the Super Achiever strategy to determine if it is unique to the United States in the 1980's or is perhaps a new generic strategy found in all advanced economies.

A second important addition to the inventory of new venture strategies is the Equivocator. Equivocator new firms were found in both distribution and retail (downstream) and are highly focused on service. The presence of the Equivocator suggests that a niche for providing service to buyers is an important opportunity. Again, the dynamics of the culture and market place may have created this niche. With greater numbers of households emphasizing "active leisure" time and dual working conditions, service regardless of price and product characteristics may be a premium in the market place. Furthermore, this may be the least expensive strategy for new ventures to mount.

While we can speculate about the descriptions of the strategies, it is not clear from the data which will achieve the greatest success. The variations of the strategies however, imply that strategies among new ventures are more robust than many theorists and researchers have thought. More work is needed in the examination of the variation in strategies of firms in the first year and continued years to determine which are most susceptible to failure. In addition, more work is needed to assess whether Super Achievers and Equivocators are strategies that will be prominent among corporations in the future, or whether these strategies are artifacts of culture and economic conditions of the United States or the constraints that accompany the founding of autonomous new firms.

REFERENCES

Aldenderfer, M. S. and Blashfield, R. K. 1984. *Cluster Analysis*. Beverly Hills, Ca.: Sage Publications.

Biggadike, R. E. 1976. *Corporate Diversification: Entry, Strategy and Performance*. Boston: Harvard University.

Boeker, W. 1989. "Strategic Change: The Effects of Founding and History" *Academy of Management Review*, 32 (3), 489-515.

Bourgeois, L. J., III. 1980. "Strategy and Environment: A Conceptual Integration" *Academy of Management Journal*, 5 (1), 25-39.

Broom, H. N. and Longenecker, J. G. 1971. *Small Business Management*, 3rd ed. Cincinnati, OH: South-Western.

Carter, N. M. 1990. "Small Firm Adaptation: Responses of Physicians' Organizations to Regulatory and Competitive Uncertainty" *Academy of Management Journal*, 33 (2), 307-333.

Changanti, R., Changanti, R. and Mahajan, V. 1989. "Profitable Small Business Strategies Under Different Types of Competition" *Entrepreneurship Theory and Practice*, 21-35.

Cohn T. and Lindberg, R. A. 1974. *Survival and Growth: Management Strategies for the Small Firm.* New York: AMACOM.

Cronbach, L. J. 1951. "Coefficient Alpha and the Internal Structure of Tests" *Psychometrika*, 16, 297-334.

Deeks, J. 1976. *The Small Firm Owner-Manager*. New York: Praeger.

Dess, G. G. and Davis, P. S. 1984. "Porter's (1980) Generic Strategies as Determinants of Strategic Group Membership and Organizational Performance" *Academy of Management Journal*, 27 (3), 467-488.

Eisenhardt, K. M. and Schoonhoven, C. B. 1990 "Organizational Growth: Linking Founding Team, Strategy, Environment, and Growth among U.S. Semiconductor Ventures, 1978-1988" *Administrative Science Quarterly*, 35, 504-529.

Feeser, H. R. and Willard, G. E. 1990. "Founding Strategy and Performance: A Comparison of High and Low Growth High Tech Firms" *Strategic Management Journal* 11, 87-98.

Glueck, W. F. 1980. *Business Policy and Strategic Management*. New York: McGraw-Hill.

Galbraith, J. R. 1983. "Strategy and Organization Planning" Human Resource Management 22 (12), 64-77.

Hambrick, D.C. 1983. "High Profit Strategies in Mature Capital Goods Industries: A Contingency Approach" Academy of Management Journal, 26 (4), 687-707.

Herbert, T. T. and Deresky, H. 1987. "Generic Strategies: An Empirical Investigation of Typology Validity and Strategy Content" Strategic Management Journal 8, 135-147.

Hofer, C. W., and Schendel, D. 1978. Strategy Formulation: Analytical Concepts. St. Paul, MN: West.

Hosmer, L. 1957. "Small Manufacturing Enterprises" Harvard Business Review 35, 111-122.

Lawrence, P. R. and Dyer, D. 1983. Renewing American Industry. New York: Free Press.

MacMillan, I. C. and Day, D. L. 1987. "Corporate Venturing into Industrial Markets: Dynamics of Aggressive Entry" Journal of Business Venturing 2 (1), 29-40.

McDougall, P. and Robinson, R. B., Jr. 1990. "New Venture Strategies: An Empirical Identification of Eight 'Archetypes' of Competitive Strategies for Entry" Strategic Management Journal 11, 447-467.

Miles, R. E. 1982. Coffin Nails and Corporate Strategies. Englewood Cliffs, N.J.: Prentice-Hall.

Miles, R. E., Snow, C.C., Meyer, A. D. and Coleman, H.J., Jr. 1978. "Organizational Strategy, Structure and Process" Academy of Management Review, 3 (3), 546-562.

Miller, A. and Camp, B. 1985. "Exploring Determinants of Success in Corporate Ventures" Journal of Business Venturing, 1 (1), 87-105.

Mintzberg, H. 1984. "A Typology of Organizational Structure." In D. Miller & P.H. Friesen (Eds.), Organizations: A Quantum View : 68-86. Englewood Cliffs, N.J.: Prentice Hall.

Mojena, R. 1977. "Hierarchical Grouping Methods and Stopping Rules - An Evaluation" Computer Journal, 20, 359-363.

Nunnally, J. C. 1978. Psychometric Theory, 2nd ed. New York: McGraw-Hill.

Porter, M. E. 1980 Competitive Strategy -- Techniques for Analyzing Industries and Competitors. New York: Free Press.

Punj, G. and Stewart, D. W. 1983. "Cluster Analysis in Marketing Research: Review and Suggestions for Application" Journal of Marketing Research, 20, 134-148.

Reynolds, P. D. and Miller, B. 1988. 1987 Minnesota New Firm Survey. Minneapolis, MN: U of Minnesota Center for Urban and Regional Affairs.

Shortell, S.M. and Zajac, E. J. 1990. " Perceptual and Archival Measures of Miles and Snow's Strategic Types: A Comprehensive Assessment of Reliability and Validity" Academy of Management Journal, 33 (4), 817-832.

Stegall, D. P., Steinmetz, L. L. and Kline, J. B. 1976. Managing the Small Business. Homewood, IL: Irwin.

Stinchcombe, A. 1965. "Social Structure and Organizations." In James G. March (Ed.), Handbook of Organizations: 142-193. Chicago: Rand McNally.

Venkatraman, N. and Prescott, J. E. 1990. "Environment-Strategy Coalignment: An Empirical Test of Its Performance Implications" Strategic Management Journal, 11, 1-23.

Ward, J. 1963. "Hierarchical Grouping to Optimize and Objective Function" Journal of the American Statistical Association, 58, 236-244.

A Venture Capital Price Index

Critique
by
Ian C. MacMillan, *The Wharton School, University Of Pennsylvania,*
Rita Gunther McGrath, *The Wharton School, University Of Pennsylvania*

IN GENERAL

1. Overall

    Given the opaqueness of the venture capital markets, one's interest in building a price index is particularly significant. In our view, this work could have significant practical benefits for those who are considering investing in venture capital stocks.

    We want to stress that we consider the creation of a venture capital index to be valuable. In our view, it is important that some things are added to it which will make it even more valuable.

2. Theoretical framework

    The paper needs to be grounded in theoretical discussion. The real problem with an index like the one being developed here is related to the debate on the efficiency of the venture capital market and the nature of the risk associated with owning venture stock.

    There is currently a debate on the extent to which the venture capitalist is exposed to agency risk, business risk or both. As opposed to publicly traded stocks, where there are immense amounts of public information, venture capital investments are likely to be far more susceptible to agency risk. In fact, Amit demonstrates theoretically that venture capitalists, because of the asymmetry of information with respect to the entrepreneur, should end up funding only second-rate investments since the entrepreneurs preserve for themselves those which are most likely to generate excess rents.

    Two references are:

    "Entrepreneurial Ability, Venture investment and Risk Sharing" <u>Management Science</u> Vol 36, No.10, October 1990.

    "Does Venture Capital Foster the Most Promising Entrepreneurial Firms?"

California Management Review Vol 32, No.3, Spring 1990.

Fiet has recently completed a study which also addresses this issue and finds that venture capitalists focus on managing business risk, while "business angels" focus on managing agency risks. If the index that is being developed is to be valuable for pricing venture capital stocks, it is important to deal with the issue of agency risk.

There is clear evidence here of an enormous amount of work having gone into constructing the index as carefully and usefully as possible. Having taken this extensive effort, it is important to be very explicit about any limitations of the model. Our concern is that future readers of this paper are apt to be far more naive than the authors are in using the index, and must be made aware of its limitations by the people who know it best. The authors would be well advised to adopt the approach of being their own worst critics, and lay out as many caveats as they can think of for the use of this index. In particular, they must be explicit about the areas in which the index cannot be appropriately used.

Finally, we encourage them to move aggressively on the development of a standard error measure, given the significantly larger standard errors one could expect with venture capital market indices as opposed to public market indices.

IN PARTICULAR

1. The model index discussed on page 2 in inconsistent with the actual index discussed later.

    On page 12 it is stated that index 1 "reflects an equally weighted buy and hold strategy". On page 2, it is suggested "the implied investment strategy of the equally weighted index is to sell and reallocate at each time interval", whereas the investment strategy implied by a price or value-weighted index "is to buy and hold".

    It appears that the authors have used an equally weighted index simply because these data are available, and are selecting the weighting procedure on the basis of convenience. The concern we have here is that in the initial discussion, the implied strategy is to sell and reallocate, but this is not the strategy followed in developing the index. If this is the case, explicit reference must be made as less-than-careful readers are apt to be mislead.

2. In the discussion of the properties of an index early in the paper, the authors are careful to recognise that high transaction costs are a factor (page 3). This needs to be addressed when the actual index is constructed. In fact, where the model differs from the assumptions in the price estimation model, (such as zero transaction costs, and ease of finding a buyer for the stock), this should be

Critique 171

pointed out explicitly. This is another case in which the authors should assume that they know a great deal more than the reader about the index, and include an appropriate critique of it themselves. Every point at which the index departs from established models should be documented, together with some discussion as to the possible effects of these departures.

3. Page 8: There is a discussion about utilising the NASDAQ 60 index as justification for the way this index has been developed. This is based on the reasonable assumption that for the 60 stocks in the index statistical independence exists. However, there is no evidence that this assumption necessarily applies to the stocks in the venture capital funds that are studied. Before simply accepting this, we would like to see some evidence that the stocks in venture capital funds vary independently.

4. Page 10, Table 3: We found it remarkable and deserving of comment that of 52 transactions, only 3 were written off. Common wisdom suggests that in most cases ventures do not have a 49 out of 52 success rate. This further suggests that the authors were working with a most unusual fund. This point should be explicitly addressed, as should any difficulties a lower success rate would pose for the index.

5. Table 5: We also found it surprising that the time intervals were quite short.

6. Page 10: The categorization of "any" to some endpoint in Tables 3, 5 and 7 creates confusion because clearly this could refer to many different stages that precede the particular endpoint.

7. There is a need to demonstrate that the two funds compared are sufficiently similar that they may be pooled without creating problems in the sample. We suggest that a t test for group means be done to ensure that there are no significant differences between means for A and B.

8. Page 13: It is not at all clear how the growth factor of 47.1 is obtained by adding to the original index each time a new stock is issued. The investment patterns and resulting returns should be very clearly documented. In our view, we may be comparing apples to oranges by comparing indices 1 and 2 with CRSP and Standards and Poors.

9. It seems to us that an interesting question, deserving of comment, raised by the indication in Table 6 that the annual rates of return are systematically decreasing. Is this a sign that the market is becoming more mature or efficient, or is it simply a reflection of a general price decline in financial markets?

10. We also feel that there is probably a relationship, insufficiently explored here, between the stages of ventures in the portfolio and the returns to be expected. The current approach implies that the index is appropriate for all stages, when in fact there was a systematic shift in portfolio during this time period, as Table

7 indicates. Over the time period of the index, there was a general shift in the venture capital industry from early stage investments to leveraged buyout type investments.

11. A final problem is in Appendix A, in which it is stated that the divisor, "approaches $1 as it becomes large". How valid is that assumption for the two funds in the sample?

In conclusion, we are convinced that the development of such an index will be very valuable, particularly once the authors have developed their estimates of the standard errors of the index on a much larger sample of venture capital investments, so that interested parties have a sense of the range of possible values of prices. Once again, we stress that they should be their own worst enemies in terms of very clearly highlighting places where the naive user of the index could run unwittingly afoul of its limitations.

A VENTURE CAPITAL PRICE INDEX

ROBERT H. KEELEY, *STANFORD UNIVERSITY*
LASSAAD A. TURKI, *STANFORD UNIVERSITY*

ABSTRACT

This paper develops a method to estimate private company values at any time between market transactions. Using such estimates, we develop a stock price index. A simulation on public stocks performs well, so we develop a venture capital index using a pilot sample of 477 transactions from 124 companies. Using this method, a full scale venture capital index may be developed, which would greatly aid institutional investors, venture capitalists and entrepreneurs in assessing price levels and trends in the venture capital market.

1. INTRODUCTION

Stock market indices, such as the Dow-Jones Industrial Average or the Financial Times 100 Index, are probably the most widely followed economic indicators in the world. They serve many purposes, including

* summarizing many thousands of transactions each day into a single measure of the market's price level and its direction,
* guiding investors and traders as they consider transactions in individual securities,
* assisting investors in evaluating the performance of their portfolios, and
* serving as a focus of many research studies (e.g. Fisher (1966), Ohlson & Rosenberg (1982), Schwert (1990) as well as providing a key piece of data in many, many others (e.g. Brophy & Guthner (1987).

Indices exist for most equity markets, but not for the venture capital market. Although an index of venture capital prices would be useful to investors for all of the purposes noted above, to date none has been created. This paper is a step towards rectifying that situation.

In this paper we present a method for constructing an index of private venture capital transactions, which takes account of their unique aspects. To verify that the proposed method provides reasonable estimates, it is tested on a sample of 60 public stocks -- stocks for which a true index value may be calculated. Then a venture capital index is estimated for the years 1980-1987 using a pilot sample of about 60 companies.

Venture capital markets are private, and that privacy, in addition to the technical problems considered here, has been a barrier to the creation of an index. However, as the venture capital industry has grown, several organizations have collected enough data with which they could create such an index for the United States and for some European countries. We believe that the proposed method solves the problems of constructing a venture capital price index, and hope that one of those organizations will begin providing it as a service to the industry.

2. STOCK MARKET INDICES

Most stock market indices are based on the following formula[1]:

Where:

$$I_t = B_0 A_t \sum_{i=1}^{N} \varpi_{it} \left(\frac{P_{it}}{P_{i0}} \right)$$

I_t = the price level of the index at time t.
w_{it} = the relative weight given to stock i for purposes of computing the index at time t.
P_{it} = the value of stock i at time t (for some indices "value" may include dividends orother cash equivalent distributions during the interval t - 1 to t).
P_{i0} = the price of stock i at t = 0
A_t = an adjustment factor which allows for changes in the membership of the index and capitalization changes in companies comprising the index.
B_0 = a base value of the index at t = 0.

All indices assume that a price is known for times 0 and t, which implies that a transaction has occurred at both of those times. In fact most stocks in the index will have traded somewhat before the relevant times , and have changed somewhat in value. However, indices routinely assume that the last trade is the correct price. As long as the probable change in stock price is small, this does not cause much error. However, with young private companies, for which transactions are very infrequent and price volatility is high, such a fiction is untenable.

Various indices can be created depending on how one selects weights, and on how often one changes them. Three important classes of American indices are

* Price weighted: the Dow-Jones Industrial Index is a leading example. Weights are set as $P_{i0} / \sum P_{i0}$
* Value weighted: the S & P 500 Index, the New York Stock Exchange Index, the CRSP Value Weighted Index (Center for Research in Security Prices, University of Chicago) and the NASDAQ Composite Index are

---

[1]The indices discussed in the paper will all use arithmetic averages. "Geometric" indices, such as the Value Line Index, exist but are relatively unusual.

examples. Weights are set as $n_{i0}P_{i0}/\sum n_{i0}P_{i0}$ where n_{i0} is the number of shares outstanding at t = 0 for company i.

* Equally weighted: the CRSP Equally Weighted Index is a leading example. Weights are 1/N where N is the number of stocks in the index.

Each index corresponds to a particular investment strategy:

Price weighted--buy one share of each firm in the index.
Value weighted--buy one percent of each firm in the index.
Equally weighted--buy $1 of stock in each firm in the index.

If no dividends or adjustments have occurred, a price or value weighted index (at time t) can be updated from any prior value (say at time t - n) by setting $B_o = I_{t-n}$ and applying the general formula to the ratio (P_t/P_{t-n}) with t - n being substituted for t = 0 for purposes of calculating weights. The index value will be the same as if the general formula had been applied from t = 0. This process of multiplying index level changes may be applied over any number of periods. Equivalently, the investment strategy implied by the index is to buy and hold.

In contrast, the equally weighted index will give different values depending on the interval over which it is calculated. For example, a value calculated for a one year interval will generally be different from the value obtained by multiplying 12 monthly changes. The reason is that the portfolio is reallocated at the end of each interval. Putting equal amounts in each security means that holdings of the high performing stocks of the previous interval will be reduced, and holdings of the low performers will be increased. When returns are positively correlated over time,[2] then the shorter the calculation interval for the equally weighted index, the lower its performance. The implied investment strategy of the equally weighted index is to sell and reallocate at each time interval.

The form chosen for a venture capital index should approximate the investment policy of a typical venture capitalist. This suggests some type of an equally weighted index, because a venture capital fund tends to diversify through relatively equal investments in a number of companies. It also suggests a buy and hold formulation. For example, if a fund invested $1 simultaneously in each of 30 companies, the index would be the total value of the investments at any given time divided by 30.[3]

---

[2]For example, high risk stocks have higher returns on the average than low risk stocks. In an index comprised of stocks with varying risks, returns of individual stocks will have positive correlations over time.

[3]If a subsequent investment were made in another company, the index would be adjusted. The adjustment procedure satisfies two criteria. It causes no change in the index at the moment the new security is added, and the new security has a weight of $\dfrac{1}{(1tN/B_o)+1}$ of the index. This adjustment procedure is common to many stock indices and will be illustrated

An equally weighted index has the additional benefits of not requiring knowledge of a company's total value, as a value weighted index would, and it makes efficient use of the company in the sample as having equal importance.

3. VENTURE CAPITAL MARKETS COMPARED TO PUBLIC EQUITY MARKETS

The nature of public markets facilitates creation of an index:

1. There are many potential buyers and sellers who bid in an open market. Their transactions involve relatively low fees. This tends to minimize price distortions caused by thin markets, lack of knowledge, or high transaction costs.

2. Trades occur frequently and prices are publicly announced. Thus the information necessary to construct an index is readily available.

3. Companies are relatively mature and remain a part of the index for several years; the maturity of the average company in the index can be viewed as unchanging. In such a case the index reflects overall market conditions and company performance, not changes in the age or composition of its constituents.

Private venture capital markets are different. An investment involves high transaction costs, including search costs by issuer and investor, investigation, and legal costs. This usually precludes any sort of auction market. However, the pool of issuers and investors at any time numbers in the hundreds. Except for some start-up companies, both investors and companies (through their current investors) have expert knowledge of the venture capital market. Thus we suggest that venture capital transactions occur at prices close to those which would prevail in a perfect market, and they are unbiased estimates of the prices in a perfect market.

The high transaction cost of private investment also implies infrequent trading -- our sample shows a typical interval of about 13 months. This, coupled with high volatility of stock prices (the standard deviation of the price ratio between one transaction and the next is about 174 percent in our sample), means that the last transaction in a private company is not likely to be close to the true value on the date the index is computed. However, one can obtain estimates between (but not beyond) the points at which prices are known. Although the individual estimates are subject to wide errors, the error shrinks as the number of securities in the index increases.

An index, which relies on estimated prices, will always have a lag. One must wait for a sufficient number of transactions before estimating the index. In the United States, venture capital transactions occur at a rate of about 100 companies/month. Thus a reasonably broad index can be estimated with a one month lag, similar lags

---

in a later section.

typify many important economic statistics.

A venture capital index will have a greater turnover of constituent companies than a typical public market index. However, changes in composition occur with all indices and attract minimal notice. If one company is on the average a good substitute for another, changes in composition will have a minor effect.

Venture capital investments tend to have labels reflecting a company's maturity, such as "seed," "startup," and "first round." Although we have neither theory nor data on which to base a hypothesis, returns may vary with the maturity of a company. Thus a change in average maturity may influence an index of venture capital prices. In addition, indices reflecting a single type of transaction can be useful. For example, one may wish to compare the returns from investing in start-ups with the returns from later stage investments.

The final problem with venture capital markets is their privacy. Prices are not publicly available. However, in the United States, and to a lesser degree in Europe, certain large investors participate in many venture capital funds and have access to transaction data for those funds. In addition, many venture capital funds provide transaction data to Venture Economics, the publisher of Venture Capital Journal. We believe that several groups have sufficient data to create an index of venture capital prices.

Although the venture capital markets differ from public markets in all important respects, none of these seems to prevent the construction of a venture capital price index. The greatest limitation is that it can only be constructed with a lag, in order to allow a body of transactions to build up. Although this means the index will never be reported on the evening news, it can be current enough for many research purposes and, in view of the typical lag in a venture capital transaction, it can be useful to investors and issuers as well.

4. CONSTRUCTION OF A VENTURE CAPITAL PRICE INDEX

Construction of a venture capital index involves three steps:

1. Transaction data must be assembled for a number of companies. Transactions will occur infrequently, e.g. once per year for a given company. Seldom will two companies have a transaction on the same date. This pilot study uses a sample of 124 companies which engaged in 477 transactions between 1980 and 1988. Very few of the 124 are represented over the entire time interval. They either started a business after 1980 or dropped out of the sample before 1988 (because they became public, were acquired, went out of business, or did not have a sale of stock in 1988).

2. Prices must be estimated for dates between the actual transactions. This

provides a set of price estimates for specific times, e.g., the end of each month.

3. An index is calculated for each time of interest.

We will defer discussion of the pilot sample until the next section, and will describe the construction of an index in the remainder of this section.

4.1. COMPUTING THE MISSING SHARE PRICES

Given that only a few share prices can be collected for each company included in the Venture Capital Price Index, the first task is to determine the value of the share price at any time as if there is a secondary or implicit market where the firm's shares are traded continuously. One way of achieving this goal is to assume that the firm's stock price follows a random walk process with a constant variance, i.e., the returns between consecutive time periods are independent of each other and are normally distributed. In that case, one can show that given the share prices at two different times t_1 and t_2, the share price at any time t between t_1 and t_2 can be computed by interpolating on the logs of the share price ratios.[4] Figure 1 graphically illustrates the estimation procedure.

4.2. CONSTRUCTING THE INDEX

For reasons noted at the end of the section "Stock Market Indices", the Venture Capital Index is equally weighted with an assumed "buy and hold" policy. If the number of stocks making up the index remains constant, if all the share prices are available throughout the period of interest, and if all the stocks in the index start with a value of one at the beginning of the period, then the value of the index at time t can be computed as:

$$I_t = B_0 \frac{1}{N} \sum_{i=1}^{N} \left(\frac{P_{it}}{P_{i0}} \right)$$

---

[4]Mathematically speaking, the firm's share price is the solution to the stochastic differential equation:

$$dP_t = P_t\mu dt + P_t\sigma dB, \quad P_o > 0$$

where σ are nonnegative constants and B denotes a Standard Brownian Motion. If P_1 is the share price at time $t_1 < t < t_2$ is a normal density with mean $\ln(P_1/P_1) + \{\ln(P_2/P_1) - \ln(P_1/P_1)\}\{t-t_1\}$. The exponential of the mean of the conditional density multiplied by P_1 is then taken as an unbiased estimate of the share price at time t.

A Venture Capital Price Index

Figure 1: A Procedure for Estimating Prices

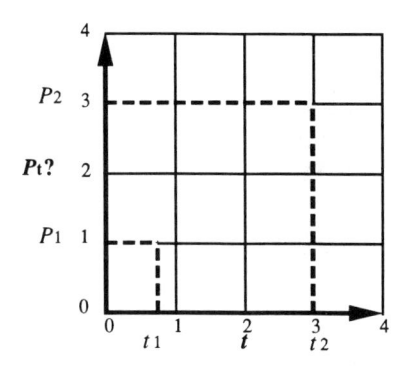

(a) Assume that $P_1 = 1$ and $P_2 = 3$ as obtained from the Venture Capital Index data set. We wish to obtain an estimate for P_t where $t_1 < t < t_2$.

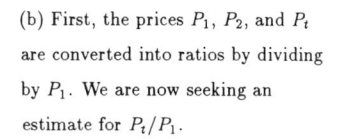

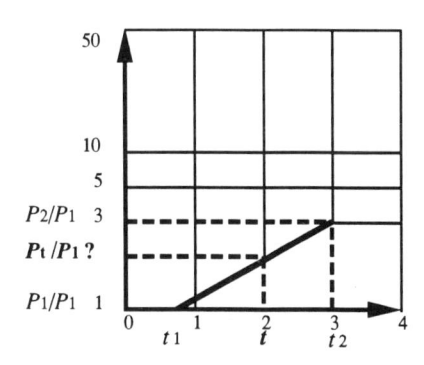

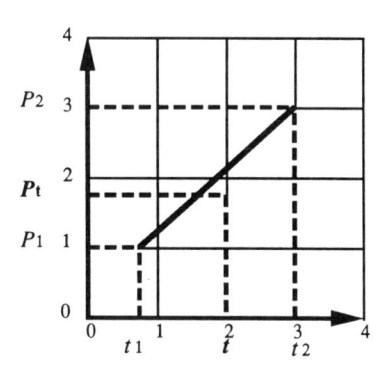

(b) First, the prices P_1, P_2, and P_t are converted into ratios by dividing by P_1. We are now seeking an estimate for P_t/P_1.

(c) Second, the price ratios are plotted on a log scale. The estimate for P_t is obtained by drawing a straight line between $(P_2/P_1, t_2)$ and $(P_1/P_1, t_1)$ and taking the y-coordinate of the intersection of the line with t. In this case, $P_t/P_1 = P_t$ can be directly read as 1.84.

(d) The equation for the estimate of P_t obtained by interpolation on the logs is:
$P_t = P_1 \exp\left[\ln(P_2/P_1) \times \frac{(t-t_1)}{(t_2-t_1)}\right]$
If the ratios instead of their logs are used in the interpolation, the estimate for P_t would have been $2.11 > 1.84$.

In the terms of equation (1) w_{it} = 1/N and A_t = 1. Actually the index composition varies over time, that is, stocks are added to and deleted from the index. The following adjustment, similar to that applied to the NASDAQ Composite Index to account for its varying composition over time, is also used in computing the values of the Venture Capital Index. The adjustment prevents any change in the index at the moment a stock is added or deleted, and amounts to a change in the divisor (N in equation (2)). Appendix A shows how to calculate the adjusted divisor (D_t).

The following simple numerical example illustrates the PC Index computation mechanism. Consider the case where only two stocks make up the index in period 1. At the end of period 2, stock #3 joins the index, while at the end of period 3, stock #1 drops out of the index. Table 1 contains the share prices for each stock over the four time-period horizon.

Table 1: Example of Equally Weighted Index
with Additions and Deletions

Stock #	Period 1	2	3	4
1	1	2	2	–
2	1	2	1	4
3	–	1	2	2
D_t	2	2	2.5	1.5
I_t	100	200	200	400

The share price of any stock is adjusted such that the initial value is 1 as if $1 in new funds is initially invested by the index in that stock. Therefore, equal percentage changes in the share prices of two different stocks equally affect the value of the index (regardless of the changes in their respective unadjusted absolute levels).

We set the level of the index in period 1 at 100, i.e., I_1 = B_o = 100. The divisor in period 1 is equal to the number of stocks making up the index which is 2. In period 2, the current value of the index portfolio is 2 + 2 = 4. The value of stock #3 is not included since the one dollar investment is assumed to be made at the end of period 2 and the stock will not start trading until the beginning of period 3. Since the composition of the index did not change between periods 1 and 2, no adjustment of the time 1 divisor is necessary. Therefore, the divisor in period 2 is (100 ÷ 100) x 2 = 2, and the level of the index is (4 ÷ 2) x 100 = 200.

In period 3, an adjustment needs to be made to account for the addition of stock #3 to the index. In this case, the beginning period sum of price ratios in the index is 2 + 2 + 1 = 5, taking into account the initial value of stock #3. Therefore, the divisor in period 3 is (100 ÷ 200) x 5 = 2.5. Since the current sum of price ratios of the index is 2 + 1 + 2 = 5, then the level of the index in period 3 is (5 ÷ 2.5

) x 100 = 200. Similar calculations are carried out in period 4. Now the adjustment has to account for the deletion of stock #1 from the index. The after adjustment sum of price ratios of the index at the beginning of period 4 is 1 + 2 = 3, assuming that the value of the deleted stock is its last trading price. Therefore, the divisor in period 4 is equal to (100 ÷ 200) x 3 = 1.5. The level of the index is ((4 + 2) ÷ 1.5) x 100 = 400.

4.3. A TEST OF THE METHOD

Because the Private Venture Index must be constructed from estimated share prices, one can never know its true value. However, we can test the properties of an estimated index by constructing one from public stocks (whose market values are continuously observable) and comparing it with a "true" index based on actual market prices. The test index uses 60 securities because that is the typical number of private companies in our sample. The 60 companies are randomly chosen among the more than 9000 companies listed in the 1989 NASDAQ daily return tapes prepared by CRSP.[5] Using daily returns, the share price ratio at any time T is computed by the following equation:

$$P_T/P_1 = \prod_{t}^{T} = 1(1 + r_t)$$

where $\prod(1 + r_t)$ denotes the products of one plus the daily return from t = 1 to T.

---

[5] The authors would like to thank Nazeh Ben Arnmar, a research assistant, for his helping in obtaining the data used in this section.

Figure 2: NASDAQ-60 Indices

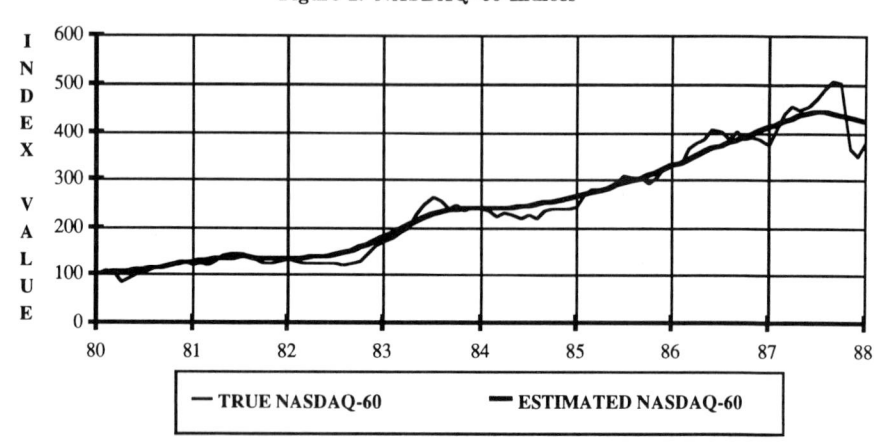

Figure 3: Monthly Returns for NASDAQ-60 Indices

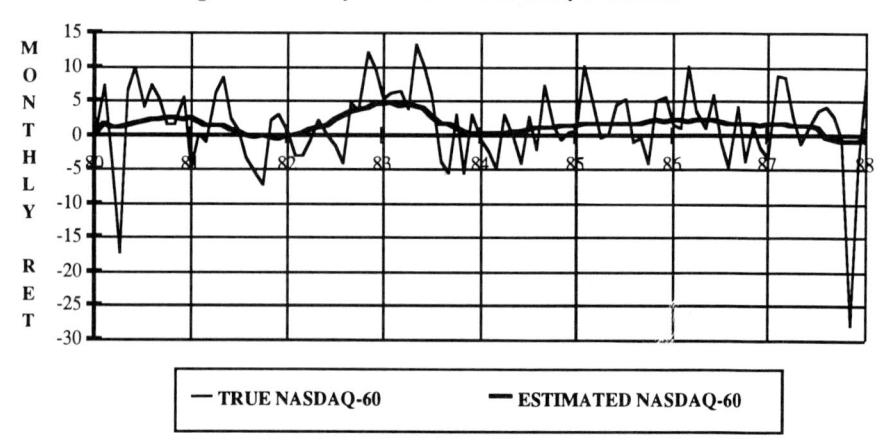

A Venture Capital Price Index

To construct the simulated index (NASDAQ-60), share price ratios, approximately a year apart, are picked for each of the 60 companies of the index. The transactions are roughly evenly distributed throughout the year. The procedure described for estimating the venture capital index is applied to get an estimated NASDAQ-60 index. In addition, the true index is calculated using the known prices at the end of each month. Figures 2 and 3 and Table 2 show the results of the test on the NASDAQ-60 index. The estimated NASDAQ-60 index has properties one would expect:

1. Figure 2 shows the estimated index to be a smoothed version of the true index. The estimated index value is nearly always within 10 percent of the true index value, and it matches the long term performance well.

2. Figure 3 shows that monthly returns of the estimated index (measured as the ratio of successive monthly values minus one) deviate widely from the monthly returns of the true index. They appear to be a smoothed version of the true returns.

3. Table 2 reinforces the impressions provided by the two figures. The estimated index matches the true index fairly well on an annual basis. For the eight year period, its average return is 0.3 percent/year less than the true return. As one would expect, it understates the amount of variation; the standard deviation of the difference between the true index and the estimated index is 5.4 percent. On a month-to-month comparison the errors are larger, because the estimated index is by nature much less volatile than the true index, True monthly returns average 1.6 percent with a standard deviation of 5.9 percent. Comparable values of the estimated index are 1.5 percent and 1.3 percent respectively. Thus the month to month variation of the estimated index is between a fourth and a fifth of the true variation.

Overall the test shows the estimated index to be reasonably successful. It follows the overall movement of the true index, with a root-mean-squared error of 5.4 percent. Although this is more than one would like, Table 2 shows that the interpolated index gives a good qualitative view of returns in all years except 1986.

Table 2: Results of Test on NASDAQ-60 Index

	True Index	Estimated Index	Error
Monthly Returns (percent/month)			
Average	1.6	1.5	
Std. Deviation	5.9	1.3	
Minimum	(27.7)	(1.0)	
Maximum	13.4	4.7	
Yearly Returns (percent/year)			
1980	23.1	20.2	(2.9)
1981	7.1	6.1	(1.0)
1982	28.1	32.7	4.6
1983	42.1	34.2	(7.9)
1984	8.4	10.6	2.2
1985	36.0	24.3	(11.7)
1986	13.1	24.8	11.7
1987	1.5	3.8	2.3
Average	19.9	19.6	(0.3)

As might be expected, the estimated index performs less well on a short term basis, and fails to capture the monthly volatility of the true index. In principle the estimated index could accurately map monthly values, if movements in the 60 stocks were statistically independent of each other. In that case, the errors of the individual estimates would tend to offset each other, and the central limit theorem implies that the error for the estimated index would decline in proportion to the square root of the number of stocks in the index. The fact that the month to month error is fairly large stems from the tendency of individual public stock prices to be influenced by the overall movement of the market. The estimated index would be improved by correcting for overall market movement (This is an extension which we are pursuing). Public stocks are known to move with the overall stock market. The NASDAQ-60 portfolio moves 0.83 percent for every 1.0 percent change in the S & P 500 index on the average. That is, it has a beta coefficient of 0.83.

The sensitivity of private stocks to movements in the market has not been estimated. Our first efforts to do so indicate a very low average beta coefficient (about 0.1). If this is a valid estimate, the true Venture Capital index may be much smoother than the NASDAQ-60 index, or other public market indices. In any case, once an estimate of average beta exists, one can correct for overall movement of the stock market.

5. DATA COLLECTION FOR THE VENTURE CAPITAL INDEX

Two venture capital funds, which requested anonymity, allowed the authors to collect data on their transactions during the period from 1975 through 1988.

Funds A and B are similar in many respects, which made us optimistic that the two sets of transactions would not differ greatly. They are of similar size, age and standing -- being among the leading firms in the industry. They prefer to invest in technology based, start-up companies. Their internal records were different so the collection procedure varied. Fund A did not keep its transactions on a database, but did have most of the documents related to the transactions available. These often included investment agreements (which summarized the firm's capitalization and identified the new investors), as well as state securities filings, financial statements, financial projections, and business plans. They provided information about stock splits, liquidation preferences, anti-dilution provisions, changes in management options, sweeteners and other elements which could influence the company's value. And in most cases they allowed us to determine the company's maturity. The fund's annual audited statements and investments logs served to verify that we had recorded all of its transactions.

Reasonable agreement exists on terms which describe the financing stages of a firm. We classified transactions by these standard terms to the extent possible.[6] Two new designations were needed:

* "start-up plus" refers to a financing between the "start-up" financing at which product development formally begins and the first stage financing at which marketing of the developed product begins.
* "sustaining" refers to a financing for a company which has significant problems. The standard designations refer only to successful companies.

From fund A we collected 333 transactions in 73 companies. Allowing for the fact that a typical transaction had several investors, 190 different venture capital funds were identified as participants in one or more of these financings. For venture capital fund A we also investigated how often financing would include a new investor. In 14 percent of the transactions (48 of 333) the records were insufficient to determine whether any new investor was involved. In 21 percent of the financings, no new outside investor was involved, and 65 percent of the transactions had at least one new investor.

Fund B provided a summary of its transactions from a database. It had 204 transactions in 57 companies. The information included the share price (adjusted for

---

[6]Definitions of financing stages are in <u>Venture Capital Journal</u> (e.g. May 1987, p. 16) in its annual report on industry disbursements. Ruhnka & Young's (1987) survey of venture capitalists shows some variations in use of these terms. We found the standard terms easy to apply to most financings.

stock splits), the size of the transaction, the overall value of the company, and a code designating the company's maturity.[7] This allowed us to increase the sample by over two-thirds; however, the data do not allow a verification of the company's maturity, or whether it had new investors in a given transaction.

Before deciding which transactions could properly be used in an index, we analyzed the effects of the presence or absence of new investors on prices. In any financing without a new investor, the existing investors provide the entire amount. Conservatism or the desire for an attractive price may produce pricing below that which would prevail if an outsider participated, and therefore, below a market price. The absence of a new investor may also indicate that a company's problems make it unattractive. Those problems lead to a relatively low price, but the price is not necessarily below market value, defined as the price a fully informed outsider would pay.

To be useful in an index, transactions must be evaluated as ratios, which implies using them in adjacent pairs. Regarding the presence of new investors, three types of ratios may exist: 1) those with a new investor only in the first transaction, 2) those with a new investor in each of the pair; and 3) those with a new investor only in the second transaction. If new investors influence pricing, the ratio 3 should be the highest on the average, and ratio 1 the lowest.

To study the influence of new investors, we considered price ratios of fund A. Ratios, whose last transaction occurred before 1980 were dropped, because there were relatively few of them -- not enough to form an index in any case. This left 273 transactions in 67 companies which formed 224 price ratios. Of these we could identify a new investor in 186. Fifty-two had a new investor in the first transaction, 92 in both, and 42 in the second[8]. As shown in Table 3 the three types of price ratios were classified according to investment stage.

---

[7]These codes covered all cases from fund A except "start-up plus" and "sustaining." We categorize any later stage financing involving a price reduction as a "sustaining" financing.

[8]When a new investor participated in only one half of the ratio, the other half might definitely not have a new investor or it might be unknown. These were combined in order to get a reasonable number of transactons in each classification.

Table 3: Fund A's Transactions classified by
New Investor Participation

New Investors?	y– #	y– Ave. Ret.	yy #	yy Ave. Ret.	–y #	–y Ave. Ret.
Stage						
1. seed – start	4	86.8	1	35.1	0	
2. start – 1st	4	71.0	11	102.6	3	125.6
3. start – start+	2	28.9	3	105.5	0	
4. start+ – 1st	2	35.3	20	103.4	4	147.9
5. 1st – 2nd	7	66.5	21	40.3	3	50.4
6. 2nd – expansion	4	14.4	3	25.5	2	84.6
7. exp – exp	4	(1.4)	9	42.8	0	
8. any – sustain	8	(126.5)	7	(59.7)	5	8.4
9. any – IPO	1	24.8	6	192.7	8	126.8
10. any – acquired	0		5	31.1	9	10.2
11. any – write–off	3	(895.0)	0		0	
12. any – unknown	13	(23.3)	6	16.2	8	46.1
Total/Average	52	(51.9)	92	63.6	42	63.6

Notes: (1) New investor codes apply to the <u>two</u> transactions used to evaluate each return.
y– means a new investor participated in the first but not necessarily in the second.
yy means new investors (outsiders) participated in both.
–y means a new investor participated in the second but not necessarily in the first.
(2) Returns are in percent/year. They are continuous compounding, which can be less than -100 percent/year.
(3) "any" refers to any prior round. It is used to limit the number of stages. The results for the stages that have "any" are not usually sensitive to the prior round.

For a given stage, returns should increase as one moves from left to right in Table 3, and this appears to be the case. Although the number of price ratios in many of the cells is low, one can still apply a binomial test. If new investors do not influence prices, we would expect the higher return of a pairwise comparison between adjacent columns (for those financing stages which have returns in both columns) to have a 50 percent chance of being in either column. Table 4 performs this test and rejects equal likelihood at a 0.015 level.

Table 4: Test of Hypothesized Ordering of Returns
from Table 3

Ordering	True	False
$-y > yy$?	6	2
$yy > y-$?	8	2
Total	14	4

Notes: (1) Binomial test (one tail) rejects equal likelihood of true and false at p = 0.015.
(2) Eliminating sustaining rounds and "any - IPO" of y- changes results to 11 true and 4 false. Binomial test (one tail) rejects equal likelihood of true and false at p = 0.059.

To allow for the most obvious cases where the absence of a new investor may indicate internal problems, we removed the "sustaining" stage.[9] A binomial test still rejects equal price ratios at a 0.059 level.

The absence of a new investor apparently correlates with a low price, which causes some price ratios to be overstated (compared to the values which would occur if new investors participated in both financings) and some to be understated. However, they may still lead to an unbiased price index if the two influences offset each other in a typical sample. Additionally our evidence cannot show whether the absence of a new investor signals that internal problems exist. If so, the lower price may well be an appropriate market price. A binomial test (not shown), which compares the combined left and right columns of Table 4 with the center column, shows equal likelihood. Thus, the effects offset each other. We conclude that transactions may be included in the index without regard to the presence of new investors.

Not needing to identify the investor group means all the data from fund A may be used. The data from fund B, which has no data on investor groups, may also be

---

[9]We also removed one initial public offering where it was not obvious that any new investors participated in the public financing.

used. To the extent it matches the return distribution of fund A the index will be improved, because shifts over time in the proportions of price ratios from each fund will not impart a spurious movement to the index. Table 5 compares the returns from the two funds for each financing stage.

Table 5: Comparison of Funds A and B:
Types of Transactions, Price Ratios, Intervals

Stage	A percent of trans.	B percent of trans.	A Average Ratio	B Average Ratio	A Average Interval	B Average Interval
1. early – 1st	24.9	36.1	2.89	2.76	0.97	0.90
2. 1st – 2nd	16.1	22.5	1.93	1.85	1.14	0.88
3. 2nd – expansion	4.9	9.5	1.54	1.31	1.09	0.99
4. exp – exp	9.3	6.1	1.56	1.19	1.15	1.63
5. any – sustain	12.0	9.5	0.65	0.36	1.16	1.39
6. any – IPO	6.6	8.8	2.73	2.55	0.71	1.14
7. any – acquired	6.2	1.4	2.26	0.70	2.37	1.00
8. any – write-off	3.5	6.1	0.01	0.01	1.15	1.00
9. any – unknown	16.5		1.28		1.30	
Total/Average	100.0	100.0	1.87	1.88	1.18	1.03

Notes: (1) Average price ratio is presented here because ratios are used in calculating estimated prices.
(2) Average interval (in years) is the time between the two transactions used to calculate the price ratios.
(3) Fund A provided 224 values (price ratios) from 67 companies. Fund B provided 147 values from 57 companies.
(4) "Early - lst" includes "seed - start" , "start - lst" , "start - start+" , and "start+ - lst." It combines some small, similar categories.
(5) Because fund A has 16.5 percent of transactions in a "any - unknown" category, the percentage of transactions in other categories will on the average be only 84.5 of those in fund B.

Table 5 shows a high degree of similarity between funds A and B with respect to investment stages, price ratios and investment intervals. We conclude that the two data sets may properly be combined.

6. INDEX OF VENTURE CAPITAL EQUITY PRICES

The pilot database from two funds provides about 50 estimated prices for most months of the period 1980 to 1988. These include transactions from all states. Figure 4 shows two indices created from the pilot sample.[10]

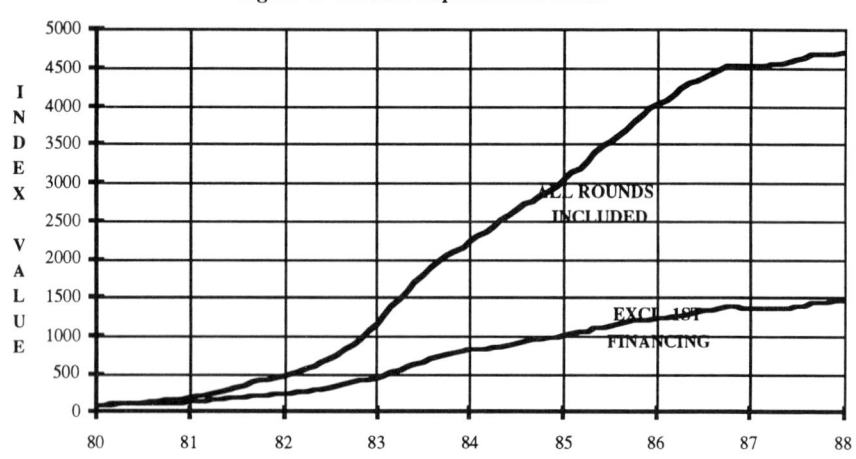

Figure 4: Venture Capital Price Index

The index with the higher value, Index I, includes all transactions in the sample. Because it reflects an equally weighted, buy and hold strategy, it is equivalent to investing only in the first outside financing by a company-which is usually at start-up. Further financing rounds by a company set prices for the stock purchased at the initial investment but no further purchase is implied. A further purchase would change the weights.

---

[10] Index1 has only 20 companies on January 1, 1980 but grows to 50 by mid 1982 and stays above that level until late 1986. By January 1, 1988 it drops to 13 companies. That is, only 20 companies in this database had transactions before January 1, 1980 and only 13 had transactions after January 1, 1988. One company is dropped from the sample because it has only one price ratio (about 400), which far exceeds all others and distorts the index, Index2 begins with 12 companies and reaches 40 by mid 1982. It stays above that level until late 1986. By January 1, 1988 it drops to 10 companies.

Index 2 excludes all initial investments by venture capitalists. It reflects the return to an investor who invests in the second external financing of a company. It is substantially lower than Index I, which implies that initial investments (largely start-ups) earn higher returns than follow-on investments on the average.

The performance of the two venture capital indices is dramatic, when compared to the public indices for the same period. Index I increases by a multiple of 47.1, Index 2 by 14.6. During the same interval, indices representing major public markets in the United States rose by a multiples of 3 to 4.5, as shown in Figure 5.

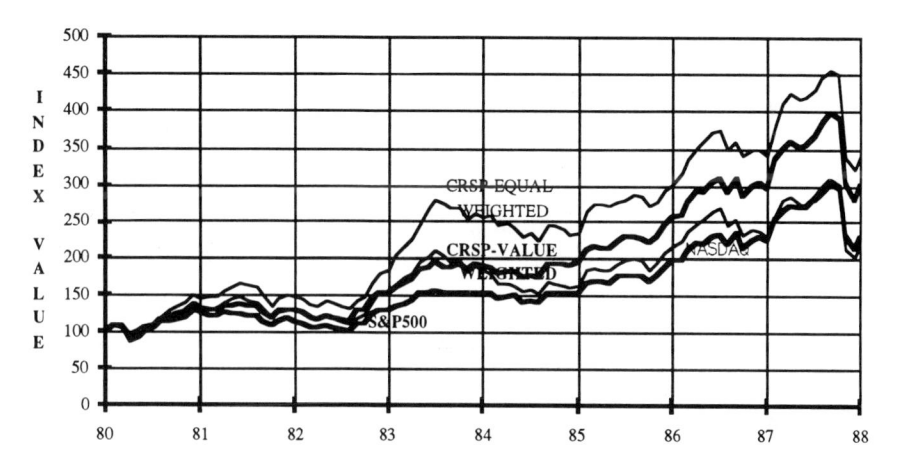

Figure 5: Major Public Market Indices

Much of the performance comes from investing in the initial external financings as indicated by the difference between Index 1 and Index 2. The implied investment strategy of the Index clearly influences its performance. Index1 is a "buy and hold" strategy of investing $1 (with minor variations, described in the Appendix, for stocks which enter the index after inception) in the first external financing of each company with no further investment in subsequent financings. Index 2 is the same, except the investment occurs only in the second financing.

Although equal investment may characterize venture capitalists, investing in only one financing round does not. Thus we could (but do not) calculate an index based on a strategy of investing $1 (approximately) in every financing round. It would lie between Index 1 and Index 2.

A second type of index would focus on a single financing stage. A security would drop out of the index when the financing of the next stage occurred. Although this does not follow a realistic strategy, it would provide useful guidance to investors.

The growth by a factor of 47.1 in Index 1 does mean that a typical investment in the initial financings of our sample companies grew by a factor of 47.1 over the 1980-1987 period. It means that one could realize a multiple of 47.1 by following a "buy and hold"[11] policy in which one invests approximately $1 (see the appendix for an exact expression) in any new opportunity and reinvests any realized returns in the remaining securities in proportion to their values. The actual portfolio changes substantially over time. Our sample of 134 companies produces a set of about 60 estimated prices at most times, which suggests that about 2.2 companies are needed to produce 8 years of prices. Thus the portfolio turns over in about 3.6 years.

Public indices should be interpreted the same way. However their turnover in membership is much lower, which allows one to view them as reflecting the change in an average stock. That is, one can ignore the occasional changes in the index portfolio without changing the results very much.

Although the private firms in our index exceed the public indices by a wide margin, Table 6 shows that the advantage occurred early in the decade. In the three years 1985-87 the returns on the CRSP Value Weighted Index,[12] which is a good proxy for the stock market as a whole, are about the same as the returns on Venture IndexI, and are slightly above the returns of Index2.

---

[11]"Hold" in this case means holding until an initial public offering, a sale of the company, or a write-off. If none of these events have happened by 1988, a security is removed from the index at the date of its latest private transaction, because extrapolating beyond the last price would be inappropriate. The movement of prices described in footnote 4 means that any extrapolation would reflect only the drift (μdt) in prices, not the random element (dB). Since the appropriate estimate of the drift at any specific time is the movement of the index itself, extrapolation would provide no additional information.

[12]The CRSP Value Weighted Index has two advantages over the S@P 500: it covers all stocks on the New York Stock Exchange, and it includes dividends. The latter accounts for most of its 3.9 percent annual advantage over the S@@P 500.

Table 6: Annual Rates of Return of Venture Capital Index
and of Other Stock Market Indices

Year	VC Index1	VC Index2	S&P 500	NASDAQ	CRSP VW	CRSP EW
1980	86.2	31.7	25.8	33.8	33.2	45.0
1981	151.0	78.4	(9.7)	(3.2)	(4.1)	0.7
1982	142.1	91.3	14.8	18.7	20.5	26.7
1983	96.5	77.2	17.2	19.8	22.7	38.9
1984	36.1	25.2	1.5	(11.3)	3.0	(8.8)
1985	33.2	23.8	26.3	31.4	31.3	28.9
1986	12.3	10.4	14.7	7.3	15.7	12.4
1987	4.1	7.0	2.0	(5.3)	1.7	(0.3)
Average	70.2	43.1	11.6	11.4	15.5	17.9
Std. Dev.	65.4	38.5	14.4	19.5	16.0	22.6

Notes: (1) VC Index1 is the Venture Capital Index with all the financing rounds included.
(2) VC Index2 is the Venture Capital Index with the first financing excluded.
(3) CRSP VW is the CRSP Value Weighted Index.
(4) CRSP EW is the CRSP Equally Weighted Index.
(5) Venture Capital Indices are equally weighted with a "buy and hold" approach.
Month end prices are estimated.
(6) S & P 500, NASDAQ, and CRSP Value Weighted are value weighted.
(7) CRSP Equally Weighted Index assumes monthly reallocation of portfolio to equalize holdings.

The advantage of Index1 over Index2 also narrowed considerably after 1983. The decline in returns in the later years could have two sources: a decrease in returns for each stage of investment, or a shift in the mix of investments toward stages with lower returns. Table 7 divides the price ratios into those ending prior to 1985 and those ending in 1985 and beyond. It suggests that in 1985-1987 both a decline in price ratios at most financing stages and a shift in mix contribute to a 0.78 decline in the average price ratio. That drop can be allocated as follows:

$$\overline{R}_E - \overline{R}_L = \sum [p_{E_i}(\overline{R}_{E_i} - \overline{R}_{L_i}) + (p_{E_i} - p_{L_i})\overline{R}_{E_i} - (p_{E_i} - p_{L_i})(\overline{R}_{E_i} - \overline{R}_{L_i})]$$

where p_{E_i} and p_{L_i} are the Proportions of investments, R_{e_i} and R_{l_i} are the average price ratios in stage i in 1980-84 and 1985-87 respectively. The first term shows the effect of the average change in price ratio, assuming a constant mix of stages. Its value is 0.72. The second term comes from a changing mix of stages, assuming no change in price ratios. Its value is 0.17. These two imply a drop in the average price ratio of 0.89. The third term subtracts the covariance of changes in price ratios and changes in mix. Its value is -0.11. This indicates a positive covariance-stages whose proportions declined also had larger than average declines in price ratios.

Table 7: Comparison of Two Periods: 1980–84 and 1985–87
Types of Transactions, Price Ratios,[3] Intervals[3]

Stage	80–84 percent of trans.	85–87 percent of trans.	80–84 Average Ratio	85–87 Average Ratio	80–84 Average Interval	85–87 Average Interval
1. early – 1st[3]	37.2	19.5	3.12	2.076	0.93	0.97
2. 1st – 2nd	19.8	17.6	2.04	1.67	0.90	1.19
3. 2nd – expansion	5.7	8.5	1.59	1.24	0.93	1.13
4. exp – exp	5.2	12.5	1.34	1.51	0.87	1.54
5. any – sustain	10.8	9.1	0.63	0.40	1.23	1.26
6. any – IPO	7.6	5.9	3.19	1.66	0.82	1.15
7. any – acquired	0.5	9.8	6.00	1.80	1.11	2.27
8. any – write–off	4.7	4.6	0.01	0.01	0.82	1.44
9. any – unknown	8.5	12.5	1.62	0.95	1.32	1.28
Total/Average (all)	100.0	100.0	2.20	1.42	0.97	1.32
Total/Average (2–9)	62.8	80.5	1.66	1.26	1.00	1.40

Notes:
(1) Combined data from funds A and B.
(2) Time periods are 1/1/80 to 31/12/84 and 1/1/85 to 31/12/87.
(3) These terms are defined in notes to Table 5.
(4) The period 1980-84 includes 216 values. The period 1985-87 includes 155 values, for a total of 371. Timing of an observation is given by the year of the second of two transactions.

Leaving out line 1 of Table 7 we may perform the same analysis for the transactions of Index2. The overall decline in the average price ratio is 0.40. The three effects are respectively 0.48 , -0.44 and 0.36. The decline in price ratios within stages is about offset by an improved mix of stages. However, a negative correlation between changes in price ratios for each stage, and the change in proportion of that stage almost nullifies an otherwise favourable shift in the transaction mix.

Although we do not analyze the effect of the longer interval between investments in the latter period, it causes a further lowering of rates of return beyond the effect of the declining average price ratio.

Annual returns on Indexl and Index2 also converge in the 1985-1987 period. The advantage of investing in start-up companies almost disappears.

7. DISCUSSION

How closely the estimated index follows the true index depends on the standard errors of the individual price estimates, the extent to which the errors at any time are correlated, and the number of securities in the index. We believe the correlated portion of the errors can be largely eliminated because they should follow the overall stock market (e.g. the S & P 500) and are therefore predictable. The uncorrelated errors can be reduced by increasing the number of securities in the index. We are currently working on an estimate of the standard error of the index.

One concern about using a broader data set is the degree to which the price ratios reflect market prices-participation by a new investor is a sufficient but not necessary condition. Our data from fund A, in which the investor group was known for almost 100 price ratios, suggests that prices without new investors, although they are different, tend to produce offsetting under- and over-estimates. Thus a broad data set can probably be used without careful checking into the circumstances of each transaction.

A possible barrier to the creation of a venture capital index is the value venture capitalists attach to their private information about prices. Such information may give a competitive advantage to a venture capitalist in negotiating a transaction. However, each venture capitalist knows only a small fraction of the recent transaction prices and those prices are inherently "noisy". In effect, no individual has enough private information to derive much benefit from it, but the value of pooling the information into a common index can benefit everyone.

Venture capitalists consider their fund's performance to be highly confidential. The index is benign in the extent to which it invades a fund's privacy. It does not require detailed, information about any fund's investments, because it does not tie transactions to funds. Individual prices are not widely publicized, but they are less confidential than individual fund performance. Additionally, the index uses prices of actual transactions, whereas fund performance may in some cases include adjustments based on judgement. Thus it represents a consistent formula for summarizing the level and movement of the venture capital market.

Bygrave, et.al. (1989) and Brophy & Guthner (1988) have recently examined the performance of venture capital portfolios, so we might briefly compare results and methods.

Our annual returns are generally above theirs although patterns are similar.[13] Brophy & Guthner (1988) study the twelve venture capital funds which were publicly traded during 1981-1985. Their average annual return (using market values of the funds) is 18.5 percent. Our sample shows annual average returns of 91.8 percent and 59.2 percent for Indexl and Index2 respectively.

Bygrave. et. al. (1987) appear to find returns which are close to zero during 1984 and 1985, following a period of high returns. The pattern is the same as shown by our indices, although returns from our pilot sample are higher than theirs. Thus our sample represents an above average set of companies, and the specific values of the index should not be viewed as indicative of industry performance.

Bygrave, et. al. measure compound rates of return from the inception of individual funds. This is a geometric average of performance over individual years. Thus it will change more slowly than our index. It also reflects each fund's continuing investment activity. An index such as ours has advantages for many, but not all, purposes. First, it may be calculated with a shorter lag, because it does not require overall data about fund performance, which is usually available only once a year. Second, its construction is very similar to that of other stock market indices, allowing relatively easy comparison. Third, it responds more quickly to market changes. It is an efficient use of the information contained in individual prices. Thus it can reduce the "recognition lag" of venture capitalists or investors as to changes of price levels in the market. Fourth, it makes possible a new way to judge the performance of individual portfolios. Their changes in value on a year to year basis can be compared against an index, which if broadly based will represent the industry's average performance.

With further work we believe reliable estimates of dispersion (lr in footnote 4) are possible. This will allow one to estimate whether a fund's performance represents a "random" deviation from the index, or whether it truly represents a systematic difference.

---

[13]This is a pilot study of a method and uses data from only two funds. We do not suggest it is representative. However, very little has been published on the performance of venture capital investments; so our pilot sample of 477 transactions in 124 companies (in which over 200 venture capital firms invested) is a significant database.

APPENDIX A

Since stocks may enter at times other then $t = 0$, the reference will be to the entry time of each stock ($t = e_i$) as it enters the index. The price ratios in (2) become P_{it}/P_{ie}. At any time a new security is added-say at $t+$ which is an instant after the close of period t- the adjustment is changed as follows:

$$B_0 \frac{A_{t+}}{N+1} \sum_{i=1}^{N+1} \left(\frac{P_{it}}{P_{ie_i}}\right) = I_{t+} = I_t = B_0 \frac{A_t}{N} \sum_{i=1}^{N} \left(\frac{P_{it}}{P_{ie_i}}\right)$$

It is helpful to think of $A_{t+}/N + 1$ and A_t/N as "index divisors." Thus, the left-hand side of expression (1A) can be written as:

$$\frac{B_0}{D_{t+}} \sum_{i=1}^{N+1} \left(\frac{P_{it}}{P_{ie_i}}\right) = I_{t+} \text{, where } D_{t+} = \frac{N+1}{A_{t+}}$$

The index divisor can be calculated directly as:

$$D_{t+} = \frac{B_0}{I_t} \sum_{i=1}^{N+1} \left(\frac{P_{it}}{P_{ie_i}}\right)$$

This procedure amounts to selling equal fractions of each holding when a new stock enters. The amount sold is sufficient to acquire $\$_t$ is somewhat less than $1, but approaches it as I_tN becomes large. The proportion of the portfolio which is sold is When a stock leaves the index (think of it as being sold), its value is allocated to the remaining holdings by purchasing equal number of shares of each.

For stock splits the adjustment is different, P_{it} and P_{ie}, are each divided by the split ratio which means P_{it}/P_{ie}, is unchanged, and the future path of the index is unaffected by the split. In contrast, adjusting for a split via the divisor would change the future path of the index because it would lower $P_{it}/P_{it'}$; namely, P_{it} would drop to the post split value and P_{ie}, would be unchanged.

REFERENCES

Brophy, D.J. and Guthner, M.W. 1988. Publicly traded venture capital funds: Implications for institutional "Funds of Funds" investors. Journal of Business Venturing 3(3): 187-206.

Bygrave, W., Fast, N., Khoylian, R., Vincent, L. and Yue, W. 1989. Early rates of return of 131 venture capital funds started 1978-1984. Journal of Business Venturing 4(2): 93-105.

Fisher, L. 1966 Some new stock market indexes. Journal of Business 29(1): 191-225.

Ohlson, J. and Rosenberg, B. 1982. Systematic risk of the CRSP equal-weighted common stock index: A history estimated by stochastic-parameter regression. Journal of Business 55(1): 121-145.

Ruhnka, J.C. and Young, J.E. 1987. A venture capital model of the development process for new ventures. Journal of Business Venturing 2(2): 167-184.

Schwert, G.W. 1990. Indexes of U.S. stock prices from 1802 to 1987. Journal of Business 63(3): 399-426.

Venture Capital Journal annual Survey of Venture Capital Fund Disbursements. e.g. May, 1987.

Interplay Among Strategy, Environment, Competitive Behavior and Performance on Entering Industrial Markets

Critique
by
Tone Ostgaard, *Imperial College*

DEFINING THE WORLD

Investigators' practice of sampling from different populations has been argued to have hindered progress of empirical entrepreneurship research, and despite extensive debate, no consensus on the definition of entrepreneurship has appeared (VanderWerf and Rosh, 1989). The alternative to a consensual definition of the field is to make the differences in populations sampled explicit in order to achieve sample comparability or progress. VanderWerf and Brush (1989) recommend that every empirical study specify its population on each of the selection criteria commonly used and restated as dimensions of variations of business units: age and size of business unit, industry and relation to parent. For those dimensions that are not used as sample selection criteria, researchers are recommended to measure and report the range of variation in the final sample. Such a practice will facilitate decisions about which populations to study by making the alternatives more precise and explicit. It will also facilitate comparisons.

Unfortunately the paper adds to the list of papers giving few or no descriptions of the population, sample size and sample characteristics, e.g. industry and initial and present firm size. And yet, start-up size has been found to have an effect both on new venture survival (Birley, 1986; Kirchhoff and Phillips, 1989; Cooper et al, 1988) and on subsequent growth (Bannock and Gray, 1989; Cooper, et al, 1989). Firm size may further moderate the relationship between competitive aggressiveness and performance under hostile environmental conditions in terms of a minimum size level before they can benefit from the implementation of aggressive strategies.

The sample appears to be biased in favor of high-potential businesses both in terms of their very size as well as the potential resource base of the parent. The authors contend that the findings may have no relevance to smaller firms or independent start-ups. As to what size a new venture, corporate or independent, must have in order to be affected is not known.

The reader is further given little information as to what constitutes market share, ROI, and further share gains and improvements in ROI. No figures are given. What comprises "promising initial performance" for ROI to be positive is somewhat unclear.

COMPETITIVE CHANGE

The topic of the paper is undoubtedly interesting as it attempts to clarify relations among competitive environment, strategy, competitive response and performance _over time_. Unfortunately, measures of munificence are determined only once in the data base: at the pre-entry stage of a new product. The authors argue that degree of munificence is unlikely to change very much in four years. As the measures of munificence include product life cycle maturity, the number of immediate customers and market growth rate, the extent of change may however be dependent upon the industry in question even in industrial markets.

The only environmental measure, beside competitor response, in years 3-4 of the venture is one of hostility. These limitations in the data put constraints on the results pertinent to hypotheses 6, 7, and 8 and should also be considered in view of the conclusions on munificence being a predictor of investment aggressiveness and competitor response at later stages of the corporate venture.

Despite uniform agreement in the literature on the combined impact of strategy and environment on performance (McDougall, 1987; Hofer and Sandberg, 1987), no such implications are drawn directly in the paper, other than for competitive response. Competitive reaction and strategy are modelled as shaping market share performance.

AGGRESSIVENESS--A SUCCESSFUL STRATEGY?

Tsai, MacMillan and McGrath conclude that market aggressiveness has "a profound and consistent positive correlation with market share gains". The same holds for investment aggressiveness. Are the results to be interpreted as implying that _low_ market and investment aggressiveness have a corresponding negative relationship to market share and ROI?

Despite the larger pool of resources that corporate ventures enjoy, aggressive market entry strategies have not been proven equally successful under all environmental conditions (Woo and Cooper, 1981; McDougall, 1987).

Covin and Slevin (1990) found an entrepreneurial strategic posture, measured by innovation, risk taking and proactivity, to be most positively related to performance in _emerging_ (munificent) industries. The relationship was less positive among firms in growing industries and negative among firms in mature industries. Operating efficiency and cost competitiveness are suggested to be more predictive of high performance in mature industries. Performance was measured on a range of financial indicators as well as sales and growth measures. Behaving in an "entrepreneurial" manner then may not be a viable goal for new ventures in all industry life cycle stages. Their results are supported in this paper, as environmental munificence was found to relate positively to both investment and marketing aggressiveness.

Woo and Cooper (1982) studied 40 high-performing low-share manufacturing firms over a three-year period. Most of them were divisions of large corporations. The majority of profitable low market share companies were found in less turbulent industries characterized by slow growth (i.e. less munificent) and few product and process changes. This finding was explained as providing a more stable environment, in which there is less elbowing to gain market share. No substantial differences in the environment could be found between effective and ineffective low-share businesses. The differences between these two groups of companies related more to how they competed in each environment. The absence of a clear focus seemed to characterize ineffective businesses as they competed aggressively along many fronts: broad product lines, advertising, selling expenses, product R&D, and vertical integration; all of which demand still more resources. Low-share businesses that pursue a specific focused competitive strategy, often emphasizing quality and cost, seemed to do best.

In a study of independent and corporate ventures from 7 industry sectors, McDougall (1987) identified three distinctly different strategies that fell within the aggressive entry category. Little commonality however, was found among the groups other than large scale entry and rapid growth objectives. Two clusters shared a joint emphasis on cost and price control, but no other similarities. In terms of performance, none of the three large scale venture groups achieved success by Biggadike's market share standard or by ROS and ROI measures.

The above discussion suggests that market aggressiveness is by no means a uni-dimensional strategy and that no single strategy appears to always work best on every performance measure.

Market aggressiveness is measured by the degree of emphasis on product quality, promotion expenditure and price. Promotion expenditures may, however, not be a critical strategy variable in industrial markets. Also, is market aggressiveness a uni-dimensional construct, or are there in fact several ways of aggressively competing in the market?

Quality and promotion can be argued to constitute two distinct competitive strategies. Luchs (1990) argues that quality in itself can constitute a competitive weapon; and lead to high profitability and market share. Woo and Cooper (1981) found effective low-share businesses in mature markets adopting an aggressive marketing strategy with less emphasis on quality, competitive prices, or R&D.

CONCLUSION

The strategic options available to small firms and their relative impact should be somewhat further analyzed before concluding that "little is gained by timidly entering the markets". This is even more important considering the dramatic effects of an aggressive entry when such a strategy in fact should not have been undertaken. The content of new venture strategy may need to be identified along several dimensions, including dimensions within the aggressive entry category. McDougall concludes that an emerging taxonomy of new venture strategies could start with a scale of entry (large and aggressive versus small and limited growth) at one level and then proceed to other key elements like vertical integration, channel usage, product characteristics, cost/price emphasis, innovation, service, and customer market orientation, which would help map out alternative strategies.

REFERENCES

Birley, S.J. The Role of New Firms: Births, Deaths and Job Generation, Strategic Management Journal, Vol.7, 1986, 361-376.

Bannock, G. and Gray, C. The Growing Small Business in Britain: Trends in Quarterly Profiles of Growing Small Firms 1984-88, Piccola impresa/Small business, No.3, 1989, 3-25.

Cooper, A.C., Woo, C.Y. and Dunkelberg, W.C. Entrepreneurship and the Initial Size of Firms, Journal of Business Venturing, 4, 1989, 317-332.

Cooper, A.C., Dunkelberg, W.C. and Woo, C.Y. Survival and Failure: A Longitudinal Study, Frontiers of Entrepreneurship Research, Babson College, 1988, 225-237.

Covin, J.G. and Slevin, D.P. New Venture Strategic Posture, Structure, and Performance: An Industry Life Cycle Analysis, Journal of Business Venturing, No.5, 1990, 12-35.

Hofer, C.W. and Sandberg, W.R. Improving New Venture Performance: Some Guidelines for Success, American Journal of Small Business, Summer 1987, 11-25.

Kirchhoff, B.A. and Phillips, B.D. Innovation and Growth Among New Firms in the U.S. Economy, Frontiers of Entrepreneurship Research, Babson College, 1989, 173-188.

Luchs, B. Quality as a Strategic Weapon: Measuring Relative Quality, Value, and Market Differentiation, European Business Journal, Vol.2, 4, 1990, 34-47.

McDougall, P.P. An Analysis of Strategy, Entry Barriers, and Origin as Factors Explaining New Venture Performance, PhD Dissertation, University of South Carolina, 1987.

VanderWerf, P.A. and Brush, C.G. Achieving Empirical Progress in an Undefined Field, Entrepreneurship Theory and Practice, Vol.14, No.2, Winter 1989, 45-58.

Woo, C.Y. and Cooper, A. Strategies of Effective Low Share Businesses, Strategic Management Journal, 2, 1981, 301-318.

International Perspectives on Entrepreneurship Research 1991
S. Birley, I.C. MacMillan (editors) / S. Subramony (technical editor)
© 1992 Elsevier Science Publishers B.V. All rights reserved.

INTERPLAY AMONG STRATEGY, ENVIRONMENT, COMPETITIVE BEHAVIOR AND PERFORMANCE ON ENTERING INDUSTRIAL MARKETS

MING HONE TSAI, *NATIONAL CENTRAL UNIVERSITY OF TAIWAN*
IAN C. MACMILLAN, *THE WHARTON SCHOOL, UNIVERSITY OF PENNSYLVANIA*
RITA GUNTHER McGRATH, *THE WHARTON SCHOOL, UNIVERSITY OF PENNSYLVANIA*[1]

SUMMARY:

Ten hypotheses about the relations among environmental, strategic and competitive factors are tested, utilizing longitudinal data from the PIMS start-up database. Two key environmental constructs, hostility and munificence, are found to be of importance in predicting aggressiveness of entry into industrial markets, which together with environmental conditions then correlates with competitor response and initial market share. Market share success, competitor response and environmental conditions predict subsequent strategic aggressiveness and venture performance four years after entry.

INTRODUCTION

It is generally accepted that firm strategy and environment are of critical importance in determining the outcome of a corporate venturing effort (Biggadike, 1979; Cooper, 1979, 1983; Hobson and Morrison, 1983; MacMillan and Day, 1987; Tsai, MacMillan and Low, 1990). Although a stream of research has concerned itself with this question, very little clarifies the complex relations among competitive environment, firm strategy, competitive response and performance over time.

A model linking these constructs is proposed here. Its essence is that performance (defined as market share) of a corporate venture in a new industrial market can be viewed as a function of competitive conditions, strategic conduct and competitive response over time. This study links these variables together in such a way that their temporal relations become clearer. To develop this model, the Profit Impact of Market Strategy (PIMS) STR4 database was utilized. This database contains information about start-up ventures over several time periods.

---

[1]The authors wish to thank the Sol C. Snider Entrepreneurial Center of the Wharton School, University of Pennsylvannia, and the Ministry of Education of Taiwan for their support.

According to the proposed model, at the time of entry two key features of the competitive environment for a corporate venture are munificence and hostility. Management's view of munificence and hostility shapes aggressiveness of entry into the market. Competitors face a similar situation, so their response to the entry of a new venture is due in part to hostility and munificence, and also in part to the new entrants' level of aggressiveness. As the venture progresses, the new entrant must, in light of competitive response and changes in competitive environment, again decide on the aggressiveness of its strategy, initiating a new round of competitive responses and venture outcomes.

A major purpose of this paper is to explore the usefulness of two important constructs, munificence and hostility, in explaining the relations among strategy, environment, competitive response and performance.

REVIEW OF THE "AGGRESSIVE ENTRY PERSPECTIVE IN STRATEGY AND ORGANIZATIONAL RESEARCH

Two perspectives have dominated discussions about the relations among environment, strategy and venture performance in the 1970s and 1980s. The population ecology perspective suggests that organizations survive on the basis of selection by the environment (Hannan and Freeman, 1977, 1984; Aldrich 1979; Greenfield and Strickon, 1986). In the most extreme examples of this view, deliberate management strategies have a limited influence over firm survival, while a far larger influence is exerted by conditions in the environment. A contrasting perspective is offered by the strategic adaptation model discussed in Child (1972); Andrews (1980); Porter (1980); Vesper (1980), and Timmons (1982). In this view, choices made by a venture's decision-makers profoundly influence the venture's future.

With both theoretical perspectives gaining substantiation in ongoing empirical research programs, there has been increased interest on the part of several authors to reconcile the two (Tushman and Anderson, 1986; Van de Ven, Hudson & Schroeder, 1984; Singh, House & Tucker, 1986; Aldrich and Auster, 1986). This paper is included in this stream of work. The view taken here is that both perspectives are necessary to understand the complex relations among strategy and environment in firms' struggles to bring new products to market. Without the element of randomness in the population ecology perspective, one would underestimate the enormous influence of environmental conditions at the time of birth for a new venture. Without a strategic management perspective, one would overlook the role of conscious choice in achieving (or not achieving) a given result.

Given this background, how should one proceed to begin an empirical study of the relations of strategy and environment to new corporate venture performance?

One point of departure is provided by writers who stress the importance of entry aggressiveness in achieving results. Several studies (Biggadike, 1979; Hobson and Morrison, 1983; MacMillan and Day, 1986) conclude that corporations entering an established industrial market should do so aggressively. In other words, they should be prepared to heavily promote products, price them competitively and make sure that they are of superior quality in order to build market share from the start.

If these results are correct it should be possible to develop a model which demonstrates the time relation among environmental, strategy, and competitive response variables and performance of the venture, provided longitudinal data can be found. The PIMS STR4 database is a reasonably large longitudinal database focusing exclusively on corporate start-ups, which therefore permits such a time-related study. Consequently, a model is proposed and tested below, which builds upon the propositions of research advocating an aggressive entry position for a new venture, and which takes into account the temporal linkages among strategic conduct, environmental conditions, competitive reaction and performance.

CHARACTERISTICS OF ENVIRONMENT, STRATEGIC BEHAVIOR, COMPETITIVE RESPONSE AND PERFORMANCE

Munificence and Hostility

The analysis of Tsai et al (1990) identified two important constructs that shape this view of the venturing process for entering firms. The first is the "munificence" of the environment (Staw and Szwajkowski, 1975; Tussle and Gerwin, 1980; Dess and Oriser, 1987; Yasai-Arkedeni, 1989). Munificence reflects the "quality" of the opportunity - the degree of richness or sparseness of the niche being entered. In ecological terms this compares with the availability of nutrients in an ecological niche.

The second characteristic of the environment is its "hostility" (Grinyer, Al-bazazz and Yasai-Arkedeni, 1980; Miller and Friesen, 1983; Covin and Slevin, 1989). In ecological terms hostility compares with the population density of organisms competing for nutrients in the niche. Hostility reflects the fierceness of competition that the firm encounters when it attempts to enter.

Some theorists have conceived of munificence and hostility as opposite ends of a continuum. While we acknowledge that the two concepts are related, there is value in conceiving each as a related but separate distinct construct. Again, using an ecological analogy: from the point of view of human beings, the plains of Africa are both munificent and hostile, whereas the plains of North America are munificent and benign, there being less predators, disease and so on in North America than Africa. Munificence captures the structure and nature of the market being entered, while hostility captures the structure and nature of the firms competing for that market. Thus, some new venture opportunities have much more potential than others, and holding the quality potential of the opportunity constant, some markets are more hotly contested than others. Obviously, the most favorable circumstance for a new venture is to pursue an opportunity with high munificence under conditions of limited hostility. Tsai, MacMillan and Low (1990) demonstrated that munificence and hostility are separately related to performance.

Sahlman and Stevenson (1985) provide an interesting practical illustration of the distinction between munificence and hostility in their discussion of the fate of new entrants into the Winchester Disk Drive industry from 1977 to 1984. The industry was broadly recognized as munificent, in that it had very high growth, and many customers in a rapidly broadening customer base. This recognition prompted the entrance of over 70 drive manufacturers, each vying for a small share of this rich market. Once this many players entered the market, an industry that had been high in munificence and relatively low in hostility rapidly became one that was high in both munificence and hostility.

Managerial choice: Aggressiveness of entry

While environment is important, it is not the only influence on venture outcome. The ecological model, in its pure form, fails to address the effects of conscious managerial choice. In so doing, we feel that it does not adequately treat the factors that differentiate the performances of firms from one another. The ecological perspective requires supplementation from the strategic adaptation camp -- managers in firms make deliberate choices for the deployment of resources. The choices made affect, not only the individual firm, but the competitive environment as well (Porter, 1980; Miles and Snow, 1978; Hofer and Schendel, 1978; Miller, 1987).

Those in charge of introducing a corporate venture are faced with the task of determining how best to take advantage of whatever environment appears to exist in the industry they are entering. In exercising this judgment, the crucial entry decision is the aggressiveness of entry - the aggressiveness with which the firm will market the product and the aggressiveness with which it will invest in the venture. This strategic conduct on entry is influenced by environmental hostility and munificence, providing the link between environment and strategic behavior. Next, the aggressiveness of entry and environmental conditions together shape the aggressiveness of competitive response. Finally strategic conduct and competitive reaction will determine the initial outcome for the venture, and this outcome sets the stage for the next round of competition.

The above model is therefore specific in both predicted relations among variables and in the predicted sequences:

- competitive conditions in the environment shape the aggressiveness of strategic conduct on entry.

- together, competitiveness of the market and aggressiveness of entry shape competitive response.

- strategic conduct on entry and competitive reaction shape first-cycle market share performance.[1]

- initial performance and competitive reaction are associated with the subsequent aggressiveness of later strategic conduct.

- this aggressiveness again shapes competitive response, and the cycle is repeated.

An important issue in such a study is how to assess outcomes of the venture. In our view, there has yet to be a truly satisfactory resolution for the problem of how organizational performance is to be defined. The approach offered by the population ecologists (avoidance of organizational death) lumps together the organization enjoying spectacular growth and profitability with the organization in poor economic health.[2] Other commonly used measures of performance, such as growth in people, growth in income, growth in sales, return on investment, or various relative measures of these factors have all been found to be problematic, particularly for start-up businesses (see Miller, Wilson & Adams, 1988, for a discussion of performance measure shortcomings).

There are fewer problems associated with relative market share gain than with any of the other commonly utilized measures (see Woo & Cooper, 1981; Buzzell, Gale and Sultan 1975; and Prescott, Kohli & Venkatraman, 1986 for discussions of the relation between market share and long-term profitability). Market share gain reflects the market acceptance of the new entrant's product. In this way, the firm's exploitation of munificence in the environment can be determined. Similarly, since the firm is being measured against other firms in the market, rather than against its own earlier performance, market share gain captures how the firm copes with environmental hostility. Finally, since this study focuses on firms entering existing markets, rather than on firms who create new markets from scratch, the problem of beginning with 100% of the market and losing share over time (Miller, Wilson & Adams, 1988) is not an issue here.

THE STUDY, VARIABLES AND MEASURES

Since the focus here is on the relations among strategic variables over time, this study used the PIMS STR4 database. This is a large, longitudinal database focusing exclusively on corporate business start-ups -- corporate ventures that represent "a business marketing a product or service that the parent company has not previously marketed and that requires the parent company to obtain new equipment or new people or new knowledge" (Biggadike, 1979:104). The sample selected from this database contains information on corporate ventures into industrial markets, collected over four years. The ventures are "divisions or profit centers which sell a distinct set of products or services within a well-defined industrial market and competitive setting" (Tsai, MacMillan and Low, 1990:9). In a limited number of cases, our study utilizes information at year one through four, then again for years two through five for the same venture. This increases the number of data points in the study.

As Tsai, MacMillan and Low (1990) note, the STR4 database and the associated main PIMS database have several well-documented drawbacks which render them less than perfect. Limitations include variability in the ways respondents interpret questionnaire items, the constraints imposed by anonymity and limitations of the AQD statistical analysis package. Overall, however, those who have worked with the STR4 and main PIMS database (Anderson and Paine, 1978; Ramanujam and Venkatraman, 1984; Woo & Cooper, 1981; Hambrick, MacMillan and Day, 1982; Lambkin, 1988) have concluded that PIMS data are reliable and of high quality. In addition, STR4 remains one of the largest and most comprehensive sources of available data on corporate venturing. The reader should note that the database utilized for this study is not the main PIMS database, but rather was collected by Biggadike specifically to study corporate ventures.

Variable Selection

Environmental variables were chosen from among those available in the STR4 database to measure the constructs described above. Variables were selected on the basis of their promise to adequately operationalize the constructs and to convey the behavior of these constructs over time.

MUNIFICENCE

Three measures in the STR4 database portray the munificence of the market prior to entry of the new firm. They are: Product life cycle maturity, Number of immediate customers, and Market growth rate.

In general, the earlier in the life-cycle of a product, the better the quality of the opportunities associated with that product (Rink & Swan, 1979; Tellis & Crawford, 1981). As a product matures, new entrants will find it increasingly difficult to find "easy" sales and gain a substantial share of the market. So, a high score on this variable is designated to be associated with lower degrees of munificence.

Similarly, the larger the <u>number of immediate customers</u>, the more difficult for the firm to reach them, hence the less accessible that particular market will be to the new entrant[3], so, a large number of immediate customers is presumed to be associated with lower munificence.

Finally, a rapid <u>market growth</u> will tend to be more munificent than a stable one. In this case, a high number is associated with high munificence.

The construct "munificence" is measured by the combination of values for these three variables. Scores for each individual variable were first divided into thirds, generating a low, medium and high category for each variable. Then each category was assigned a value from 1 to 3. Life cycle maturity and number of customers were assigned a value of 1 for the top third and 3 for the bottom third because higher scores meant lower munificence. Market growth was assigned a value of 1 for the bottom third and 3 for the top third because higher scores mean higher munificence. Thus every variable now had a that which ranged from low (one point) to high (3 points). To measure munificence, a combined score was then calculated by summing the individual values for each of the three variables. Thus a combined score of 3 reflected low munificence (values of 1 for each variable) while a score of 9 reflected high munificence (values of 3 on all three of the variables).

The variables included in the munificence measure are determined only once in the STR4 database: at the pre-entry stage of a new product. Although it would be interesting to note whether changes in these values occurred over time, this information is not available in STR4. Furthermore, these basic environmental conditions are unlikely to change much for the four years we studied in the database.

HOSTILITY (INITIAL AND LATER)

Two measures in the STR4 database relate to the degree of competitiveness in the environment (Tsai, Low and MacMillan, 1990): Largest competitor dependence and Top three competitors share.

A competitor who is heavily <u>dependent</u> upon a given marketplace is likely to fight very hard to retain its position in that marketplace. It would be reasonable, therefore, to conclude that heavy dependence of the largest competitor on the market would increase the hostility of the environment for the new entrant.

Similarly, well-entrenched competitors, as would be suggested by <u>large shares for the top three number of competitors at the start of the venture</u>, indicate that this marketplace is likely to be heavily contested and more hostile to a newcomer. The "hostility" construct was created in a similar manner to that of "munificence": responses were divided into thirds, and a combined score developed which ranged from low (2) to high (6) for each response.

A second variable, Later Hostility, is used to measure hostility in the second cycle of the study. Largest competitor dependence continues to form the first part of the construct, but the second is changed to top three competitor's share (end). This represents the top three competitors combined market shares in years 3-4 of the corporate venture.

STRATEGIC CONDUCT: AGGRESSIVENESS

Entry can be aggressive along two dimensions: marketing aggressiveness and investment aggressiveness.

Marketing aggressiveness. For marketing aggressiveness we chose measures that tapped firm's marketing efforts relative to competitors in order to minimize the problem of differences across industry. These marketing aggressiveness measures were: Relative product quality, Relative promotion expenditure, and Relative price.

An overall aggressiveness index for these three variables was constructed in the same manner as for munificence (above). Thus marketing aggressiveness scores could range from 3 to 9 depending on the degree to which firms used high quality and promotion and low price to enter. Two marketing aggressiveness indices were developed for the study. Marketing aggressiveness (beginning) refers to the average of values for years 1 and 2, in other words the aggressiveness at initial cycles of entry for a new corporate venture. Marketing aggressiveness (end) refers to the average of values for years 3 and 4, the end of the period we studied.

Investment aggressiveness. Only one measure taps investment aggressiveness, and that is Capacity installed as a percentage of the served market. This reflects the degree to which the firm is prepared to invest its resources in going after market share. A low percentage indicates a cautious approach, a high percentage an aggressive one. Just as with the marketing aggressiveness variables, we used beginning (year 1 and 2) and end (year 3 and 4) time periods to assess the effects of changes in this variable over time.

COMPETITIVE RESPONSE

STR4 contains a number of measures that reflect a competitors' response to the new entrant at the beginning and end of time cycles. We found consistent multicollinearity among the five competitive responses, so an overall competitive response measure was created. A score was developed which aggregated all the major competitors' responses to entry via decreases in price or increases in production capacity, new product introduction, quality and marketing and distribution expenses, measured separately for year 1 and year 2. For this study, as the competitive response variable goes higher, competition is more fierce (this is to keep things less confusing than in PIMS, where fierce competition has a lower score). In our study the associated response variables are called Competitive Response Beginning and Competitive Response End.

PERFORMANCE

As noted above, our primary measure of performance for evaluating corporate start-ups is market share. Two indicators of market share relate to different times in the study: Actual market share obtained in year 2 (2 years after entry) and Actual market share obtained in year 4 (four years after entry).

Return on investment is a second commonly utilized measure for evaluating business performance. Although for reasons noted above we are reluctant to rely on ROI as a primary indicator of performance for new ventures, we felt it should be included in the analysis as a complement to market share performance measures. Variables utilized here are: Return on investment, beginning (average of year 1 and 2); and Return on investment, end (average of year 3 and 4). Averages of the performance variables were selected in order to minimize the effects of extreme observations and year-to-year fluctuations.

HYPOTHESES

Based on the above arguments and the measures developed for the study, the following hypotheses were generated:

H1: Higher marketing aggressiveness will be positively associated with greater environmental munificence and lower initial hostility.

H2: Higher investment aggressiveness will be positively associated with greater environmental munificence and lower initial hostility.

H3: Higher competitive response will be associated with less munificence, higher initial hostility, and less aggressive investment and marketing behavior.

H4: Higher initial market share performance will be associated with higher marketing and investment aggressiveness and with lower competitive response.

H5: After the launch, investments in building share should depress ROI.

H6: After the launch of the venture, higher marketing aggressiveness will be positively associated with greater environmental munificence, lower later hostility, lower competitive response and greater market share gain.

H7: After the launch of the venture, higher investment aggressiveness will be associated with greater environmental munificence, lower later hostility, lower competitive response and greater market share gain.

H8: After the launch of the venture, higher competitive response will be associated with less munificence, higher later hostility, and less aggressive investment and marketing behavior in the post-entry period.

H9: After the launch, higher market share will be related to higher marketing aggressiveness, higher investment aggressiveness and lower competitive response.

H10: After the launch, higher ending ROI will be associated with higher market share, higher marketing aggressiveness, and higher investment aggressiveness in the post-entry period.

We will test these hypotheses both for the pre-entry and the post-entry period, thus including two cycles of strategic conduct and competitive response.

RESULTS AND DISCUSSION

In order to test the specific relations of the model, a series of multiple regressions were run. Results are summarized for each cycle in the model. Regression coefficients were estimated for each cycle, using ordinary least squares (the AQD "Regress" program). Standardized results are reported in order to minimize variation due to scale.

The logical procedure for discussing the results would be to do so sequentially, discussing marketing and investment aggressiveness, response and performance first for the initial cycle and then for the second cycle. This leads to a very long and unwieldy discussion. Instead, we shall discuss the results for both cycles in parallel.

Marketing aggressiveness
H1: Higher marketing aggressiveness will be positively associated with greater environmental munificence and lower initial hostility.
H6: After the launch of the venture, higher marketing aggressiveness will be positively associated with greater environmental munificence, lower later hostility, lower competitive response and greater market share gain.

REGRESSION ON MARKETING AGGRESSIVENESS				
	INITIAL		SECOND	
CYCLE	Beta	p value	Beta	p value
Munificence	.170	<.05	.127	--(<.10)
Hostility	-.074	--	-.040	--
Competitive Response Y1	N.A.		-.031	--
Early Market Share	N.A.		.251	<.01
F	2.43	--	4.21	<.05
Sample R^2	.031		.099	
--: Not statistically significant				

Overall, the degree to which the independent variables predict marketing aggressiveness is disappointing -- R^2 values are low. However, as predicted, marketing aggressiveness is significantly and positively related to munificence at the start of the venture, and modestly related later in the venture. On the other hand, contrary to the hypotheses, there is no significant relation, at any stage, between marketing aggressiveness and hostility. It appears that it is the quality of the market that drives aggressiveness of marketing on entry, and the structure of competition does not appear to deter the resultant enthusiasm. Surprisingly, while the signs for competitive response are both in the right direction, they are not significant. Apparently vigorous competitive reaction also does not significantly deter the firms in the sample from sustaining their initial marketing stance. Perhaps this dismissal of competitive structure as well as competitive response is a function of the fact that the subscribers to the STR4 database are generally large Fortune 500 firms. Such firms generally have the resources to play a hardball game. Such firms may also not make significant strategic shifts in a four-year timeframe. Early market share gain has very strong positive relation with marketing aggressiveness.

Investment aggressiveness

H2: Higher investment aggressiveness will be positively associated with greater environmental munificence and lower initial hostility.

H7: After the launch of the venture, higher investment aggressiveness will be associated with greater environmental munificence, lower later hostility, lower competitive response and greater market share gain.

REGRESSION ON INVESTMENT AGGRESSIVENESS			
CYCLE	INITIAL		SECOND	
	Beta	p value	Beta	p value
Munificence	.460	<.001	.133	<.05
Hostility	-.054	--	-.177	<.05
Competitive Response Y1	N.A.		-.059	--
Early Market Share	N.A.		.482	<.001
F	20.7	<.001	27.5	<.001
Sample R^2	.208		.414	
--: Not statistically significant				

    The independent variables perform much better as predictors of investment aggressiveness than for marketing aggressiveness. As with marketing aggressiveness, initial investment aggressiveness is significantly related to munificence, while hostility is not a significant predictor of the initial decision to invest in capacity. It is interesting to see how investment aggressiveness changes after the launch.

    Environmental munificence continues to be positively related to investment aggressiveness. Hostility is now negatively related, as was predicted. Competitive reaction again does not appear to discourage investment.

To summarize the effects of environment on initial strategic conduct:

-- <u>Munificence</u>, or the quality of the customer market, appears to significantly enhance initial propensity to invest in capacity, and also encourages early marketing aggressiveness. As the venture progresses beyond the launch, munificence continues to be strongly related to investment aggressiveness but only modestly correlates with marketing aggressiveness. Clearly munificence as developed by Staw and Szwajkowski (1975), Tussle and Gerwin (1980), Dess and Oriser (1987), and Yasai-Arkedeni (1989) is a useful environmental construct for the study of strategic conduct in corporate ventures.

-- <u>Hostility</u> appears only to affect investment aggressiveness, and only after the venture is underway. While the signs are in the expected direction, hostility (Grinyer, Al-bazazz and Yasai-Arkedeni,1980; Miller and Friesen, 1983; and Covin and Slevin, 1989) appears to play less of a role than munificence in predicting entry aggressiveness.

-- <u>Competitive response</u>, once the venture is underway, surprisingly does not appear to have any effect on the aggressiveness of strategic conduct.

<u>Environment, strategic conduct and competitive response</u>

H3: Higher competitive response will be associated with less munificence, higher initial hostility, and less aggressive investment and marketing behavior.

H8: After the launch of the venture, higher competitive response will be associated with less munificence, higher later hostility, and less aggressive investment and marketing behavior in the post-entry period.

REGRESSION ON COMPETITIVE RESPONSE				
	INITIAL		SECOND	
CYCLE	Beta	p value	Beta	p value
Munificence	.155	<.05	.301	<.001
Hostility	-.342	<.001	.425	<.001
Investment Aggressiveness-beginning	-.279	<.001	-.065	--
Market Aggressiveness-beginning	-.194	<.05	-.036	--
F	11.1	<.001	11.2	<.001
Sample R²	.222		.223	
--: Not statistically significant				

The degree to which the independent variables predict competitive response is encouraging -- somewhat over one fifth of variance is explained with these few variables. As predicted, aggressiveness of entry by the new entrant has a depressing effect upon the responses of competitors, but this occurs only in the initial stages of the venture. Thereafter it is the texture of the environment that appears to take over as the major predictor of competitive aggressiveness. Entirely as predicted, the more hostile the environment, the greater the degree of competitive response, a pattern which persists beyond the launch and well into the venture. However, environmental munificence appears to be related to more aggressive response, not less, as we predicted. One possible explanation for this somewhat counterintuitive outcome is that new, high-growth markets with a few key direct customers are jealously defended by established competitors, who see real danger in allowing anyone to get a foothold in so attractive a business. This pattern also persists well into the venture. Despite the unexpected result for munificence, it continues to be an important construct, this time in the prediction of competitive reaction. Hostility now also emerges as an important environmental construct for predicting competitive response.

Strategic conduct, competitive response and market share performance

H4: Higher initial market share performance will be associated with higher marketing and investment aggressiveness and with lower competitive response.

H9: After the launch, higher market share will be related to higher marketing aggressiveness, higher investment aggressiveness and lower competitive response.

REGRESSION ON MARKET SHARE				
CYCLE	BEGINNING SHARE		ENDING SHARE	
	Beta	p value	Beta	p value
Marketing Aggressiveness	.321	<.001	.338	<.001
Investment Aggressiveness	.529	<.001	.624	<.001
Competitive Response	-.383	<.001	-.099	<.05
F	91.7	<.001	59.4	<.001
Sample R^2	.637		.532	
--: Not statistically significant				

The performance of the independent variables in explaining market share gains is highly gratifying -- more than sixty percent of variance is explained. As predicted, both market and investment aggressiveness are positively associated with high initial market share, and both these patterns persist well into the venture. As predicted, competitive response is negatively associated with market share and also persists well into the venture.

Strategic conduct, competitive response and ROI performance

H5: In the initial cycle, investments in building share should depress ROI.

H10: After the launch, higher ending ROI will be associated with higher market share, higher marketing aggressiveness, and higher investment aggressiveness in the post-entry period.

REGRESSION ON RETURN ON INVESTMENT				
CYCLE	INITIAL		SECOND	
	Beta	p value	Beta	p value
Market Share	.118	--	.267	<.01
Marketing Aggressiveness	-.174	<.05	-.281	<.001
Investment Aggressiveness	.012	--	.069	--
Competitive Response	.139	--	.002	--
F	1.64	--	5.61	<.001
Sample R^2	.040		.126	
--: Not statistically significant				

As prior studies have suggested, return on investment is notoriously difficult to predict in the initial stages. Our results corroborate this general conclusion. The results suggest that initial expenses incurred in aggressively seeking share during the market entry period (high marketing aggressiveness index) tend to depress ROI, and that this pattern persists. However, four years after the launch, market share is positively associated with ROI, supporting Biggadike (1979). Investment aggressiveness appears neither to harm nor help profitability. Interestingly, strong competitive response does not have the expected negative effect upon short-term ROI. It appears that competitive action affects share, particularly at the start, but that the only way that competitive action affects venture profitability is indirectly via its impact on market share.

Summary of results

The results of the study are summarized in Figures 1 and 2. Figure 1 depicts the results for the launch, while Figure 2 refers to the post start-up period. In reviewing these figures we can draw the conclusions that follow.

FIGURE 1: LAUNCH OF VENTURE

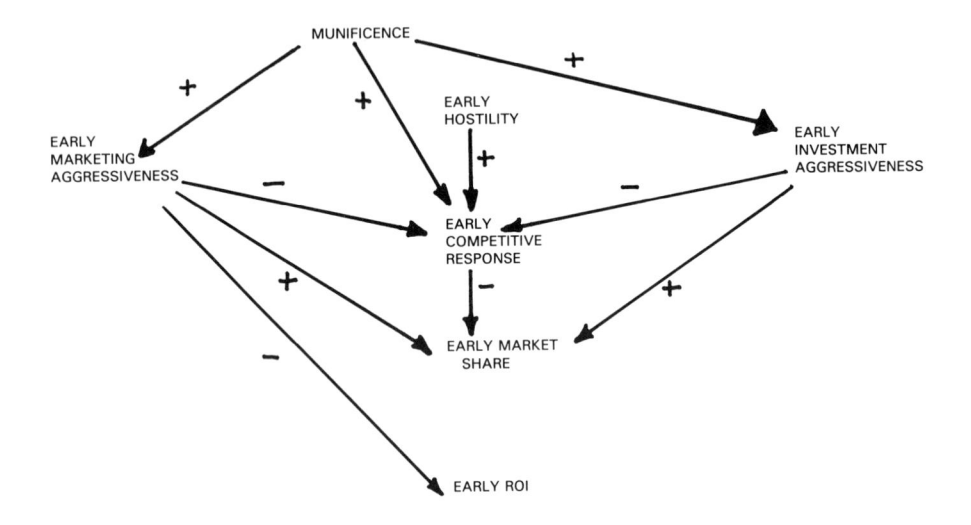

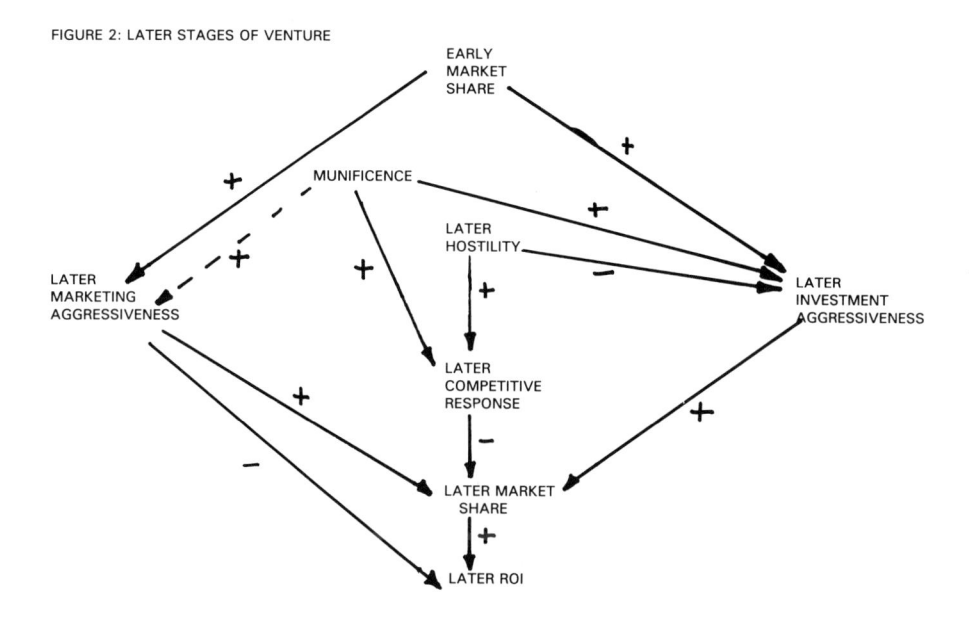

FIGURE 2: LATER STAGES OF VENTURE

CONCLUSIONS

This study was undertaken with the intention of:

1) exploring the value of two distinct environmental constructs, munificence and hostility, and

2) clarifying the relations among competitive environment, firm strategy, competitive response and performance over time.

The study found that the relations among environment, strategy, competitive reaction and performance proceed in the manner predicted in the proposed model. Unfortunately, the small sample size precludes a more sophisticated analysis using something like LISREL. However confidence in these results is considerably strengthened by the fact that the research was done with variables that are temporally sequenced -- the conditions of hostility and munificence precede strategic conduct decisions, which in turn precede competitive responses, which in turn precede performance. In addition, the results reflect similar patterns for two distinct temporal cycles, so that the relations that were found among these variables evoke more confidence than simple, cross-sectional relations.

On the basis of the two figures above, we draw the following conclusions:

1) Munificence is a useful construct for the study and understanding of the corporate venturing process. It is a predictor of investment aggressiveness both at the launch and at the later stages of the venture. This is important because investment aggressiveness is significantly related to market share gains. Munificence is also a predictor of initial marketing aggressiveness, which also correlates with market share gains. Finally, munificence is a major predictor of competitive response, both at the launch and in the later stages, and competitive response is negatively related to market share performance. Thus, munificence appears to play a major role in setting the stage for corporate ventures.

2) Hostility is another useful construct in the study and understanding of corporate ventures. It discourages investment aggressiveness later in the venture, and is the major predictor of competitive response, both at the launch and in the later stages of the venture. Thus hostility also appears to play a major role in setting the stage for corporate venturing.

3) Marketing aggressiveness, which is one type of strategic choice, has a significant impact on dynamics of the market. Throughout the venture market aggressiveness has a consistent negative relation with competitive response and also has a profound and consistent positive correlation with market share gains. Here is a refutation of the pure population ecology approach, at least for the type of corporate venture in our study, since the results provide strong

evidence that strategic choice indeed makes a difference.

4) Investment aggressiveness, another strategic choice, also has an impact on the dynamics of the market. Here is further evidence that strategic choice matters, at least for the type of corporate venture in our study. Investment aggressiveness has a sustained and consistent negative correlation with competitive response and has a profound and consistent positive relation with market share achievement.

5) Competitive response appears to be initially discouraged by aggressive strategic conduct, but this seems to wear off in the later stages of the venture, when competitive response is related more to industry conditions. There is a hint here of regression towards the mean, which in competetive terms implies that once the venture is established, environmental forces start to shape competitive decisions, rather than the strategic behavior of the entrants. It may be that the population ecology approach becomes more tenable once the entrant establishes a position in the market and competitive conditions start to stabilize.

6) In the pre-launch period when there is no performance data to drive strategic choices, industry conditions shape aggressiveness, particularly investment aggressiveness, but later market share takes over as the major predictor of both marketing and investment aggressiveness. A way of relating this conclusion to the one above is as follows: the entry of a new player is an unusual event, attracting the attention of competitors and becoming the focus of competitive decision making geared to coping with the interloper. These decisions are shaped both by the aggressiveness of the interloper and the quality and structure of the customer and competitor market conditions. If the interloper succeeds in establishing a foothold in the industry it is no longer an "event" and it soon becomes part of the "fabric" of competition. Thus the objective of denying a foothold is no longer the focus of attention and competitors revert to focussing on their own performance as the main driver of strategic choice decisions.

7) There appear to be more benefits from investment aggressiveness than marketing aggressiveness. ROI is depressed by marketing aggressiveness, both at the launch and the later stages. Later on in the venture, share gains admittedly start to kick in ROI, but this indirect positive effect of marketing aggressiveness on ROI via market share gain is still less than the direct negative effect of marketing aggressiveness. Thus in the case of marketing aggressiveness, there is a need to trade off share gain for return on investment. On the other hand, investment aggressiveness has a positive effect on market share both during the launch and in the later stages while at no time does it have a negative effect on ROI. In effect, investment aggressiveness allows one to pursue market share without compromising profitability.

Caveats

Several caveats are necessary for this study. First, the study is based on an analysis of corporate start-ups in a sample dominated by very large (Fortune 1,000) firms. Our findings may have no relevance to smaller firms, or independent start-ups. In particular the sheer size of these firms may accord them a number of "immunities" from competitive reaction that for a smaller, less powerful entrant would not be forthcoming.

Second, each of the businesses in our study have survived at least the four years of the research period. Presumably the total failures have thus already been weeded out, leaving only the somewhat-to-very-successful ventures in our study.

Third, the study examines performance four years after entry. Long-term success may not correlate with promising initial performance.

Finally, any database includes certain data and excludes others. While STR4 provides information that is generally acknowledged to be of high quality, the data are only from industrial products, and only for established markets. It would be a mistake to transplant the findings to brand-new markets or service businesses.

Implications for Practitioners

The study has some interesting implications for practitioners.

First, caution should be exercised when entering environments that appear to be munificent, and therefore are unlikely to provoke vigorous competitive reaction. The indications are that competitors will defend aggressively.

It continues to appear that little is gained by timidly entering the markets analyzed in this study. This applies even in the case of more hostile markets, although as might be expected, hostility tends to be associated with increased competitive response.

Implications for Research

A major implication for theory in strategy research is that both environment (random or uncontrollable factors, from the perspective of the firm) and strategic choices (non-random, purposive firm activity) play a significant role in the fate of new corporate ventures. Neither dominates, but both have a substantial influence upon the eventual outcome.

Second, the constructs of environmental hostility and munificence provide a parsimonious mechanism for describing environmental characteristics at the firm level of analysis. This reduces the need to rely upon exhaustive typologies or detailed descriptions of particular environmental characteristics (for example, Emery and Trist, 1965). Such constructs would contribute to tighter, more cleanly operationalized theory.

The results should be replicated using other data. Two studies that come to mind immediately would be an examination of these factors over time in service-based businesses and a study of entry into entirely new (as opposed to existing) markets.

The applicability of these ideas to firms *not* in the Fortune 1000 should also be considered, as the resource and information constraints upon these companies is apt to be quite different from those upon larger organizations.

Much current work in strategy appears to be focused on precisely the intersections among strategic behavior and environment which are central to this study. It is our hope that one contribution of the paper lies in the way our variables are operationalized. The constructs used in this study appear to hold promise as a way of operationalizing both environmental and strategic variables for future research.

FOOTNOTES

1. Another commonly used measure of performance aside from market share is Return on Investment (ROI). As has been amply documented (Hambrick, MacMillan and Day, 1982; and MacMillan and Day, 1986), ROI is far less predictable than market share, and more vulnerable to imperfect information and fluctuations over time. In particular, for new ventures, especially in the early stages, profitability has huge variability, is highly unstable and is subject to all sorts of vagaries stemming from creative accounting practices.

2. Meyer & Zucker, 1989, shed considerable light on the notion that good performance and organizational survival are not necessarily equivalent.

3. Marketplace fragmentation, defined as a large number of customers relative to the overall size of the market, is generally considered a problem for a new business. In this study, we use the number of immediate customers as a proxy for market fragmentation. This is necessary because in STR4 both number of direct customers and market size are both categorical variables.

REFERENCES

Aldrich, H. 1979. Organizations and Environments. Prentice Hall, Englewood Cliffs.

Aldrich, H. and Auster, E. 1986. Even dwarfs started small: Liabilities of age and size and their strategic implications. Research in Organizational Behavior vol 8, pp. 165-98.

Anderson, C.R. and Paine, F.T. 1978. PIMS: A reexamination. Academy of

Management Review vol 3, pp. 602-11.

Andrews, K. 1980. The Concept of Corporate Strategy. Irwin, Homewood, Ill.

Biggadike, R. 1979. The risky business of diversification. Harvard Business Review May-June, pp. 103-111.

Buzzell, R.D., Gale, B.T. and Sultan, R.G.M. 1975. Market share -- a key to profitability. Harvard Business Review Jan-Feb., pp. 97-106.

Child, J. 1972. Organization structure, environment, and performance: the role of strategic choice. Sociology pp. 1-22.

Cooper R.G. 1979. The dimension of industrial new product success and failure. Journal of Marketing 43, pp. 93-103.

Cooper R.G. 1983. Most new products do succeed. Research Management November-December, pp. 20-5.

Covin, J.G. and Slevin, D.P. 1989. Strategic management of small firms in hostile and benign environments. Strategic Management Journal vol 10, no 1, pp. 75-87.

Dess, G.G. and Oriser, N.K. 1987. Environment, structure and consensus in strategy formulation: A conceptual integration. Academy of Management Review vol 12, no 2, pp. 313-330.

Emery, F.E. and Trist, E.L. 1965. The causal texture of organizational environments. Human Relations vol 18, pp. 21-32.

Greenfield, S.M. and Strickon, A. 1986. Entrepreneurship and Social Change. Lanham, University Press.

Grinyer P., Al-bazazz S. and Yasai-Arkedeni, M. 1980. Strategy, structure, the environment and financial performance in 48 U.K. companies. Academy of Management Journal vol 23, no 2, pp. 193-220.

Hambrick, D., MacMillan, I.C. and Day, D.L. 1982. Strategic attributes and performance in the BCG Matrix -- a PIMS-based analysis of industrial product businesses. Academy of Management Journal Dec, pp. 510-31.

Hannan, M.T. and Freeman, J. 1984. Structural inertia and organizational change. American Sociological Review vol 49, pp. 149-64.

Hannan, M.T. and Freeman, J. 1979. The population ecology of organizations.

American Journal of Sociology vol 82, pp. 929-64.

Hofer, C.W. and Schendel. 1978. Strategy Formulation: Analytical Concepts. St. Paul, West.

Hobson, E.L. and Morrison, R.M. 1983. How do corporate start-up ventures fare? Frontiers of Entrepreneurship Research Wellesley, Babson, pp. 390-410.

Lambkin, M. 1988. Order of entry and performance in new markets Strategic Management Journal vol 9, pp. 127-40.

MacMillan, I.C., Block, Z., and Subba Narasimha, P.N. 1984. Obstacles and experience in corporate venturing. Frontiers of Entrepreneurship Research Wellesley, Babson, pp. 341-63.

MacMillan, I.C. and Day, D.L. 1987. Corporate ventures into industrial markets: Dynamics of aggressive entry. Journal of Business Venturing vol 2, pp. 29-39.

MacMillan, I.C. and George, R. 1985. Corporate venturing: challenges for senior managers. Journal of Business Strategy vol 5, no 3, pp. 34-44.

Meyer, Marshall M. and Zucker, L. 1989. Permanently Failing Organizations. Newbury Park, Sage.

Miles, R.E. and Snow, C.C. 1978. Organizational Strategy, Structure, and Process. New York, McGraw-Hill.

Miller, A., Wilson, B. and Adams, M. 1988. Financial performance patterns of new corporate ventures: An alternative to traditional measures. Journal of Business Venturing vol 3, no 4, pp 287-300.

Miller, D. 1987. The structural and environmental correlates of business strategy. Strategic Management Journal vol 8, pp. 55-76.

Miller, D. and Friesen, P.H. 1983. Strategy-making and environment: The third link. Strategic Management Journal vol 4, pp. 221-35.

Mitchell, W. 1989. Whether and when? Probability and timing of incumbents' entry into emerging industrial subfields. Administrative Science Quarterly vol 34, pp. 203-230.

Porter, M. 1980. Competitive Strategy. New York: Free Press.

Prescott, J.E., Kohli, A.K. and Venkatraman, N. 1986. The market share -- profitability relationship: An empirical assessment of major assertions and contradictions. Strategic Management Journal vol 7, 377-94.

Ramanujan, V. and Venkatraman, N. 1984. An inventory and critique of strategy research using the PIMS data base. Academy of Management Review vol 9, no 1, pp. 138-51.

Rink, D.R. and Swan, J.E. 1979. Product life-cycle research: A literature review. Journal of Business Research 78, pp. 219-42.

Sahlman, W. and Stevenson, H. 1985. Capital market myopia. Journal of Business Venturing vol 1, no 1, pp. 7-30.

Singh, J.V., House, R.J. and Tucker, D.J. 1986. Organizational change and organizational mortality. Administrative Science Quarterly vol 31, pp. 587-611.

Staw, M. and Szwajkowski, B.E. 1985. The scarcity-munificence component of organizational environments and the commission of illegal acts. Administrative Science Quarterly vol 20, pp. 345-54.

Tellis, G.J. and Crawford, C.M. 1981. An evolutionary approach to product growth theory. Journal of Marketing vol 45, pp. 125-32.

Timmons, J.A. 1982. New venture creation: methods and models. In C.A. Kent, D.L. Sexton, and K.H. Vesper (Eds.), Encyclopedia of Entrepreneurship (pp. 126-38). Englewood Cliffs, NJ: Prentice-Hall.

Tsai, W., MacMillan, I.C. and Low, M. 1990. Effects of Strategy and Environment on Corporate Venture Success in Industrial Markets. Working Paper, Snider Entrepreneurial Center, University of Pennsylvania.

Tushman, M. and Anderson, P. 1986. Technological discontinuities and organizational environments. Administrative Science Quarterly vol 31, pp. 439-65.

Tussle, F.D. and Gerwin, D. 1980. An information processing model of organizational perception, strategy, and choice. Management Science vol 26, no 6, pp, 575-92.

Van de Ven, A.H., Hudson, R. and Schroeder, D.M. 1984. Designing new business startups: entrepreneurial, organizational, and ecological considerations. Journal of Management vol 10, no 1, pp. 87-107.

Vesper, K.H. 1980. New Venture Strategies. Englewood Cliffs, NJ, Prentice-Hall.

Woo, C.Y. and Cooper, A.C. 1981. Strategies of effective low share businesses. Strategic Management Journal vol 2, pp. 301-18.

Yasai-Arkedeni, M. 1989. Effects of environmental scarcity and munificence on the relationship of context to organizational structure. <u>Academy of Management Journal</u> Vol 32 No 1. pp. 131-156.

ENTREPRENEURIAL STRATEGY AND BEHAVIOR

Business Start-Ups: The HRM Imperative

Critique
by
Abdul Jalil bin Ismail, *National University of Singapore*
Chong Li Choy, *National University of Singapore*

INTRODUCTION

Of late, human resource management (HRM) has become an important concern in management literature as well as in the minds of practising managers. The realization that management techniques by themselves will not help to solve organizational problems has spurred researchers to focus instead on the human element of the organization.

The paper under review is an extension of this search. It seeks to justify the importance of HRM policies in the context of entrepreneurial organizations, specifically in the starting up of such firms. With a focus on high technology firms, the paper postulates several developmental models through a discussion of several factors perceived to be salient in influencing the choice of HRM policies adopted by such firms.

STRATEGIC HRM

The basic contention of the paper is that HRM policies should be part of the strategic orientation of the firm. But what is still not known is when and how such policies get integrated into the strategic management process. The authors present the developmental and evolutionary models as possible approaches in understanding the process.

There can be no denying that the move towards integrating HRM into strategic management is sound and justifiable. However, one has to be cautious when applying such postulations within an entrepreneurial setting. An entrepreneur's intentions are important underpinnings of new venture development (Bird, 1988). Entrepreneurial intentions are aimed at creating values. In doing so, the entrepreneur may be intuitive and opportunistic. As such, there has to be a congruency between his personal ideas and the kind of organization he wishes to create and sustain. To understand his actions and intentions within the purview of organizational theories would thus be unfair to the entrepreneur. Furthermore, even if he develops any kind of system or policy as understood by academia, it would only be an after-thought based on his own personal preferences and experiences. Therefore, the conception of HRM from the viewpoint of an entrepreneur is based solely on his own needs and circumstances, and is thus very unlikely to be explicitly stated in terms of specific policies. Added to this is the fact that most small firms, at least in Singapore, are family businesses. In this context, the definition of role assignment is further complicated. In such a situation, one would expect policies with regard to acquisition, rewards and training to be based, not on a formal set of standards, but more likely, on trust.

The definition of start-ups tends to be very ambiguous. As Katz and Gartner (1988) pointed out, most studies of "new" or emerging organizations tend to identify existing organizations. What is needed in looking at the orientation of entrepreneurs is to identify organizations-in-creation. This is important because it is possible that most entrepreneurial endeavors die while emerging (Vesper, 1983). The failure to observe emerging organizations early on may result in the researcher missing out on entrepreneurial activities.

The focus on high technology firms also adds to the difficulty of assessing to what extent these entrepreneurs really understand the management of human resources. One can perhaps speculate that most of these entrepreneurs are inventors or highly specialized professionals. Can one really expect these specialists to be able to think about development of human resources, given their functional specialty? Perhaps, a look at business start-ups within other industries which utilize moderate levels of technology, such as in the service sector, may give a clearer indication of the kind of understanding these entrepreneurs have about managerial and HRM issues. As cited by the authors of the point made by Samson (1990), scientists tend to be ignorant of managerial and organizational issues when they set up their own firms.

The authors pointed out the influence of the founder in the development of HRM policies. Perhaps, the authors could have discussed further this point in the context of the kind of corporate culture the founder would like to establish in the emergent organization. As pointed out by Schein (1985), culture serves the organization in two ways: (1) survival and adaptation to external environment, and (2) integration of internal processes to ensure the capacity to survive and adapt. Clearly, the vision and conception of the type of culture he would like to have will have a direct bearing on the kinds of HRM policies he wants perpetuated in the organization, how explicit he wants the policies and values to be, and how he shares these with his employees.

CONCLUSION

As an exploratory paper which seeks to address the issue of HRM within the context of emergent organizations, this is an excellent paper and provides ample questions which call for further research in this area. However, in looking for answers with respect to how HRM policies are developed or evolved in entrepreneurial settings, academics may well be advised not to expect satisfactory and well-fitted answers. HRM, as understood by entrepreneurs working within a loose organizational framework, may not be explicitly found in terms of structural configurations such as in the creation of a department or even a crudely written policy. It may lie in the mind of the entrepreneur who has to grapple with other immediate concerns such as survival. HRM, if it exists at all, is more the result of a reaction to changes in the environment. It is an after-thought. It is an irony that in an era when we are moving away from the development of management techniques and formalization as the way to manage organizations, we are still looking towards such techniques as an asset in managing emerging entrepreneurial settings.

Perhaps, what we should be looking for are entrepreneurs in the area of human resource management. As Chong (1990) pointed out, entrepreneurship, or more simply, an entrepreneur's innovation, could be in any one or more of the functional areas of a business. An innovative management of human resources, such as in the motivation of employees, can strengthen the effectiveness of organizations.

The study of emergent organizations may well be better-founded if the sample of firms to be studied are organizations which are truly in the process of being created. Studying an existing organization may well lead us to misleading conclusions. A sample which looks at entrepreneurs who are well-versed in organizational issues may perhaps be a better way of understanding the extent to which business start-ups really concern themselves with HRM issues. Finally, the role of the culture to be inculcated by the founder needs to be understood as it will shape the HRM policies, in its content and process.

REFERENCES

Bird, B. (1988), Implementing entrepreneurial ideas: The case for intention, Academy of Management Review, Vol. 13, No.3, 442-453.

Chong, L. C. (1990), Entrepreneurial human resource management: excellence in small enterprises, presented at the ENDEC International Entrepreneurship Conference, March 21-24, Singapore.

Katz, J. & Gartner, W.B. (1988), Properties of emerging organizations, Academy Management Review, Vol. 13, No. 3, 429-441.

Schein, E.H. (1985), Organizational Culture Leadership: A Dynamic View, The Jossey-Bass Publishers, San Francisco.

BUSINESS START-UPS: THE HRM IMPERATIVE

HOWARD E. ALDRICH *UNIVERSITY OF NORTH CAROLINA AT CHAPEL HILL*
MARY ANN VON GLINOW, *UNIVERSITY OF SOUTHERN CALIFORNIA*[1]

ABSTRACT

Human resource management policies and entrepreneurship are linked. New businesses in the high technology sector are competing for employees in a tougher labor market than most businesses face. Like all businesses, they must attract, recruit, and keep skilled workers. They must also find ways of motivating these workers throughout their careers in a highly competitive and quickly changing market. We propose two perspectives on organizational change--a developmental and an evolutionary--to aid our investigation of the following questions: Do new firms start with effective HRM policies? If not, why not? If yes, how do owners learn about effective policies? If firms don't start with effective policies, do or can they eventually develop or adopt them? How quickly do effective HRM systems arise? We review the literature and suggest four sets of factors that might be used in answering these questions: characteristics of founding teams, a firm's initial workforce composition, the structure of an organization, and a firm's institutional context.

INTRODUCTION

Organizational theorists have tried to capture the growth of new organizations in a variety of ways: stage models, evolutionary models, life-cycle models, metamorphosis models, and others. Theorists argue over just whose model is the "right" model, or best predicts various organizational outcomes, including various measures of financial health or organizational health. A key issue facing new business is which human resource management (HRM) policies and practices to adopt. Research and theorizing on start-ups has almost totally neglected HRM, as most of the literature focuses on technological innovation, finance, and marketing. We believe that HRM deserves the same attention as other aspects of new ventures, particularly in an age when businesses are searching for every possible competitive advantage.

After reviewing the significance of HRM policies for high technology firms in the business environment of the 1990s, we present several models of new venture

---

[1] We thank Andrew H. Van de Ven for providing access to his cases on business start-ups.

development. We identify four sets of factors that influence new firms' HRM practices, including founding team, workforce, organizational characteristics, and institutional contexts. We review two HRM issues facing start-ups: acquiring workers, and motivating them. In our reveiw, we identify some questions that we hope to address in research on start-ups during their first few years of life.

THE SIGNIFICANCE OF HUMAN RESOURCES

During the 1980s, two great forces played an enormous role for most organizations: globalization and restructuring. Both of these altered the competitive field, transforming companies as well as national economies, and both have been exacerbated by America's endless search for higher productivity and faster growth. In addition, both have been top-down, business-driven developments (Doyle, 1989).

The 1980s was also the age of the entrepreneur, with business start-ups accounting for the bulk of new jobs that were created in the U.S. This entrepreneurial age might not have been possible without the upheaval created by corporate America's quest for higher productivity and competitive advantage via globalization and restructuring. Corporate America took out jobs, delayered, downsized, and generally restructured, while rearranging portfolios through LBOs, mergers and other attempts at becoming more globally competitive. The ensuing economic disruption structured the environment of the entrepreneurs of the 1990s, and they clearly benefited from the upheaval evident in larger corporations.

A recent Korn-Ferry (1990) report on the 21st Century identified the following core areas as most critical for CEOs of the future: strategy formulation, human resource management expertise, marketing and sales, and negotiation/conflict resolution. Changing conditions mandate that corporate America, with its "fewer people and more knowledge" (Doyle, 1989) aggressively invest in human resources for productivity and competitive advantage, but it is still unclear how most entrepreneurs, who are early on the life-cycle curve, view human resources. Considerable theoretical attention has been paid to Ghadar, 1989; Ulrich, 1989; Ulrich, Yeung, and Brockbank, 1990; von Glinow and Milliman, 1990; Wagel, 1990), yet very little empirical research has examined the HR correlates of competitive advantage in large firms. Virtually no recent studies have examined the human resource practices and policies of new firms.

Thus, we propose to focus the field's attention on what we believe are HRM imperatives for new business start-ups. We have both a normative and a research agenda. We believe that a heightened attention to HRM will become not only a competitive necessity for large firms, but also for new firms, i.e., those that have not had to go though the upheavals of the 1980s associated with downsizing. In particular, new firms that hope to compete in global markets with competitive products and services must begin with an articulate set of HRM strategies, enacted into policies. On the research front, before we develop these imperatives into test table propositions, we must examine what is known about the HRM policies and practices of new businesses.

New Business Start-Ups in High Technology

We have chosen business start-ups in high technology industries. Typically, high technology industries are defined as "industries in which (1) the ratio of R & D expenditures to sales was a least twice the average of all industries, and/or (2) the relative employment of technology-oriented workers was 300 percent of the rate of all U.S. industries" (Von Glinow, 1988). Others have noted that additional characteristics of high technology industries include: (1) how technology-oriented the goods and services are, as well as (2) the relative level of the technology employed or developed by the industry (Dorfman, 1982; Rich, Hecker, and Burgan, 1983). We believe our focus on high technology industries, and in particular, start-up businesses within that sector, is warranted because developments in this sector spill over into almost all other sectors, inducing changes that other firms must incorporate. For example, while leaving untouched the production process, micro-electronics have affected inventory control, record keeping, and office management even in highly labor intensive retail stores. Thus, we have targeted high technology start-up businesses as the focus of this manuscript.

For most high technology start-up businesses in the 1990s to compete successfully in domestic markets, a global strategy will be required. A considerable amount of foreign direct investment occurs in the high-technology arena, and there is tremendous competition for scarce resources in this sector: people, technology, and processes. Technology-intensive industries have understandably flocked to research consortia, or other cooperative alliances, to leverage knowledge. In 1970, there was fewer than one alliance per wholly-owned subsidiary, whereas in 1990, the number of alliances outnumbered wholly-owned subsidiaries by four to one.

Unlike technology-intensive firms in the 1980s, which typically engaged in allinaces for risk-spreading mechanisms, the high technology firms of today must move quickly, moving products to market in a fraction of the time it took a decade earlier. The bulk of the competition for domestic high technology firms operating in the U.S. today comes from foreign firms, or their alliances with domestic firms. For high technology start-ups, this "speed" requirement is just as real as it is for larger, better established firms. These fledgling businesses must compete with firms that have an established niche, are streamling their processes for quick turnaround of product, and are customer-sensitive. Speed is the "ability to anticipate and act, instead of react; speed is the ability to see and seize competitive advantage first" (Doyle, 1989, p.5). In addition to speed, competitive firms must also make use of technologically-sophisticated hardware and software.

Yet, a fundamental paradox underlies this rationale. Many high technology businesses, either start-ups or those that are competing with larger firms, must be globalized, and thus, at least for North America, Europe and East Asia, technology advances are less apt to contribute to competitive advantage than productivity through people. The necessary and sufficient ingredient appears to be people, and paradoxically, not technology or processes in high technology firms. Hence, we renew our emphasis on the imperative associated with managing today's human resources for competitive advantage.

But how do high tech start-ups develop or evolve human resource strategies that leverage their human assets?

HUMAN RESOURCE MANAGEMENT AND BUSINESS START-UPS

Human resource management policies and entrepreneurship are linked. New businesses in the high technology sector are competing for employees in a tougher labor market than most businesses face. Like all businesses, they must attract, recruit, and keep skilled workers. They must also find ways of motivating these workers throughout their careers in a highly competitive and quickly changing market.

Do new firms start with effective HRM policies? If not, why not? If yes, how do owners learn about effective policies? If firms don't start with effective policies, do or can they eventually develop or adopt them? How quickly do effective HRM systems arise? Under what conditions do firms develop toward more effective HRM systems? Does change in a firm's HRM policies and practices require that it grow? Or, can transformation occur without growth?[2] Are HRM policies linked to a firm's performance in its first few years?

Models of New Firms' Development

Two theoretical models shaped our thinking on new firms' development; a developmental model, and an evolutionary model.

A developmental approach to organizations assumes that change occurs in a cycle of emergence, growth, maturity, and decline (Baird and Meshoulam, 1988; Milliman, Von Glinow, and Nathan, 1990). Organizations pass through a series of stages in their life cycle, representing the maturation of the potential an organization had when it was founded. The natural unfolding of organizational structures and processes is the realization of the forces that all organizations face. The timing or pacing of events has a natural rhythm which participants create but which also constrains them (Gersick, 1990). From this perspective, the principles of organizational emergence and growth are similar for <u>all</u> organiztions, and can be learned by investigating the natural history of existing organizations.

---

[2]We do NOT assume that high growth is equivalent to high economic performance. Research has repeatedly shown that growth and profitability are only moderately associated.

An evolutionary approach is much more contingent, as it assumes that organizations do not follow a fixed path of development and have no 'natural' life cycles. External events interact with an organization's own actions to drive its pace, pattern, and direction or change. Although all organizations face similar fundamental problems of organizing, their histories--the timing and intensity of changes--are grounded in the environments they experience. From this perspective, organiztions must be studied in their environments, and generalizations must be historically grounded and limited to the domain of organizational forms sampled.

Baird and Meshoulam (1988) argued that there were four kinds of growth models, and added "stage" and "metamorphosis" models to the two we have listed. These two are actually variations on the essence of the first two, and thus we have not included them as separate models. Stage models assume a developmental sequence, but modify the developmental model by positing that organizations pause in various steps, during which managers can take adaptive actions (Scott, 1971). Metamorphosis models may be based on either developmental or evolutionary foundations, but modify both in positing that changes are provided when an organization's structure is mis-matched with its environment (Starbuck, 1965). Change thus occurs abruptly and in discontinuous bursts, rather than gradually and smoothly.[3]

One problem with some developmental models is that they imply little managerial choice or dominance by external forces (Lengnick-Hall and Lengnick-Hall, 1988). By contrast, evolutionary models allow room for managerial choice, as a firm's trajectory of development is treated as resulting from the interaction of firms' actions with the resources and constraints made available by their environments. Stage models of development also allow room for managerial choice within the confines of an unfolding natural history. However, evolutionary models probably allow more rein for managerial creativity and luck than stage models.

Clearly, both developmental and evolutionary models are heuristics, meant to orient research and raise certain kinds of questions about organizational change. Adjudicating between them is an empirical task, and at this stage we propose simply to use them to set up expectations about what should be included in our review.

Four factors

---

[3]Some misreadings of the evolutionary model presume that it ONLY posits smooth, incremental changes in organizations. Actually, the essence of the evolutionary model is the absence of any prior notion of a fixed pace at which changes occur. Thus, a metamorphosis model can easily be treated as a special case of a more general evolutionary model. However, over the long run, most changes in organizations are small and incremental, rather than large and monumental.

Four sets of factors influence a new firm's human resource policies: (1) the founding team's characteristics of the initial workforce; (3) key features of the organization itself; and 4) the institutional context. In formulating our argument, we have reviewed the literatures on human resource management and entrepreneurship, searching for articles that linked HRM policies with firms' development. Whereas we found many cross-sectional studies of both HRM and entrepreneurship, we found almost no empirical longituidnal studies of HRM in new and growing firms.[4] Also the literature on HRM and strategy, although couched in general terms, uses very large corporations almost exclusively in the examples it presents, e.g., Lengnick-Hall and Lengnick-Hall (1988) used General Electric, Apple, Anheuser-Busch, and American Express, among others.

Founding Teams. First, we expect that business founders' prior experience and training, as well as their strategic plan for the firm, set up strong expectations as to what an effective HRM system looks like. Imitation and borrowing play a large role, and they depend heavily on what industry the founders worked in previously. From a developmental perspective, such initial endowments fundamentally circumscribe future development. From an evolutionary perspective, initial endowments are the raw materials with which subsequent environments interact.

Founding team size and composition affect the development of start-ups, although most studies of these variables have focused on economic rather than human resource outcomes. Van de Ven, Hudson, and Schroeder (1984) discovered that software firms founded by a single owner did significantly better than those founded by partnerships. Of the seven (out of 14) firms founded by partners, five encountered serious troubles in their development, including severe power struggles in five firms.

In our pilot study, an entrepreneur described setting up a new cellular phone company and bringing in an executive from a large firm. The executive had been the CEO of a fairly large company, and he almost immediately began to develop formal structures that resembled those of his old firm. The entrepreneurial team, by contrast, was still very concerned with expanding their niche--"getting customers," as one entrepreneur put it--and were surprised by the CEO's emphasis on formal policies. (The firm had less than twenty employees at this point). They asked him to hold off on formalization until the firm's growth warranted it.

Scientists who leave their laboratories to start new ventures are often blind to managerial and organizational issues (Samson, 1990). They tend to be technology driven, and to ignore human resource issues.

---

[4]Studies of growing firms are not the same as studies of start-ups--the two populations are not the same. E.g., in Buller and Napier's (1990) study of fast growth versus other mid-sized firms, the average fast growth firm as 14 years old. Given their sample selection criteria, based on Business Week's list of the 100 fastest growing firms and 100 randomly selected firms from Dun & Bradstreet's DMI file, few if any start-ups (or even young firms) could have been included.

The management team's understanding of, and tolerance for, ambiguity will affect the speed with which a new firm moves toward role closure (Meyerson, 1990). Some theorists argue that maintaining a fairly high level of ambiguity is the key to sustaining innovation in growing firms (McCaskey, 1982; Peters, 1987; Pascale, 1990). Others argue that ambiguity is a source of stress and conflict, and that it will subside as a firm matures (Kahn et al., 1964).

Policies are also shaped by founders' networks of contacts. Founders with extensive networks across different industries have access to different information and HRM experiences than founders whose networks are mainly limited to a single industry. Founders' networks might be extended through trade and professional associations, consortia, and the like. Van de Ven, Hudson, and Schroeder's (1984) study of 14 software start-ups suggested that entrepreneurs who engaged in more externally-oriented networking were more successful than others.

The HRM literature is increasingly emphasizing the extent to which human resource planning figures in a firm's strategic plans (Dyer, 1983; Fombrun, Tichy, and Devanna, 1984). Typically, this literature deals with large firms that already have fairly sizeable HRM or personnel departments, and so its direct applicability to start-ups is questionable. However, its emphasis on the importance of a match between firms' competitive strategies and their HRM policies alert us to the need to consider founders strategies in our model. Firms pursuing a low cost, efficiency strategy undoubtedly view their employees differently than firms pursuing an innovation-driven differentiation strategy (Porter, 1980). Whether current strategy typologies make sense for start-ups is an open question, but the matter is worth pursuing.[5] As Lengnick-Hall and Lengnick-Hall (1988:468) noted, "to date, there is little <u>empirical</u> evidence to suggest that strategic human resource management directly influences organizational performance or competitive advantage," and so research on start-ups will fill an important need.

<u>Initial Workforce.</u> Second, employees' prior education and training shape the founding team's beliefs about how much attention the HRM policies deserve, given their other priorities. From a developmental perspective, employees are a resource that can be transformed by organizational policies, but only within certain limits. Thus, firms that intend to make substantial demands on their workers would be expected to pay a great deal of attention to recruitment and selection. Start-ups that are constrained from making such up-front investments in recruiting and selecting workers might be forced to make massive adjustments later in their life cycle.

From an evolutionary perspective, characteristics of the labor market from which a firm recruits shape the composition of its initial workforce. Thus, because labor markets are continually undergoing change as labor force demographics

---

[5]Indeed, a recent theory of organizational development argued that taking action, rather than elaborate planning, was the key to a successful firm (Brunson, 1985).

fluctuate over time, when a firm is founded will have a substantial affect on its development (Lawrence, 1990). "Good" employees will be more readily available during some eras than others, and the consequences of being founded in a period when highly qualifed workers are scarce will linger with a firm for years afterward.

Organizational Structure. Third, firm's initial size, technology, strategic orientation (e.g., specialis/generalist), as well as other organiztional chacteristics, will affect its HRM practices. Organizational size is implicated in nearly all aspects of organizational structures and processes, and is clearly central to HRM. O'Reilly and Anderson (1982:7) collected survey data on 127 firms in the Los Angeles area, and found that "the personnel function in firms of fewer than 300 employees was either non-existent or rudimentary." They followed this pilot study with a survey of 143 Fortune 500 firms. Based on the combined sample of 290 firms, they concluded that "firms with less than 1000 employees typically have no separate personnel function unless there is an extensive legislative burden, rapid growth, or special circumstances such as being a subsidiary of a large firm. In these circumstances the personnel function is almost invariably a bureaucracy with no influence. Only when there are more than 2000 employees does the personnel function appear to develop to the point that college-trained personnel officers are employed" (O'Reilly and Anderson, 1982:11). They argued that top management's support for professionalization of the HRM staff and innovative HRM policies was crucial.

The consequences of growth for the amount of organizational resources allocated to HRM is evident in the experience of Glaxo, an intenational ethical drugs firm, with a large base in the Research Triangle Area of North Carolina, that has experienced rapid growth in the past decade. In 1984, it had about 200 employees and only 3 people working in the HRM area. Six years later, it had about 5000 employees and 94 HRM people, and had moved from a very centralized to a decentralized HRM policy. Clearly, expanding size forced Glaxo executives to make major changes in HRM. The question is: is their experience typical?

Evidence linking new firms' size to subsquent performance is rather mixed. If the outcome criterion is survival, than most studies show that larger firms survive at higher rates than small ones (Birch, 1979; Carroll, 1984). If the outcome criterion is innovativeness, then some research shows that smaller might be better. Greiner (1970) argued that unsuccessful innovation attempts were brought on, in part, by beginning on too large a scale and expanding too quickly. Van de Ven, Hudson, and Schroeder (1984) replicated this finding in their study of software start-ups.

We know that most start-ups will not have formal HRM departments, but all have HRM policies, even if they are only implicit. Our interest lies in these implicit policies, as well as in the issue of when growing firms adopt formal HRM functions and departments.

Institutional Context. Fourth, the institutional context creates another set of expectations and standards: What are the prevailing HRM practices in the industry? In the region? Industry and firm life cycle stage is very important--are effective forms available to be copied? Fombrun (1982) identified changes in the technological and social environment of business as constituting the most critical institutional factors, but he also listed a host of other factors: demographic changes, interest group politics, inter-organizational relations, and many others.

State and national government are a critical part of the institutional environment of new firms. In the U.S., national regulations affect many aspects of a firm's relations with its employees: health and safety--OSHA; pensions--ERISA; race and sex discrimination--EEOC, OFCC; unions--NLRB; taxes--IRS; and so forth. Changes in the laws and the legal system also affect start-ups relations with employees. For example, suits challenging employers, assertions of the traditional "employment at will" doctrine have expanded claims of wrongful discharge, and a growing number of women have turned to the courts for settlement of sexual harassment and discrimination claims.

The four sets of factors we have identified--founding team, workforce, organizational, and institutional--must be investigated further before generalizations can be drawn. In the next section, we use them implicitly to set forth some questions about two critical processes facing start-ups.

HRM ISSUES FACING START-UPS

We have organized our review of the HRM issues facing start-ups around two critical processes: acquiring workers, and motivating them. We have not used more elaborate, traditional HRM functions or system components because most start-ups do not have complex system in place when they begin. Instead, the founding teams and their top managers are faced with concrete problems requiring immediate attention. Structures accumulate as problems are dealt with, within an organizational and institutional context.

Acquiring Workers

Start-up founders face an immediate issue of what proportion of their employees to hire as part of ther permanent workforce versus hiring them under other arrangements (Pfeffer and Baron, 1988). Firms that are trying to minimize fixed costs have a number of options. First, they may split their workforce into a core of workers who are (nearly) guaranteed permanent employment, and another set of workers who are explicitly temporary. Second, they can lease some of their employees from a temporary help agency, externalizing the costs of recruiting, record keeping, and so forth (Carey and Hazelbaker, 1986). Third, they can structure their operations so that some fraction can be contracted out to other firms, including professional services such as advertising and legal affairs, and support services such as mailing and maintenance.

Deciding what fraction of the workforce to hire into the core of the new firm involves several tradeoffs. The smaller the core workforce, the lower the fixed overhead expenses, and thus the more flexible the firm can be if it runs into cash flow problems, as many start-ups do. However, a small core workforce means that many of the benefits of learning by doing are lost to the new firm, as the temporary and leased employees gain experience which they take with them. Employees pick up a great deal of implicit knowledge which they will have no stake in passing on if they are not in the core (Shaiken, 1986). Creating a segmented workforce complicates human resource management for young firms, especially if they do not have a full time person overseeing personnel issues. Most of our discussion focuses on the permanent employees of new businesses, but we must keep in mind the other alternatives.

How do newly founded high technology firms communicate their organization's appeal and attract workers? Larger firms have the advantage of highly visible names, an ongoing recruitment process that reaches into many universities, head hunter firms, employment agencies, and indirectly into other firms through ex-employees. Young firms start with almost none of these advantages. How do they make themselves known? They face added pressures because unlike established firms, they are often recruiting employees for positions that have never been filled, and so position descriptions as well as job expectations may be difficult to articulate (Aldrich and Auster, 1986; Stinchcombe, 1965).

We might expect that social networks play an important role in alerting potential employees to the young firms' existence. Founders must communicate information about the nature and mission of the firm, including information about its unique characteristics, culture, and work opportunities. Research on high technology professionals has identified the following factors as being critical in attracting such employees: "the type of work they would be engaged in; the type of rewards and benefits that the firm had to ofer; the geographical location; the image of the company in its industry as 'leading,' or cutting-edge; the type of project team, including the reputation of the key players' new employees would initially be assigned to work with; the career advancement associated with the position; and finally, the challenge" (Von Glinow, 1988:48).

Recruiting Processes. Recruitment is the next step in the process, once potential employees. Having been made aware of the young firms' existence and desire to hire employees, uncertainty is likely to be very high in the process, because of imperfect knowledge on the part of both the employer and employee. "The information workers hold about the value of a prospective job is highly imperfect because certain properties of jobs--what economists call experience properties--are difficult to assess in the absence of actual employment" (Halaby, 1988:12). To the extent that workers have incorrectly anticipated what a job will be like, a firm may incur increased recruiting and retention costs (Jovanovic, 1984). To what extent do young firms attempt to send accurate signals about the nature of the jobs they offer, and what factors impede the signaling process?

A central concern for young firms is how many <u>strangers</u> to recruit--what franction of the workforce will be unknown to one another? The higher the proportion of strangers, the greater the potential problems in molding a coherent organization out of the raw materials available to the founders.

One possible recruiting method is for the founders to return to the firms where they formerly worked and try to entice colleagues to leave to join them. Another possibility is that the founders make use of networks and informal contacts to recruit persons whom they don't know personally, but who are known to them through a trusted intermediary. The recruitment process, unlike the annual hiring visits of big firms to college campuses, takes place under a great deal of time pressure, and so we might expect short cuts to be taken, and also the normal process to be somewhat distorted.

Do young firms use executive search agencies? We suspect not, because when the founders are putting together their work force, they will have neither the time nor the resources to contract with others to hire new employees. However, firms that do use executive search firms or employment agencies might develop differently than those which do not, and so we should pay close attention to this possibility. Unlike established firms, the young firm cannot trade on its name, its reputation in the field, or its market share, because none of these things are firmly established yet.

In what career stages are the persons recruited to young firms? Is it really true that professionals and highly skilled persons are attracted to high tech firms because of the challenge, and not because of the potential career building or profit-participation schemes these firms might make possible. And what about employees who are looking for career stability? We know age-related differences occur when managers design reward systems and wonder to what extent founders consider the relative salience of rewards.

We also know that in many cases, the founders of new high tech firms are bright individuals fleeing from organizations that have not met their needs, or have become overly bureaucratic (Aldrich and Wiedenmayer, 1991). We would expect these people to bring other committed professionals with them to the new venture.

Studies show that new employees are very concerned about being told the truth regarding the firm, but what can recruiters for new firms tell potential employees? What expectations do they create for their work force, when the work force and the job themselves are still evolving?

Whether a young firm has put together a counseling or career plan for its new employees may be very important in recruiting and in retaining employees. Do firms that begin, early on, with a well developed human resource plan do better at attracting and recruiting employees than othe firms? We suspect that few young firms have such plans. Indeed, how many young firms give much though to attracting employees with a well developed career planning scheme?

Sex differences in work force composition will affect counseling plans. In wafer producton and most laboratories, there is an abudance of female workers. Do any of these firms systematically develop counseling systems or other support systems specifically for female employees (e.g., day care)?

Selecting employees out of the recruits who present themselves to the firms is another critical stage in the human resource development of young firms. Who makes the decisions? How formalized is the plan for selecting employees? Is the person who does the recruiting the same as the person who does the selecting? What role do project leaders within the growing firm play in selecting employees? Is there a coherent selection plan for the entire firm, or does each division, project, or section select its own people?

Informal interviews with directors of young firms suggest that the human resource function is one of the last to be formalized, and perhaps one of the most neglected aspects of the firm-building process. Who does the searching, screening, and interviewing of potential employees? For high technology firms, we know that technical specialists are selected by other technical specialists, rather than the finance or marketing person. Is there such a division of labor in selection in most firms? Or, is the picture painted in some descriptions of high technology firms accurate: a founder, with a vision of the firm's future, attracts and selects employees on the basis of his/her charisma or forceful personality?

Motivating Employees: What do Workers Want?

The concept of a reward system encompasses more than the income and material benefits made available by firms to their employees. Reward system also include any other incentives which firms have available to motivate employees, which can include identification with the firm (commitment and loyalty), career development possibilities (mobility within the firm as well as within one's professional or occupational culture), and perhaps even other incentive systems. Van de Ven, Hudson, and Schroeder (1984:100), in their study of new software ventures, argued that personnel stability was extremely important for young companies, as it "promotes program continuity, decreases the time needed to search for and train qualified personnel, stimulates commitment, and increases opportunities to learn from mistakes."

Reward and compensation systems must include procedures for: (1) directing the work of employees; (2) appraising the performance of employees; and (3) rewarding or compensating employees, not only for their direct job performance but perhaps also for other, more indirect contributions to the firm (Edwards, 1979). These three requirements are so closely bound up with one another that it is difficult to theorize about them independently.

Underlying all reward systems is the issue of their perceived legitimacy in the eyes of employees. Halaby (1986:646) argued that in the U.S., workers' attachment to their jobs "is partly the outcome of a process whereby workers grade governance practices and calculate authority costs by reference to a belief in legality." His conception of work place authority as a key feature of the connection between workers and owners highlights the social context for what takes place within new firms. Workers in the U.S. bring to their job a set of expectations about what principles will guide an employer's reward, discipline, and other practices. Such principles include: universalism (equality and fairness), due process, and non-arbitrary evaluatons of achievement. For purposes of our analyses, these principles are an institutional constant, a feature of the American landscape which all new firms must confront. At the firm level, however, some do a better job than others in convincing workers that they follow the principles of legality.

What are the rewards most valued by high technology and professional workers. Von Glinow (1988) compiled the list shown in Figure 1.

Research has shown that professional and job content rewards are more significant for high technology professionals than financial rewards. Employees respond differently to these rewards, also, depending on their values and career and stage in life. Younger people are more likely to respond to job content rewards, whereas older people are more likely to respond to financial rewards. Similarly, geographic location has been hypothesized to make a difference in attracting employees to high tech firms. Sunbelt and technopolis areas are often claimed to have a lifestyle advantage over other locations. Young firms will have to decide what mix of the above rewards to offer, and to target their rewards to the type of employees they have recruited and wish to retain.

Are there some rewards which young firms simply cannot offer? Are there some rewards which are especially available to young firms which are not available to older firms, such as career or job content rewards?

Young firms and their founders must decide not only what mix of rewards to offer, but also how to allocate them (cf Kerr, 1988). Two questions are central in allocating rewards: will they be contingent or non-contingent on performance, and will they be based on individual or collective characteristics. Contingent rewards are based on either an individual's or a group's performance level, whereas non-contingent rewards are benefits that flow simply from affiliation with an organization or from being in a particular status in an organization. Individual rewards are based on a specific individual's characteristics, whereas collective rewards are given equally to all who qualify. In Figure 2, we have cross-classified these two dimensions to produce a two by two table, with an example for each cell.

Figure 1. Rewards Most Valued by High Technology and Professional Workers

A. Professional Rewards

　　1. Opportunity to work with top-flight professionals
　　2. Freedom to make the most of your own work decisions
　　3. Intellectually stimulating work environment
　　4. Not working on repeating yesterday, but working on tomorrow
　　5. Having an impact on national legislation

B. Job Content Rewards

　　1. A productive atmosphere
　　2. Flexible work hours
　　3. Long-term project stability
　　4. Opportunities to address significant human needs
　　5. Diversity of busness, which creates continuing new opportunities
　　6. Patriotic projects
　　7. Projects of an altruistic nature

C. Career Rewards

　　1. Working for a leading-edge company
　　2. Diverse opportunities for personal growth and advancement
　　3. Opportunity to participate in the company's success
　　4. Career opportunities to stay ahead of the crowd
　　5. The chance to get in on the ground floor of important projects
　　6. Opportunities for self-expression
　　7. Being able to play a role in the company's future

D. Social Status or Prestige Rewards

　　1. Beautiful location
　　2. Open-door management
　　3. Extensive recreational facilities

D. Financial Rewards

　　1. Twice yearly salary reviews
　　2. Compensation for unused leave
　　3. Cash bonuses

Figure 2. Bases on Which Job Rewards Can be Given

	Individual	Collective
Contingent	Individual's performance e.g. productivity bonus	Group/unit's performance, e.g. quality bonuses
Non-Contingent	Membership benefits, e.g. ownership stake	Collective benefits, e.g. status or prestige of firm

Firms that begin with an emphasis on individual rewards may have a very hard time switching to collective rewards, and vice-versa. Individually-focused reward systems direct employees' attentions to their own responsibilities and careers, perhaps at the expense of the group. Collectively-focused reward systems emphasize a teamwork orientation, but may lead to shirking and a loss of individual initiative.

A computer software firm in a mid-Western state was founded by an entrepreneur who brought several of her friends in as programmers. Early on, they shared responsibilities for negotiating contracts with clients, pricing their services, and developing the software. The founder implicitly treated them as partners, and rewarded them accordingly. But, their status and reward system was never formalized in writing. Subsequently, as the firm grew, new employees were paid regular salaries and assigned to tasks, rather than developing their own contracts. They questioned why they did not receive the same treatment as the older employees, and the founder was faced with the dilemma of reconciling collectively-based rewards to the initial employees but individually-based rewards to all others.

To what extent do young firms systematically prepare a reward and compensation plan which clearly identifies the basis on which employees will be rewarded? Who has responsibility for drawing up the plan, and implementing it? Do young firms tend to base their plans on previous experiences in other companies, advice from consultants, or does the plan emerge form the interaction of the founders over the first few months or year of a firm's life?

Identifying rewards and deciding how to allocate them are only two of the three steps needed to understand the reward and compensation systems of young firms. In addition, we must also consider who controls the distribution of rewards. The founders may retain direct control, or they may delegate it. If they delegate reward distribution, they may centralize it in a human resource management unit, or decentralize it to managers and supervisors. Decisions may also be shared between these various possibilities. Eventually, as policies crystalize, founders may establish organizational policies and guidelines that formalize the process and thus constrain the actions of lower-level managers and supervisors.

The questions for us are, to what extent does organizational policy establish a set of priorities <u>before</u> the other bases of distributing rewards become firmly established. We would expect structural inertia to pose a difficult problem for high level management, unless drastic steps were taken to make sure that policy--and not lower level considerations--dictated reward distributions. From a developmental perspective, if there is a necessary order to the setting of priorities, then firms that grow out of sync with it will suffer inefficiencies and threaten their survival. From an evolutionary perspective, priorities might be imposed on a young firm because of its relations with banks, customers, and governmental regulations.

In a pilot study, the CEO of a rapidly growing medical services firm bemoaned the pressure he faced in trying to keep up with the human resource needs of his firm. The firm was growing too rapidly to promote from within, because young employees had not yet acquired the experience needed to fill middle-management jobs. Consequently, outsiders were brought in to fill such jobs, managing insiders who had been with the firm almost since its start-ups days.

For high technology firms, of course, the bottom line is "how well are employees performing?" What sorts of performance appraisal system do young firms establish? Where do they draw their ideas from? Some of the issues include, what should be evaluated, who should do the evaluating, and what specific procedures should be used for the evaluation?

Bureaucratically organized firms typicaly use job descriptions to direct the work of employees, and then judge employees by how well they measure up to the job description. But, we would expect high technology firms to have unclear or ambiguous job descriptions, and for the appraisal process to be much more open. How, then, is it managed? The medical services firm we studied had evolved a policy of continually pushing responsibility for evelution and training down onto the immediate supervisors, rather than creating a full-scale personnel department. Employees could thus check with their supervisors and know immediately how they were being evaluated, but the policy had an unforeseen side effect. Employees had difficulty determining their chances of advancement and what they should do about them. Promotion chains wee not clearly drawn, and it appeared to some employees that favoritism and luck were the major factors in promotions.

Education and Training

If employees must be re-trained, re-educatd, re-socialized, how do the founders accomplish this? Externally or internally? And how do founders pay for it?

Over time, we would expect high tech professionals to build upon skills and expertise learned previously. Training and development activities are provided, either through in-house trainers, videotapes, and consultants, or externally, such as through university training. What mix of training and development are young firms likely to use? We know the half life of some engineering specialties is extremely short (e.g., six months for laser optics engineering specialists) and thus the concept of keeping up one's skills is critically important in a high tech firm, almost as much as getting a product to market in a timely fashion. What provisions for training and development are made by the founders for their employees over the early (and later) stages of a firm's growth?

Training can be oriented toward individuals, work groups, or the total firm. Consequences for 'culture'. . . Training can be continuous, built into the structure of the firm, but does this have to be done at the start, before inertia sets in?

There are a host of other HRM questions that could be asked of new founders--however, the essence of this research focuses on how human assets are deployed at the outset in new high tech start-ups.

CONCLUSIONS

The developmental and evolutionary models lead to different expectations about the trajectory of HRM in start-ups. The developmental model, in its extreme form, implies that firms MUST go through a sequence of stages as the firm ages. Failure to fully develop a prior stage dooms a firm to ineffective HRM at a later stage. The evolutionary model, by contrast, makes fewer assumptions about the precise path of changes a start-up firm undergoes as it ages. Structural inertia obligates firms to build later stages on earlier states, but some firms may never break out of an earlier stage. Institutional forces may swamp developmental forces so that firms living through the same legal/political era look more like each other than like firms of the same age but from different eras.

The developmental model contains clear prescriptions for HRM in start-ups, as well as a blueprint for growth: the strategic components of HRM must be congruent with a firm's stage of development, and they must fit into a coherent whole (Baird and Meshoulam, 1988). If one component is developed more fully than another, resources will be wasted and effectiveness lowered. HRM policies and practices should be built in a modular fashion, one block on top of another, until a comprehensive, effective fit is achieved.

As a normative ideal, the developmental model is very clear. As a description of actual firm growth, however, the jury is still out on it. Although the four case studies they conducted seemed to show stage-like development, Baird and Meshoulam (1988:125) noted that in all 24 firms they studied, "human resource management lagged far behind the organization's stage of development." In their case studies, they also found many instances of firms prematurely adopting HRM practices that did not fit their developmental stage.

Lengnick-Hall and Lengnick-Hall (1988) have criticized many strategic HRm models because they over-emphasize the need for fit between the components of HRM and also between an organization and its context. When firms are pursuing multiple or conflicting goals, or when environmental conditions are changing rapidly, a tight fit may be neither feasible nor desirable.

From an evolutionary perspective, whether firms pass through a series of _a priori_ stages is an empirical question. Moreover, given the conditions under which most start-ups are formed, we suspect that new ventures contain a melange of HRM policies and practices, rather than a tidy set of modules on which successive blocks are built. Until research is conducted on start-ups which are followed over the first few years of their lives, we have few grounds--other than _a priori_ theorizing--for choosing between developmental and evolutionary models.

REFERENCES

Adler, Nancy and F. Ghadar 1989 "Globalization and Human Resource Management." In A. Rugman (ed.) Research In Global Strategic Management: A Canadian Perspective, I. Greenwich, CT: JAI Press.

Aldrich, Howard E. and Ellen R. Auster 1986 "Even Dwarfs Started Small: Liabilities of Age and Size and Their Strategic Implications" In Barry Staw and L.L. Cummings (eds.) Researhc in Organizational Behavior, Vol. 8. Grennwich, CT: JAI Press.

Aldrich, Howard E. and Gabriele Wiedenmayer 1991 "From Traits to Rates: An Ecological Perspective on Organizational Foundings: In Jerome Katz and Robert Brockhaus (Eds.), Advances in Entrepreneurship, Firm Emergence, and Growth, Vol I. JAI Press.

Baird, Lloyd and Ian Meshoulam 1988 "Managing Two Fits of Strategic Human Resource Management" Academy of Management Review 13:116-128.

Birch, David 1979 The Job Generation Process. MIT Program on Neighborhood and Regional Change.

Buller, Paul F. and Nancy K. Napier 1990 "Strategy and Human Resource Management Integration in Fast Growth Versus Other Mid-Sized Firms" Presented at the 1990 Academy of Management Meeting, Personnel/Human Resources Division.

Carey, M.L. and K.L. Hazelbaker 1986 "Employment Growth in the Temporary Help Industry" Monthly Labor Review (April):37-44.

Carroll, Glen R. 1984 "Organizational Ecology." Annual Review of Sociology, 10: 71-93.

Dyer, Lee 1983 "Bringing Human Resources into the Strategy Formulation Process" Human Resource Management 22:257-271.

Edwards, Richard 1979 Contested Terrain New York: Basic.

Fombrun, Charles 1982 "Environmental Trends Create New Pressures on Human Resources" Journal of Business Strategy 3:61-69.

Gersick, Connie J.G. 1990 "Temporal Pacing in Organizational Development: The case of a New Venture" Unpublished paper, UCLA Graduate School of Management.

Greiner, Larry E. 1970 "Patterns of Organizatonal Change" pp. 213-229 in G.

Dalton and Paul R.Lawrence (Eds.), Organizational Changes and Development Homewood, IL: Irwin-Dorsey.

Halaby, Charles N. 1986 "Worker Attachment and Workplace Authority" American Sociological Review 51 (October): 634-649.

Halaby, Charles N. 1988 "Action and Information in the Job Mobility Process: The Search Decision" American Sociological Review 53 (February): 9-25.
Jovanovic, Boyan 1984 "Matching, Turnover, and Unemployment" Journal of Political Economy 87:1246-60.

Kahn, Robert G., Donald M. Wolfe, Robert Quinn, J.D. Snoek, and R.A. Rosenthal 1964 Organizational Stress: Studies in Role Conflict and Ambiguity New York: Wiley.

Kerr, Stephen 1988 "Some Characteristics and Consequences of Organizational Reward Systems" In David Schoorman and Benjamin Schneider (Eds.), Facilitating Work Effectiveness: Concepts and Procedures (pp.43-76) Lexington, MA: Lexington Books.

Lengnick-Hall, Cynthia A. and Mark L. Lengnick-Hall 1988 "Strategic Human Resources Management: A Review of the Literature and a Proposed Typology: Academy of Management Review 13:454-470.

McCaskey, Michael B. 1982 The Executive Challenge: Managing Ambiguity and Change Marshfield, MA: Pittman.

Meyerson, Debra 1990 "On Acknowledging and Uncovering Ambiguities in Cultures" In P. Frost, L. Moore, C. Lundberg, M. Louis, and J. Martin (Eds.), Reframing Organizational Culture Newbury Park, CA: Sage.

Milliman, John, Mary Ann Von Glinow, and Maria Nathan 1990 "Organizational Life Cycles and Strategic International Human Resources Mangment in MNCs: Implications for Contingency Theory." Unpublished paper, School of Business Administration, University of Southern California.

O'Reilly, Charles A. and John Anderson 1982 "Personnel/Human Resource Management in the U.S.: Some Evidence of change" Journal of Irish Business and Administrtive Research 4,2 (October): 3-12.

Pascale, Richard T. 1990 Managing on the Edge New York: Simon and Schuster.

Peters, Tom J. 1987 Thriving on Chaos: Handbook for a Management Revolution New York: Knopf.

Pfeffer, Jeffrey and James N. Baron 1988 "Recent Trends in the Structuring of

Employment" In Barry M. Staw and L.L. Cummings (eds.), Research in Organizational Behavior Greenwich, CT: JAI Press.

Scott, B.R. 1971 "Stages of Corporate Development" [9-371-294 EP 998] cambridge, MA: Intercase Clearing House Harvard University Business School.

Stinchcombe, Arthur 1965 "Social Structure and Organizations" In J.G. March (Ed.), Handbook of Organizations Chicago: Rand McNally.

Van de Ven, Andrew H., Roger Hudson, and Dean M. Schroeder 1984 "Designing New Business Start-ups: Entrepreneurial, Organiztional, and Ecological Considerations" Journal of Management 10, 1:87-107.

Von Glinow, Mary Ann 1988 The New Professionals: Managing Today's High Tech Employees Cambridge, MA: Ballinger.

Planning Meeting Intensity In Small Firms

Critique
by
Yves-Frédéric Livian, *IRE/Groupe ESC Lyon*
Stéphane Marion, *IRE/Groupe ESC Lyon*

    The problem of the role and consequences of planning on the behaviour of firms has been the subject of extensive research, as this survey makes clear. These studies, however, differ widely in their findings on the relationship between levels of strategic planning and firm performance.

    The literature survey undertaken in the paper is very useful in highlighting both the sampling problems specific to this discipline and the issue of the causal relationship between planning and performance.

    As some of the past research presented in the paper shows, the decision to plan or not itself indicates a certain kind of entrepreneur and firm. We believe therefore, that planning is merely one aspect of the behaviour of firms and this could explain the differences in the results seen in other research. In this view, researching correlations between the 'strategic profile' of a firm and the actual planning activity is a good basis to work from.

    Focusing the study on small firms avoids the sterile discussion of the difference in planning between small and large firms. We agree with the authors that the strategic planning of small firms has special characteristics and takes diverse forms. We accept that "planning takes the form of regular discussion with all those concerned with the strategic development of the firm". But it is excessive to extrapolate that all forms of regualar discussions are a sign of planning. Are there no meetings that are not concerned with planning? For the purposes of this research, which definition of the term 'planning meeting' is used? What differences are there between 'planning meetings' and other meetings?

    If meetings with and between partners of the firm is a sign of planning, is it enough to take into account only the frequency of meetings? It would have been equally interesting and revealing to analyse the content of the meetings. The choice of 'frequency' measurement seems to be a direct result of the methodology used, which in turn was suggested by the available data base and the quantitative analyses that could be undertaken with it.

    The choice of the three short-listed types of meetings is relevant. At the same time, from a methodological point of view, it may have been more useful to have taken very small firms, i.e., those with less than 10 employees, out of the sample. It is difficult to study "management and board planning meetings" in this size of firm.

The number of variables taken into consideration to define the strategic profile is too large. Their number may in part explain the difficulties met with in finding meaningful results. It might have been more interesting to have defined a limited number of variables and questioned the relevance of others to the definition of strategic profile. We also question the usefulness of looking for correlations between frequency of meetings and information such as the fact that the entrepreneurs own their sales vehicles. It is not clear what conclusion is to be drawn from the finding that, "the smaller firms in the sample, as reflected by the number of employees, appear to be those most likely to use the expertise of their business contacts. However, this only applies to those firms which have invested in personnel life insurance".

If, as is pointed out, with a touch of courage and humour, in the conclusion, the univariate analysis perhaps "defeated" the authors, the paper does show the difficulty of apprehending the notion of planning action in small firms. In this area, the definition of planning itself remains an important field of research, when the formal rational system has been abandoned. These research directions need to take account of the specific nature of small firm context. These specificities should lead to more qualitative analyses of the planning process.

However, this does not mean the rejection of quantitative methods. In conclusion, it would be more interesting if the authors could make clear the basic hypothesis they have drawn from the paper and the direction they intend to take for future research on the topic.

PLANNING MEETING INTENSITY IN SMALL FIRMS

SUE BIRLEY, *IMPERIAL COLLEGE*
PAUL WESTHEAD, *IMPERIAL COLLEGE*

INTRODUCTION

Strategic planning is increasingly being seen as a crucial ingredient in the survival of any small business. Indeed, research suggests that firms with a long history of planning outperform those with shorter planning histories (Bracker and Pearson, 1986). As Kelly and Young (1983, p.28) note, "The importance of planning is repeatedly emphasized by academics, consultants, and practitioners," and as a corollary, "its adequacy or absence is repeatedly cited as a primary cause of the high failure rate of small businesses," a conclusion which also finds support from other empirical studies (Timmons et al., 1977; Tootalain and Gaedeke, 1978; Robinson, 1980; Vozikis and Glueck, 1980; Sanford, 1982). However, whilst there is general consensus that planning is important, there is less agreement on its exact nature -- what it is and the way in which it contributes to superior performance. Some researchers have been concerned with its formality, some with its content, and some with the individuals within the firm who are involved in the process. All agree, however, that it is a process that owner-managers must adapt to the peculiar circumstances of their firm and to their own particular skills and needs. As Shuman and Seeger (1986, p.16) note, "...continued empirical work is needed to develop a resource-sensitive strategic planning process that accurately takes into consideration the unique size-related circumstances of these firms." This view is also supported by Stoner (1983, p.41), who concluded that "specification of the relationships between firm performance and the types of planning activities utilized is a fertile area for future research. Such research should help to clarify the role and importance of strategic planning in the small firm."

This paper argues that the previous focus on the planning/performance dimension is too narrow and that planning is but one aspect of the strategic profile of the firm which accounts for its performance. Moreover, within the small firm, where managerial systems and structures are being developed, formal planning procedures modelled on those in large, established firms are inappropriate. More relevant is the extent to which the owner-manager consults with those individuals most knowledgeable about the business and most concerned about its long term survival -- its customers and suppliers, its advisers and investors, and its managers.

PREVIOUS RESEARCH

In their review of the literature, Pearce et al. (1987) identified three major thrusts of research surrounding the importance of strategic planning in small firms. The first thrust, generally conducted in the United States, recognised planning as "...an essential management function in a resource constrained business organisation" (Robinson et al., 1986a, p. 19), and devoted considerable empirical attention to its the role within the firm as reflected in the relationship between strategic planning and company performance. The results are, however, mixed. Some researchers found a positive relationship in firms of all sizes (Thune and House, 1970; Ansoff et al., 1971; Herold, 1972; Rue, 1973; Karger and Malik, 1975; Burt, 1978; Wood and LaForge, 1979; Robinson, 1980; Unni, 1981; Jones, 1982; Rhyne, 1983; Robinson and Pearce, 1984; Robinson et al., 1984; Acklesburg and Arlow, 1985; Sexton and van Auken, 1985; Braker and Pearson, 1986; Rhyne, 1986; Pearce et al., 1987) and, indeed, that small firms which engaged in systematic planning tended to out perform their non-planning counterparts (Reeser, 1981; Robinson, 1982; Bracker, 1982); and others identified a negative relationship (Grinyer and Norburn, 1975; Shuman, 1975; Kudla, 1980; Leontiades and Tezel, 1980; Fredrickson and Mitchell, 1984; Lindsay et al., 1982; Sexton and van Auken, 1985; Robinson and Pearce, 1983; Robinson et al., 1986b; Gable and Tople, 1987). Shuman and Seeger (1986, p.15) found no statistical significance between the planning process used by companies in their sample and sales growth, although their results did suggest that by conducting planning activities, decision-making abilities were enhanced, thus leading to increased profitability. Moreover, Orpen (1985) concluded that through planning activities, the marketability of the business was increased, thus creating a more secure financial base. Unfortunately, this concentration on the identification of the planning process and its relationship to performance begs the question of the perceived value to the decision-maker and the owner-manager, an assumption not always supported directly. For example, in a study of ninety-four owner-managers in the Perth metropolitan area of Australia, Kelmar and Noy (1989) found that, whilst 85% of small businesses engaged in planning activities, 15% did not. Moreover, rather than increased profitability, most perceived the greatest benefit in an improvement in the level of sales, a better competitive position, greater cost-savings and reduced cash-flow problems.

Whilst most of the above studies have concentrated solely upon the planning/performance relationship, some researchers have widened the debate to include other firm characteristics. For example, Hofer (1975), Vozikis and Glueck (1980), and Lindsay and Rue (1980) found that organisational effectiveness in planning was contingent on the stage of development of the firm, a result not supported by Robinson et al. (1984, p.52) who found superior performance in "planning" firms at all stages of development. This latter result is perhaps explained in part by Shuman and Seeger (1986) who noted that as the company's profitability level declined (often suggested to be the point at which firms move from one stage to another), there was an increased propensity for businesses to change their planning process, a point also made by Lindsay et al. (1982) who found no consistent relationship between planning and performance and concluded that this could be due to the fact that businesses did not plan until performance was unsatisfactory.

In the 'second wave' of planning research, Pearce et al., (1987) suggest that researchers have attempted to seek more rigourous methods for guaging the formality of the strategic planning process. For example, in their study of small banks in South Carolina in the United States, Robinson and Pearce (1983, p.202) found that firms engaging in formal planning failed to out-perform non-formal planners on four performance measures. These results contradicted the earlier results presented by Wood and LaForge (1979) who found that formal planners outperformed non-formal planners in the banking industry. However, Leontiades and Tezel (1980) argue that there are significant difficulties associated with measuring the formality of the process, and that the simplistic and subjective operationalisation of planning formality used in prior research has led to the presentation of potentially dubious results, a point supported by Wood and LaForge (1981) and by Ramanujam et al.(1986). In a later study, Bracker et al (1988, p.594) departed from the crude formal/informal planning dichotomy and focussed upon the level of planning sophistication. They found (p.601) that "...planning for the sake of planning does not lead to increased financial performance. What does seem important is the type of planning process employed, and the length of time the firm has been planning. The structured strategic planning categorisation, coupled with a long planning history, outperformed all other planning categorisations with regard to financial performance". This empirical evidence led the authors to conclude that "...the quality of planning rather than the time spent on planning is the most appropriate determinant of financial performance" (p.599).

Pearce et al. (1987, p.126) suggest that the findings of these later studies led to the start of a 'third wave' of empirical research on the planning/performance issue. Characteristic of the 'third wave' is the use of classification schemes which facilitate the recognition of the multidimensional nature of the strategic planning formality construct (Fredrickson and Mitchell, 1984). Associated with this wave was the development and use of more sophisticated Guttman scaling procedures to produce planning formality classification schemes (Robinson and Pearce, 1983; Wood and LaForge, 1979, 1981). Interestingly, in a recent study Carland et al. (1989) broadened the arena by exploring the relationship between established personality traits of owners of small firms and the incidence of planning. They also examined the relationship between planning and demographic factors. The results of their study indicated that formal planners had traits associated with the traditional view of the entrepreneur including a high need for achievement, innovative preference and risk-taking propensity. In their conclusions (p. 31) they suggest that "these managers may utilise planning activities to better understand the risks inherent in their operations and to guide their risk taking", and that the implication of these finding are that "...most 'entrepreneurs' can be expected to plan while 'small business owners' cannot be expected to plan to the same depth".

It is clear from this preliminary analysis of both the entrepreneurship and strategic management literature that the relationship between 'strategic' planning and organisational performance has been extensively researched. However, the results are fragmented and contradictory. Ramanujam et al. (1986, p.348) claim that this is due to two major conceptual shortcomings. First, most studies have used rather simplistic conceptualizations of the notion of planning such that researchers have attempted to show differences in financial performance between "planners" and "nonplanners" or "formal planners" and "informal planners". Second, most studies have been solely preoccupied with the linkage between planning and financial aspects of corporate performance, even though conceptual writings on the formal planning systems stress several non financial, intangible benefits (Camillus, 1975; Steiner, 1979).

Following this theme, Hansen and Wernerfelt (1989, p.399) propose two major determinants of firm performance. "One is based primarily upon an economic tradition, emphasizing the importance of external market factors in determining firm success. The other line of research builds on behavioural and sociological paradigms and sees organizational factors and their fit with the environment as the major determinants of success". Related to these themes, various authors have implied that the business environment is composed of physical, cultural and technological components and that the organisational environment can be broken down into 'external' and 'internal' factors (Duncan, 1972). The 'external' environment includes competitors, suppliers, consumers, stockholders, governments, regulatory agencies and labour markets (Dill, 1958; Estafen, 1971); and the 'internal' environment the physical and nominal factors within the boundaries of the organisation that influence the decision making behaviour of individuals in the organisation (Duncan, 1972). This latter includes the resources of the firm, the extent of the division of management labour, the control system and the extent to which planning is built into it (Gibb and Scott, 1985), the human potential of the organisation in terms of skills and flexibility of the work force, the financial situation of the company, and the physical asset base of the company in terms of age and quality of machinery and equipment.

More relevant to the small firm and to this research is the approach proposed by Dutton and Duncan (1987, p.108) which encapsulates the natural inclination of the owner-manager to use informal, discursive methods to analyse and develop his strategy -- "the scope of strategic issues considered in a more intensive planning process is broader because the amount of time expended trying to understand issues collaboratively is greater. When individuals get together frequently, and spend more time discussing issues verbally, there is greater potential to understand the complexities of the strategic issues than with a less intensive process. As more time is spent sharing information about issues, interrelationships between issues become visible, and issues are framed more generally."

PROBLEMS ASSOCIATED WITH PREVIOUS RESEARCH

The literature reported above shows that there is clearly significant disagreement as to the contribution which planning makes to the performance of the smaller firm. However, this may be due in part to the fact that analysis is usually based upon the type of structured planning reflected in the normative models (Golde,

1964; Still, 1974; Rice and Hamilton, 1979; Robinson, 1982; Robinson and Pearce, 1984; for a dissenting view see Moyer, 1982; Thurston, 1983). For example, Sexton and van Auken (1985, p.15) have argued that, "strategic planning appears to be a scarce, fragile commodity in the small business environment. Most small firms do not engage in true strategic planning at all, and the rest may do so only sporadically or temporarily, despite the evidence that strategic planning can help firms to survive and prosper." Recently, however, this approach has been called into question on definitional grounds by Shuman and Seeger (1986, p.8) who suggest such findings "...appear to be a function of how the researcher(s) defined strategic planning and how they evaluated organisational performance." Further, in a fierce and comprehensive criticism of the literature, Bracker and Pearson (1986, p.505-506) find that studies of the empirical relationship between planning and financial performance suffer from a number of methodological problems which "....include small sample sizes, short-time frames, failure to measure the degree of congruence of the planning process or comprehensive strategic management models, ignoring the role of CEO or entrepreneur in the process, inappropriate and non-robust statistical procedures, non-homogeneity of data, and inappropriate financial performance measures. Other major shortcomings of past research are failure to distinguish between entrepreneurs and small businesses or between young and old firms; and inattention to firm size and the dynamic or static nature of the firm's environment." Unfortunately, this list is not complete. Previous studies of planning in small firms:

*   have not controlled for inter-industry differences (Beard and Dess, 1981) even though industry has been suggested as a key determinant of the level of profitability.

*   have placed small firms into a small number of planning categories based upon self selection by responding owner-managers (Robinson et al, 1986b; Bracker, 1982; Reeser, 1981). Leontiades and Tezel (1980) argue that such simplistic and arbitrary approaches are more a reflection of the researcher's opinion than of the true character of the planning system.

*   have associated the relationship between planning and performance with a large firm bias in the samples studied. Consequently, there has been limited research which has examined the strategic planning performance relationship per se in small firms. As Robinson and Pearce (1983, p.205-206) have argued, "....contrary, to the frequently encountered (contingency) notion that strategic management is solely a large firm phenomenon, this study suggests that the small firm is an important arena for strategic management research."

*   have tended to focus on firms less than five years old. In the opinion of Bracker and Pearson (1986, p.504), "the short operating time frames for these businesses may lead to inadequately developed strategic planning systems. This leads researchers to make prescriptions for all small firms based on a sample that differs significantly from older, mature small businesses."

* fail to address the varying degrees of sophistication of planning processes employed by small firms (Bracker and Pearson, 1986, p.504).

* have dealt almost exclusively with manufacturing firms.

* have concentrated on formal planning systems and consequently the characteristics of informal planning processes have not been captured (Rhyne, 1986, p.435).

THIS RESEARCH

This research starts from the premise that small firms are not a homogeneous group. They differ in resource base, management style, sophistication of managerial practices, level of maturity, and performance. Therefore, research which studies the planning process must take into account that unique nature of the individual firm (Bracker et al. 1988, p.593). Moreover, rather than taking the simple dichotomies of planning/no planning or formal planning/informal planning, this research starts from the presumption that all firms plan but that in many this is often "...on an informal, ad hoc basis, with little evidence of formal written plans from which to refer in order to analyse the resultant change in performance measures" (Kelmar and Noy, 1989, p.13). Thus planning takes the form of regular discussion with all those concerned with the strategic development of the firm. In this way, the development of a strategy is an evolving process which can change as regularly as circumstances require. As Dutton and Duncan (1987, p.104) argue, "....organizations vary in the extent to which their issue array is large or small (array, size). Organizations vary in the diversity of issues considered at one time (array, variety) and the frequency with which any one issue is replaced by another (array, turnover). .....some organizations may have issues that are very narrowly defined, while others consider issues that are much broader in scope (issue scope)." Due to these contrasting conditions, these authors have argued that, "...organizational planning processes vary in terms of the frequency of contact of planning participants. In some organizations the planning cycle requires frequent, lengthy, face-to-face contacts between planning participants. In other organizations participants communicate once a year, and when they do, it is through written and not verbal contact. Planning intensity captures the level of personal resources participants must devote to the planning process. It is assumed that intensity is highest when participants meet frequently, in person, over longer periods of time. It is proposed that the intensity of the planning process expands the scope of the issues considered, decreases the size of the issue array, and increases the frequency of issue turnover" (1987, p.107-108).

Whilst the extent of planning is a function of the individual circumstances of the firm, it is also related to the inclinations of the owner-manager. For example, it has been suggested that owner-managers do not plan due to little training, lack of necessary skills, lack of time and resources and a fear of planning itself (Golde, 1964). More recent research has indicated that they consider planning irrelevant and unnecessary (Steiner, 1967), too time consuming (Robinson and Littlejohn, 1981) and feel it leads to the development of a fear of the unknown with rapidly changing external circumstances (van Auken and Ireland, 1980).

This research examines the type and "frequency" of the planning activity within small firms in two stages. The researchers accept that planning is not a sterile activity but rather that it requires continuous debate and discussion. Therefore this study attempts to capture the nature of planning inputs through the frequency and regularity with which the owner-manager meets with those directly concerned with the commercial development of the firm -- the managers, customers and suppliers, investors and professional advisers. Drawing for support upon the networking theories which argue that successful owner-managers are those who are also active networkers (Aldrich and Zimmer, 1986; Aldrich et al., 1987; Birley et al., 1990), the assumption inherent in the study is that all of these meetings are crucial to the strategic process and so will have some strategic component.

The literature described above suggests that the variables most likely to explain variation in planning activity within the firm are:

- Industry
- Age of the Firm
- Size of the Firm
- Performance of the Firm

The first stage of the paper analyses these four factors individually. However, the definition of planning used in this study implies a constant exchange between all those concerned with the development of the firm. Therefore, it is likely that other characteristics will also explain variability in activity. For example:

- Firms with a large number of customers and suppliers are likely to meet them frequently.

- Firms with complex financial or cost structures are likely to meet their advisors frequently.

- Firms with complex ownership and management structures, and employee profiles, are likely to meet regularly.

These characteristics are defined by the researchers as the strategic profile of the firm. Figure 1 below shows the structure of the study.

Figure 1

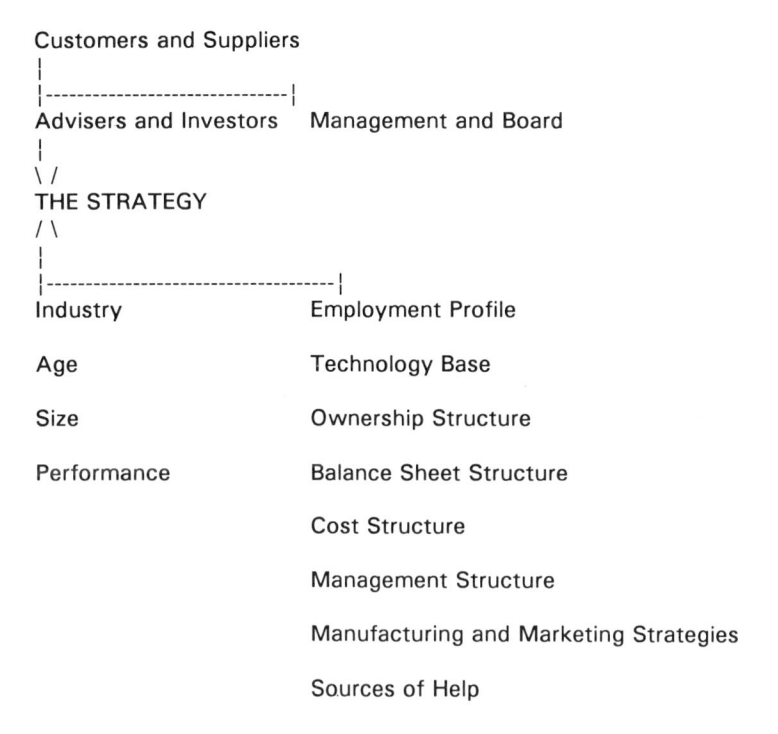

Customers and Suppliers
|
|-------------------------------|
Advisers and Investors   Management and Board
|
\ /
THE STRATEGY
/ \
|
|----------------------------------|
Industry   Employment Profile

Age   Technology Base

Size   Ownership Structure

Performance   Balance Sheet Structure

                          Cost Structure

                          Management Structure

                          Manufacturing and Marketing Strategies

                          Sources of Help

The second stage of the paper uses stepwise regression analysis to isolate those factors which <u>best describe</u> the variability in planning scores.

Data Collected:

This paper draws upon data from 249 small firms in the Cranfield Small Firms Data Base (CSFDB) established by the authors. The CSFDB was set up to monitor the changes in the strategic profiles of a sample of small firms. Firms in the sample are from a diverse range of industries, both service and manufacturing, employ approximately 8,000 people, account for approximately £318 million of sales revenue, range in size from 1 to 181 employees, and from less than £100,000 in sales to greater than £10 million. For a full description of the data collection methods, see Birley and Westhead (1988a), and for the sample characteristics, see Birley and Westhead (1988b).

Three types of planning meetings were studied -

* Management and Board
* Bank, Accountant and Lawyer
* Major Customers and Suppliers

In each case, owner managers were asked to indicate the frequency and regularity of the meetings from the following list. The responses were scored as indicated:

Never	1
Irregular	2
Annually	3
Six Monthly	4
Quarterly	5
Monthly	6
Weekly	7

Thus the score for management and board, and customers and suppliers could range between 2 and 14, and for bank, accountant and lawyer between 3 and 21. In order to compare the three groups for the preliminary analysis, the data were then standardised to the range 1 to 7. Subsequent analysis was conducted using the raw scores.

Only those firms which responded to all the questions in the sections were included in the analysis. After using this criterion to eliminate all those cases with missing values, the size of the four samples analysed is shown in below:

Type of Meeting	Code	Sample Size
Management and Board	PLANMAN	200
Bank, Accountant, and Lawyer	PROFMAN	221
Customers and Suppliers	BUSMAN	219
Total	PLANTOT	177

In order to explore the relationship between the frequency of formal planning meetings and the strategic profile of surveyed small firms, either Pearson Product-Moment correlation coefficients were calculated or Chi-squared analyses conducted. Each calculation was computed using cases which had complete data for the pairs (or groups) of variables correlated. To explore the multivariate relationships between total planning meetings (PLANTOT) and strategic profile measures, the data were further subjected to multiple regression analysis. This statistical technique allows the association of each independent strategic profile measure with the total planning score to be examined while controlling for the effects of other independent strategic profile variables. The multivariate regression equations were calculated using the 'stepwise inclusion method'. The 0.05 level of significance was the selected level for the stepwise inclusion of significant independent variables for the first equation, whilst the second equation included variables found to be significant at the 0.01 level.

RESULTS

The evidence presented in Table 1 shows that the majority of firms in the sample tend to meet most regularly with those most immediately concerned with the business -- the management meetings, the Board and major customers. There is no apparent pattern in the meetings with suppliers; meetings with the bank and accountant are regular but not usually frequent; and meetings with lawyers are generally irregular depending upon particular circumstances and needs.

STAGE 1:

Table 2 shows the results of the univariate analysis of the four primary variables identified in the literature. As can be seen, only two significant results emerge. Thus, the older firms are less likely to have frequent meetings with their professional advisors, and those with a large number of employees are less likely to meet with their business contacts. Neither industry nor performance effects are significant. Moreover, when taking into account the planning activity as a whole, none of these variables emerges as significant.

STAGE 2: Frequency of Management Planning Meetings

Despite the large number of variables analysed in this section, only three -- the percentage of costs spent on sales and marketing, the use of Export Credit Guarantee, and workforce training - show any significant correlation with the frequency with which the board and the management meet. Whilst it would not be sensible to place much credence on this without further support, it is both interesting and intuitively acceptable that the management of firms which appear to be marketing oriented, whatever their size, performance, or complexity are also the firms which meet frequently and regularly to discuss the progress of the business.

Breaking the primary results down into their constituent parts, six further significant results emerge. Frequent planners tend to own their own sales vehicles but not necessarily their premises, plant and equipment, or computers; to have employees as investors; to include production, operations management, and quality control as functions within the firm; and to use their lawyers as a primary source of information. They are less likely to delegate the stores function.

Frequency of Meetings with Professional Advisors

The extent to which firms met with their professional advisers was significantly associated with eleven of the primary variables in the strategic profile.

Thus firms which consulted with their bankers, accountants and lawyers frequently and regularly tended to have a broad customer base, high insurance and interest costs, and to invest in owners' or directors' personal liability insurance, their life insurance, management training, personal computers, and market research.

Breaking the primary variables into their constituent parts, nine significant results emerged. Thus, these frequent planners tended to:

* lease their plant and equipment
* had sought the help of both their accountant and their banks in the previous 3 months
* had sought commercial information from their accountant, bank, lawyer, and the planning and estates department of their local authority in the pr previous three months.

They were less likely to operate transport and purchasing as managerial functions within the firm.

Frequency of Meetings with Business Contacts

Firms which frequently meet their business contacts are those which have invested in personal life insurance and insurance to guarantee export credits, and who have applied for Government grants. Counter-intuitively, those firms in which one person is responsible for a large number of managerial functions are also most likely to consult their commercial colleagues. However, when this variable is compared with the total number of managerial functions operated within the firm in order to compute a delegation index, it would seem that this result only applies to those owner-managers who have begun to create structure through delegation. This theme continued, in part, when the constituent parts of the primary data are analysed. Thus, frequent planners also tended to:

* lease both premises and plant and equipment
* operate manual control systems for payroll and production
* not to operate engineering and production functions although the frequent planning manufacturing firms tended to delegate the management of both engineering and purchasing,

although they were also less likely to be the manufacturing firms in the sample since they tended not to operate engineering and production functions.

Frequency of Total Planning Meetings

The results in each of the sections above do not present a consistent pattern although they appear to suggest some internal coherence. Thus, for example, those firms which meet their advisors regularly do appear to seek information and advice from them.

However, the data also shows considerable divergence between the three sets of analyses. Of the 43 significant results identified, only the following five variables occur more than once (See Table 3):

Export Credit Guarantee Insurance
Insurance of the Owners Life
Leasing of Plant and Equipment
Production/Operations Function Operated within the Firm
Information from Lawyers Sought in the Previous 3 Months

Overall, the variables which occur most frequently are those of management structure and finance. The question which remains, therefore, is the extent to which these variables describe the total planning activity of the firm. All of the 177 businesses for which complete data was available were involved in management meetings and meetings with customers and professional advisers at some level of frequency, but only two firms replied that they conducted all seven types of meeting on a 'weekly' basis. Generally, firms held meetings either every six months (39.0%) or annually (31.1%). Table 4 lists the results of the analysis of variables for this section.

Strategic Profile

Industry: No statistically significant difference was recorded between firms in each of the groups with regard to the industrial characteristics. Over 45% of firms in each of the groups were engaged in manufacturing activities, although a slightly larger proportion of '6 monthly' firms were engaged in service activities (48.0%).

Age: Approximately half the firms in each of the meeting groups were less than sixteen years of age.

Employment: In total, 6,311 people were employed in the 176 firms that supplied employment data with 71.7% of total employment accounted for by '6 monthly' firms (2,280 total employees) and 'annually' firms (2,248 total employees). Moreover, by far the largest number were full-time employees in each of the meeting groups. No difference was recorded between the types of firms with regard to the total employment sizes of the surveyed small firms. However, it is interesting to note that markedly more 'annually or more' firms employed 50 or more people.

Over 45% of firms in the meeting groups employed no part-time directors (i.e. non-executive directors).

Sales: No difference was recorded between the four groups of firms in terms of levels of sales for the previous financial year. Similarly, no difference was recorded between firms with regard to the percentage of sales revenue accounted for by the major product line or service group, although a slightly larger proportion of 'annually or more' firms obtained over 80% of their sales revenue on the basis of their major product line or service group.

Profitability: In each of the groups, over 67% of firms had made a profit in the last financial year and, over 54% of firms rated their businesses profit performance as being better than average relative to competition.

Location: Significantly more '6 monthly' and 'irregular' firms were located in the less affluent and buoyant 'north' of the United Kingdom (all standard regions of the United Kingdom excluding East Anglia, the South East and the South West of England).

Ownership: There was no relationship between the groups and the family relationship of the current majority owners to the original founder, with over 54% of firms having 'first generation' owners, although a slightly larger proportion of 'quarterly' firms had 'family succession' current owners. Over 39% of each type of business had 'first generation' current senior executives.

No significant difference was recorded between the groups with regard to the number of founders who are still partners or shareholders, nor between firms in the three groups with regard to the number of shareholders or partners. Indeed, 40% of firms in each of the groups had only 2 shareholders / partners .

Product Base: No significant difference was recorded between firms in terms of the total number of major product lines or service groups. However, a larger percentage of those firms which tended to meet quarterly had added more than one new major product line or service group in the last twelve months. Interestingly, over 38% of firms in each of the meeting groups had not introduced a new major product line or major service group in the last twelve months.

Customers: Over 47% of firms in each of the meeting groups had over 100 customers. During the past twelve months, over 59% of firms in each of the groups had acquired between 1 and 50 new customers. Significantly, more '6 monthly' firms had the majority of their customers in nationwide or overseas locations, whilst 'annually or more' firms had a greater propensity to serve 'local' customers within a radius of twenty miles from their operational premises.

Suppliers: Over 45% of firms in the three groups had less than 51 suppliers; over 70% had contacted between 1 and 10 new suppliers in the past twelve months; and over 30% purchased locally from suppliers situated less than 20 miles from their operational premises, whilst a further 29% purchased from locations over 100 miles from their main operational premises.

Competition: In each of the groups, over 35% of the firms stated they had between 1 and 10 direct competitors, and more than 40% of firms in each of the groups stated they were in direct competition with fellow small firms with less than 51 employees.

Technology base

Production systems: More than three quarters of the manufacturing firms in the sample used small batch or unit production processes and manual technology for the major manufacturing product lines.

There was no significant difference between the groups with regard to the age of the oldest piece of production equipment although the mean age of the oldest piece of production equipment was highest in 'irregular' firms (194.7 months) and lowest in 'quarterly' firms (117.2 months). Similarly, there was no significant difference between the meeting groups with regard to the age of the newest piece of production equipment where the mean age ranged from only 8.0 months in 'quarterly' firms to 12.4 months in '6 monthly' firms.

The mean cost of the most important piece of production equipment bought in the previous year was not significantly different between the types of firms, although it ranged from £15,850 in 'annually' firms to £58,887 in '6 monthly' firms.

The leading technology used in control systems in each of the meeting groups was manual. In only a few instances in each of the groups were personal computers, mini computers, computer mainframes and computer bureaus found to be appropriate control technologies.

Financial data

Asset base: The majority of firms in the sample preferred to own rather than to hire or lease their assets with one exception. A significantly larger proportion of 'quarterly' firms preferred to lease sales vehicles.

Cost base: The leading component of the cost base of all the firms was salaries and wages, with the second leading mean percentage cost being sales and marketing. When all aspects of the cost base were subjected to a Pearson Product-Moment Correlation, only percentage training costs and absolute interest costs were significantly higher in frequent planning firms. Over 38% of firms in each of the three groups stated that their interest cost was between £1,000 and £5,000 although a slightly larger proportion of 'quarterly' firms (55.9%) had an interest cost of more than £10,000.

Investment: The leading sources of received financial investment in each type of firm were the essentially 'local' ones of employees and family. Interestingly, a significantly larger proportion of 'irregular or more' and 'annually' firms had not obtained financial investment from any source, whilst frequent planning firms had a tendency to have received financial investment from more than one source.

Insurance: All the firms studied had the usual types of insurance cover such as employers liability, vehicles, theft, flood, etc. and plant/equipment. However, a significantly larger proportion of 'annually' and 'irregular firms did not hold any owners or directors personal liability insurance cover.

Management of the firm

Managerial functions: The leading functions operated in the majority of firms were general management, finance, accounting, marketing, sales and purchasing and no significant differences were recorded between the planning groups. However, a significantly larger proportion of 'irregular' firms had operated the functions of general management, transport, and stores, which were the sole responsibility of one person. Over 43% of firms in each of the groups currently operated between 6 and 12 managerial functions. Interestingly, a larger proportion of the 'annually or more' firms did not have their managerial functions under the sole responsibility of one person.

There was no significant difference between the groups with regard to the level of managerial delegation as indicated by a managerial delegation score (number of managerial functions currently operated / number of managerial functions currently operated under the sole responsibility of one person).

Training: Over 42% of firms in each of the groups stated that their management had undertaken some form of management training, although by contrast the majority also stated that their staff had never attended any training courses. Over 84% of firms had not applied for local or central Government training schemes in the previous three months. Also, over 59% of firms in each group had not employed Youth Training Scheme (YTS) trainees.

Market research: A significantly larger proportion of 'quarterly' firms had conducted formal in-house market research studies and, as a result, had not received any financial assistance. '6 monthly' firms tended to utilise the services of consultants and to have spent more than £1,000 on their last formal market research study.

Agencies: The vast majority of firms in each of the four groups had not applied for any Government grants nor had they made any contact with their local small firms assistance agencies, although those which had tended to be satisfied with the advice which they received.

Sources of help: The leading sources of both advice and information in all the groups remains the traditional sources of the accountant, the lawyer, and the bank. It is, however, interesting to note that significantly more 'quarterly' and '6 monthly' firms had sought help from the bank. Also, markedly more 'quarterly' firms had sought information from a lawyer and the bank. The leading sources of consultancy in the groups were accountants, followed by lawyers, and the small amount of training was mainly provided by a local educational institution.

Firms in each of the groups ranked the usefulness of the sources of advice and assistance on a scale from 1 ('not at all useful)' to 5 ('very useful)'. On average 'quarterly' and 'monthly' firms stated that they found the advice and assistance provided by professional advisers (e.g. accountant, bank, consultants and lawyer) (mean scores of 3.70 and 4.25, respectively) the most consistently helpful. In contrast, 'annually' and '6 monthly' firms stated they found the advice and assistance provided by business contacts (e.g. business contacts, customer, supplier and trade association) the most consistently helpful (mean scores of 3.39 and 3.70, respectively). 'Irregular' firms stated that the advice provided by social contacts (e.g. family and friends) was the most helpful (mean score of 3.07).

Regression Analysis

The following fourteen of the more than two hundred and thirty primary and secondary variables analysed in stage 2 of the study of total planning scores were found to be related to total planning activity at a 5% level of significance and, as is shown below, six had not emerged in the previous analysis. Moreover, all but one of the remaining eight are also related to the level of consultation with professional advisers.

Location of the Business	-
Geographic Location of Customers	PROFMAN
%Training Cost	-
Interest Payments	PROFMAN
Sources of Finance	-
Sales Vehicles Leased	-
Owners Personal Liability	PROFMAN
General Management Sole Responsibility of one Person	-
Transport Delegated	-
Stores Delegated	PLANMAN
Market Research Study	PROFMAN
Bank Help	PROFMAN
Information from Lawyers	PLANMAN/PROFMAN
Information from Bank	PROFMAN

In order to find which combination of variables best described the planning activity of the firms studied, the above variables were subjected to a stepwise multiple regression analysis. Taking account of the missing values in the data base, ninety four cases were used to produce Equation 1 below:

Equation 1

PLANTOT = 3.82 +   0.57LAWINF + 0.15 TRAINCOST +   0.38BANKHELP
           30.19***   2.73**   2.59*   2.22*

MR = 0.4443, Adjusted R^2 = 0.1707, SEE = 0.8088

F = 7.38, Sig. = 0.0002, Regression = 3df, Residual = 90df

*** = $p<0.001$, ** = $p<0.01$, * = $p<0.05$

Thus it would seem that firms which frequently met internally, with their professional advisers, and with their customers and suppliers generally consult their lawyers for information, and their bankers for help, and have committed a considerable amount of their expenditure to training.

To interrogate the data even more closely, and to include more of the cases, only those five variables which were significant at the 1% level were included in a second stepwise regression. See Equation 2.

Equation 2:

PLANTOT = 3.79 +   0.10ABINTEREST + 0.40BANKHELP
           32.25***   2.79**   2.75**

MR = 0.3205, Adjusted R^2 = 0.0908, SEE = 0.8618

F = 8.64, Sig. = 0.0003, Regression = 2df, Residual = 152df, n = 154

*** = $p<0.001$, ** = $p<0.01$, * = $p<0.05$

Finally, and appealingly -- the frequent planners in this sample were likely to be those with high absolute interest costs and who had recently sought help from their bank!

CONCLUSION

The first and, in view of the literature to date, most important finding from this study is that no measures of performance and only one of size (total number of employees) have survived the analysis. Second, our suspicion that other factors in the strategic profile of the firm may explain planning activity would appear to find some support. Interestingly, this is more true for consultation with those outside the organisation than for the management itself. Further, some of the variables which appear to emerge do intuitively make sense. It is reasonable, for example, to assume that a firm which has high interest costs is likely to be in close contact with its bankers, and that a firm which states that it meets regularly with its professional advisors also appears to do so! Nevertheless, the initial reaction to the findings of this research are likely to be that it has all the attributes of a "damp squib". The researchers have some sympathy with this view. After all, whilst a number of significant results have emerged, it is hard to specify any sensible pattern when stepwise regression analysis is applied. It is, therefore, worth reflecting on the origins of the analysis. Previous research has made much of relating formal planning systems to ONE or TWO variables in the firm, usually some type of financial performance. Based upon the theory that formal planning must pay (else why would we do it?), researchers have produced "lo and behold" results which give no indication of the direction or underlying reasons for any causality identified. Such univariate analysis makes these researchers nervous.

In their study of attitudes to planning, Welsch and Plaschka (1990) found that "planning zealots are characterised by a higher profit, greater initial investment and place greater emphasis on growth." They conclude that "the question is whether these successful attributes are the result of their following through with implementation behaviours based on their intense planning conviction." We would agree with their scepticism. Therefore, this analysis attempted to take into account all the variables in the strategic profile and to relate them to a surrogate for planning activity which we believe is more representative of the owner-manager's world than the formal planning systems prescribed in much of the literature. It goes without saying that we accept the limitations of this approach: that we have not included any analysis of the content of the meetings, and that we have assumed that all meetings reported are likely to have some planning content.

At the outset we had hoped to indulge in sophisticated statistical analysis to isolate those variables which best described the planning activity of our sample. Unfortunately perhaps, our univariate analysis defeated us. Quite simply, despite the large number of variables analysed, there were few which were identified as significant and these few did not present a particularly convincing pattern. Thus it would seem that the relationship between planning activity and other attributes in the firm are not as clear cut as the literature would have us believe. There are, however, some indications of areas for future research. For example, whilst these findings aid our understanding of planning in small firms, the results from this paper do not delineate what small firm planners should do (Robinson et al., 1986a, p.20). The question of what specific planning activities and issues comprise effective small firm planning still remains an area of research interest and debate. We agree with Robinson et al. (1986a, p.26) that future research should simultaneously study both the 'process' of planning in small firms and its 'nature and content' as determinants of small firm performance and growth. However, we also believe that such research should also include measures of the context of the firm itself -- the strategic profile

TABLE 1

Frequency of Planning Meetings

Type of planning meeting	Never (1)	Irr. (2)	Anlly. (3)	6 Mo. (4)	Qtrly. (5)	Mo. (6)	Wkly. (7)	No. of cases	Mean	Median
Board	12	27	42	18	41	57	23	220	4.42	5
Management	9	25	1	4	14	63	101	217	5.68	6
Bank	13	42	53	54	61	13	1	237	3.64	4
Accountant	2	25	56	60	56	24	15	238	4.16	4
Lawyer	26	142	17	14	21	8	4	232	2.58	2
Maj. cust.	8	45	10	13	38	64	49	227	4.83	5
Maj. suppl.	17	77	16	19	30	48	22	229	3.87	4

TABLE 2: Statistically Significant Differences Between Planning Meetings and the Four Primary Variables

Variable	Management and Board	Professional Advisors	Business Contacts	Total
Industry	$X^2 = 4.32$ $DF = 8$	$X^2 = 5.94$ $DF = 4$	$X^2 = 9.31$ $DF = 8$	$X^2 = 6.84$ $DF = 6$
Age	$R = -0.04$	$R = -0.16^*$	$R = -0.08$	$R = -0.13$
Size Employees	$R = 0.02$	$R = -0.02$	$R = 0.05^*$	$R = -0.10$
Sales	$X^2 = 10.02$ $DF = 8$	$X^2 = 5.01$ $DF = 6$	$X^2 = 3.99$ $DF = 8$	$X^2 = 6.52$ $DF = 6$
Profits[1]	$X^2 = 13.50$ $DF = 12$	$X^2 = 13.50$ $DF = 12$	$X^2 = 7.96$ $DF = 12$	$X^2 = 9.79$ $DF = 8$

[1] relative to competition
* significant at 5% level

TABLE 3: Significant Differences Between Small Firms for PLANMAN, PROFMAN, AND BUSMAN

	PLANMAN	PROFMAN	BUSMAN
Corporate Structure			
Age		*	
Total Employment			*
Total Number of Customers		* (-)	
Geographic Location of Customers		*	
Market Research		*	
Technology Base			
Total number of PCs		*	
Manual Payroll Systems			*
Manual Production Control			*
Financial Base			
%Sales and Marketing Cost	*		
%Insurance Cost		*	
%Interest Cost		*	
Interest Payment		*	
Export Credit Guarantee Insurance	*		*
Owners Personal Liability		*	
Owners Life		*	*
Sales Vehicles Owned	*		
Plant and Equipment Leased		*	*
Premises Leased			*
Employees invest in firm	*		
Management of the Firm			
Training for Workforce	* (-)		
Management Training		*	
Managerial Functions Sole Responsibility of one Person			*
Managerial Delegation			*
Production/Operations Function	*		* (-)
Engineering Function			* (-)
Quality Control Function	*		
Transport Function		* (-)	
Purchasing Function		* (-)	
Stores Delegated	* [1](-)		

(-) indicates a negative relationship

Engineering Delegated			*
Purchasing Delegated			*
<u>Sources of Help</u>			
Government Grants			*
Information from Lawyers	*	*	
Information from Accountant		*	
Information from Bank		*	
Information from Local Authority		*	
Estates and Planning			
Help from Accountants		*	
Help from Bank		*	

Table 4:
Statistically Significant Differences Between Small Firms by the Frequency of Total Planning Meetings

Criteria	Chi-square (X^2)	Degrees of freedom (d.f)	Significance level	Pearson correlation coefficient (r)	Sig. level
1. Industry	6.84	6			
2. Location	10.93	3	0.05		
3. Legal entity	n.a.				
4. Is the small business a franchise?	n.a.				
5. Family relationship of current majority owners	1.86	6			
6. Family relationship of current senior exec.	2.59	6			
7. Number of original founders who are still partners of shareholders				0.09	
8. Number of shareholders/partners if other than a sole proprietorship				-0.05	
9. Age of the business				-0.13	
10. Total employment size				-0.10	
11. If the company is inc. the number of the dirs. who don't work full-time in the firm	0.33	4			
12. Level of sales for the last fin. year	6.52	6			
13. Percentage of sales rev. acct. for by the maj. product line or service group				-0.13	

Table 4 cont:
Statistically Significant Differences Between Small Firms by the Frequency of Total Planning Meetings

Criteria	Chi-square (X^2)	Degrees of freedom (d.f)	Significance level	Pearson correlation coefficient (r)	Sign. level
14. Level of profitability for the last financial year	n.a.				
15. Rating the business profit performance relative to compet.	9.79	8			
16. Total number of maj. product lines or maj. service groups				0.06	
17. Total number of new maj. product lines or maj. service groups added in the last 12 mos.				0.10	
18. Total number of customer	4.74	6			
19. Number of new customers in the past 12 mos.	n.a.				
20. Geographic loc. of majority of customers	14.08	4	0.10		
21. Total number of suppliers	2.86	4			
22. Number of suppliers in the past 12 mos.	n.a.				
23. Geograp. loc. of maj. of supplier	4.38	9			
24. No. of direct competitor	4.29	8			
25. Employment size of major compet.	1.27	4			
26. Technology of production	n.a.				

Table 4 cont:

Statistically Significant Differences Between Small Firms by the Frequency of Total Planning Meetings

Criteria	Chi-square (X^2)	Degrees of freedom (d.f)	Significance level	Pearson correlation coefficient (r)	Sign. level
27. Control Technology used for the maj. product lines	n.a.				
28. Total no. of personal computers				0.03	
29. % of total costs by salaries & wages costs				0.09	
30. % of total costs by sales & mktg. goods				0.14	
31. % of total costs by training costs				0.24	0.05
32. % of total costs by rents costs				-0.01	
33. % of total costs by rates costs				0.01	
34. % of total costs by insurance costs				0.09	
35. % of total costs by research & development costs				0.08	
36. % of total costs by interest payment costs				0.16	
37. Interest costs for the last fin. yr. (€'000s)				0.23	0.01

Table 4 cont:

Statistically Significant Differences Between Small Firms by the Frequency of Total Planning Meetings

Criteria	Chi-square (X^2)	Degrees of freedom (d.f)	Significance level	Pearson correlation coefficient (r)	Sign. level
38. No. of sources of received financials investment				0.18	0.05
39. Owners of directors personal liability insurance	3.82	3	0.05		
40. Employers liability insurance	n.a.				
41. Life of the owners/ partners ins.	6.82	3			
42. Professional indemnity insurance	4.70	3			
43. Export credit guarantee insurance	0.27	2			
44. Product liability insurance	5.44	3			
45. Credit ins.	0.23	2			
46. Vehicle ins.	n.a				
47. Theft, flood ins.	0.66	2			
48. Bdgs. insurance	0.35	2			
49. Plant/equipment ins.	2.82	2			
50. Other ins.	5.35	3			
51. No. of managerial functions currently operated				0.00	

Table 4 cont:

Statistically Significant Differences Between Small Firms by the Frequency of Total Planning Meetings

Criteria	Chi-square (X^2)	Degrees of freedom (d.f)	Significance level	Pearson correlation coefficient (r)	Sign. level
52. No. of managerial operated the sole responsibility of one person				0.07	
53. Managerial delegation score				0.10	
54. Mgmt. training	5.40	3			
55. Training for the workforce	0.59	2			
56. Has the business applied for any local or central gov't training schemes?	0.95	2			
57. No. of Youth Training Scheme (YTS) trainees curently employed	3.96	4			
58. Has a mkt. research study been conducted?	9.50	3	0.05		
59. Who conducted the last formal mkt. research study?	n.a.				
60. Cost of last mkt. research study (є's)				-0.13	
61. Was the last formal mkt. research study subsidised?	0.88	2			

Table 4 cont:

Statistically Significant Differences Between Small Firms by the Frequency of Total Planning Meetings

Criteria	Chi-square (X^2)	Degrees of freedom (d.f)	Significance level	Pearson correlation coefficient (r)	Sign. level
62. Has the small business applied for any gov't grants?	0.50	3			
63. Contact with small firms asst. agencies	3.93	3			
64. Satisfied with the advice/asst. given by the small firms asst. agencies	n.a.				
65. Sales vehicles-leased	10.93	3	0.05		
66. General mgmt. managerial functions the sole responsibility of one person	11.37	3	0.10		
67. Transport managerial functions the sole responsibility of one person	11.74	3	0.01		
68. Stores managerial functions the sole responsibility of one person					
69. Bank source of help	10.59	3	0.05		
70. Lawyer source of info.	12.78	3	0.01		
71. Bank source of info.	10.65	3	0.05		
	9.39	3	0.05		

REFERENCES

Acklesburg, R., and Arlow, P. (1985), Small Businesses Do Plan and It Pays Off. Long Range Planning, 8, p 61-67.

Aldrich, H., Rosen,B., and Woodward, E. (1987), The Impact of Social Networks on Business Foundings and Profit. In N.C. Churchill, J.A. Hornaday, B.A. Kirchhoff, O.J. Krasner, and K.H. Vesper (eds.) Frontiers of Entrepreneurship Research. Wellesley, MA: Babson, p154-168.

Aldrich, H., and Zimmer, C. (1986), Entrepreneurship Through Social Networks. In D. Sexton and R. Smilor (eds.) The Art and Science of Entrepreneurship. Cambridge, MA: Ballinger.

Ansoff, H. I., Brandenburg, R.G., and Radosevich, R. (1971), Acquisition Behaviour of U.S. Manufacturing Firms, 1946-1965. Nashville:Vanderbilt Press.

Beard, D., and Dess, G. (1981), Corporate-Level Strategy, Business-Level Strategy, and Firm Performance. Academy of Management Journal, 24, p.663-688.

Birley, S., Cromie,S., and Myers, A. (1990), Entrepreneurial Networks in Northern Ireland. Belfast: University of Ulster, Northern Ireland.

Birley, S., and Westhead, P. (1988a), Establishing the Small Firms Data Base: the Exploratory Investigation. Proceedings of the 33rd World Conference of the International Council for Small Business. Boston, MA:ICSB, p. 33-38.

Birley, S., and Westhead, P. (1988b), The Cranfield Small Firms Database. 1988. Report 1: Small Firm Characteristics. Cranfield, England: Cranfield School of Management.

Bracker, J. (1982), Planning and Financial Performance Among Small Entrepreneurial Firms: An Industry Study. Georgia State University, Unpublished Doctoral Dissertation.

Bracker, J.S., Keats, B.W., and Pearson, J.N. (1988), Planning and Financial Performance Among Small Firms in a Growth Industry. Strategic Management Journal, 9, p. 591-603.

Bracker, J.S., and Pearson, J.N. (1986), Planning and Financial Performance of Small, Mature Firms. Strategic Management Journal, 7, p. 503-522.

Burt, D.(1978), Planning and Performance in Australian Retailing. Long Range Planning, 11, p. 62-68.

Camillus, J.C. (1975), Evaluating the Benefits of Formal Planning. Long Range Planning, 8, p.33-40.

Carland, J.W., Carland, J.A.C., Aby, C.D. (1989), An Assessment of the Psychological Determinants of Planning in Small Businesses. International Small Business Journal, 7, No. 4, p. 23-34.

Dill, W.R. (1958), Environment as an Influence on Managerial Autonomy. Administrative Science Quarterly, p. 409-443.

Duncan, R.B. (1972), Characteristics of Organizational Environments and Perceived Environmental Uncertainty. Administrative Science Quarterly, 1972, 17, p 313-327.

Dutton, J.E., and Duncan, R.B. (1987), The Influence of the Strategic Planning Process on Strategic Change. Strategic Management Journal, 8, p. 103-116.

Estafen, B.D. (1971), Methods for Management Research in the 1970's: An Ecological Systems Approach. Academy of Management Journal, p. 51-63.

Fredrickson, J.W., and Mitchell, T.R. (1984), Strategic Decision Processes:Comprehensiveness and Performance in an Industry with an Unstable Environment. Academy of Management Journal, 27, p. 445-466.

Gable, M., and Topol, M.T. (1987), Planning Practices of Small-Scale Retailers. American Journal of Small Business, 12, Fall, p. 19-32.

Gibb, A., and Scott, M. (1985), Strategic Awareness, Personal Commitment and the Process of Planing in the Small Business. Journal of Management Studies, 22, p. 597-631.

Golde, R.A. (1964), Practical Planning for Small Businesses. Harvard Business Review, 42, p. 147-161.

Grinyer, P. H., and Norburn, D. (1975), Planning for Existing Markets: Perceptions of Chief Executives and Financial Performance. The Journal of the Royal Statistical Society, 138, Series A, p. 70-97.

Hansen, G.S., and Wernerfelt, B. (1989), Determinants of Firm Performance: The Relative Importance of Economic and Organisational Factors. Strategic Management Journal, 10, p. 399-411.

Herold, D. (1972), Long Range Planning and Organizational Performance: A Cross Validation Study. Academy of Management Journal, p. 784-810.

Hofer, C.W. (1982), Towards a Contingency Theory of Business Strategy. Academy of Management Journal, 18, p. 31-40.

Jones, W.D. (1982), Characteristics of Planning in Small Firms. Journal of Small Business Management, July, p. 15-19.

Karger, D., and Malik, Z. (1975), Long Range Planning and Organizational Performance. Long Range Planning, 8,p. 60-64.

Kelly, C.A., and Young, J.E. (1983), Is Your Small Business Ready for Planning?. Journal of Small Business Management, 21, p.28-33.

Kelmar, J.H., and Noy, S. (1989), Profit and Growth in Small Firms - The Strategic Planning Influence. Paper Presented at the Twelve National Small Firms Policy and Research Conference, London Docklands Business School, London.

Kudia, R.J. (1980), The Effects of Strategic Planning on Common Stock Returns. Academy of Management Journal, 23, p. 5-20.

Leontiades, M., and Tezel, A. (1980), Planning Perception and Planning Results. Strategic Management Journal, 1, p. 56-76.

Lindsay, W.M., Boulton, W.R., Franklin, S., and Rue, L. W. (1982), Strategic Planning: Determining the Impact of Environmental Characteristics and Uncertainty. Academy of Management Journal, 25, p. 55-509.

Lindsay, W. M., and Rue, L. W. (1980), Impact of the Organization Environment on the Long Range Planning Process: A Contingency View. Academy of Management Journal, 23, p.385-404.

Moyer, R. (1982). Strategic Planning for the Small Firm. Journal of Small Business Management, 9, p. 8-14.

Orpen, C. (1985), The Effects of Long Range Planning on Small Business Performance: A Further Examination. Journal of Small Business Management, 23, p. 16-23.

Pearce, J.A., Robbins, D.K., and Robinson, R.B. (1987), The Impact of Grand Strategy and Planning Formality on Financial Performance. Strategic Management Journal, 8, p. 125-134.

Ramanujam, V., Venkatraman, N., and Camillus, J.C, (1986), Multi-objective Assessment of Effectiveness of Strategic Planning: A Discriminate Analysis Approach. Academy of Management Journal, 29, 1986, p. 347-372.

Reeser, C. (1981). Tactical Planning. Mangerial Planning, 24, p. 27-34.

Rhyne, L.C. (1983), The Impact of Strategic Planning on Financial Performance. Paper presented at the 43rd Annual Academy of Management Meeting, Dallas.

Rhyne, L.C. (1986), The Relationship of Strategic Planning to Financial Performance. Strategic Management Journal, 7, p. 423-436.

Rice, G.H., and Hamilton, R.E. (1979), Decision Theory and the Small Businessman. American Journal of Small Business, 4, p. 1-9.

Robinson, R.B. (1980), An Empirical Investigation of the Impact of SBDC-Strategic Planning Consultation Upon the Short-Term Effectiveness of Small Business in Georgia. University of Georgia unpublished Doctoral Dissertation.

Robinson, R. B. (1982), The Importance of 'Outsiders' in Small Firm Strategic Planning. Academy of Management Journal, 25, p. 80-83.

Robinson, R.B., and Littlejohn, W.F. (1981), Improtant Contingencies in Samll Firm Planning. Journal of Small Business Management, July, p. 45-48.

Robinson, R.B., Salem, M.Y., Logan, J.E. and Pearce II, J.A. (1986a), Planning Activities Related to Independent Retail Firm Performance. American Journal of Small Business, 11,p. 19-26.

Robinson, R.B., Logan, J.E., and Salem, M. (1986b), Am Empirical Investigation of Strategic Versus Operational Planning in Small Independent Retail Firms. American Journal of Small Business, 10, p. 7-16.

Robinson, R.B., Pearce, J.A., Vozikis, G.S., and Mescon, T.S. (1984), The Relationship Between Stage of Development and Small Firm Planning and Performance. Journal of Small Business Management, 22, p. 45-52.

Robinson, R.B., and Pearce, J.A. (1983), Research Thrusts in Small Firm Strategic Planning. Academy of Management Review, 9, p.128-137.

Rue, L.W. (1973), Theoretical and Operational Implications of Long-Range Planning on Selected Measures of Financial Performance in U.S. Industry. Georgia State University, Unpublished Doctoral Dissertation.

Sanford, M. (1982), New Enterprise Management. Reston: Reston Publishing Co.

Sexton, D.L., and van Auken, P. (1985), A Longitudinal Study ofSmall Business Strategic Planning. Journal of Small Business Management, 23, p. 7-15.

Shuman, J.C. (1975), Corporate Planning in Small Companies - A Survey. Long Range Planning, October, p. 81-90.

Shuman, J.C., and Seeger, J.A. (1986), The Theory and Practice of Strategic Management in Smaller Rapid Growth Firms. American Journal of Small Business, 11, p. 7-18.

Steiner, G.A. (1967), Approaches to Long Range Planning for Small Business. California Management Review, 10, p. 3-16.

Steiner, G.A. (1979), Strategic Planning: What Every Manager Must Know. New York: Free Press.

Still, T.W., (1974), An Exploratory Investigation of Strategic Planning Behavior in Small Businesses. The Florida State University, Unpublished Doctoral Dissertation.

Stoner, C.R. (1983), Planning in Small Manufacturing Firms: A Survey. Journal of Small Business Management, 21, p. 34-41.

Thune, S., and House, R.J. (1970). Where Long Range Planning Pays Off. Business Horizons, 13, August, p. 81-87.

Thurston, P.A. (1983), Should Smaller Companies Make Formal Plans? Harvard Business Review, 61, p. 162-188.

Timmons, J., Smallen, L., and Dingee, A. (1977), New Venture Creation: A Guide to Small Busines Development. Homewood, IL:R.D. Irwin.

Tootelian, P.H., and Gaedeke, R.M. (1978), Small Business Management: Operations and Profiles. Santa Monica: Goodyear.

Unni, U.K. (1981), Corporate Planning and Entrepreneurial Success: An Empirical Analysis. Southern Management Association Proceedings. p. 177-180.

van Auken,P.M., and Ireland, D.I. (1980), An Input-Output Approach to Practical Small Business Planning. Journal of Small Business Management, January, p. 44-50.

Vozikis, G.S., and Glueck, W.F. (1980), Small Business Problems and Stages of Development. Academy of Management Proceedings.

Welsch, H.P., and Plaschka, J.R. (1990), Intensity of Planning Conviction Among Entrepreneurs: Differences Between Zealots and Non-Believers. Proceedings of Rent I-V Research in Entrepreneurship 4th Workshop. Cologne, Germany:November.

Wood, D.R., and LaForge, R.L. (1979), The Impact of Comprehensive Planning on Financial Performance. Academy of Management Journal, 22, p. 516-526.

Wood, D.R., and LaForge, R.L. (1981), Toward the Development of a Planning Scale: An Example from the Banking Industry. <u>Strategic Management Journal</u>, 2, p. 209-216.

From Evaluation of Business Ventures to Prognosis of Success: Results of a Longitudinal Study of 11 French Cases

Critique
by
Nancy M. Carter, *Marquette University*

Livian and Marion have presented a timely and critical argument for considering the process of gestation as a predictor of business venture success. Their study contributes to the growing recognition that new ventures are not instantaneously formed. Indeed, the founding may take several months, sometimes as long as a year. Livian and Marion contend that firms' future success depends upon the learning founders' influence during this time period.

To demonstrate their argument, the authors follow 11 French new ventures that were part of an entrepreneurship program. By comparing "experts'" evaluations with the firms' actual outcomes, the authors illustrate the influence of "coaching" and the entrepreneur's capacity for embracing change.

As a pilot study, the project holds considerable promise. The authors' use of previous literature to guide their inquiry is noteworthy, as is the breadth of the evaluation process used to compare the ventures over a two year period. Before extending the research however, there are several theoretical and methodological issues that warrant consideration.

Drawing on their comparisons of successful versus non-successful "launchings", Livian and Marion conclude that the content of the business plan is secondary to the entrepreneur's ability to adapt and adjust as the project takes shape. Implicit in this conclusion is the supposition that entrepreneurs' capacity for learning is a significant predictor of new venture success. As problems are encountered, successful entrepreneurs seemingly are those who can work through the process, banking the experience in the firms's memory for use in recognizing and responding to future challenges. This argument is increasingly finding its way into the literatures of strategic management, organizational theory and organizational behavior. Integration and extension of this literature to new venture gestation would make a significant contribution to our understanding of entrepreneurship. In particular, an elaboration of the process of problem recognition may reveal why certain firms in Livian and Marions' study succeeded, while others failed. Was it because the "successful" entrepreneurs were more adept at problem recognition, and could thus adjust their plans to meet the challenges posed? Extant theoretical models of problem recognition, such as Cowan's (1986) process model, offer opportunities for developing a bridge between learning theory and new venture gestation.

Central to Livian and Marion's argument that the process of planning deserves equal consideration with the plan content, is the role played by coaches or judges. Each of the 11 cases described in the study represented new ventures that were part of an entrepreneurs' program sponsored by Groupe ESC Lyon. Admittance to the program was gained through a juring process in which the individual (or team), the idea (project), and the feasibility of the project were evaluated. Once accepted, the participants engaged in coaching situations where the initial business plans were developed and modified over several months. Livian and Marion concluded that compatibility between the judges (coaches) and the candidate (entrepreneur) during this time period paralleled candidates' capability and willingness to adapt, the key determinant for firm success.

A promising line of inquiry for future research is the elaboration of the coaching phenomena described by Livian and Marion. For example, what factors led to establishing the compatible relationship that facilitated successful gestation? Is a shared professional business background between the judge and the candidate necessary? What role do personalities or shared visions play in forming the relationship? How can judges be matched to candidates to maximize the coaching benefits? Insight in answering these questions, among others relative to coaching, can be gained by applying theoretical models from other areas to the process of new venture formation. Social information processing theory (SIP) (Salancik & Pfeffer, 1977, 1978), for example, seems particularly appropriate. According to SIP, individuals react not only to the objective reality of work environments, but they also construct a perceptual reality that is influenced by the social context of the situation. As cogent sources of social information, coaches or judges are in a unique position to provide cues that guide entrepreneurs in constructing their particular version of reality. Therefore, further examination of how these agents or conduits of influence shape the perceptions of entrepreneurs seems warranted.

Finally, extensions of Livian and Marion's research will benefit from the inclusion of control groups. By adding cases in which the entrepreneur had no formal written plan, and cases where the entrepreneur did not participate in the coaching process, the authors' preliminary conclusions about the process and content of planning can be verified.

REFERENCES

Cowan, D. A. 1986. Developing a process model of problem recognition. Academy of Management Review, 11 (4), 763-776.

Salancik, G. R. & Pfeffer, J. 1977. An examination of need-satisfaction models and job attitudes. Administrative Science Quarterly, 22, 427-456.

1978. A social information processing approach to job attitudes and task design. Administrative Science Quarterly, 23, 224-253.

FROM EVALUATION OF BUSINESS VENTURES TO PROGNOSIS OF SUCCESS : RESULTS OF A LONGITUDINAL STUDY OF 11 FRENCH CASES

YVES-FRÉDÉRIC LIVIAN, *IRE/GROUPE ESC LYON (MANAGEMENT RESEARCH CENTER)*
STÉPHANE MARION, *INNOVATION AND ENTREPRENEURSHIP CENTER/GROUPE ESC LYON*

ABSTRACT

It is well known that designing criteria for new business venture evaluation which have a predictive value, is a very difficult task.

This article presents the results of a study on a sample of eleven cases of new business ventures in France. Its purpose was to compare evaluations made on the same ventures at 3 points in time over a two year period, in order to test the quality of new business venture evaluation.

This study shows that a few elements which appeared as critical afterwards had been neglected in the first evaluation, but that a "time skidding" phenomenon occurred frequently.

The evaluation of the business plan and the existence of a clear vision of the business by the entrepreneur, are both good predictors for sucess. On the other hand, using the evaluation of an entrepreneur's personal capacities has been found to be a poor predictor by several studies.

The practical consequences of evaluation methods can be drawn from this study, although further research is necessary.

In addition to the inevitable question of what the key factors for success are in building new businesses, there has recently arisen scepticism about the true capacities of the project selection processes in anticipating these factors on precise projects. As in other areas, this passage from the "ex-post" analysis -- which indicates after the event what has "made the difference" -- in the recommendation of criteria having some form of forecast value is very difficult.

Amongst others, recent studies such as those carried out by P.DUBINI (1989 and 1990) moreover, insist upon these difficulties. On the one hand they underline the specific nature of the criteria related to company start-ups -- by the complexity, the dynamic nature and the rapidity of changes within the process -- and, on the other hand, the predominance of research work referring to the selection process of venture capital companies.

From the latter, OOGHE (OOGHE et al. 1988) proposes a division into two groups of criteria used in project analyses. The first group is composed of all of the criteria related to the analysis of the entrepreneur or the team and the management skills which surround the project. The second groups together the criteria linked to the analyses of the activity which is normally described in a business plan.

The importance given to the factors in the first group were pointed out by MacMILLAN, SIEGEL and SUBBA NARASIMHA (1985) in a study of the factors used by venture capital companies in order to evaluate a project. Amongst the ten criteria which were regarded as being the most significant, five were directly related to the experience and the personality of the entrepreneur or of the team.

STUART and ABETTI (1988) distinguish three major areas in the composition of this first group :

1. personality analysis,

2. the study of accumulated knowledge (background),

3. the examination of the management characteristics, which correspond to the capacities and to the vision of the new entrepreneur or the team.

On the first point, research which was carried out in order to distinguish a specific profile of the entrepreneur having great potential for success has often had limited results. Thus, studies based on the use of various batteries of psychological tests (SEXTON AND BOWMAN, 1986 ; LIVIAN, 1989 ; BEVERINA, 1989) or inquiries established from significant samples (BEGLEY and BOYD, 1987) only very partially distinguish new entrepreneurs from other populations. The conclusions often come up with the observation of a greater need for achievements on the part of new entrepreneurs, a greater capacity to take risks, a greater tenacity and a greater propensity to accept the unknown.

On the second point underlined by STUART and ABETTI, numerous studies have sought to point out the correlations between the educational level, age, sex, experience, and the different role models of the entrepreneur and the success of the new entreprise. COOPER, DUNKELBERG and WOO (1988) have in this respect carried out some very interesting work through a longitudinal study, over 3 years, of 2994 firms. The results show for example : that men are more successful than women or entrepreneurs from minority groups ; that new entrepreneurs with professional experience and a higher level of studies obtain better results ; that initial management experience has no correlation with a strong probability of success wheras technical experience does. The role of initial experience is examined in many other studies (NEISWANDER and DROLLINGER, 1986; STUART and ABETTI, 1987) and appears to be a key element.

On the third point, studies initiated by SMITH has given rise to a whole collection of research with a typological nature (PETERSON and SMITH, 1986 ; SMITH et al. 1987 ; WOO, COOPER and DUNKELBERG, 1988) and has tried to associate types of entrepreneurs with types of firms. Again, this area has also produced other studies which demonstrate the relationships between the development of the company and the various different networks to which the entrepreneur has access (BIRLEY, 1985 ; ALDRICH, ROSEN and WOODWARD, 1987 ; WARD and RANDALL, 1989). Several pieces of research also underline the importance to be given to the strategy employed, and to the structure of the sector within which the firm is liable to develop (SANBERG and HOFER, 1986 ; STEINER and SOLEM, 1988).

This last point enables us to move directly to the second group of analysis factors as defined by OOGHE, i.e., those which concern the study of the activity. The latter assumes that a business plan always exists. This document, which tends to become generalised, has moreover caught the attention of many researchers who are interested in its limits, its structure and content (FRANK, PLASHKA and ROESSL, 1988). The characteristics of the product or of the service, the market, the finance plan and the financial performances, human resources management, the strategy and organisation are generally touched upon in this document.

STUART and ABETTI (1987) for instance, define in this respect, the initial success of a new company as a function of the market, the degree of innovation, the strategy, the organisation and the managerial capacities of the management team. They therefore note that it is preferable to have a strategy and a structure which reflects the behaviour of other firms in the sector, or be in a stable market, than in a new and rapidly growing market.

MACMILLAN, ZAMANN and SUBBA NARASIMHA (1987) distinguish three major classes of failures. Apart from teams of poorly qualified entrepreneurs who have products which are poorly differentiated, we also find : qualified teams who very quickly come up against the competition and who have insufficient resistance to face it, and those who, having both of these characteristics, end by losing their initial advantage because they do not have adequate protection of the project.

The nature of the product-market couple, the type of the manufacturing process, the degree of innovation, and the degree of inexperience of the new entrepreneur are also put forward as being factors which determine how risky the project is (MASSACRIER and RIGAUD, 1984 ; GORMAN and SHALMAN, 1984 ; RIGAUD, 1987 ; RAMUS, 1989).

Economic and financial performance indicators are also frequently mentioned. Several different authors underline, for example, the importance of evaluating the risk associated with a lack of liquidity, due on the one hand to the tendency to have insufficient capital and, on the other hand, to the gaps generally met between forecasts and achievements (FOURCADE, 1985; RIGAUD, 1987; NEISWANDER and DROLLINGER, 1986).

In spite of all of the interest and the content of this research, it remains difficult to make the connection between these risks or these success criteria and concrete evaluation practices (COLOMBO, 1989 ; DEPPERU, 1989 ; RAMUS, 1989).

We wished to work in this direction by attempting to see in which way the project selection and monitoring practices used, on entry to and during the course of an Entrepreneurs' Programme [1] could have had a predictive value. In order to do this we compared the results of these evaluations with the real outcome of a group of projects which were analysed 24 to 36 months later.

I. PRESENTATION OF THE OBJECTIVES OF THE STUDY AND THE PROJECTS STUDIED

A. Objectives of the study

The aim of the study was to determine what degree of forecast had been obtained in the selection and monitoring process of the project, by comparing the assessments made of the projects during the course of the support programme, and the actual growth during the course of the first two or three years.

The analysis which may be made of these projects cannot reach a conclusion of a definitive success after just two to three years from the launch date. Our analysis only seeks to understand what really happened during at least the first 24 months of their activity in relation to the evaluations made at the beginning by specialists based on a complete dossier and interviews with the entrepreneur.

More precisely, this study bases itself on certain hypotheses, taken both from the literature and the practical experience of the evaluation experts, about the key factors to be analysed in the project.

We wanted to check :

- The overall quality of the forecast about the viability of the projects, during their start-up phase, by enquiring into their situation two to three years after they had left the programme, i.e. about 30 to 36 monts after their first formulation and especially the materialisation of the project, the evolution of its content and how closely the timetable had been followed.

- The relationship which may exist between the evaluation of the business plan carried out at the end of the programme and the situation of the company 24 to 36 months afterwards.

- The existence of unforeseeable factors or events and their influence on the start of the project.

- The quality of the evaluation which had been carried out on the personal characteristics of the new entrepreneur, by comparing the analysis made at the beginning with the personal elements observed during the course of the launch period.

- The role played in the running of the start up phase by the level of innovation contained in the project.

B. <u>Methodology</u>

The choice fell upon a methodology enabling us to follow the evolution of the project and using data gathered every year from entrepreneurs having followed this Entrepreneurs' Programme.

This type of longitudinal study, which is rather rare in the appropriate literature, has the advantage of enabling a judgment to be made on the changes, and not just rely on assessments made on a study carried out at a single point in time, even if it can only be carried out on a reduced number of samples.

Eleven projects were chosen at random in May 1987, from a total population of 36^2. The entrepreneurs and authors of these projects participated in the Entrepreneurs' Programme N°3 which took place in 1986 (3 projects), Nos. 4 and 5 which took place in 1987 (4 projects each).

Eight projects concerned service activities, and 3 had an industrial activity. For each of them, we carried out an analysis of 3 evaluations.

. The evaluations were made on entry to the programme by the team of experts, based on the dossiers completed during the admission session, and an interview with the entrepreneur. This dossier comprises 5 areas of analysis on the entrepreneur and those immediately surrounding him, and 4 areas on the project itself as well as a synthesis on the "special opportunities and threats to the project" (see Appendix 2).

. The evaluation was carried out by the programme experts on the business plan handed in by each new entrepreneur at the end of the programme (about 6 monts after their initial entry) and presented during the course of a jury session composed of the experts of the programme and possibly interested bankers. These assessments were noted in the dossiers which were then systematically studied[3].

The data was collected on each company with the help of the Data Bank set up in the Innovation and Entrepreneurship Centre of the Groupe ESC Lyon and an interview carried out with the new entrepreneur.

We have summarized below some of the characteristics of the eleven projects and their current situation.

- BC was a company which printed textiles using an original concept. It was launched by a single person, who disposed of a network of important relationships in the area of his products.

  An ambitious promotional campaign turned out to be a heavy financial loss. The company filed for bankruptcy after 18 months of activity.

- PM is a company which designs and manufactures items made of wood aimed at public institutions, launched by a person who had registered a patent on the manufacturing process.

  The company is still continuing in activity after a relatively slow start up phase.

- JC is an innovative distribution project in the Agri-Food Industry sector which did not take off.

- GV is an R & D company based on high-tech products, founded by 2 partners with professional experience in this area.

  Having started up later than foreseen, the company is still in operation and is growing.

- FD is a company which provides services to other firms and was launched by one individual with an innovative idea. A slower start-up in business than had been foreseen, along with a somewhat erratic management, led the company to file for bankruptcy after 24 months.

- AL is an industrial data processing consultancy firm launched by an individual entrepreneur and it is still in business.

- ES is a company which distributes a supplier's product, launched by one person alone and which filed for bankruptcy after only 6 months of activity.

- SV is a company which manufactures and sells an innovative product for the home launched by two persons and which is continuing to develop.

- SI is a service company, which creates and sells specialised software in a new market, which was launched by one person alone. After nearly 3 years of existence and faced with the difficulties in breaking into the market the new entrepreneur sold his business.

- DB is a data processing service company project which has not been launched.

- MM is a service and consultancy firm to other companies, launched by an individual and which continues in business, albeit by providing a service that is very different from that described in the initial project.

The appendix 1 sums up certain characteristics of the projects and provides the available figures.

II. GLOBAL OBSERVATIONS ON THE PROJECTS

A. A contrasted but not very surprising assessment of new business ventures

The first observation to be made here : out of the 11 projects chosen at random, 2 have not reached fruition:

The project DB did not result in a new business start up. The evaluation on the personality of the new entrepreneur was positive, he was considered to be serious and competent, but he did not succeed in penetrating the market, he became discouraged in face of all the difficulties and abandoned it.

The project JC, based on a single supplier activity, came up against a increase in prices of the products to be distributed. The evaluation noted the vulnerability of the project, but the products seemed good and the new entrepreneur quite capable.

Out of the 9 companies which were founded, 3 filed for bankruptcy : ES, BC and FD, and one company SI was sold. There therefore remain 5 companies still in business, of which one is carrying on a different activity to that of the initial project.

The failure rate after 3 years is not surprising and is very close to those generally predicted[4].

What is striking in the comparison between the outcome of the projects and the initial evaluations is that the elements of evaluation taken into account in the Entrepreneurs' Programme evaluation process covers fairly extensively the reality which can be observed after a certain length of time.

Several remarks may, in fact, be made in this respect.

First of all, in the 2 cases where the projects did not reach fruition, the acceptances of the product by the market -- under certain price conditions in the second case -- was the determining element. This acceptance had been noticed in the evaluation, although at various different degrees. The risk undertaken by JC was obvious : the evolutions in price could not simply be foreseen, but from the moment where the risk of dependence existed, the essential question put forward by the project was the absence of a possible alternative. It is true that, for DB, this difficulty had not been so well evaluated, and what perhaps appeared to be insufficient tenacity on the part of the entrepreneur had not been foreseen.

Next, a certain number of obstacles which were really met by the new entrepreneurs, had been noted by the experts.

For instance, the current difficulties met by AL in the commercial area, connected to a lack of interest in sales, admitted to by the new entrepreneur himself, correspond well to a evaluation carried out right from the start by the experts.

JC's dependence on a partner had also been observed and important reservations had been expressed on the clarity and the ambition of the project.

Moreover, several essential reasons for the four "failures" correspond to elements which had been spotted, not to say diagnosed, right from the entry into the Programme, as withnessed by the dossiers which were analyzed.

Thus, the absence of ambition and of risktaking observed by the experts in project ES were, from the beginning, considered to be a serious problem, as well as the gap between the potential of the individual (Marketing Manager of a large Agri-Food Industry group) and the size of the project.

The importance, no doubt exaggerated, of the stakes represented by BC's first export sales operation had also been underlined before its realization, as well as the relative fragility of the financial construction of the project.

To a lesser extent the difficulties connected with the necessity to create the market for FD and SI had been touched upon. In both cases it is more likely that the factors linked with the personalities of the new entrepreneurs which could have been underestimated.

The analysis "two years later" also revealed few really surprising elements. Of course, certain phenomena had accelerated, or on the contrary, the new entrepreneurs felt that certain delays had been underestimated. However, for the moment, one does not find important factors which were decisive for the evolution of the project, and which were of a different nature than those brought out in the evaluation.

Does this then mean that the experts have finally discovered an infallible evaluation method ? Of course not, first of all because there has been relative surprises, such as that of a success following a rather reserved evaluation (Project GV). Next, what appears to be more at stake is the rhythm and relative importance of the different factors of evolution of the project, which in every case contribute to the development of the firm, pushed back in time in relation to the forecasts[5].

In the nature of the judgment of the projects, one finds analogies with medical diagnosis and prognosis : a certain structure of the factors can be detected, and in a great number of cases, thanks to an empirical know-how, this enables a valid diagnosis to be formulated.

The task of making a prognosis is quite another thing, because it has to take into account : the specificity of the case, a gamble taken with the time-scale, the resistance of the subject concerned, etc. The symptoms and potential risks have been detected : if the person falls ill, we could then almost say what illness afflicts him... but then again : will he fall ill ? and when ? At this point contingent factors come into play making an accurate prognosis difficult, even on the basis of a diagnosis which reveals the essentials[6].

B. "Time Skidding"

Another remarkable point is that the start-up is almost always more difficult to create than was foreseen. Although there were few really unforeseen elements in their nature, there are numerous cases where certain foreseen difficulties achieved a greater importance than was imagined. The negotiation with the banks (BC, FD), the length of time in reaching the purchasing decision (AL, PM), the difficulty in recruiting and forming a team (FD, PM) are some of the most remarkable examples.

There again, it is not so much a case of the nature of the obstacle, but more of its size or the time necessary to get over it which is surprising.

FD considered that he first of all had to create the market for his service, and admits to having underestimated the length of time needed for launching it. The SI case is very similar to this. PM underestimated the slowness in the purchasing decision process. GV underestimated the time necessary for recruiting properly trained employees.

This point reinforces the importance of tenacity and motivation as criteria for the personal evaluation of the new entrepreneur, as has been pointed out by many researchers and practitioners.

"It was foreseen (that it would be difficult), but in fact it certainly is even more !" declare two new entrepreneurs questioned, in almost identical terms.

The appropriateness of having sufficient financial resources in order to face irreducible fixed costs therefore becomes an element of prognosis which is all the more important where these costs are high, and the risks of increases are very important (an innovative product, a market to be created, purchasing decisions which are long and submitted to seasonal or "political" factors, etc.)

C. The Importance of the Evaluation of the Business Plan

The study carried out on our sample shows that the evaluation of the business plan provides a very useful element of judgment on the project, even if, of course, it is not sufficient.

The evaluation of the business plan, such as it has been defined by the team of evaluating experts, brings to light the coherence of the project, the direction of its strategy, and its force of conviction with regard to eventual financiers. Its formal qualities may also be considered as indicative of the quality of the reasoning and communication.

Precisely, it should be noted, in at least 4 out of the 6 cases where the ventures were not launched or resulted in failure, three were the subject of adverse evaluations of their projects, and in one of the cases, reservations were expressed on its clarity.

GC's business plan was considered as being "vague", without objective references. The financial dossier was judged to be very weak. That of JC had a very unenthusiastic response: it was seen as "lacking in ambition" and not very clear. That of DB was judged as being "simply descriptive", "shallow and lacking in soul". Only that of ES was the object of an acceptable evaluation, with certain reservations however.

In the same way, there was a general positive view taken of SV and PM whose plans were judged to be good. Of course, this analysis was not totally predictive, since a project which improved was originally the object of an adverse evaluation of its plan (GV), and since certain projects having an excellent plan have not met up with expectations (FD and SI).

However, we can keep in mind that the criteria used in the appreciation enable one to detect the qualities of the project which constitute an indispensable basis for its success. This does not mean that the new entrepreneur who succeeds is the one who draws up detailed and well presented plans. But the fact that the existence of detailed plans do not characterize the entrepreneur who succeeds, in the growth phase, does not invalidate in any way the examination of the business plan as an important feature of evaluation, especially at the moment of launching the project itself. We can use the business plan at the beginning of the new venture as an exercise which may or may not reveal certain qualities of the project. It is not so much the content which brings into play a predictive element, as rather the capacities which are manifested by the entrepreneur, especially if the latter knows how to make this change over a certain length of time as the project takes shape.

Therefore, we reach agreement with the conclusions of certain previous studies, which insist more at the start-up phase on the quality of the business plan than on its scope and its structure. It is a question of judging the capacity of the new entrepreneur in distinguishing what is important and what is accessory. The business plan exercise can be a useful tool in contributing to the evaluation of the new entrepreneur's strategic capacity.

Thus we arrive at another observation in the same order of ideas, relating to the vision which the new entrepreneurs possesses. It appears that the existence of a clear "vision" on the part of the new entrepreneur about the future of his project may be considered to be a possible criterion of prognosis. This can be seen in the two cases where the new venture was not launched, in the one case of failure out of three, and in the venture which showed a strong potential for success.

Without going as far as the "visionary" conception of the entrepreneur which is the fashion in the United States, this notion corresponds sufficiently well with other research (notably those which precisely define the leadership through this characteristic) to merit its inclusion[7].

The capacity to represent the future of his project with sufficient accuracy and clarity, not only in its strategic dimension, but also in certain everyday elements, may in fact be a considerable asset, since this may enable the entrepreneur to anticipate, to choose, and to convince. JC, and DB, two cases of failure, had been given an adverse judgment in respect of this capacity.

Of course, the existence or not of this vision is more important during certain phases of the project than others (in order to go from the rough project to the final project, for example).

Nevertheless it appears that any expression on the part of the new entrepreneur which leads him to formulate how he represents his business venture, can particularly help the evaluating experts.

D. The Difficulties of Evaluating New Entrepreneurs

The evaluation of the new entrepreneur himself has played a prime part in the evaluations carried out on the projects.

This is first of all observed by the the fact that, in certain cases, it was the person himself who, more than anything else, caught the attention of the jury.

The analysis of the project evaluation dossiers in fact reveals the importance of the weight exerted by the new entrepreneur himself in the overall examination of the project, which can be reckoned to be greater than the interest shown in the project in five cases out of eleven ; and in only two cases (SV and GV) the project appears to have been of more interest than the person himself.

This interest is not abnormal compared with pedagogical preoccupations (the Entrepreneurs' Programme) and compared with the fact that, in many cases, admission to this programme is carried out at a very early stage in the project. However, it has to be recognized that this evaluation is exposed to a considerable number of hazards.

In at least five out of six cases where the venture was not launched or resulted in failure, the judgment made on the person himself, by the experts, proved to be largely positive.

In the case of DB, the new entrepreneur was originally considered to be earnest and competent. The entrepreneur of ES was seen as having had a very wide experience, only one doubted his capacity for working in a team. As for the new entrepreneurs in BC, FD and SI, they appeared as being "determined", competent in their field, and highly "motivated".

It will be noted that in these cases, certain mechanisms, inherent in the evaluation in a face to face situation, may explain what appeared, afterwards, as being "errors" of judgment :

.   a certain seduction exerted on the evaluating experts by the person himself (the case of BC's project). A situation close to this can also be found in FD and SI's evaluations.

.   a certain appearance of competence and of a serious attitude which could have been "worked upon" by the candidate in preparing for the interviews (such as the case of DB, and perhaps ES).

This observation brings up the problem of the relationship between the evaluation expert and the new entrepreneur "evaluated", and of the quality of the personal relationships between them. The interest shown in the project by the expert, the "technological halo" which surrounds it in the eyes of the expert, may greatly distort the judgment made and cause it to move away from the required impartiality[8].

Conversely, two interesting new ventures were set up with a new entrepreneur who was the object, at least at the beginning, of reservations expressed by, or disagreements between, the experts on his personal characteristics (GV, SV).

This observation underlines the changing character in the human phenomena related with the new venture, and spotlights an essential element, which is the capacity for learning, on the part of the new entrepreneur.

In several cases, what has been observed or what is still doubtful is less the personal characteristics of the new entrepreneur, taken as a whole, rather than his capacity, taken from these characteristics (whatever they may be), to evolve in a positive fashion. In this we come back to the medical analogy mentioned earlier.

In GV and SV's case the new entrepreneurs appear to have evolved favourably, whilst ES perhaps not enough. The new entrepreneur in AL has been awarded a reserved judgment which stresses his commercial capacities. As for the new entrepreneur in BC, could he have acquired certain complementary capabilities which would have enabled him to have avoided failure ? As for the new entrepreneur in MM, he recognizes that he had not taken account of certain advice given to him and he explains, himself, certain difficulties that he met through his "refusal to change".

In every case, the decisive element in the prognosis is the new entrepreneurs's capacity for learning and for accepting changes.

This prognosis (or forecast) is therefore greatly facilited when one sees the new entrepreneur evolving between two interviews, or during the training period under consideration, bearing in mind that this delay in observation also enables the efficiency of the new entrepreneur to be tested in the resolution of the problems he encounters.

Another individual aspect confirms its importance and is itself easier to judge: this is the past professional experience of the new entrepreneur. The results in our sample really do go in the direction of previous research : one of the cases of failure was that of a person who, although qualified and having good backing available to him, did not have experience which was precisely centred on the activities. On the other hand, the only firm whose current turnover is above the initial forecasts, (GV), was founded by two partners who have specialized in this field for a long time. Another company in good condition also has a similar background.

E. The Difficulties Specific to Innovation

Another research hypothesis, as confirmed by our observations, resides in the difficulty which is specific to the most innovative products.

Although it will always be difficult to establish a hierarchy in innovation, it appears that certain projects in our sample, which have in common a higher degree of innovation, met with more serious difficulties than foreseen, as in their access to the market.

SI, and to a certain extent SD, experimented to their cost, upon the importance of reputation and the difficulty of entering into a highly structured market. In these cases, the conventional sales techniques proved to be inadequate for penetrating a market whose potential is however not called into question. SI sold his business, and this shows that the products offered were not without interest, whereas FD's entrepreneur started up a new company after filing for bankruptcy by again using approximately the same basic idea. SV and AL also met with the same kind of problems.

This observation underlines the importance, for the most innovative projects, of the reputation network established earlier by the new entrepreneur, and of the solidity of the financial backing which he has to arrange in order to face a long period for market penetration.

Beyond the difficulties of finding access to the market, other problems have appeared in the development of the products and in the passage to large scale production.

SV, who had manufactured his prototypes in a craftsmanlike manner, met with some difficulties in carrying out batch production. The setting up of an industrial process brings about a certain number of drawbacks which were not foreseen during the development of the prototype. In the same way, partial recourse to subcontractors who do not meet up to expected standards in terms of quality and of lead time, is a penalizing factor which is initially underestimated.

SI, and GV, for whom a large amount of research and development work was carried out, experienced important gaps in the development of marketable products. However, the setting up of a service activity, from the first developments, in these cases appears as a palliative, which enables them to put up with these gaps. Both of these observations on the development of products, and on the passage towards an industrial manufacturing process, confirm all of the difficulty there is in measuring the state of advancement of a product, and particularly in evaluating the period of time required between its final improvement and putting it on the market. Here we have one of the major causes for the gaps between the forecasts and achievements mentioned earlier.

We cannot, of course, draw general conclusions, from a study covering a small number of companies, about the conditions for success for new business ventures. On the other hand, the study of the quality of prediction of an evaluation method (even if it does not pretend to be infallible) enables us to say, in our opinion, that it goes beyond that of the "ex-post" analysis of the success criteria, and brings about several interesting points about project evaluation practices.

It is relatively easy to detect the principal strong points and weak points of the project, by using a rather large number of analysis criteria, related to the project and to its environment, both in the relationship between the project and the individual or the team carrying it out, as well as by accumulating evaluation experience. In our study, the quality of prediction of the method used, if it were to be analysed in this sense, would be very good. The commercial aspects in particular, considered as being determinant, were analyzed accurately. On the other hand, new business start-ups' equilibrium is fragile, and has a dynamic force which may give a variable importance, over a period of time, to one or other of the aspects (commercial quality, importance of investments, capacity of reaction by the people involved etc.). It is the change in this dynamic equilibrium which is difficult to predict.

To go from a "good" evaluation to a valid prognosis, the evolution of the project over a certain lenght of time will have to be taken into account.

This, therefore, pleads the case for dynamic evaluation processes which are capable, not only of analysing the value of the different criteria which are now well known, at a given moment in time, but also of observing the type of structuring of these different aspects on successive occasions. With this in mind, one can only deplore the weakness of research carried out on the evaluation of new business ventures which take into account the rhythm at which the project reaches maturity.

This account taken of the time element could be developed by diachronic evaluation means. It could also be developed by accentuating the study of two dimensions which could well be of predictive value : adequation of financial resources in order to meet the frequent gaps, and the capacity for learning and the tenacity of the new entrepreneur.

The evaluation of the personal characteristics of the new entrepreneur poses quite considerable problems.

The new entrepreneur's capacities are determinant but must be specially examined in the light of his professional experience, by completing the judgment arising from the study of the dossier, at a given point in time, by a diachronic vision which may enable one to evaluate his personal potential for evolution. This observation confirms the importance that one has to give to the experience of the new entrepreneur or that of his team.

In the same way, the effects which distort the judgment of the person himself which we have mentioned, may be partially compensated for by a confrontation of diverse opinions between the evaluation experts and by a developed formalization of the evaluation process (analysis grids, evaluation reports, etc.).

The evaluation of the business plan, and especially of the business "vision" it gives and of its solidity, provides a good method of studying several determinant aspects. We are not, of course, putting forward the hypothesis of a capacity, on the part of the new entrepreneur, to accurately forecast what is going to happen. Many studies have even shown that there exists no direct correlation between the existence of the business plan and the success of the new business venture. It is more a question of considering the business plan as a formal occasion for evaluating certain aptitudes on the part of the new entrepreneur, which may have a predictive value, such as the capacity for formulating a clear image of his project and of the emphasis it gives to the available resources. In addition, it enables the demonstration of trust by the new entrepreneur towards the partners which he will need in the future.

Naturally, these conclusions need to be developed. However, we considered that they could, as of now, inspire certain improvements in evaluation practices which we have moreover begun to apply in our institution.

In view of the distance that still has to be covered in the area of project evaluation, it appears to us that increased efforts in longitudinal research should be precisely undertaken. It will be lead to elaborate concrete forecasting methods and practices, which alone are capable of helping the "evaluation experts" in their difficult task.

APPENDIX 1

PROJECT CHARACTERISTICS

Projects	No. of Entrepreneurs	N°. of yrs. Prof. exp. activity	Company activity	Turnover Forecast (B.P) (in KF)	Turnover achieved 1 year later (in KF)	Remarks
BC	1	0	Editing and printing artistic products			Filed for bankruptcy after 18 months
PM	1	0	Designed marketing of wooden items	3,800	1,600	Start-up of a second company
JC	1	yes	Distribution Agri-Food products	/	/	Abandoned
GV	2	5 and 10 years	R.& D. in high-tech products	4,626	6,900	Business dropped in in n+1
FD	1	10 years	Services to other companies	6,080	3,700	Filed for bankruptcy after 24 months
AL	1	0	Industrial D.P. consultancy	711	300	The turnover achieved in n+1 met the forecasts
ES	1	10 years	Sales of Agri-Food products	2,464	/	Filed for bankruptcy after 6 months

Evaluation of Business Ventures   309

SV	2	10 years for one of the two	Manufacture and sales household equipment	4,213	2,200	On partner left
SI	1	5 years	Design and sales Computer software	1,072	600	Sale of the business after 36 months
DB	1	yes	Data Processing Services	/	/	Abandoned
MM	1	10 years	Consultancy services to small to medium sized firms	2,464	700	Change of activity

Legend : KF = 1,000 FF.

APPENDIX 2

Simplified outline of the evaluation chart used on entry to the Entrepreneurs' Programme

1. THE CANDIDATE(1)
    1. Personal capacities (7 factors)
    2. Motivation (3 factors)
    3. Attitude from personal environment (4 factors)
    4. Quality of the team (5 factors)
    5. Know-how (7 factors)

2. THE PROJECT
    1. Attractiveness, market quality (4 factors)
    2. Degree of knowledge of the market (6 factors)
    3. Competitive advantages of the product (3 factors)
    4. Project assets (6 factors)

3. SPECIAL OPPORTUNITIES AND THREATS PRESENTED BY THE PROJECT

4. SYNTHESIS
    1. Synthesis of the evaluation made of the project (3 criteria)
    2. Synthesis of the evaluation made of the new entrepreneur (3 criteria)
    3. State of advancement of the project
    4. Principal assets and handicaps.

(1) For the majority of the factors proposed, the evaluating experts are asked to mark between 1 and 4. A detailed commentary explains, for certain factors, the meaning that should be given to them.

APPENDIX 3

RESEARCH EVALUATION OF NEW BUSINESS VENTURE PROJECTS

NAME :

COMPANY :

Business plan evaluation Grid

1. Clarity of vision of the future
   of the firm

   . Coherence, accuracy, evolutive
   nature of the project.

2. Solidity of business plan

   . Clarity of the outline strategy
   . Internal coherence of the B.p.
   (Objectives, markets, products,
   fiancial resources)
   . Existing objective information
   (Products, markets).

3. Description and evaluation
   of the existing human resources

   . Lucidity in the expose of the
   resources
   . Convincing character of their evaluation.

4. Explanation of the demands
   for resources

   . Capacity to convince others of joining him.

5. Quality of the presentation

   . Rigour
   . Precision
   . Quality of the synthesis.

General appreciation:

ENDNOTES

(1) This is the Programme d'Appui (the Entrepreneurs'Programme) of the Groupe ESC LYON created in 1985 and which welcomes about 30 projects per year.

(2) Out of a parent population of 36 projects, we eliminated from the random selection those where success appeared to be too closely linded to a single "veto" factor and those which corresponded to an already created company. There remained 25 projects, out of which a random selection was carried out.

(3) Appendix 3 presents the analysis grid used for the business plans.

(4) An enquiry conducted on a national scale by the French National Institute of Statistics and Economic Studies (INSEE) on a sample of 20,000 firms started up between September 1984 and August 1985 shows that less than one company in two reaches their fourth anniversary (VIENNET 1990).

(5) Moreover, as can be seen in Table 1, out of the 7 projects still alive, 5 already appear to have reached volumes of business beyond the forecasts, and sometimes in quite considerable proportions.

(6) This observation is similar to that given by certain researchers who underline that starting up a new business is always an experience which is based on hypotheses concerned with the relationships between products, markets and competitors. Some going as far as saying that it is only possible to test them...just by launching the company. They also underline the importance of the information gathered at each stage of the starting-up process (and that it is not possible to have it beforehand). See Z. BLOCK and I.C. MacMILLAN : "Milestones for successful venture planning" Harvard Business Review, 85, n°5.

(7) For example, the study by A. VAN DEN VEN, R. HUSTON and D.M. SCHROEDER which indicates that a "clear and widespread idea of his business" is one of the elements which differentiate efficient entrepreneurs from the others, in "Designing new business startups", Journal of Management 10 (1), 1984.

(8) These points are developped in V. RAMUS' text : "A longitudinal study of new business projects, First results", Groupe ESC Lyon, February 1988, 4-5. Cf. P. DUBINI (Ed.), in the bibliography.

BIBLIOGRAPHY

ALDRICH H., ROSEN B., WOODWARD W. (1987) "The impact of social networks on business foundings and profits : a longitudinal study", in <u>Frontiers of Entrepreneurship</u>

Research, Babson College, 154-168.

BEGLEY T.M., BOYD D.P. (1987) "Psychological characteristic associated with performance in entrepreneurial firms and smaller businesses", Journal of Business Venturing, Vol 2, 1, 79-93.

BERRYMAN J.(1983) "Small business failure and bankruptcy : a survey of the literature", European Business Journal, vol 1, 4, 41-59.

BEVERINA R. (1989) "The evaluation of entrepreneurial profiles", in Dubini P. Ed. The evaluation of entrepreneurial projects and profiles, Milan : EGEA, 15-28.

BIRLEY S. (1985) "The role of networks in the entrepreneurial process", Journal of Business Venturing, Vol 1, 1, 107-118.

BLOCK Z., MacMILLAN I.C. (1985) "Milestones for successful venture planning", Harvard Business Review, 5.

BOWMAN-UPTON N., SCAMAN S.L., SEXTON D.L. (1989) "Innovation evaluation programs : do they help the inventors ?", Journal of Small Business Management, vol 27, 3, 23-30.

CAPIEZ A. (1988) "Conditions et modalités d'émergence des TPE et PE ; l'exemple du Maine-et-Loire (France)", Revue Internationale PME, vol 1, 2, 127-155.

CARSRUD A.L., OLM K.W., THOMAS J.B. (1989), "Predicting entrepreneurial succes : effects of multi-dimensional achievement motivation, level of ownership, and cooperative relationships.", Entrepreneurship and Regional Development, Vol.1,3,237-244

COLOMBO G. (1989) "The selection of entrepreneurial profile and projects", in Dubini P. Ed. The evaluation of entrepreneurial projects and profiles, Milan : EGEA, 1-14.

COOPER A., DUNKELBERG W., WOO C.Y. (1988) "Survival and failure : a longitudinal study", in Frontiers of Entrepreneurship Research, Babson College, 225-237.

DEAN B.V., GIGLIERANO J.J. (1990), "Multistage financing of technical start-up companies in Silicon Valley.", Journal of Business Venturing, Vol.5,4,375-390.

DEPPERU D. (1989) "The selection of new entrepreneurial projects for training purposes", in DUBINI P. Ed. The evaluation of entrepreneurial projects and profiles, Milan : EGEA, 73-92.

DUBINI P. (1990) "Assessing new ventures success", in BIRLEY S. (Ed) Building European ventures, Amsterdam : Elservier Science Publishers B.V., 179-197.

DUBINI P. (1989) "The evaluation of new ventures and entrepreneurs : methodological considerations", in DUBINI P. Ed. The evaluation of entrepreneurial projects and profiles, Milan : EGEA, 103-122.

DUBINI P., MacMILLAN I.C. (1988) "The evaluation of entrepreneurial profiles in venture capital backed projects", in Frontiers of Entrepreneurship Research, Babson College, 46-58.

DUCHESNEAU D.A., GARTNER W.B. (1990), "A profile of new venture success and failure in an emerging industry", Journal of Business Venturing, Vol.5,5,297-312.

FOURCADE C. (1984) "The "démarrage" of firms : international comparisons", International Small Business Journal, vol 3, 2, 20-32.

FRANK H., PLASHKA G., ROESSL D. (1988) "Planning behavior of succesful and non-successful founders of new ventures", European Small Business Seminar, Gent-Brussels, 25 p.

GORMAN M., SAHLMAN W.A. (1986) "What do venture capitalists do ?", in Frontiers of Entrepreneurship Research, Babson College, 414-436.

GOSLIN J., BARGE B. (1986) "Entrepreneurial qualities considered in venture capital support", in Frontiers of Entrepreneurship Research, Babson College, 366-379.

HISRICH R.D., JANKOWICZ A.D. (1990) "Intuition in venture capital decisions : an exploratory study using a new technique", Journal of Business Venturing, Vol 5, 1, 49-62.

KHAN A.M. (1987) "Assessing venture capital investments with noncompensatory behavioral decision models", Journal of Business Venturing, vol. 2, 3, 193-206.

LIVIAN Y.F. (1989) "An evaluation of the personal characteristics of new entrepreneurs: an empirical study", in Dubini P. Ed. The evaluation of entrepreneurial projects and profiles, Milan : EGEA, 29-42.

MARION St. (1990) "Evaluation de projets de création d'entreprises innovantes",Banque, 504, 406-412.

MASSACRIER G., RIGAUD G. (1984) "Le démarrage d'activités nouvelles : aléas et processus", Revue Française de Gestion, mars-mai, 5-18.

MacMILLAN I.C., SIEGEL R., SUBBANARASIMHA P.N. (1985) "Criteria used by venture capitalist to evaluate new venture proposals", Journal of Business Venturing, Vol 1, 1, 119-128

MacMILLAN I.C., ZEMANN L., SUBBANARASIMHA P.N. (1987) "Criteria distinguishing successful from unsuccessful ventures in the venture screening process", Journal of Business Venturing, Vol 2, 2, 123-138.

NEISWANDER D.K., DROLLINGER J.M. (1986) "Origins of successful start-up ventures", in Frontiers of Entrepreneurship Research, Babson College, 328-334.

O'NEILL H.M., DUKER J. (1986) "Survival and failure in small business", Journal of Small Business Management, vol 24, 1, 38-46.

OOGHE H., VAN WYMEERSCH C., ERNST M., VAN DEN BOSSCHE P. (1988) "Empirical analysis of the differences between successful and unsuccessful new enterprise", European Small Business Seminar, Gent-Brussels, 21 p .

PETERSON R., SMITH N.R. (1986) "Entrepreneurship : a culturally appropriate combination of craft and opportunity", in Frontiers of Entrepreneurship Research, Babson College, 1-11.

RAMUS V., LIVIAN Y-F. (1990), "Relations between types of risks and new ventures success" in BIRLEY S. (Ed). Building European ventures, Amsterdam : Elsevier Science Publishers B.V., 198-213.

RAMUS V. (1989)"A longitidunal study of new business projects : first results about the early development of new ventures", in DUBINI P. Ed. The evaluation of entrepreneurial projects and profiles, Milan : EGEA, 73-92

RIGAUD G. (1987) "Le démarrage d'activités nouvelles : typologie des risques et financement des projets", Banque, 504, 244-260.

ROURE J.B., KEELEY R.H. (1990), " Predictors of success in new technology based ventures", Journal of Business Venturing, Vol.5,4,201-220.

SANDBERG W.R., HOFER C.W. (1987) "Improving new venture performance : the role of strategy, industry structure, and the entrepreneur", Journal of Business Venturing, Vol 2, 1, 5-28.

SEXTON D.L., BOWMAN N.B. (1986) "Validation of a personnality index : comparative psychological characteristics analysis of female entrepreneurs, managers, entrepreneuship students and business students", in Frontiers of Entrepreneurship Research, Babson College, 40-51.

SHAILER G. (1989) "The predictability of small enterprise failures : evidence and issues", International Small Business Journal, vol 7, 4, 54-58.

SMALLBONE D. (1990) "Success and failure in new business start-ups", International Small Business Journal, vol 8, 2, 34-47.

SMITH N.R., BRACKER J.S., MINER J.B. (1987) "Correlates of firm and entrepreneur success in technologically innovative companies", in Frontiers of Entrepreneurship Research, Babson College, 337-353.

STEINER M.P., SOLEM O. (1988) "Factors for success in small manufacturing firms", Journal of Small Business Management, vol 26, 1, 51-56.

STUART R., ABETTI P. (1987) "Start up ventures : towards the prediction of initial success", Journal of Business Venturing, Vol 2, 3, 215-230.

STUART R., ABETTI P. (1988) "Field study of technical ventures - Part III : the impact of entrepreneurial and management experience on early performance", in Frontiers of Entrepreneurship Research, Babson College, 177-193.

STUART R., ABETTI P. (1990), "Impact of entrepreneurial and management experience on early performance", Journal of Business Venturing, Vol.5,3,151-162.

VAN DE VEN A., HUDSON R., SCHROEDER D.M. (1984) "Designing new business start-ups", Journal of Management, 10,1.

VIENNET H. (1990) "Survivre : premier souci des jeunes entreprises", INSEE Première, 110, Nov. 1990, 4 p.

WARD R., RANDALL R. (1989) "Competitive advantage in the new business venture : the role of social networks" in DUBINI P. (Ed) The evaluation of entrepreneurial projects and profiles, Milan : EGEA, 43-60

WOO C.Y., COOPER A., DUNKELBERG W. (1988) "Entrepreneurial typologies : definitions and implications" in Frontiers of Entrepreneurship Research, Babson College, 165-176.

New Business Strategies: An Exploratory Examination

Critique
by
Paola Dubini, *Luigi Bocconi University*

The goal of the paper is to define the "structure of strategy" as applied to new ventures; the authors follow an entrepreneurial approach in gradually defining and testing hypotheses. The article clearly identifies a weak spot in strategy literature, as existing models hardly apply to new companies.

The dimensions identified by the authors are: domain, objectives, means and resources; together, they enable us to look at new companies' strategies according to Hambrick's (1983) as well as Mintzberg's (in Quinn et al. 1988) definition of strategy. This study is particularly significant, as it calls for a deeper understanding of strategy process as applied to new companies.

First, results indicate that three dimensions of the strategy typology -- domain, objectives and resources -- are independent one from the other and explain nearly 53 percent of the variance in new firm sales growth. This calls for a further analysis in two directions:

* can we better define the strategy typology, so as to capture part of the missing variance?

* is new firm sales growth the best indicator for success? The following paragraphs briefly examine both issues.

1. The significant dimensions in defining strategy typology

The problem of strategy definition is intimately linked with the way the firm positions itself in the market; in other words, the firm determines first which is the strategic territory (Normann 1983) in which to compete, and subsequently identifies possible ways to get there. The definition of the firm's strategic territory in turn, is functional to its core competences (Prahlad, Hamel 1990), that enable the firm to build a competitive advantage. In other words, the company tends to position itself within the industry so as to maximize the effect of its core competences.

If this hypothesis makes sense, the definition of strategy typology becomes more subjective, and rigid classification of significant variables might become misleading. Core competence identification may be a hard or fruitless task in the case of new companies, because the concept calls for a learning process occurring over time; yet, many companies are created around a basic core skill (Irvin, Michaels, 1989) that dominates future growth and development.

The perspective of core competences as the leading force influencing the company's strategy requires a different definition of domain from the one offered by the article.

As far as domain variability is concerned, one problem might arise in determining the novelty of the products or services offered. Some products may be relatively well known in the market (for example, bicycles) and still be perceived as significantly different products (i.e., mountain bikes), so that discussions may arise on whether mountain bikes are new products or not.

Classification on the basis of product range may therefore be misleading; an alternative way to define domain variability could be to analyze the needs served (product based vs service based vs style based (Sinatra 1989)). In this way, we can relate the novelty of the product/service offered by the new firm to the development of the industry in which the firm operates: in some industries, customers tend to choose their suppliers on the basis of the intrinsic characteristics of the product system (consumer goods), while in others service becomes a key variable in the success of the firm (software). Viewed from a different perspective, the novelty of the product or service offered may depend on the way the company decides to compete, according to Porter's (1980) definition; service strategy (through a resegmentation of the market) may be a way to bypass established competitors.

Another element to take into consideration is the issue of innovation, in the case in which it is not related to new product development. Although many new firms are me-too businesses from many points of view, a lot of new firms change their industries' rules of the game by being innovative from the organizational point of view (see for instance the case of McCornick hairdressing chain in the US). Therefore, distinctive capabilities (Sinatra 1989) could be added as a dimension for evaluating domain, by analyzing whether they are based on management of core technology or on the generation of innovation.

One key ingredient for new business strategy seems to be missing from the article, although it is generally acknowledged as a critical element in shaping the new firm: the entrepreneurial profile. In the article, the entrepreneur is directly taken into consideration only to assess wealth maximization. The entrepreneurial dichotomy (opportunistic versus craftsman) could be added as a dimension to explain the role of the founder in the new company.

2. Indicators for new firm's success

Another critical element to consider is whether sales growth is the best indicator for assessing new firms' success. Success can be defined as the consistency over time between the characteristics of the product system, the market served and the company's structure (Coda 1984); however, this definition hardly applies to a new venture, as the Coda model loses validity if it is applied ex ante (Dubini 1989).

The identification of growth rate rather than stock level as an indicator of new venture performance is consistent with previous studies on new firms' performance; as Miller et al (1990) point out, "a new venture is best evaluated on the basis of its progress towards a desirable end, rather than the end itself". Sales growth rate could be combined with ROI growth rate, so as to take into consideration not only revenue dynamism, but also costs and investments. Both parameters could be weighed according to industry characteristics.

References

Coda V. "La valutazione della formula imprenditoriale" SviluDo e Organizzazione, 92, 1984.

Dubini P. "Assessing New Ventures Success" in Birley (ed) Building European Ventures, EFER, 1989.

Hambrick D.C. "Some tests of the Effectiveness and Functional Attributes of Miles and Snow's Strategic Types" Academy of Management Journal, 26,1 5-26.

Irvin R.A., Michaels III "Core skills: Doing the Right Things Right" The McKinsey Quarterly, Summer 1989, 4-19.

Miller A., Wilson B., Adams M. "Financial Performance Patterns of New Corporate Ventures: An Alternative to Traditional Measures", Journal of Business Venturing, Vol. 3, n. 4.

Porter M. Competitive Strategy The Free Press 1980.

Prahalad C.K., Hamel G. "The Core Competence of the Corporation" Harvard Business Review, May - June 1990.

Quinn J.B., H.Mintzberg, James R.M. The Strategy Process: Concepts Contexts and Cases, Prentice Hall 1988.

Sinatra A. Strateaie di innovazione e strateaie di consolidamento UTET 1989.

NEW BUSINESS STRATEGIES: AN EXPLORATORY EXAMINATION

JOHN W. MULLINS, *UNIVERSITY OF MINNESOTA*
RICHARD N. CARDOZO, *UNIVERSITY OF MINNESOTA*
PAUL D. REYNOLDS, *MARQUETTE UNIVERSITY*
BRENDA MILLER, *UNIVERSITY OF MINNESOTA*

ABSTRACT

Two existing typologies of business level strategy are determined to be inadequate for empirical use in the study of new business strategies. An inductive approach to the construction of new typologies for new business strategies is proposed. Dimensions of a proposed typology are examined, using available data from a sample of 126 new firms.

INTRODUCTION

The purpose of this paper is to stimulate thinking about the dimensions on which typologies of new business strategies might be based, in order to encourage development of one or more typologies of strategies for new businesses. We are concerned here with strategies at the business level, as opposed to corporate or functional strategies (Hambrick, 1980).

We seek a typology of strategies for new businesses because new business survival and success have been linked to the strategies employed by new businesses (see, for example, Shimanski, Cardozo, Mullins, Reynolds, and Miller, 1990; Cardozo, McLaughlin, Harmon, Reynolds, and Miller, 1990b). Unfortunately, our quest is hampered by (1) differences in definitions of strategy in the literature; and (2) in the use of typologies that are incomplete, and that have been developed from the study of large, well-established organizations.

Recent years have seen a growing volume of entrepreneurship research. Much of this work is phenomenological in nature, as researchers attempt to identify and describe the various forms of phenomena related to entrepreneurs and entrepreneurship. The study of new business strategies is typical of this pattern. Researchers have identified differences among new business strategies (e.g., Shimanski, et al., 1990), but presently lack suitable means of organizing their knowledge about such strategies. Various typologies of business strategies exist in the strategic management literature (e.g., Miles and Snow, 1978; Porter, 1980). These typologies, however, have been inductively developed from populations of large, generally multi-divisional businesses. Useful as they are for facilitating the development and testing of theories about the relationships of strategies with other variables such as structure and performance (Hambrick, 1980), these typologies are inadequate in capturing key elements of the variability in new firm strategies.

For example, Porter (1980) divides strategies on the basis of their central means of competitive advantage: cost, leadership, differentiation, and focus. Many new firms, however, are copycat cat firms which lack clear bases for competitive advantage. Many of them may be regarded, in the Porter framework, as having focus strategies, since most start small with a limited line of products or services offered, and have a limited target market. Hence the Porter framework doesn't facilitate study of the proliferation of "me-too" businesses which start (and sometimes fail) every year.

Another example is the Miles and Snow (1978) typology, which classified businesses into four types, based on their orientation toward new product development. Prospectors aggressively seek out new product-markets; defenders attempt to build barriers to insulate themselves from competition as they defend their present product markets; analyzers are an intermediate form between prospectors and defenders; reactors are firms with no clearly defined product-market orientation. The Miles and Snow typology lacks relevance to new business settings for two reasons. First, new businesses often lack the resources to be prospectors, as borne out by evidence that there is not much prospectors-like behavior occurring among new businesses (Shimanski, et al., 1990). Second, it seems inappropriate to think of new businesses as defenders, since, at birth, they have neither products nor markets, and hence nothing to defend.

The fact that these typologies are not adequate in the new business context, however, does not indicate that new firms are undifferentiated with respect to their strategies. Although a case may be made for lack of differentiation [observation of no differences in firm performance across industries, or in founding circumstances (Cardozo, Reynolds, Miller and Ford, 1990s; Cardozo, et al., 1990b)], anecdotal evidence suggests that there are differences among strategies of new firms, but that current typologies are not as helpful as they might be in describing those strategies and differences among them.

Hence, typologies which take into consideration the varied conditions which often accompany the founding of new businesses are needed. These include such conditions as severely limited capital resources, diverse motivations for starting the business, including non-financial considerations and a lack of sustainable competitive advantage.

TYPOLOGIES

Typologies are classification systems which utilize one or more dimensions of a phenomenon or construct to group those members of the class sharing similar levels of the dimension(s) into types. Well designed typologies yield types which are mutually exclusive and collectively exhaustive, and prove to be useful for their intended purpose (Hunt, 1983). In the context of new business strategies, new typologies would be used for building and testing theory about the relationship of strategic types to other variables as firm performance, firm survival, and adaptation to environmental conditions, to name just a few variables of interest.

Typologies may be constructed from a single dimension, as with the Miles and Snow typology which is based on the firm's orientation toward the development of new products and new markets. Typologies may be constructed from more than one dimension as well. This approach is useful where the dimensions interact with one another, or where one dimension moderates the relationship of another with regard to other variables of interest. An example of a two dimensional typology is the Ansoff growth matrix (Ansoff, 1957), whose dimensions are markets (old and new), and products (old and new). The 2 X 2 matrix produces a typology of four strategies for growth, as follows:

	Markets Old	Markets New
Old	Growth in old markets with old products	Growth into new markets
New	Growth into new products	Growth into new markets and new products

Products

An important factor in determining the utility of a typology is the extent to which it captures variability across the population of interest in meaningful and explanatory ways. In the present context, then, useful dimensions on which to build typologies of new business strategies would be those which vary across the population, and which have main or interaction effects with selected dependent variables. If such dimensions can be identified, they can be used as potential building blocks for the creation of typologies.

DIMENSIONS OF BUSINESS STRATEGIES

"A strategy may be considered a pattern in a stream of decisions (past or intended) that (a) guides the organization's ongoing alignment with its environment and (b) shapes internal policies and procedures" (Hambrick, 1983).

A strategy may be thought of as consisting of four dimensions: domain or scope, objectives, means, and resources (Boyd and Walker, 1990). Domain refers to the customer groups and customer functions to be served, and the choice of a technology to be employed in doing so (Abell, 1980). Objectives may be financial or otherwise (for example, the desire to be one's own boss), may differ in the measures used to assess attainment (profit, sales growth, market share, survival of the business, etc.), and may vary in their level of specificity and difficulty. Those who start new businesses appear often to have objectives other than the maximization of profit (Reynolds and West, 1985). Means refer to the bases for competitive advantage (Porter, 1980) on which the organization depends for satisfying the wants and needs of its customers. Resources in the new business setting concern the amount of each of several types of resources (including capital and human resources) available, and their allocation across product-markets and across the elements of the marketing mix. Since all resources can conceptually be converted to money terms, we can discuss resources in terms of funds available and funds deployed across various functional activities and product-markets.

These four dimensions of strategy are the basic building blocks with which we shall explore the building of typologies of new business strategies. We shall first address some alternative ways of conceptualizing variability on each of the four dimensions.

Domain

Three approaches to conceptualizing domain variability among new businesses are the following:

- Novelty of the products or service offered: Some firms introduce innovative products or services, such as the personal computer (Apple Computer), overnight delivery (Federal Express), or in-line roller skates (Rollerblade). Each of these firms came to market with products or services which served new customer functions, or provided new technology to existing functions. In contrast, other firms offer "Me-too" products or services, such as a new dry cleaning shop, an office supply store, or a new brand of spaghetti sauce. Thus, new versus "me-too" may be a useful dichotomy for building a new business strategy typology.

- Breadth of market targeted: Some firms focus on a narrow niche, such as selling extraction technology to owners of low-yield oil wells. Other seek a mass market, such as the market for microwave popcorn or pizza delivery. Thus a niche versus mass approach may be a second way to characterize domain differences among new business strategies.

- Breadth of products/services offered: Many new firms offer a limited product in start-up. The Apple II is an example. Others offer a broad range, such as new firms which manufacture accessories for personal computer users. Thus a dichotomy based on a narrow versus broad product line is a third approach.

Objectives

The goal setting literature suggests that goal difficulty and goal specificity are significant mediators of performance (Locke, Saari, Shaw, and Latham, 1981). One way to conceptualize goal difficulty in the new business setting is:

- Maximizing versus satisfying objectives for economic performance: Some founders do not intend to make large amounts of money. They may only hope to earn a reasonable living for their family, or they may have non-financial objectives which rule out maximizing behaviors. This dichotomy may be particularly useful, especially when evaluating the performance of different kinds of new business strategies. Appropriate measures for assessing performance will vary, depending on the objectives of the business.

The notion of goal specificity implies that goals should be stated in terms of some clearly specified unit of measure. Numerous measurers of goal attainment are possible of course, depending on the nature of the goal. Two such measures which may be useful in the present context are profitability and revenue growth:

- Profit versus revenue goals: Objectives to grow quickly, versus objectives to maximize short-term profits can lead to very different courses of action. This dichotomy may provide insights into new business strategies.

Means

There are many ways to describe the means of pursuing a new business strategy. Means refers to a combination and configuration of functional strategy elements, combined together into a gestalt on which competitive advantage is to be based. One potentially useful way which may encompass a relatively broad notion of means is derived from Porter's (1980) bases of competitive advantage:

- Price leadership versus differentiation: Does the new firm seek to establish a price advantage or a differentiated quality advantage over its competitors?

Resources

The issue of resources is central to entrepreneurship. The notion of under capitalization pervades much thinking about new businesses. Hence a fruitful way to characterize the variability along this dimension may be:

- Amount of financial resources: The strategies of new businesses having substantial resources may differ significantly from those having to bootstrap their way into existence.

A multidimensional typology based on the foregoing characterizations would include the following dimensions:

- Domain: Novelty (new versus "me-too")
- Domain: Product Breadth (broad versus narrow)
- Domain: Market Breadth (broad versus narrow)
- Objectives: Maximizing versus satisfying income or wealth
- Means: Basic competitive advantage (price versus non-price)
- Financial Resources: Amount (few versus many)

Generating combinations of these six dimensions, each of which would have more than two values, becomes an enormously complex undertaking. Therefore, to illustrate how the typology might work, we can use subsets of the six dimensions to specify likely strategies and to generate hypotheses. To do so, we use product breadth or product novelty to measure domain, and set aside the means dimension for the present. This procedure allows us to demonstrate two variations of the proposed typology.

TWO PLAUSIBLE VARIATION OF THE PROPOSED TYPOLOGY

In this section of the paper, we develop two variations of the proposed typology, and provide examples of research questions which might be explored through their use.

Variation 1

The first variation includes two levels each of domain, objectives, and resources, using novelty as the domain dimension:

- Domain: Firms are classified as to whether they address a new domain (i.e., new customer group, new customer function, or new technology) versus a "me-too" approach with regard to customer groups, functions, or technology. It is unlikely that a new business will find new customers (though perhaps pet psychology would fit such a definition!), so the essence of newness will typically be either new technology or making it possible for customers to perform new functions (e.g., travel to the moon, or perform highly complex analyses on a super computer).
- Objectives: Is it the intent of the founders of the new firm to maximize financial performance or satisfice financially!
- Resources: Is the firm well capitalized, or is it under funded?

This set of dimensions creates a 2 X 2 X 2 typology of strategic types as follows:

A: New domain, maximizing, high resources

B: Me-too domain, maximizing, high resources
C: New domain, satisficing, high resources
D: Me-too domain, satisficing, high resources
E: New domain, maximizing, low resources
F: Me-too domain, maximizing, low resources
G: New domain, satisficing, low resources
H: Me-too domain, satisficing, low resources

An examination of the interrelations among the three dimensions leads to some interesting speculation. First, one might expect four of the types not to exist at all, or to fail soon if they did occur:

> B: One does not expect to see high resources together with a maximizing strategy unless there is something new (i.e. new technology, or newly identified customer groups or functions) being brought to the party.

C & D: One does not expect to see satisficing strategies employed when high resources are invested. The use of high levels of resources usually implies a maximization strategy.

> G: One does not expect to see a satisficing strategy when a new technology is brought to an enterprise, or a new market is identified. Such situations and their attendant risk typically suggest a maximizing strategy.

We are left with four types of strategies we would expect to find in the population of new businesses:

> A: New domain, maximizing, high resources, e.g., Apple computer. One might call this an Innovative Growth Strategy.
>
> E. New domain, maximizing, low resources, e.g., many franchisors, some franchisees. One might call this an Innovative Bootstrapping Strategy.
>
> F: Me-too domain, maximizing, low resources, e.g., Orville Redenbacher popcorn. One might call this an Imitative Bootstrapping Strategy.
>
> H: Me-too domain, satisficing, low resources, e.g., many mom and pop businesses. Call this an Imitation Strategy.

Several hypotheses which might be explored using this typology come to mind:

> H1: We would expect to see higher variance in growth rates among the two innovative types (Types A and E) compared to the imitative types (Types F and H), because of the uncertainty about whether the market

will support the new idea.

H2. We might also expect higher average growth rates for the innovative types compared to the imitators as a result of less competition in the new domain situation, compared to the "me-too" situation.

H3. We would expect higher survival rates for Type A than Type E, due to the slack provided by higher financial resources.

H4. We would expect to find the innovative types in more volatile environments, the imitative types in less volatile environments.

It should be noted that numerous issues related to construct definition (What constitutes new technology?) and measurement (What level of start-up resources is high versus low?) will need to be addressed in order to empirically employ such a typology.

Variation 2

The second variation, also three-dimensional, conceptualizes domain in a different way:

- Domain: Firms are classified according to whether the product-market domain they target is broad or narrow. A broad domain would be one which encompasses a broad range of products or product lines, and/or a broad range of customer groups or customer functions. Though the use of a broad range of technologies would also constitute a broad domain, such a circumstance is probably unlikely for a new business. A narrow domain would be one in which a clearly defined set of customers and customer functions are targeted, based on a chosen technology.
- Objectives Is it the intent of the founders of the new firm to maximize financial performance or satisfy financially? (Same as in Variation 1).
- Resources: Is the firm well capitalized , or is it under funded? (Same as in Variation 1).

This set of dimensions again creates a 2 X 2 X 2 typology or strategic types as follows:

A: Broad domain, maximizing, high resources

B: Narrow domain, maximizing, high resources

C: Broad domain, satisficing, high resources

D: Narrow domain, satisficing, high resources

E: Broad domain, maximizing, low resources

F: Narrow domain, maximizing, low resources

G: Broad domain, satisficing, low resources

H: Narrow domain, satisficing, low resources

An examination of the eight types again leads to some interesting speculation. Again one expects that some types will typically not occur.

A: Broad domain, maximizing, high resources. Such a firm targets many markets at the outset, a plausible strategy, given high resources, but probably an unlikely one, given that most firms begin with a narrower focus.

C & D: As in typology 1, one does not expect to see satisficing strategies employed when high resources are invested. The use of high levels of resources usually implies a maximization strategy.

We are left with five remaining types of strategies we would expect to find in the population of new businesses:

B: Narrow domain, maximizing, high resources, e.g., Apple Computer or Federal Express. One might call this the Focused Growth Strategy.

E: Broad domain, maximizing, low resources. This represents the classic overextended, undercapitalized entrepreneur who tries many avenues, hoping that one will succeed. Call it Overambitious and Under funded.

F: Narrow domain, maximizing, low resources, e.g., Orville Redenbacher's Popcorn. Call this the Bootstrap Strategy.

G: Broad domain, satisficing, low resources. Call this group Overextended and Under funded.

H: Narrow domain, satisfying, low resources, e.g., many mom and pop businesses. Call this the Family Livelihood Strategy.

Several hypotheses come to mind:

H1: Survival rates will be poor for the Overambitious and Overextended, and Overextended and Under funded types E and G. Survival rates will be higher for Types F and H, which have low resources, but target narrower domains.

H2. Average revenue growth rates will be highest for the Focused Growth Strategy, and lowest for the Family Livelihood Strategy, due to the interaction of objectives and resources. Bootstrap growth rates will be intermediate.

H3: In terms of the Ansoff Growth Matrix, firms with Focused Growth Strategies will tend to grow into both new products and new markets, given their superior resources. Family Livelihood businesses will likely do neither. The other three types will add new products or new markets, but at a lesser rate than Focused Growth firms.

H4: In terms of the Porter bases for competitive advantage after start-up, firms with Bootstrap Strategies will tend to pursue focus strategies, firms with Family Livelihood strategies will tend to pursue cost based strategies. The other three types will use any of the Porter types.

Again, numerous issues related to measurement (What constitutes a broad or narrow domain? What level of start-up resources is high versus low?) will need to be addressed in order to employ this typology empirically.

The examples outlined above suggest the potential utility of developing typologies of new business strategies. We intend in due course to evaluate the proposed typology in an empirical setting that will allow us to examine both the structure of the typology and the extent to which it helps to explain variance in a variety of response measures.

Because the empirical study(ies) necessary to perform such analyses are costly in money and time, we wish first to explore inductively some elements of the typology, and the ability of the typology to explain variance in at least one measure of new firm performance. For this exploration, we chose an existing data base that contained (1) measures of most of the constructs we needed to examine the structure of proposed typology, and (2) a continuous measure of new firm performance -- sales growth -- that would allow us to make a preliminary assessment of the usefulness of the proposed typology in explaining variation among new firms. Although the sample size is insufficient to permit classification of firms into eight types and test fully hypotheses such as those which have been proposed, the available data are sufficient to undertake an exploratory analysis to determine whether the dimensions chosen explain variance across the population and whether there are interactions present that suggest the development of a multi-dimensional, rather than uni-dimensional typology.

SAMPLE

Our sample consisted of a sub sample from a probability sample of 2,000 Minnesota firms drawn from a Dun's Marketing Identifier's file of firms that reported a start date in 1979 through 1982. After discarding subsidiaries, branches, firms that were not new, firms that were no longer active, listings that were not new business firms, and reducing the sample in retail and consumer services, 724 were eligible for the study (Reynolds, West & Finch, 1985). Of the 724 eligible firms, 550 provided the requested information (details in Reynolds and West, 1985). Follow ups were completed with this sample in 1985, 1986, 1988, and 1989.

Of the initial firms, 430 (78%) were still in business in 1988. Consistent with their original distribution, almost two-thirds of these survivors were in the Minneapolis-St. Paul Metropolitan area. Phone, mail, and fact-to-face interviews with management personnel in 126 firms (approximately half of the metropolitan area active survivors) were completed in 1989. Complete data were available from 56 firms. We excluded from the analysis any firms for which even a single data point was missing.

Both the original sample and this sub sample contained a mix of businesses representative of the industry mix in the population. Other analyses have shown high similarity in results between this Minnesota panel and two other surveys, a 1986 survey of Pennsylvania and a (second) 1987 Minnesota survey (Reynolds and West, 1985; Reynolds and Freeman, 1987; Reynolds and Miller, 1987). As Pennsylvania has a quite different economic and political context, there is reason to expect that the results from this analysis may be generalized to most new U.S. firms in urban contexts.

ANALYSIS

To evaluate the proposed typology, we defined the constructs operationally in a manner consistent with variation 2:

Domain was defined as the number of products the new firm offered in its first year.

Objective: We defined objective in terms of the expressed importance of maximizing wealth (critical, important, not important).

Resources were measured by the level of funding available before start up (lowest one-third of the distribution of funds, middle one-third, highest one-third).

Sales growth, the dependent measure, was defined as a growth multiple, sales in the firm's sixth year divided by sales in the firm's first year. Because the distribution of both sixth and first year sales were highly skewed and non-normal, we used a log transformation of that measure to perform an analysis of variance.

RESULTS AND DISCUSSION

Results indicate that three dimensions of the strategy typology--domain, objective and resources--are independent of one another (See Table 1), and together explain nearly 53% of the variance in new firm sales growth. Of particular interest is the finding that most of the explanatory power of the typology resides in interactions, rather than in main effects of the domain, objective and resource variable (See Table 2).

These observations suggest that new firm strategy is indeed a multidimensional construct, and that our proposed typology has identified three independent, important dimensions of new firm strategy. The observation that the interactions are more important than the main effects themselves implies that particular combinations (as yet unspecified) of values on each structural variable affect new firm growth; and that relationships between strategy variables, on the one hand, and measures like growth, on the other, may be much more complex than we have imagined.

Of interest is the finding that "objective" accounts for most of the variation within main effects, and approaches statistical significance. Evidently, differences in objectives among entrepreneurs influence the growth that their firm experience.

FUTURE RESEARCH

Results from this exploration of the "structure of strategy" and relationship of that structure to new firm growth embolden us to pursue the project. That pursuit includes conceptual effort, methodological refinements and extensive data collection. Conceptual work involves (1) broadening our definition of strategy (if broadening appears appropriate) to enrich the structure of the framework proposed here; (2) specifying and supporting hypotheses relating elements of that framework to a variety of measures of new firm performance; and (30 identifying classification factors (e.g., industry classification, initial size, location, etc.) and external environmental influences (competitors' actions, demand fluctuations and the like) that likely moderate the relationships hypothesized, in order to move forward the process of developing a contingency theory of new firm strategy and performance.

Methodological refinements include (1) writing operational definitions of the terms in the proposed framework, which definitions can be readily extended to become questionnaire or interview schedule items; (2) providing uniform or comparable response scales for these items, which scales can be verified for reliability; and (3) exploring alternative models to ANOVA and its components for data analysis.

Expansion of the framework to six independent dimensions, each of which had, say, three values, would generate a 3^6 per 729-cell design. A minimum of 10 observations per cell would require nearly 7300 new firms, if each firm was a simple data point. Even creative collapsing of dimensions, and use of nested and alternative designs, will clearly require very large amounts of data. Simply to render tractable the research program implied here will require piecemeal empirical evaluation, even on large data sets.

Our immediate plans are to pursue a portion of this effort within the context of a resurvey of panels of new businesses begun in Minnesota and Pennsylvania in the mid-1980's. These panels should provide us with approximately 2,000 firms.

IMPLICATIONS

As we progress in this endeavor, we expect to generate knowledge about relationships between new firms' strategy and performance under specified conditions. This knowledge should (1) increase our understanding of new firms' strategies themselves; (2) enable us to draw inference about strategy -- performance relationships, which inference can form a basis for recommendations to entrepreneurs; (3) contribute to a richer and more useful definition of strategy itself, and in turn enhance our understanding of strategy in firms of all ages, stages and sizes.

SUMMARY

We have proposed a typology for classifying strategies of new firms, which typology is based on multiple components or dimensions of "strategy." A partial, exploratory empirical evaluation of that typology revealed that constituent elements appeared independent of one another, and that the typology might explain, principally through interactions rather than main effects, more than half the variance in a single performance measure, new firm sales growth. The typology and this approach hold promise for future research.

REFERENCES

Abell, D.F. (1980), Defining the Business: The Starting Point of Strategic Planning, Englewood Cliffs, N.J.: Prentice-Hall.

Ansoff, H. T., "Strategies for Diversification,". Harvard Business Review, September- October 1957, 35 (5) pp. 113-24.

Boyd, H. W., Jr. and O. C. Walker, Jr. Marketing Management: A Strategic Approach Homewood, IL: Irwin.

Cardozo, R. N., P. D., Reynolds, B. Miller, and D. Ford, "Mapping Sales of New Businesses Over Time,: (1990a) paper presented to American Marketing Association, 1990 Winter Marketing Educators' Conference, Scottsdale, Arizona, February 24-27, 1990.

Cardozo, R., K. McLaughlin, B. Harmon, P. Reynolds, and B. Miller (1990b),

"Product-Market Strategies and New Business Growth," in L. E. Apple and T. P. Hustad (eds.), Product Development: Prospering in a Rapidly Changing World, Product Development and Management Association.

Hambrick, D. C. (1980) "Operationalizing the Concept of Business-Level Strategy in Research," Academy of Management Review, 5, 567-575.

Hunts, S. D. 1983) Marketing Theory: The Philosophy of Marketing Science, Homewood, IL: Irwin.

Locke, E. A., L. M. Saari, K. N. Shaw, and G. P. Latham (1981) "Goal Setting and Task Performance: 1969-1980, Psychological Bulletin, 90, 1, 125-152.

Miles, R. E. and C. C. Snow (1978) Organizational Strategy, Structure and Process. McGraw-Hill, New York.

Porter, Michael (1980) Competitive Strategy, New York: The Free Press.

Reynolds, P. D. and B. Miller, 1987. 1987 minnesota New Firm Survey. Minneapolis, Minnesota: University of Minnesota, Center for Urban and Regional Affairs.

Reynolds, P. D. and S. Freeman, 1987. 1986 Pennsylvania New Firm Survey. Washington, D.C: Appalachia Regional Commission.

Reynolds, P. D. and S. West, 1985. New Firms in Minnesota: Their Contributions to Employment and Exports, Start-up Problems and Current Status. Minneapolis, Minnesota: University of Minnesota Center for Urban and Regional Affairs.

Reynolds, P. D., S. West, and m. Finch, (1985) "Estimating New Firms and New Jobs: Considerations in Using the Dun and Bradstreet Files," Frontiers of Entrepreneurial Research, Babson College, Wellesley, Massachusetts, 383-397.

Shimanski, J. M., R. M. Cardozo, J. W. Mullins, P. D. Reynolds, and B. Miller (1990), "Evolution of Competitive Strategy in New Firms," Proceedings of 1990 AMA Entrepreneurship Symposium, Chicago: AMA, forthcoming.

TABLE 1
CORRELATION MATRIX

	Domain	Objective	Resources
Domain	1.00	0.09	-0.16
Objective		1.90	-0.23
Resources			1.00

TABLE 2
ANALYSIS OF VARIANCE
LOG OF GROWTH MULTIPLE

Source of Variation	Sum of Squares	DF	Mean Square	F	Sig. of F
Main Effects	1.516	5	.303	1.336	.268
Resources	.801	2	.401	1.765	.183
Domain	.228	1	.228	1.006	.321
Objective	1.110	2	.555	2.445	.099
2-Way Interactions	3.420	8	.427	1.883	.088
Resource X Domain	1.304	2	.652	2.872	.067
Resource X Objective	2.962	4	.741	3.262	.020
Domain X Objective	.298	2	.149	.657	.524
3-Way Interactions Resources, Domain Objective	6.025	3	2.008	8.846	.001
	6.025	3	2.008	8.846	.001
Explained	10.961	16	.685	3.018	.002
Residual	9.762	43	.227		
Total	20.723	59	.351		

The Second Time Around: The Outcomes, Assets And Liabilities Of Prior Start-Up Experience

Critique
by
Robert H. Keeley, *Stanford University*
Lassaad A. Turki, *Stanford University*

Jennifer Starr and Bill Bygrave ask whether prior start-up experience is an asset or a liability for entrepreneurs. By examining second, or "n"th, time entrepreneurs they provide us with an interesting overview of what researchers know and do not yet know about entrepreneurship. This is an important, fascinating subject and they cover it well. Some of their more important references date from the 1960's and before, suggesting that despite the subject's importance, in some areas we have not made much progress.

Starr and Bygrave suggest a perspective in which successful entrepreneurship involves the intersection of a <u>career trajectory</u> and an opportunity for an appropriate <u>scale</u> situated within an <u>industry's</u> <u>life-cycle.</u> We believe that it will prove valuable in synthesizing the various strands of research on entrepreneurship.

The use of second time entrepreneurs is not necessary to their study, but it gives a second data point on each subject. Rather than simply throwing out the ones which do not get the same score each time -- i.e., success-success or fail-fail -- they suggest that repeated success may involve a special skill at learning. The habitual entrepreneur may be better able to gather transferable assets from each venture without dragging along some liabilities. They propose a framework to explain how that may happen.

These comments will first summarize Starr and Bygrave's paper. Then we will discuss a few of their subjects, including the industry life cycle as an influence, the changeable nature of entrepreneurship, the value of studying second time entrepreneurs as a window on entrepreneurial learning, and the implications of their work for the teaching of entrepreneurship.

The literature on entrepreneurship, surveyed by Starr and Bygrave, has multiple origins, including:

*Studies of small business entrepreneurs (Collins and Moore, 1964; Vesper, 1980)

*Studies of career trajectories (Schein, 1978 & 1986)

*Distillation of venture capitalist perceptions (MacMillan, Zemann, & SubbaNarasimha, 1985; Dubini, 1989).

*Theories and empirical studies of "fit" among environment, strategy, and founders (Romanelli, 1989a, 1989b).

*Studies of technological start-ups (Eisenhardt & Schoonhoven, 1990).

They begin with a "population ecology" perspective in which entrepreneurshp stems from appropriately qualified individuals stepping forward at appropriate points in the industry life cycle. From this they develop a set of six propositions relating a founder's experience, the scale of the new enterprise, and the stage of the industry's development.

Although this perspective may explain broad aspects of any industry, and of entrepreneurship, they note that it cannot identify who will step forward and why. To address this they examine the literature on career trajectories and on entrepreneurs. They conclude that the research on entrepreneurs, at least that part that deals with their learning and skills, is too shallow for today's environment (e.g. Collins & Moore, 1964; Lamont, 1972), and lacks a unifying framework. As a framework they adapt Schein's (1978, 1986) work on career dynamics. This allows them to combine several qualities:

*personal energy, moral development, wealth and aspirations
*"career anchoring" preferences regarding incentives of recognition
*business assets such as networks, reputation, and management style.

They suggest that these dimensions may provide the basis for understanding an individual's fitness for entrepreneurship, and for understanding how prior start-up experience may contribute to that fitness. They begin by stating that experience is paradoxical -- it teaches important lessons, but they may not be the right ones for the next time around.

The first attribute of fitness they propose is entrepreneurial expertise -- an approach to understanding one's environment. Start-up experience offers an opportunity to develop such expertise, which usually leads toward a more intuitive mode of analysis and an ability to view a situation broadly. A second attribute is a network of relations, which is an economical way to locate resources, and tap the know-how of others. The third is reputation. A good reputation opens doors -- they specifically mention venture capital doors, but the same may be said of customers, suppliers, and strategic allies.

But the same experiences which breeds fitness also imposes liabilities. Intuition enables shortcuts and saves time, but in new situations, the shortcuts may be different, and the seasoned entrepreneur may have too much faith in the past. The issue is that one needs second order learning, and may only have obtained first order.

The strong ties of a network may be the wrong ones; this seems particularly likely if an industry changes rapidly, or if an entrepreneur enters a new industry. And finally, the "success syndrome" may cause the entrepreneur to abandon the "roll up your sleeves" attitude that helped create the earlier success.

Necessarily, our summary cannot convey the breadth of research which the authors bring to their ideas. They pull together many studies, and achieve a considerable unity. Second time entrepreneurs may be a very good vehicle indeed for discovering which learning and skills really matter. They also give a broader view of careers than first time entrepreneus and can illuminate whether career anchors, wealth, energy, and aspirations change over time, and if so how.

We would suggest to Starr and Bygrave, as an extension of this work, that they might try to integrate industry life cycles with career dynamics more closely. This may only add complexity, but their theories suggest the two will be interrelated in many interesting ways.

For example, in industries undergoing prolonged growth such as electronics, first order learning may be sufficient to carry an entrepreneur through multiple companies. With respect to computer systems, start-up companies tend to rely on product innovation as their main advantage. Manufacturing strategies aim at meeting industry norms through extensive reliance on suppliers, and marketing tends to be a copy of industry norms as well. These organizations are designed to move quickly, and to respond to market shifts. Disk drives, semiconductors or medical equipment vary in some important ways, but within each industry, the modus operandi shows considerable uniformity.

On the other hand, as an industry tries to emerge from a pre-commercial state -- the case of the start-ups in Ven de Ven, Angle & Poole (1989) -- the circumstances may be very different. An infrastructure of suppliers, distributors and knowledgeable executives does not exist. The circumstances of this early stage seem to call for different knowledge, backgrounds, and attitudes than in a growth stage.

An additional dimension, which might receive more attention, is scale. In a large scale start-up, people can be more specialized, and the likelihood that their competitors will also be large puts a premium on efficiency, and speed. These do not always coexist comfortably, and founders with knowledge of how to balance them become important.

Starr and Bygrave have already begun to integrate industry life cycles and individual careers, but their initial propositions are aimed at rather broad tests -- as expressed in Propositions 1 through 6. Broad propositions may be widely enough embraced that they convey only a tiny comptetive advantage. The more important secrets, as far as performance is concerned, may require a finer partition.

A first step toward a finer partition with respect to life cycle would recognize subindustries, and look at breadth of product line, absolute scale, degrees of vertical integration and the like. The semiconductor industry has been in a growth stage for over 30 years, but the skills needed to succeed today may be very different because of the availabilies of foundry facilities, overseas alliances and so on.

As a final comment, we might reflect on what Starr and Bygrave's work implies for the teaching of entrepreneurship. It recognizes that entrepreneurship has several dimensions:

*The personality and career dynamics of the (co)founders of a business;

*The economic function, whose specifics may vary with the nature and stage of the industry;

*The knowledge and skills which make a person an effective manager in the specific situation, and

*The organizational role played by each (co)founder.

Studies of entrepreneurship, even when they propose to be integrative, tend to focus on one of these. To the reader remains the the difficult task of fitting the pieces together, and knowing what to apply when.

Starr and Bygrave have some help for us. They provide the unifying themes of accumulation of managerial knowledge, career trajectories, and industry characteristics. They also implicitly recognize the possible need for second order learning -- when, and how to change the way one does business. And finally, they suggest that learning is a balancing act -- one must learn from limited data, but must be cautious about deriving the wrong lesson.

THE SECOND TIME AROUND: THE OUTCOMES, ASSETS AND LIABILITIES OF PRIOR START-UP EXPERIENCE

JENNIFER A. STARR[1], *BABSON COLLEGE*
WILLIAM D. BYGRAVE, *BABSON COLLEGE*

ABSTRACT

The entrepreneurship literature has assumed that prior experience, and particularly start-up experience, is associated with successful new venture performance. However, the results of empirical studies have been inconclusive. This paper argues that the outcomes of prior entrepreneurial experience may have both positive and negative effects on the performance of subsequent ventures. We discuss four liabilities of prior successful performance which may constrain the innovative potential and financial performance of future ventures -- the liabilities of staleness, sameness, priciness and costliness.

INTRODUCTION

The last two decades of entrepreneurial enthusiasm in the United States have yielded a growing roster of entrepreneurs who have been involved in the creation of not one, but several start-up ventures. As modern folk heros and industry idols, Steve Jobs of Apple Computer and NEXT, Seymour Cray of Control Data, Cray Research and Cray Computer, Mitch Kapor of Lotus Development Corporation and ON Technology, and many others are joining the historic ranks of prolific business founders. These business generators prefer to specialize in the entrepreneurial function throughout their careers, rather than rest on their laurels as originators of innovative products, high growth companies, path-breaking technologies, and billion dollar industries. "Starting pitchers", entrepreneurs with successful venturing backgrounds who are ready to "do it again", are considered to be a desirable, but scarce, commodity by connoisseurs of entrepreneurial talent in the venture capital community. Yet, although scholars of

---

[1]The authors gratefully acknowledges the support of the Sol C. Snider Entrepreneurial Center at The Wharton School of University of Pennsylvania and the encouragement and wisdom of Ian C. MacMillan who has served as adviser for the dissertation research which provides the background for this paper. In addition, we recognize the valuable discussions with entrepreneurs and members of the entrepreneurial community who have been influential in shaping our understanding of Habitual Entrepreneurship. We also appreciate the efforts of Shirley J. Jafari at The Wharton School and Daniel Munson at Babson College who conducted library research and contributed early stage intellectual capital to this project.

Entrepreneurship have been avid students of these highly visible success stories, the phenomenon of multiple venture entrepreneurship has received limited attention.

Multiple venture entrepreneurs warrant further investigation because they challenge popular views of entrepreneurial success. The experience of Ken Olsen, founder of Digital Equipment Company, typifies the traditional American dream. Olsen started a successful technology-based company that gave birth to the minicomputer revolution and then "graduated" to CEO of a prosperous, professionally-managed, multi-product, multinational firm. At the other extreme, less ambitious individuals with entrepreneurial aspirations aim for a comfortable _early_ retirement, financed by the profitable sale or public offering of their first start-up. In contrast to the two aforementioned distinctive paths to entrepreneurial fortune, prolific business founders choose to continue a career of self-employment by starting multiple independent ventures. Although there is some evidence that involvement in multiple new ventures may be more prevalent than is commonly believed, second (and _several_) time around entrepreneurs seem to be a breed which we know very little about (MacMillan, 1986; Starr, 1990).

Despite the lack of specific focus on multiple venture entrepreneurs, prior entrepreneurial experience has been considered to be an important determinant of successful new venture performance. Prior start-up experience is typically defined as prior participation in the formation of at least one independent start-up venture. Most studies have measured prior start-up experience as a simple categorical, independent variable, rather than consider the characteristics of the entrepreneurial experience curve which would further our understanding of the entrepreneurial phenomenon (Starr, 1990). Researchers have asked standard demographic questions: started a prior business? yes/no; in the same industry? yes/no; prior performance? successful/unsuccessful; years in earlier business?. At first glance, the preparation offered by the first start-up seems readily apparent, warranting little intellectual exploration. However, given that entrepreneurial careers begin at various times, vary in duration, and follow a variety of paths, it is not surprising that the empirical investigations that have attempted to identify a positive association between prior experience and venture success have demonstrated _mixed_ results (Cooper and Gascon, Forthcoming; Starr, 1990).[2] This suggests that further conceptual work is needed to augment our understanding of the impact of this particular entrepreneurial characteristic on venture performance (Gartner, 1989).

Although the advantages of prior start-up experience may seem intuitively obvious, few studies have presented well-developed theories to justify causal linkages between this background and future venture results. Similarly, there has been limited

---

[2]For a comprehensive review of the literature and references regarding prior industry start-up and joint team experience see Cooper and Gascon, forthcoming. Given the space limitations and scope of material covered here, we have necessarily limited our review.

attention paid to the differential contributions of industry experience and start-up experience. And no studies have considered the ways in which the founder's prior experience might be detrimental or dysfunctional to the second, third, fourth, tenth or fiftieth new business. To fill this gap, this paper explores some of the logical linkages between prior start-up experience and subsequent firm performance.

Briefly stated, this paper argues that the outcomes of prior venturing experience can be both an asset and a liability to an entrepreneur's successive ventures. While the advantages of start-up experience have been assumed, experienced business founders also face certain liabilities of prior performance which constrain the innovative potential and results of future ventures. These are similar to the "liabilities of age and size" facing large, old organizations (Aldrich and Auster, 1986). In this paper, we outline some of the effects of the liabilities of prior successful performance. This analysis would also suggest differences between entrepreneurs with early track records of success and those that failed or achieved moderate success before building subsequent ventures. But, that discussion is left for future development. At this juncture, we embrace the opportunity to explore the different assumptions, theoretical inconsistencies, contradictory explanatory principles and problems posed by this seemingly paradoxical role of prior successful start-up experience (Poole and Van de Ven, 1989).

Thus, a consideration of the theoretical construct, prior start-up experience, lands us squarely in the ongoing dialogue between strategic choice and population ecology theorists, and the inherent theoretical tension between stability and change. Even Schumpeter doubted that Entrepreneurship could be embodied and institutionalized in a single individual throughout a lifetime: "being an entrepreneur is not a profession and as a rule not a lasting condition..." (Schumpeter, 1934, p. 78). Several scholars grounded in the population ecology tradition have included entrepreneurial experience as a critical variable in their predictive models of new venture outcomes and theoretical explanations for the sources of variety among organizational forms (Boeker, 1989; Romanelli, 1989; Schoonhoven, Eisenhardt and Lyman, 1990; and Eisenhardt and Schoonhoven, 1990). However, they have not considered the personal limits of adaptation and the inherent inertia in human and career life cycles in detail.

This paper is exploratory in nature. Since no single theory offers sufficient guidance for model development and hypothesis generation, several theoretical perspectives are integrated to consider the critical dimensions of entrepreneurial experience and explanations for expected relationships between the founder's prior venturing experience and the performance of subsequent ventures. The empirical foundation for the analysis presented here draws upon an ongoing study of numerous in-depth interviews with multiple venture entrepreneurs in a variety of industries (Starr, 1990), as well as a review of historical coverage and archival information about high visibility multiple venture entrepreneurs in the business and trade press (Starr and Bygrave, 1991).

The paper begins with a brief review of the Entrepreneurship literature to help understand the basic driving forces and some of the effects of prior entrepreneurial experience. Building upon this background, the next section identifies the perspectives which contend that prior start-up experience is an asset and categorizes some of the benefits of on-the-job entrepreneurial training for successive entrepreneurial ventures. This viewpoint is contrasted with some potential drawbacks, negative repercussions, and unintended consequences of prior performance. Based on the theories developed throughout the paper, we derive some preliminary propositions about the role of prior entrepreneurial experience and its relationship to other factors which may influence venture performance. The scope of our analysis is necessarily limited to a few key areas where we believe a closer assessment is warranted. Our hope is that this line of inquiry will encourage researchers to examine second time around entrepreneurs in a variety of contexts, finding new ways to prospect and delve into the gold mine of entrepreneurial expertise.

THE OUTCOMES OF PRIOR START-UP EXPERIENCE

Entrepreneurship researchers have viewed prior start-up experience as a special type of on-the-job training, distinctive from the business curricula provided by formal education and former employers. Yet, with a few textbook exceptions, there has been little effort made to identify the unique contributions and outcomes of early venturing episodes. In order to clarify the dimensions of start-up experience, we briefly discuss what is known about launching the maiden business voyage and highlight some features of the generic entrepreneurial process. Building upon Romanelli's concept of an entrepreneurial work setting, some pertinent distinctions are drawn between prior industry experience and prior start-up experience, particularly as it pertains to stages in the industry life cycle. Next, we consider how prior start-up experience influences the career development of entrepreneurs. This review reinforces the viewpoint that there is not an "average" first time experience or collective entrepreneurial experience that is equally weighted and can be compared across all entrepreneurs.

The Maiden Voyage

The challenge for the would-be entrepreneur is to mobilize ideas, people, resources and markets into a self-sustaining, profit-making venture. Although there is no single formula for success, standard models of new venture creation identify a combination of interdependent forces driving the entrepreneurial process--the Founders, the Opportunity and the Necessary Resources (Timmons, Smollen and Dingee, 1985; Cooper and Gascon, forthcoming). The art and science of new venture management lies in the founders' ability to transform these raw materials into a viable organization. The founders' capability to develop the necessary connections and combinations between opportunities and resources hinges upon their readiness to handle the task at hand (Liles, 1974).

An individual's window of opportunity for entrepreneurship is integrally linked to career and biosocial life cycles (Liles, 1974). The typical career trend commences with rapid experience gains between the ages of 20 and 30; and is modified and reversed over time as the marginal learning curve decreases, the relative risks increase, and the counter-entrepreneurial forces of successful employment plus non-career and family-related interests and obligations change. The optimism and enthusiasm, physical stamina and emotional energy required to launch a venture generally decreases with age. Simultaneously, over time, industry knowledge deepens, together with increasing expertise, network contacts and reputation. Identifying and managing the "fit" of personal resources to organizational contexts is fundamentally a personal career decision; choosing to start a business is one of many options (Schein, 1978). But, the dynamic forces which promote entrepreneurial activity and the creation of viable new organizations vary over the industry life cycle.

Romanelli's theory of entrepreneurial work settings (1989b) specifies a limited set of relationships between stages of industry evolution[3] and incentives for career advancement that precipitate the founding of new firms by individuals with prior industry experience. It is based on the notion that organizations provide the information, resources and incentives that encourage certain individuals to found new companies (Granovetter, 1973). Thus, individuals will choose to start a company when they have access to the information and resources regarding viable opportunities; and, their analysis of the incentives of entrepreneurial possibilities outweighs alternative employment opportunities. It also recognizes that patterns of resource utilization vary over product and industry life cycles (Hambrick, MacMillan and Day, 1982). Building on Romanelli's analysis of origins and variations in entrepreneurial activity over the industry life cycle, we suggest a set of propositions that elaborate the relationship between prior experience and the founding resources typically required by industry evolutionary processes.

Proposition 1. The earlier the stage of an industry, the less need there is to possess a particular set of experiences (occupational, industry or start-up) to start a venture. In the pioneering or "ajar" stage, relevant prior experience, skills, expertise, roles and routines have not yet been defined. Potential entrants approach from a variety of market-related arenas. Yet, there are few visionary founders who have the information and incentives to "see" the opportunity at this early stage. The historical record shows that entrepreneurs who revolutionize industries have a headstart on the relevant information for these emerging market opportunities.

Proposition 2. The earlier the stage of the industry, the fewer the resources that are needed to start a venture. In emerging markets, no single bundle of resources is specified for the new firm. Further, since emergent markets are characterized by

---

[3]Given the limited scope of this paper, the authors assume general familiarity with industry evolutionary processes (for an overview, see Porter, 1980).

low demand and high uncertainty, substantial resource commitments may not even be justified (Hambrick, MacMillan and Day, 1982; Hambrick and MacMillan, 1984). The production of the production function is necessarily ambiguous and a variety of resource combinations are possible (Rumelt, 1989). Investments made at this point will result in a unique combination of resources and novel relationships that will define firm-specific sources of profitability and competitive position. In fact, potential returns from these strategic investments may be as much a matter of luck as skill ("being in the right place at the right time") (Barney, 1986).

Proposition 3. In the growth stage, firms will be founded by entrepreneurs with prior industry experience and prior entrepreneurial experience. Growth markets provide many resource opportunities for new firms. Individuals who have a background in the emerging industry have access to information and incentives to start new companies in this next stage of evolution. Eisenhardt and Schoonhoven (1990) found that technology-based firms initiated in growth-stage markets are more likely to become large compared with those founded in emergent or mature markets. Thus, entrepreneurs involved in the pioneering stage may see new opportunities that promise to exceed the potential of the earlier founding strategy. If they are unable to persuade the initial team to fund the new area of growth as a product-line extension or new business frontier, starting a second venture offers the promise for further career advancement in growth-stage markets where substantial resources are available. Many founding entrepreneurs may perceive no other career alternative than to start another company. Having had an early taste of personal freedom and achievement in an entrepreneurial venture, they cannot conceive of working for others. Thus, unless they start another business, they are unemployable.

Proposition 4. In the maturing stages of an industry, there is a greater need to possess prior industry experience to start a new venture. As an industry's market potential grows and matures, pioneering entrepreneurs no longer have a monopoly on industry-specific knowledge and skills. Prior industry experience in both independent start-ups and established firms is broadly shared among a cohort of individuals with entrepreneurial potential. Given the increasing industry concentration and specialization among a number of large competitors who dominate the field, these potential founders face possible career displacement which may cause them to consider entrepreneurial alternatives.

Proposition 5. The later the stage of an industry, the more resources that are needed to start a new venture. New entrants in the later stages of growth and maturing markets face greater competition for all the necessary resources. Industry inertia predetermines the standard operating procedures and acceptable rules for performance. Many organizational roles, routines, patterns of exchange, and technological design are fixed. Competitive pressures for aggressive entry increase resource requirements and dictate certain types of expenditures (Romanelli, 1989a; MacMillan and Day, 1989). Entrepreneurs who start a new business in this environment must be able to raise significant resources to enter at this stage of industry development. Since "starting from scratch" is significantly resource-intensive, only a few individuals with extraordinary prior start-up experience will have sufficient entrepreneurial insight, expertise, reputation and network contacts to mobilize the level of resources needed to pursue an aggressive entry strategy at this stage of development.

This analysis highlights some of the ways in which an industry's competitive dynamics are connected with career choices. The availability of start-up experience among the population of potential business founders changes over the industry life cycle, and varies with resource availability and resource requirements for starting new firms. Career advancement may be a powerful incentive driving first time founders, and some displaced "niche playing" entrepreneurs starting their second or third companies. But, it is an insufficient sole explanatory factor for the multiple venture entrepreneurial process. The population ecology perspective cannot address the complexity of personal career choices and the details of on-the-job entrepreneurial career development. The next section explores some of these dimensions.

The Second Time Around

Multiple venture careers are more prevalent than conventional wisdom would suggest. In a representative sample of new firms in Pennsylvania and Minnesota drawn from the Dun and Bradstreet database, Reynolds and Miller (1990) found that less than 20% had started two or more other businesses. In a large sample of undergraduate alumni from five U.S. colleges who identified themselves as having had a career as an independent founding entrepreneur, 63% of the currently practicing entrepreneurs and 40% of all ex-entrepreneurs had created more than one venture (Ronstadt, 1986). And, 51% of the respondents to a questionnaire of entrepreneurs in Southern California reported involvement in two or more ventures (Schollhammer, 1991). Thus, there is mounting evidence that there are a group of entrepreneurs who continue to proliferate new ventures throughout their careers.

In the study of college alumni, Ronstadt noted that age at initial start-up increased the likelihood of developing a multiple venture career. Most practicing multiple venture entrepreneurs in this study started their first business in their early twenties. This observation can be explained by appreciating that frequency of involvement in new ventures tends to be a function of time. 26% of the multiple venture entrepreneurs had initiated a second venture within two years of the first; and another 39% had started a second business within six years of the first venture. Thus, it follows that entrepreneurs who were involved in multiple start-ups had longer entrepreneurial careers than those involved in single venture initiatives. Unfortunately, this study does not report pertinent demographic characteristics regarding the initial venture, such as firm size, or success or failure rates, which would provide further insight into the nature of the career transition from venture to venture.

Proposition 6. Through entrepreneurial experience, founders begin to recognize their strengths, weaknesses, and work preferences, and develop a "career anchor". Although age alone is not a reliable predictor of venture initiation or success (Cooper and Gascon, Forthcoming), it is interesting to speculate how early career experiences influence the decision to become a "starting pitcher" who initiates several companies during an entrepreneurial career. Based on many years of research of several hundred individual job biographies and the reasons given for career decisions, Schein (1978) suggested that through early work experience, feedback and self-evaluation, an individual develops an occupational self-concept, a career anchor, based on self-perceptions and patterns of talents, abilities, motives, needs, attitudes and values. The career anchor influences preferences for the type of work, pay, benefits, promotion and recognition. And, this self-knowledge "serves to guide, constrain, stabilize and integrate the person's career", as individuals attempt to fit their career anchor with available career options. Nine different career anchors are described in detail: security, autonomy/ independence, technical/functional expertise, managerial, entrepreneurial creativity, service, pure challenge, and lifestyle (Schein, 1978, 1986). However, a detailed discussion of the definitions of these career anchors will not be provided here, for any of these categories might form the basis for a multiple venture career (similar to the taxonomy of entrepreneurs and new business ventures developed by Gartner, Mitchell and Vesper, 1989).

Yet, in Schein's lifetime sample of over 1000 interviews, he identified only 23 who possessed <u>entrepreneurial creativity</u> as a career anchor (Schein, 1986). These business generators had definite preferences for using ideas, capital, people, and markets as the media for discovery and their outlet for original expression. This is in keeping with MacMillan's (1986) assertion that "habitual" entrepreneurs enjoy the excitement and the challenge of the startup process and so, they continue to get involved in new ventures. Thus, the career anchor concept may differentiate the "habitual" entrepreneurs from other multiple venture entrepreneurs who are compelled to start multiple businesses by other predominating factors. Further, the limited number of individuals with an entrepreneurial creativity career anchor suggests that habitual entrepreneurs may be a rare breed, even among a population of entrepreneurs, and therefore, may be difficult to locate (Starr, 1990).

Proposition 7. Throughout their venturing careers, entrepreneurs encounter specific developmental events which shift their management style and business practices in subsequent ventures. The premium placed on Prior Start-up Experience is based on the assumption that there is much that can only be learned by practice: "Learning-while-Doing". Yet, we know very little about entrepreneurial on-the-job training and what skills entrepreneurs learn from experience. Researchers at the Center for Creative Leadership interviewed a large group of successful senior executives about the key lessons gleaned from their managerial careers (McCall, Lombardo and Morrison, 1982). This study reported that the potential key lessons learned from "starting from scratch" within the corporate context, included:

1) Out of chaos and demands, managers learned how to identify what is important and how to organize themselves to get it done.

2) Creating a staff taught them how to select, train and motivate subordinates.

3) Living through the event successfully taught them "I could survive". This raw endurance carried with it increased confidence and willingness to take risks.

4) They learned firsthand how much leadership matters and how lonely the role can be.

But, although these are familiar themes in entrepreneurship, a similar study has not been conducted with experienced entrepreneurs.

Based on interviews with a group of Midwestern entrepreneurs in the classic study <u>The Enterprising Man</u>, Collins and Moore (1964) outlined a representative catalogue of "The School for Entrepreneurs". In this academy, "credits are counted by lost jobs, broken partnerships, exploited sponsors and number of appeararances in the bankruptcy courts" (Collins and Moore, 1964, p. 100)". The curriculum includes lessons in dealmaking skills as the result of exercises which attempt to bring ideas, people, and resources together to make profits. Vesper summarized this intensive program,

"Many of these experiences will have intensely uncomfortable aspects, such as being disdained by acquaintances as a hustler, having to solicit funds and being turned down, being squeezed out of deals by associates so they need share less, learning too that what looked like the long end of a bargain was in fact the short end, and being accused of double dealing by associates who believe they got the short end. These may not be directly sought after lessons; but they are often the consequences of experiences in arranging deals that do exercise and develop entrepreneurial ability (Vesper, 1980, p. 35-36).

The lessons learned from "Basic Dealing" suggest that there are issues related to ethics and moral development which also change over time. Although these have not been directly explored in the Entrepreneurship literature, Dees and Starr (Forthcoming) suggest several ethical challenges which may be elements of entrepreneurial practice: promoter dilemmas, relationship dilemmas, innovators' dilemmas, and finders' keepers dilemmas. The ability to anticipate ethical difficulties, to prevent them when possible, and to effectively manage them when they occur is an important ingredient in the mix of skills needed for entrepreneurial management. Thus, the ways in which entrepreneurs meet and wrestle with these situations and demands over time, and from venture to venture, remains a subject for future research.

TABLE 1: VARIABLES THAT MAY CHANGE WITH ENTREPRENEURIAL EXPERIENCE

Stamina, enthusiasm and energy	Ethics and moral development
Motivations and aspirations	Expertise
Wealth and other rewards	Wisdom
Career anchor	Network relationships
Management style and practices	Reputation

Only one study has systematically examined the influence of entrepreneurial "on-the-job" training on strategic activities and firm performance (Lamont, 1972). This study compared a matched sample of 24 technology-based firms, 12 founded by individuals with no previous entrepreneurial experience, and 12 founded by individuals with a background of at least one technical venture. In comparison to first-time founders, experienced entrepreneurs: 1) started businesses with a product rather than a contract orientation; 2) obtained larger initial financing; 3) had a better balance of business skills on the venture team; 4) achieved greater sales and profitability earlier in the life cycle; 5) were financially stronger, and 6) had better credit ratings by a leading business information service. These measurable outcomes of improved performance suggest that technical entrepreneurs do learn from previous venturing activity. But, the key lessons the author attributes to first venture experiences -- the benefits of market planning, financial planning and a balanced management team -- are basic curriculum requirements, so basic, that they appear to be truisms rather than contribute much to our knowledge base of entrepreneurship.

This brief review, and the pages that follow, propose an initial set of variables which may change with entrepreneurial experience (summarized in Table 1). We begin to understand why studies which have measured start-up experience as a simple dichotomous independent variable have shown mixed results. Personal preparedness for entrepreneurship varies across a population and over time. And, the lessons from experience are generally the product of personal _and_ contextual factors (McCall, Lombardo and Morrison, 1988). Thus, future research should probe more deeply into the quality rather than the quantity of entrepreneurial experience, and consider the various ways in which entrepreneurs transfer and leverage their past into future ventures. In the next sections we propose ways in which prior experience can be both an asset and a liability in the development of successive ventures.

THE ASSETS AND LIABILITIES OF PRIOR START-UP EXPERIENCE

The organizational theory literature has catalogued the generic internal and external obstacles which threaten a new venture's survival, the "liabilities of newness and smallness". The negative effects of the liabilities of newness are associated with the difficulties encountered due to the need to develop and learn new roles, negotiate and organize different roles, and form trusting relationships with strangers (Stinchcombe, 1965). Simultaneously, the entrepreneur must overcome various barriers to entry and develop linkages with customers (Aldrich and Auster, 1986). In addition, the new firm often suffers from the liabilities of small size which make it difficult to raise capital, locate labor and meet regulatory burdens (Aldrich and Auster, 1986). Prior start-up experience has the potential to obviate many of the difficulties of resource poverty typically encountered by first time entrepreneurs.

Through experience, entrepreneurs accumulate the "wealth, power and legitimacy" to found new organizations (Stinchcombe, 1965; Romanelli, 1989b). Coupled with prior industry experience, start-up experience generally serves as a proxy for a wide range of developed skills and competencies, a rolodex of network contacts, and a business reputation and track record (Vesper, 1980). But, unlike industry experience, prior start-up experience yields a customized set of abilities and expertise, network contacts and a track record which filter information and resources particularly relevant to venturing. Rather than "starting from scratch", the seasoned entrepreneur is well-acquainted with the innovation journey and is able to quickly initiate new venture operations.

However, the positive relationship between prior industry and start-up experience and future firm performance is based on two critical assumptions. First, it presupposes prior successful performance. Given the mortality statistics of start-up companies, this is an inaccurate assumption. Second, even a proven venturing track record is no guarantee of another command performance. Second time around entrepreneurs may be better able to shape the odds in their favor. However, the expectation that "nothing succeeds like success" is not a given in the new venture management arena. Instead, experienced business founders also face the liabilities of prior performance which constrain the innovative potential and financial returns of their successive ventures, akin to the "liabilities of old age and large size" attributed to large, established firms (Aldrich and Auster, 1986).

The remainder of this paper focuses on this seemingly paradoxical role of prior start-up experience. For the purposes of this paper, we necessarily limit our discussion to the assets and liabilities of prior successful performance. First, for the benefit of comparison, we briefly review the familiar assets of prior successful start-up performance -- expertise, network contacts and reputation. The advantages of these personal resources are contrasted with the pitfalls -- biases and blindspots, strong ties, and the success syndrome. This analysis leads to a set of propositions regarding the relationship between prior success and the fundraising capacity and resource expenditures of firms started by previously successful entrepreneurs. The liabilities of prior successful performance have the surprising effect of potentially hampering the outcomes of firms founded by second time around entrepreneurs.

Assets of Prior Successful Performance

Most studies that have examined the role of prior entrepreneurial experience have substantiated the advantages of past successes. Case studies provide "thick descriptions" of the ways in which prior venturing experience can be used in future start-ups. Mitton (1984) and MacMillan (1986) reported cases of multiple venture entrepreneurs who are consistently able to leverage their expertise, networks and reputations to quickly organize new ventures. And, Starr and MacMillan (1990) demonstrated ways in which these social assets can be strategic currency in new venture management.

Survey and archival based studies substantiate some of these anecdotal claims. Van de Ven et al. (1984) observed that previous competencies of founders in the educational software industry could speed new firms towards developmental milestones. Roure and Maidique (1987) noted that founders of more successful venture-backed high technology companies had previously been employed in growing subunits of medium and large size companies where they held fast-track positions. As noted above, Lamont observed that technical entrepreneurs with prior start-up experience performed better than novices (Lamont, 1972). In a study of the semiconductor industry, although entrepreneurial experience was highly correlated with bringing products to market; it did not have a significant impact when weighed against other independent variables (Schoonhoven, Eisenhardt and Lyman, 1990). However, in another analysis of this industry, the top management team was highly influential and a key ingredient was prior team experience (Eisenhardt and Schoonhoven, 1990). Although the authors do not state the organizational origins of this prior team experience, nor the composition of the team (ie., previous company founders vis established firm employees), nonetheless, this finding suggests that one advantage of prior experience is the cultivation of future venturing partners.

Entrepreneurial Expertise and Wisdom. Entrepreneurship educators have speculated on the wide range of skills needed for new venture management, such as creative problem-solving, negotiations, venture financing. Yet, there have been few empirical investigations which catalogue a common body of professional knowledge and areas of entrepreneurial expertise (Starr, 1990). Similar to other practitioners, entrepreneurs develop their professional skills through repetitive action and interaction with certain similar types of situations (Schon, 1982). Over time, they accumulate a repertoire of models and images of phenomenon, expectations and theories of action, and methods and techniques of control. Much of this becomes tacit knowledge, "mastery" or "art", which is difficult to verbalize or explain except by example, through instruction of novices and in direct interaction with the phenomenon. But, unlike the major professions (ie., lawyers, doctors and architects), there is no single accepted body of knowledge which entrepreneurs are expected to master. As such, each venture can provide the opportunity to practice certain skills, but not others. Even experienced entrepreneurs may find new things to learn in subsequent ventures. Many successful entrepreneurs eagerly seek these learning challenges (Bailey, 1986).

Studies which have compared experts to novices (ie., physicists, chess players, winetasters and negotiators) have observed differences in their problem-solving capabilities (Larkin et al., 1980). The literature on human expert performance would suggest that recognized entrepreneurial talent is just another word for expert's skill -- perceptual knowledge, recognition capabilities and the way in which information is represented in long-term memory (Hayes, 1985). The expert has a catalogue of accumulated information and general principles, and a history of observing familiar patterns and situations, which are readily at his disposal. In contrast, the novice must build a database, consciously searching and deliberating over alternatives. Without this experience base, he cannot recognize the various ways in which a set of events can unfold and may vigorously follow courses with unforeseen dead-ends. Following this logic, seasoned entrepreneurs will develop a set of expert skills. These personal experience curves can provide cost savings to subsequent ventures.

In the "late career" stage -- age 40 to retirement -- one of the major career development tasks is to "learn to substitute wisdom based on experience for immediate technical skills" (Schein, 1978, p. 44). Wisdom is the ability to gather and communicate a multitude of life experiences into meaningful patterns and creative visions (Erikson, 1988). Building on Erikson's life-cycle theory of human development, entrepreneurial wisdom is accumulated through lessons learned over a lifetime in the school of hard knocks and gentle touches. Unlike practitioner skill development which considers the superior abilities of the expert compared to the novice, entrepreneurial wisdom is judgment seasoned by pragmatic concerns for resiliency and continuous adaptation. Thus, it fosters a sense of wonder, discovery, humility and "beginner's mind", akin to the novice. It enables the experienced entrepreneur to keep up with the changing times; balancing the need to modify strategies, revise approaches and refresh their knowledge base with the need to keep certain patterns constant. A seasoned entrepreneur's capacity to communicate and share this cultivated wisdom is certainly another strength of the second time around entrepreneur.

Network Relationships. New venture development is both a social and an economic enterprise, characterized by face-to-face relationships and informal interpersonal exchange. Previous working relationships, voluntary connections, kinship, and community ties lay the groundwork for independent new ventures (Birley, 1985; Aldrich and Zimmer, 1986). By using social relationships, entrepreneurs "cash in" on the patterns of expectations, norms, governance structures and social resources built into these previous interactions (Johannisson, 1987; Starr and MacMillan, 1990). Using social assets, such as friendship, trust, gratitude and obligation reduces the costs and the risks of startups (Starr and MacMillan, 1990). And, network relationships offer many benefits to entrepreneurial ventures where innovation and access is a priority, including: know-how and technology transfer, speed and richness of communication, and cooperation and mutual exchange. In addition, long-term friendships: "strong ties", provide a safe haven for entrepreneurs to express and share their concerns and commiserations (Kanai, 1989; Starr, MacMillan and Thompson, 1989). Thus, the decision to start the first business moves the entrepreneur down a venture corridor which leads to additional knowledge, access to information, extended networks and attractive new business opportunities which would not have been perceived, offered or actionable without the initiation of the first venture (Mitton, 1984; Ronstadt, 1988).

Reputation. With a rolodex of familiar acquaintances, business colleagues, and potential venturing partners and investors, the experienced entrepreneur possesses a pre-existing innovation infrastructure of personal relationships based on his past reputation. This image of prior success lends legitimacy to the new enterprise in the eyes of outside observers (Starr and MacMillan, 1990). The "reach" and leveragability of an entrepreneur's reputation will depend on the arena and scope of past ventures.

The advantages of prior experience appear to reduce the liabilities of smallness and newness, suggesting the following propositions.

Proposition 8. The more experienced the entrepreneur, the easier it is to raise start-up financing.

Proposition 9. The more experienced the entrepreneur, the easier it is to raise larger amounts of start-up capital.

The Liabilities of Prior Successful Performance

There have been no studies that have intentionally focused on the liabilities of prior successful performance, although there is some evidence that past experience is not always advantageous in subsequent start-ups. Thus, this section is necessarily speculative, raising questions, rather than offering answers. But, our arguments parallel some of the liabilities of aging and large size for old, established firms elaborated by Aldrich and Auster (1986). Drawing upon the extant literature, we propose three potential pitfalls of prior successful performance which mirror the benefits discussed above -- biases and blind spots, strong ties, and success syndrome. These factors lead to four liabilities of prior successful performance -- liabilities of staleness, sameness, priciness, and costliness. These liabilities of prior successful performance have the surprising effect of potentially hampering the financial outcomes of firms founded by Second Time Around entrepreneurs.

Biases and Blindspots. Some studies which have examined the role of prior experience and firm performance have documented evidence of biases and blindspots. Chambers et al. (1988) observed differences in the subjective assessments of measures of organizational performance between founders with and without prior start-up experience. Founders with previous start-up experience focused on overall company performance; while those with prior experience in established firms emphasized product design and development performance. In Boeker's study, founders in the semi-conductor industry tended to favor their functional training (ie., R&D, sales and marketing, manufacturing and production) in the assembly and allocation of resources for the founding strategy regardless of the "fit" with product-market needs (Boeker, 1989). Similarly, Schoonhoven and Eisenhardt found that entrepreneurs tended to start ventures in markets that they knew well rather than in markets that were objectively attractive (Eisenhardt and Schoonhoven, 1990). Another study noted that entrepreneurs may suffer certain learning disabilities and superstitious learning (Dornblaser, et al, 1989). And, an in-depth case study of the lessons by one novice entrepreneur over a one year period identified the biases of overconfidence noted in behavior decision theory (Guth et. al., 1990). These studies suggest that entrepreneurs may suffer from biases and blindspots that influence their decisions.

The entrepreneurial experience curve premise is based on the assumption that entrepreneurs can learn from experience and that the skills gained in an earlier venture are transferable to subsequent start-ups. Cognitive psychologists have demonstrated that individuals do not always learn from experience, at least not when the experience consists of a series of cases (Brehmer, 1980). An industry-specific rule-of thumb or a personal catastrophe that has impressed a lesson, may not be universally applicable. Often, experiential knowledge is the result of trying to confirm hypotheses; rather than seeking to refute them. The search for confirmatory evidence is colored by cognitive biases and may positively reinforce incorrect decision rules (Einhorn, 1982). Knowledge acquired in action-oriented contexts necessarily precludes the testing of alternatives which may have been equally viable (Brehmer, 1980). And, the lessons learned via specific cases are highly context dependent. The way the problem is represented and framed influences decision rules, behavior, and action (Einhorn, 1982). Ironically, through experience, the second time around entrepreneur can develop the inertia of conventional wisdom, which may be challenged by others who bring a fresher perspective. The negative impact of expertise might be considered the liability of staleness.

Strong Ties. While the advantages of network relationships have been emphasized, they also may pose certain problems particularly for entrepreneurs with prior start-up experience. In a detailed study of two networking entrepreneurial-oriented organizations, MIT Forum and SBANE, Kanai found that older participants perceived fewer networking benefits in these organizations. He suggested that these older entrepreneurs were more established in their careers and were less interested in career alternatives or the novel information available through "weak-tie" relationships. He speculated that older entrepreneurs preferred their "clubs", established social networks of old buddies ("strong ties") that comfortably share common experiences and stories. Experienced entrepreneurs must manage the social obligations built into prior (and perhaps, continuing) relationships. Since "weak-tie" relationships bridge established configurations of socially structured relationships, they are important sources of diverse information and resources for new ventures. Experienced entrepreneurs who favor familiar circles and customary relationships over the unknown and the obscure may be stuck in routine patterns of interpersonal interactions that hinder their ability to continuously innovate. Thus, prior "club"-like network relationships are not always positive for venture performance, suggesting the drawbacks of the liability of sameness.

Success Syndrome. Finally, although experience can command a premium in the capital markets, an entrepreneur with a track record of prior success(es) may be particularly vulnerable to the hazards of success. Hambrick and Crozier (1985) observed this sense of invincibility in fast-growing INC 500 companies. These hyperconfident firms believed their own publicity, and doubted the capabilities and new approaches of entering competitors. While this problem has been documented as an organizational phenomenon, we believe that the successful entrepreneur, and particularly the mega-successful entrepreneur, faces some similar problems. As a result of "great expectations", the second time around entrepreneurial process may be quite different from the first. The successful entrepreneur may become more confident and attempt more difficult or complex ventures. Outsiders (including investors) defer to the superstar's status. In turn, the experienced entrepreneur may be reluctant or embarrassed to show ignorance, which was easy to do as a novice. Thus, tough questions may not get asked in subsequent ventures. Similarly, certain tasks and activities are now considered beneath the "superstar" and are delegated to others. The division of labor and poor communication may hinder the next venture's performance. In addition, customers may be less willing to provide the necessary assistance or forgive divergences that might be offered to a struggling novice. The second time around start-up company operates in a more visible arena, which reduces managerial discretion (Hambrick and Finkelstein, 1987). Thus, second time around entrepreneurs and their ventures can be disadvantaged by the reputation and image of prior successes. Particularly, the fundraising ability and price paid premiums for ventures founded by entrepreneurs with a reputation and track record for success may place unrealistic performance expectations on the start-up which may lead to the liability of priciness.

Thus, as a result of industry forces and the assets of prior experience, experienced entrepreneurs are likely to raise and spend more capital in subsequent ventures. Competitive pressures for aggressive entry into maturing markets compel the entrepreneur to make large upfront commitments in the next venture. But, easy access to capital reinforces the success syndrome. And, easy money is easily spent. Habits developed in previous high-growth, success-oriented environments of an adolescent company may be transferred to the new start-up which is hampered by excessive expenditures. The second time around entrepreneur no longer spends the time and imagination that was applied to the resource-constrained first ventures. Frugal resource management strategies of Resource Parsimony and Resourcefulness have the pronounced material advantages of reducing fixed costs, increasing flexibility, and limiting some of the risks of new venture management (Hambrick and MacMillan, 1984; Starr, 1990). Subsequent ventures built with large amounts of capital may be subject to the liability of costliness.

Proposition 10. As a result of Propositions 4, 5, 8, and 9, the more experienced the entrepreneur, the less likely he is to implement resourceful strategies and use resources parsimoniously.

TABLE 2: THE ROLE OF PRIOR START-UP EXPERIENCE: THE ASSETS AND LIABILITIES OF PRIOR SUCCESSFUL PERFORMANCE

Assets	Liabilities
Expertise	Biases and Blinders
Network relationships	Strong Ties
Reputation	Success Syndrome
REDUCES Liabilities of newness and smallness	INCREASES Liabilities of staleness, sameness, priciness and costliness

The liabilities of prior successful performance -- the liabilities of staleness, sameness, priciness and costliness -- have the surprising effect of potentially hampering the financial performance of firms founded by Second Time Around entrepreneurs. These relationships are summarized in Table 2.

CONCLUSIONS

Joseph Schumpeter, the seminal theorist on Entrepreneurship, would be surprised by the multiple venture entrepreneurship phenomenon. Following the basic tenets of the Schumpeterian theory of economic development, the evolutionary forces of "creative destruction" erode the initial entrepreneurial advantage and the entrepreneurial function as bureaucracy attempts to rationalize and institutionalize innovation (Schumpeter, 1934).

> "Everyone is an entrepreneur only when he actually "carries out new combinations," and loses that character as soon as he has built up his business, when he settles down to running it as other people run their businesses. This is the rule, and hence, it is just as rare for anyone to remain an entrepreneur throughout the decades of his active life as it is for a businessman never to have a moment in which he is an entrepreneur, to however modest a degree (Schumpeter, 1934, p. 78-79).

But multiple venture entrepreneurs seem to defy this observation. They do not "settle down" to run their businesses. Instead, at some point during the first firm's development, the entrepreneur faces a critical series of decisions -- the decision to continue the firm or exit. The multiple venture entrepreneur chooses to exit, but continues an entrepreneurial career by starting a second independent venture; and perhaps later a third, a tenth, and a fiftieth business.

This paper begins to identify a seemingly paradoxical role of prior start-up experience for the ventures of seasoned entrepreneurs. The assets of prior entrepreneurial experience -- expertise and wisdom, network contacts and reputation -- can potentially obviate some of the difficulties typically encountered by first time entrepreneurs. But this exploratory study begins to suggest that veteran entrepreneurs may face a new set of difficulties -- the liabilities of prior performance. We discuss four liabilities of prior successful performance which may constrain the innovative potential of future ventures -- the liabilities of staleness, sameness, priciness, and costliness. These limitations may potentially limit the financial outcomes of firms founded by experienced entrepreneurs. Thus, although the interest in seasoned entrepreneurs may be an extension of the venture capital industry's conventional wisdom and practice "To Bet the Jockey, not the Horse", this study suggests that a proven venturing track record is no guarantee of successful performance the second time around. Rather, the search for founders with the "Golden Touch" may be another version of "Capital Market Myopia" (Sahlman and Stevenson, 1985). However, probing the nature of prior entrepreneurial experience raises several pertinent issues and themes of interest to entrepreneurship scholars.

First, prior start-up experience is typically defined as prior participation in the formation of at least one independent start-up venture. Although never explicitly stated, research on the role of prior start-up experience typically assumes that the entrepreneur has held a large equity position and devoted a significant proportion of time and personal energy into the birth and management of an innovative, high potential/high growth venture (Following the definitions implicit in the Entrepreneurship literature, Gartner, 1990). Yet, many entrepreneurs ease into a career of venturing, with smaller low risk ventures (Vesper, 1980; Ronstadt, 1985). Others may have invested only, as informal or formal venture capitalists, without earning their stripes and medals from hands-on day-to-day new venture management. Most studies have used multivariate analysis and have assumed that there is an "average" first time experience or collective entrepreneurial experience which is equally weighted and can be compared across all entrepreneurs (Gartner, 1985; Bygrave, 1989; Stevenson and Harmeling, 1990). Given that entrepreneurial careers begin at various times, vary in duration, and follow a variety of paths, we would expect a wide variation of multiple venture entrepreneurship experiences. As a result, prior startup experience offers a wide range of core curricula that may be both beneficial and detrimental to the next ventures.

At first glance, the probabilistic thinking and deterministic models based on the law of averages favored by the Population Ecologists, do not seem to have much relevance to practicing entrepreneurs. But, the juxtaposition of industry and career dynamics suggests that there is a relationship between entrepreneurial experience and the founding resources typically required by industry evolutionary processes. And, there may be other critical industry factors also varying and changing over the industry cycle (ie., skills, venture scale), that will influence the venture performance of successive ventures (Keeley and Turki, 1991). Further, our analysis recognizes certain limits to adaptation and an inherent inertia in human and career cycles. Just as there are limits to the bearing capacity of the ecology, there are limits to the creative capacity of individuals and the number of viable new ideas that they can put into practice (Findlay and Lumsden, 1985). As noted by Keeley and Turki (1991), the liabilities of prior successful performance need not be limited to the second time around entrepreneur, but could apply to entrepreneurs who have developed a single venture, but become less entrepreneurial with accumulated years of career experience in their business.

And, the empirical research which considers the effects of founders' characteristics, strategy, industry dynamics and new venture performance demonstrates that an entrepreneur's prior experience is an influential factor in firm formation, albeit not always an advantageous one. We have identified some of the liabilities of prior successful performance -- the liabilities of staleness, sameness, priciness, and costliness. We encourage researchers to investigate the negative effects of prior failure or moderate success on subsequent firm performance and entrepreneurial management practices as well. Muzyka (1988) found that general managers of large, complex projects with highly uncertain task environments developed techniques to minimize the rate of failure and the impact of failure because failure was part of their experience. Several venturing attempts, including a few failures, may be required before the patterns and techniques emerge which enable seasoned entrepreneurs to avoid the typical obstacles of starting new ventures (Starr, 1990). Thus, although the nature of the entrepreneurial experience curve provides a fruitful avenue for research, findings should be moderated by our appreciation of the limits of human performance and the complexity of new venture development.

Our analysis also highlights new strategic choices that entrepreneurs make throughout their careers. Many of them focus on personal and private choices, such as career strategies and ethical dilemmas, that are not typically considered in business decision-making. As such, they are often not readily discussed in the entrepreneurship literature. But if we truly want to understand the nature of on-the-job entrepreneurial training and entrepreneurial expertise, these need to be added to our research agenda.

Our review of the literature suggests that few studies have probed for this level of detail in a founder's background. Instead, most studies have measured start-up experience as a simple dichotomous or interval independent variable. Our analysis suggests that it is the quality rather than the quantity of entrepreneurial experience that can make a difference. The comparative studies of experts and novices highlight this viewpoint; it is not a matter of age, but accumulated "chunks of knowledge" which produce world class performers (Hayes, 1985). It also emphasizes the need to be creative in finding new methods and measures, which initially, may be less tractable, but potentially could be more meaningful (Cooper and Gascon, 1990). We agree with scholars who have observed that the field of entrepreneurship has pursued "rigor" by focusing on large sample sizes and the most sophisticated statistical techniques, overlooking other approaches which can shed new light on these rich dimensions of the entrepreneurial process (Bygrave, 1989; Aldrich, 1990).

Finally, the multiple venture entrepreneur challenges our traditional notions of entrepreneurial careers and career success. Like marriage, real entrepreneurial success stories are supposed to be permanent and monogamous. But, a study of multiple venture entrepreneurs necessarily tracks individuals who have not pursued a single-minded goal, but have continued to focus and refocus throughout their careers, directing and redirecting their aspirations and ambitions. They have charted a course into unknown territory, searching for and shaping new opportunities that are attuned with their past experience and visions of the future. Their perspective does not only offer new tools and techniques for new venture management, but promises to provide insights about ways to adapt and transform careers and personal resources for our changing times.[4]

REFERENCES

Aldrich, H. 1979. Organizations and Environments. Englewood Cliffs, NJ: Prentice-Hall.

Aldrich, H. Forthcoming. Methods in our Madness? Trends in Entrepreneurship Research. In D. Sexton and J. Kasarda (eds.) Entrepreneurship in the 1990s. PWS Kent Publishing.

Aldrich, H., Auster, E. 1986. Even Dwarfs Started Small: Liabilities of Age and Size and Their Strategic Implications. Research in Organizational Behavior 8: 165-198.

Aldrich, H., Zimmer, C. 1986. Entrepreneurship Through Social Networks. in D. Sexton and R. Smilor (eds.), The Art and Science of Entrepreneurship, Cambridge, MA: Ballinger Publishing Company, pp. 3-24.

Bailey, J. 1986. Learning Styles of Successful Entrepreneurs. In R. Ronstadt, J. Hornaday, R. Peterson and K. Vesper. (eds.) Frontiers of Entrepreneurship Research Wellesley, MA; Babson College.

Barney, J. 1986. Strategic Factor Markets: Expectations, Luck, and Business Strategy. Management Science 32(10): 1231-1241.

Baron, J. 1988. Thinking and Deciding. Cambridge, ENG: Cambridge University Press.

Bateson, M. 1990. Composing a Life. New York: Plume Publishing/Penguin Books USA, Inc.

Bird, B. 1989. Entrepreneurial Behavior. Glenview, ILL: Scott, Foresman and

---

[4]This parallels Mary Catherine Bateson's commentary on the lives of 5 successful women, Composing a Life (Bateson, 1990).

Company.

Birley, S. 1985. The Role of Networks in the Entrepreneurial Process. Journal of Business Venturing, 1: 107-117.

Boeker, W. 1989. The Development and Institutionalization of Subunit Power in Organizations. Administrative Science Quarterly 34: 388-410.

Brehmer, B. 1980. In One Word: Not from Experience. Acta Psychologica 45: 223-241.

Bygrave, W. 1989. The Entrepreneurship Paradigm (I): A Philosophical Look at Its Research Methodologies. Entrepreneurship: Theory and Practice Fall: 7-26.

Chambers, B., Hart, S., Denison, D. 1988. Founding Team Experience and New Firm Performance. In B. Kirchhoff, W. Long, W. McMullan, K. Vesper, W. Wetzel, Jr., (eds.) Frontiers of Entrepreneurship Research Wellesley, MA; Babson College.

Collins, O., Moore, D., Unwalla, D. 1964. The Enterprising Man. East Lansing, MI: MSU Business Studies.

Cooper, A., Gascon, F. Forthcoming. Entrepreneurs, Founding Processes and New Firm Performance. In D. Sexton and J. Kasarda (eds.) Entrepreneurship in the 1990s. PWS Kent Publishing.

Einhorn, H. 1982. Learning From Experience and Suboptimal Rules in Decisionmaking. In D. Kahneman, P. Slovic & A. Tversky (eds.) Judgment Under Uncertainty: Heuristics and Biases. Cambridge: Cambridge University Press.

Eisenhardt, K., Schoonhoven, C. 1990. Organizational Growth: Linking Founding Team, Strategy, Environment, and Growth among U.S. Semiconductor Ventures, 1978-1988, Administrative Science Quarterly 35: 504-529.

Erikson, J. 1988. Wisdom and the Senses: The Way of Creativity. New York: W.W. Norton & Company.

Findlay, C.S., Lumsden, C. 1988. The Creative Mind: Toward an Evolutionary Theory of Discovery and Innovation. Journal of Social and Biological Structures 11(1):3-56.

Gartner, W. 1985. A Conceptual Framework for Describing the Phenomenon of New Venture Creation. Academy of Management Review 10:696-706.

Gartner, W. 1989. Some Suggestions for Research on Entrepreneurial Traits and Characteristics. Entrepreneurship Theory and Practice Fall: 27-37.

Gartner, W. 1990. What Are We Talking About When We Talk About Entrepreneurship. Journal of Business Venturing 5(1): 15-28.

Gartner, W., Mitchell, T., Vesper, K. 1990. A Taxonomy of New Business Ventures. Journal of Business Venturing. 4(3):169-186.

Hambrick, D., MacMillan, I. 1984. Asset Parsimony -- Managing Assets to Manage Profits. Sloan Management Review, 25(Winter): 67-74.

Hambrick, D. Crozier, L. 1985. Stumblers and Stars in the Management of Rapid Growth. Journal of Business Venturing, 1: 31-45.

Hambrick, D., Finkelstein, S. 1987. Managerial Discretion: A Bridge Between Polar Views of Organizational Outcomes. In L. Cummings and B. Staw (eds.) Research in Organizational Behavior 9:369-406.

Hambrick, D., MacMillan, I., Day, D. 1982. Strategic Attributes and Performance in the BCG Matrix -- A PIMS-based Analysis of Industrial Product Businesses. Academy of Management Journal 25: 510-531.

Hayes, J. 1985. Three Problems in Teaching General Skills. In S. F. Chipman, J. Segal and R. Glaser (eds.), Thinking and Learning Skills: Volume 2. Research and Open Questions. Hillsdale, NJ: Erlbaum.

Johannisson, B. 1987. Anarchists and Organizers: Entrepreneurs in a Network Perspective. International Studies of Management and Organization 17:49-63.

Kanai, T. 1989. Entrepreneurial Networking: A Comparative Analysis of Networking Organizations and Their Participants in an Entrepreneurial Community. Unpublished Dissertation. Massachusetts Institute of Technology.

Keeley, R., Turki, L. 1991. Commentary on "The Second Time Around: The Outcomes, Assets and Liabilities of Prior Start-up Experience. Inaugural Global Entrepreneurship Conference. London, England.

Lamont, L. 1972. What Entrepreneurs Learn From Experience. Journal of Small Business Management July: 36-41.

Larkin, J., McDermott, J., Simon, D., Simon, H. 1980. Expert and Novice Performance in Solving Physics Problems. Science 208: 1335-1342.

Liles, P. 1974. New Business Ventures and the Entrepreneur. Homewood, IL: Richard D. Irwin, Inc.

MacMillan, I. 1986. To Really Learn About Entrepreneurship, Let's Study Habitual Entrepreneurs. Journal of Business Venturing, 1: 241-243.

McCall, M., Lombardo, M., Morrison, A. 1988. The Lessons of Experience: How Successful Executives Develop on the Job. Lexington, MA: Lexington Books.

Mitton, D. 1984. No Money, Know-How, Know-Who: Formula For Managing Venture Success and Personal Wealth. In J. Hornaday, F. Tarpley, Jr., J. Timmons and K. Vesper (eds.) Frontiers of Entrepreneurship Research Wellesley, MA; Babson College.

Muzyka, D. 1988. The Management of Failure: A Key to Organizational Entrepreneurship. In B. Kirchhoff, W. Long, W. McMullan, K. Vesper, W. Wetzel, Jr., (eds.) Frontiers of Entrepreneurship Research Wellesley, MA; Babson College.

Poole, M., Van de Ven, A. 1989. Using Paradox to Build Management and Organization Theories. Academy of Management Review 14(4): 562-578.

Porter, M. 1980. Competitive Strategy. Free Press: New York.

Reynolds, P., Miller, B. 1990. Race, Gender and Entrepreneurship: Participation in New Firm Start-Ups. Washington, D.C.: American Sociological Association Annual Meetings Presentation.

Romanelli, E. 1989a. Environments and Strategies of Organization Start-up: Effects on Early Survival. Administrative Science Quarterly 34: 369-387.

Romanelli, E. 1989b. Organization Birth and Population Variety: A Community Perspective on Origins. In L. Cummings and B. Staw (eds.) Research in Organizational Behavior 11:211-246.
Ronstadt, R. 1985. Entrepreneurship. Lord Publishing.

Ronstadt, R. The Educated Entrepreneurs: A New Era of Entrepreneurial Education is Beginning. American Journal of Small Business 10:7-23, 1985.

Ronstadt, R. 1988. The Corridor Principle. Journal of Business Venturing, 3: 31-40.

Roure, J., Maidique, M. 1986. Linking Pre-Funding Factors and Venture Success. Journal of Business Venturing, 1: 295-306.

Rumelt, R. Theory, Strategy and Entrepreneurship. In D. Teece (ed.), The Competitive Challenge: Strategies for Industrial Innovation and Renewal. Cambridge, MA: Ballinger Publishing Co. 1987.
Sahlman, W., Stevenson, H. 1985. Capital Market Myopia. Journal of Business Venturing, 3: 31-40.

Schein, E. 1978. Career Dynamics: Matching Individual and Organizational Needs. Reading, MA: Addison-Wesley Publishing Company.

Schein, E. 1986. Individuals and Careers. in J. Lorsch (ed.), Handbook of Organizational Behavior: 155-171.

Schollhammer, H. 1991. Incidence and Determinants of Multiple Venture Entrepreneurship. Babson Entrepreneurship Research Conference, Pittsburgh, PA.

Schon, D. 1983. The Reflective Practitioner. New York: Basic Books.

Schoonhoven, C., Eisenhardt, K., Lyman, K. 1990. Speeding Product to Market: Waiting Time to First Product Introduction in New Firms. Administrative Science Quarterly 35: 177-207.

Schumpeter, J. 1934. The Theory of Economic Development. Cambridge, MA: Harvard University Press.

Starr, J. 1990. Resource Parsimony and Resourcefulness in New Venture Creation: Lessons from Habitual Entrepreneurs. Unpublished Dissertation Proposal and Work-In-Progress. The Wharton School, University of Pennsylvania.

Starr, J., MacMillan, I. 1990. Resource Cooptation via Social Contracting: Resource Acquisition Strategies for New Ventures. Strategic Management Journal, 11:79-92.

Starr, J., Bygrave, W. 1991. The Assets and Liabilities of Prior Start-up Experience: An Exploratory Study of Multiple Venture Entrepreneurs. Babson Entrepreneurship Research Conference, Pittsburgh, PA.

Stevenson, H., Harmeling, S. 1990. Entrepreneurial Management's Need for a More "Chaotic" Theory. Journal of Business Venturing 5(1): 1-14.

Stinchcombe, A. 1965. Social Structure and Organizations. In J. March (eds), Handbook of Organizations. Chicago: Rand McNally.

Timmons, J., Smollen, L., Dingee, A. 1985. New Venture Creation. Homewood, IL: Irwin.

Van de Ven, A., Hudson, R., Schroeder, D. 1984. Designing New Business Startups: Entrepreneurial, Organizational, and Ecological Considerations. J. of Management 10: 87-107.

Vesper, K. 1980. New Venture Strategies. Englewood Cliffs, NJ: Prentice-Hall, Inc.

Business Creations by Quebec's Engineers: Stability of Entry from 1970 to 1987

Critique
by
John W. Mullins, *University of Minnesota*
Richard N. Cardozo, *University of Minnesota*

The paper seeks to refute the notion that entrepreneurship rates have increased over the past two decades. We concur with the authors that there is little empirical evidence and no theoretical support for this notion. While interest in entrepreneurship among public policy makers, schools of business, and the popular press has skyrocketed, we are not aware of literature which support the view that incidence of entrepreneurship has increased in any substantial way. Thus, we are not certain that the mission of the paper to refute conventional wisdom does so, regardless of the paper's findings. Nonetheless, the question of whether or not incidence of entrepreneurship has increased, and, if so, in what sectors, is a question well worth examination.

We have identified three aspects of the paper for which we would welcome clarification or additional support. These issues have to do with the simulation model used, the need for an alternative model to examine the alternative hypothesis, and certain sampling and response issues.

As for the model itself, we question the rate of entry which was used. The constant rate of entry of 3.25% results in a cumulative total of new firms equal to 44% of the initial pool of engineers. Projected out to 40 years, about the length of 3 typical careers, the curve in Figure I seems likely to reach a cumulative total of anywhere from 65 to 85% of all engineers. These estimates of new firm creation strike us as unrealistically high. Knudsen and McTavish, for example, found that 17 to 18% of college-educated males in a probability sample of Minnesota households expressed strong interest in entrepreneurship (Knudsen and McTavish 1989). Perhaps universities with engineering programs would have data on their graduates which might provide support for the rates which have been proposed . If such support can be found, it would lend support to the model and to the findings . We also wonder about the uniform rate of enterprise creation assumed by the model. A pattern related to the business cycle seems more likely.

We think a meaningful addition to the paper would be an attempt to construct a model based on the alternative hypothesis, i.e., based on an assumption of an increasing rate of entrepreneurial activity from 1970 to 1987. For example, this might be done using an increasing entry rate and an increasing exit rate. A comparison between the model presented and this additional model might yield some useful insights.

Finally there are several questions which come to mind regarding the sample used and response patterns. First, was the response rate similar across cohorts, and among those who had and had not had entrepreneurial experience within each cohort?

Answering this question would help resolve possible concerns about reporting bias. For example, is it possible that individuals in older cohorts may under-report entrepreneurial attempts early in their careers, particularly if such attempts were of a limited nature or were unsuccessful. Members of recent cohorts might find such attempts more salient.

Next, the simulation appears to model exits and place them back in the pool of potential entrepreneurs. Prior research has noted that exits occur for many reasons, including success and failure. We wonder if those re-entrants into the pool have similar entry rates to those who have never attempted to form new businesses. It would appear that their rate of reentry might be a function of prior success or failure and other factors.

We also wonder how representative engineers are of the total population of potential entrepreneurs, and how they relate to start up rates in real estate and other industries that may not rely on engineering training.

Lastly, we raise the question of cross validation. We assume the model was built to fit the data. The arguments would be strengthened if the model were built with a portion of the data, and then shown to be valid for the balance of the data.

These few issues notwithstanding, we are encouraged by the direction of this research, and find some potentially interesting extensions that might be pursued. There are some meaningful career path questions that might be addressed with the data base at hand: What are the antecedents of recidivism among entrepreneurs?, what kinds of early career experiences, in what kinds of industries, lead to entrepreneurial behavior? There are also questions relating to differences in entrepreneurial behavior across industries that suggest interesting possibilities for future work. We encourage further pursuit of the ideas developed here.

References

Knudsen, Kjell R. and Donald G. McTavish, "Modelling Interest In Entrepreneurship: Implications For Business Development" 1989 Babson Entrepreneurship Research Conference, April 1989.

Business Creations by Quebec's Engineers: Stability of Entry from 1970 to 1987

Critique
by
Paul Reynolds, *Marquette University*

The basic objective of this paper -- to explore the tendency of individuals to purse new firm creation and the factors that affect same -- is extremely important and not well developed in the literature; there is much to be learned on this topic. The findings regarding the tendency to chose an entrepreneurial career options by trained engineers is very significant, much higher than represented in the popular wisdom. It is probably true that this is relatively stable over time for different cohorts of engineers. It is also probably true that the decision to pursue entrepreneurial options is affected by the costs of inputs (e.g. interest) as well as demand for products. This paper, however, is less than fully convincing because of a number of omissions and ambiguities.

I) The basic data is a combination of those engineers that said they had "created a firm" or "acquired an important share in an enterprise." These are quite different activities -- one is a pursuit of an entrepreneurial option, the second an investment strategy that may be entirely passive. The decision to combine these responses is worthy of some attention, at the very least, the percentage indicating each response should have been indicated.

2) The data presented in Table II is a distribution of the ages of firms that had discontinued. It cannot be used to make statements about the probability of survival for firms at different ages, as implied by the last paragraph on page 3. Quite simply, the probability of survival/death at each year must be computed by dividing the number of survivors/death by the number of active firms at the beginning of each year. That information was not provided in Table II. The fact that the patterns are generally similar -- in an empirical sense -- does not justify using the wrong type of data. This is a typical problem with using data on failed firms for analysis, without a comparison with firms that had survived.

3) The discussion of how the schedule in Exhibit III was developed is quite obscure. Further, there is ample data on the survival rates of Canadian firms provided in the Stat Can publication "Small Business in Canada: 1990" and the "Annual Report on Small Business in Ontario: 1989. These suggest that the survival rate has a quite different pattern than proposed in Table III: highest death rates in first three years. . . dropping later. This is a complex area, because the definition of "a business" and the "start date" can affect the results. Further, mixing results from industry studies, which focus on "business

entities as they enter and exit and industry" with studies of business start-ups and discontinuances may be risky.

4) The assumption of a constant rate of entrepreneurial career choices for engineers, regardless of their age, would seem to require some justification. Most studies show a considerable age influence, with participation in new firm start-ups increasing up to the mid-thirties, and then dropping off to about nil by the late 50s. This is even mentioned in this analysis.

5) It is not clear what is to be gained from the "stability" tests. The variations found are small, and could be accounted for by variance in sampling the population to achieve the mailing lists, and variance associated with the non-response of those that returned the questionnaire.

6) The efforts to explore contextual factors that affect the tendency to initiate a new firm is a move in the right direction, but are incomplete. For example, Table VI, by itself, does not "speak very clearly." To start with, it is not clear why the analysis was divided into decades. Second, the percentage of variation in incorporation rate (which is undefined -- it could be based on total businesses or total human population or total workforce, etc.) accounted for by variation in interest rates is not discussed. After all, the incorporation rate was never zero --so higher interest rates must have been offset by some other factors that suggest that the entrepreneurial career option was viable.

7) It is not clear why it is useful to assume that older engineers are starting new firms because they have become outdated and obsolete and, by implication, are escaping from competition with younger engineers. First, this assumes that engineers do not learn on the job, that work experience has no value. It is not clear that the "only" way to be current with engineering technology is to be in a university degree program. Second, these older engineers may be motivated to pursue career opportunities they cannot pursue within their existing job contexts. That is, they leave their jobs to try something else, rather than to escape "competition" with the new hires. Without better evidence, it is difficult to have confidence in this assumption.

Overall, the authors are working on an important issue and have access to some useful data, but these are complicated issues. Some of the ambiguity surrounding the details detracts from the strengths of their argument.

BUSINESS CREATIONS BY QUEBEC'S ENGINEERS:
STABILITY OF ENTRY FROM 1970 TO 1987

JEAN-MARIE TOULOUSE[1], *ÉCOLE DES HAUTES ÉTUDES COMMERCIALES*
LUC VALLÉE[2], *ÉCOLE DES HAUTES ÉTUDES COMMERCIALES*

ABSTRACT

We show in this paper that the rate of entrepreneurship among Quebec's engineers over the 1970-87 period is stable. We do so by modelling the dynamic entry and exit behavior of entrepreneurs. Our result contrasts with most of the recent literature. We also show that most of the slight and recent increase in entrepreneurial activity can be attributed to the behavior of recidivists, that is of entrepreneurs who had previous entrepreneurial experience. We also examine the rates of entrepreneurship within sectors of the economy and among individuals who graduated in different areas of engineering.

INTRODUCTION

Many authors [Blais (1987); Piore (1986); Birch (1985); Toulouse(1979)] have recently written about the waves of small firm creation over the past decades. Some of these authors believe that the eighties have seen the creation of many more firms than the previous decades. There are no strong theoretical arguments nor convincing empirical evidence to back these beliefs. Due to the lack of reliable data, it is understandable that so few authors have looked carefully at the phenomenon of firm creation. There are, however, a few exceptions: Dunne, Roberts and Samuelson (1988, 1989) for the U.S., Baldwin and Gorecki (1989) for Canada. These authors have used panel data to study the pattern of entry and exit of firms while Reynolds and Miller (1989) have used a Minnesota Bank sample.[3]

In this paper we make use of a totally unexploited and relatively rich data base to test the stability of firm creation over the period covered by our sample.[4] We

---

[1]Professor of Management, Maclean Hunter Chair of Entrepreneurship, École des Hautes Études Commerciales

[2]Assistant professor, École des Hautes Études Commerciales. The authors would like to thank Caroline Gaudette, Georges Tanguay and Serge Trépanier for valuable research assistance.

[3]P. Reynolds and B. Miller (1989), pp. 159-172.

[4]Blais (1987) has used the data set once to present preliminary results.

designed the test based on reasonable and widely accepted assumptions about the entry and exit behavior of firms. We will show that entrepreneurship among Quebec's engineers is relatively stable over time.

This paper is divided into five sections. We first discuss the data very briefly. In the second section we make some assumptions about the rate of entry and the rate of exit of firms, and derive three specific schedules of firm entry. In the third section, we compare predictions about entry, which we make based on our schedules of the actual and observed entry rates for three cohorts of entrepreneurs that have been surveyed. The fourth section presents disaggregated results where we test for the stability of firm creation among entrepreneurs in different sectors of the economy and among graduates from different fields of engineering. We then conclude.

I. THE DATA

The data used in this paper was collected in 1987 and is composed of the answers of 1087 engineers to a single page questionnaire. The engineers were chosen from three cohorts. Respectively, 284, 343 and 460 questionnaires from the 1970, 1975 and 1980 cohorts were returned and retained to construct our sample. The questionnaire was initially sent to 2638 engineers, which represents 10% of all registered engineers in Quebec. [5] The engineers were asked questions regarding their occupation and their education. They were also asked if they had created a firm or acquired an important share in an enterprise since their graduation. If they answered "yes" to that question, they were then asked where their firm was located, when it had been created and in which sector of the economy it was active.

Entrepreneurs were also asked if they had had previous entrepreneurial experience.[6] Although they were asked about their current occupation, the question and the answers were unfortunately not specific enough to determine whether the individuals were still entrepreneurs at the time the survey was taken.

We were able to compute the gross number of firms created for each cohort. This was done by adding the number of individuals who indicated that they had created a firm to the number of individuals who had acquired an important share in an enterprise. To this number we also added the number of people who admitted to have had previous entrepreneurial experience.

In addition, we obtained data on the sectors in which the entrepreneurs created their firms and each engineering specialty at graduation. We then computed the

---

[5] See Blais for more statistics on the data set. The sample originally included data on 1235 individuals but after a careful inspection of the data it was decided to eliminate the answers from some 153 questionnaires for various reasons ranging from inconsistencies to typographic errors.

[6] Other questions were asked but they are less relevant to our study.

frequency of entrepreneurial activities within each sector, and for each engineering specialty. Table I gives the frequency of entrepreneurial activities among the three cohorts in the whole sample.

TABLE I

Cohort	1970	1975	1980
Number of entrepreneurs	125	113	109
Number of engineers	284	343	460
Rate of entrepreneurship	44%	33%	24%

II. ENTRY AND EXIT SCHEDULES

Firms, as is widely known, do not have an infinite life. Apart from large companies like Exxon, IBM and GM, which are long lived, most firms have a very short life. Altman (1971, 1983) has documented the phenomenon of firm exit and the pattern of firm failure. Empirically, firm failure peaks after four years of existence.[7] There is an initial two-year period characterized by a few exits which is followed by a massive exodus in the next two to three years. In the third phase, failure gradually declines.[8] See Table II below.

TABLE II Aged of Failed Business by Function (1980)

Age in Years	Manufacturing	Wholesale	Retail	Construction	Service	All Concerns
1	0.7%	0.9%	1.1%	0.5%	1.3%	0.9%
2	8.3	8.5	11.7	5.3	11.2	9.6
3	14.6	13.4	18.2	11.1	14.6	15.3
4	12.3	16.1	16.6	15.7	14.2	15.4
5	11.4	11.5	13.3	12.8	10.6	12.4
6	9.3	8.6	8.7	9.5	8.6	8.9
7	6.7	5.9	5.5	7.9	6.8	6.3
8	4.8	5.5	4.7	6.2	5.8	5.2
9	5.0	4.4	3.1	5.4	5.4	4.3
10	3.0	4.3	2.9	4.1	3.1	3.4
>10	23.9	20.9	14.2	21.5	18.4	18.3
	100%	100%	100%	100%	100%	100%
No. of failures	1,599	1,284	4,910	2,355	1,594	11,742

Altman, E., *Corporate Financial Distress* (New York: Wiley-Interscience, 1983).

---

[7]Although Roberts (1972) has found that high technology firms appear to have a low disturbance rate of only 20% after five years, pp. 126-149.

[8]In a recent paper, Murray Frank (1989) presents a very appealing theoretical model to explain the observed pattern of firm exit.

What is the extent of firm failure? More specifically, what is the failure rate among existing firms? Using data from three U.S. Censuses (1967, 1972 and 1977), Dunne, Roberts and Samuelson (1989) found that more than 60% of firms will have failed or exited the market within five years of creation and almost 80% will have done so within ten years of creation. The results are similar to those reported earlier by Shapero and Giglierano (1980).[9] After this time, the cumulative exit rate usually stabilizes: those who make it to the ten year bench-mark will often survive, for a while at least.[10] Based on these two observations we propose the following exit and cumulative exit schedules. All rates are expressed as percentages.

TABLE III

YR.	1	2	3	4	5	6	7	8	9	10	11	12	13	14	15	16	17
XR	0	5	10	15	15	10	5	5	5	5	5	0	0	0	0	0	0
CXR	0	5	15	30	45	55	60	65	70	75	80	80	80	80	80	80	80

XR: Exit Rate; CXR: Cumulative Exit Rate

It is more problematic to derive a pattern of entry as there is neither consensus nor empirical evidence to suggest a specific pattern of firm creation. We therefore assumed a constant average annual rate of entry. However, we took into account the fact that the pool of individuals from which entrepreneurs are drawn will shrink every period as individuals engage in entrepreneurial activities.

Thus, based on the above exit schedules and a constant average rate of entry of 3.25%, we derived the entry and cumulative entry rate presented in Table IV. The difficulty in deriving such a schedule is in simultaneously accounting for the entry and exit of entrepreneurs from the pool of engineers every year: some entrepreneurs leave the pool of engineers while it is being replenished by entrepreneurs who exit entrepreneurial activities and rejoin the pool of engineers. For example, according to the schedule, in year 17, 3.25% of engineers from the pool will engage in entrepreneurial activities; this will represent, however, less than 2% of the original pool, after taking into account cumulative entry and exit. After 17 years, the cumulative rate of entry will almost be 44%. Note that, the cumulative entry rate is a gross number: It is the ratio of the total number of firms that have been created, whether they still exist or not, to the number of individuals in the initial pool of engineers. We refer the reader to Appendix 1 for an explanation of how the schedules were derived.

---

[9]Shapero and Giglierano, pp. 113-141.

[10]See also Baldwin and Gorecki (1989) for different estimates.

TABLE IV

YR.	1	2	3	4	5	6	7	8	9	10	11	12	13	14	15	16	17
ER	3.2	3.1	2.0	2.9	2.8	2.8	2.7	2.6	2.5	2.4	2.4	2.3	2.2	2.1	2.1	2.0	1.98
CE	3.2	6.4	9.4	12.	15.	18.	20.	28.	30.	33.	30.	33.	35.	41.	39.	41.	48

ER: Entry Rate; CER: Cumulative Entry Rate.

Of course, in reality, the rates of firm entry and exit for each period depend heavily on the interest rates, the current and future opportunities for business as well as many other factors that we are unable to take into account. We have to admit some randomness in the two processes. However, since we are particularly interested in cumulative entry and exit rates over long periods of time, that is, averages over 7, 12 and 17 years, this methodology makes intuitive sense.[11]

Influenced by the results of Vesper (1990) on the importance of previous experience, we derived the rate of firm reentry, that is, the probability that an engineer will resume entrepreneurial activity given that he already has one previous entrepreneurial experience. This schedule (Table V) was derived from the previous exit schedules, using a constant average rate of entry of 3.25% and under the assumption that an entrepreneur who exited the market is as likely to reenter the market as an engineer who has yet to enter it for the first time. We refer the reader to Appendix 2 for the derivation of the probability of reentry. It can be shown that the probability of a second reentry (i.e third entry) is negligible.

TABLE V

YR.	1	2	3	4	5	6	7	8	9	10	11	12	13	14	15	16	17
RR	0.0	0.0	0.0	0.1	0.1	0.1	0.2	0.2	0.3	0.4	0.5	0.6	0.6	0.7	0.8	0.9	1.
CR	0.0	0.0	0.0	0.1	0.2	0.3	0.5	0.8	1.2	1.6	2.1	2.7	3.4	4.2	5.1	6.0	7.

RR: Reentry Rate; CRR: Cumulative Reentry Rate.

We concede that these schedules are approximations of entrepreneur behavior. However, our results hold up well under different hypotheses about the pattern of entry and exit. Simulations of any pattern could easily be provided on request. We next present the simulations that we judged to be the most relevant.

---

[11]However, because we do not know the conditional means and variances of entry and exit rates at every moment in time, formal statistical tests are impossible to apply here. The standard procedure that could have allowed us to estimate the conditional mean and variance of the entry and exit rates which would have been necessary to transform the data in order to make the usual statistical inference would be difficult to apply and will be the subject of future research. We still think, however, that the results presented in this paper offer valuable insights.

FIGURE 1
cumulative entry rate

→ cum. entry rate

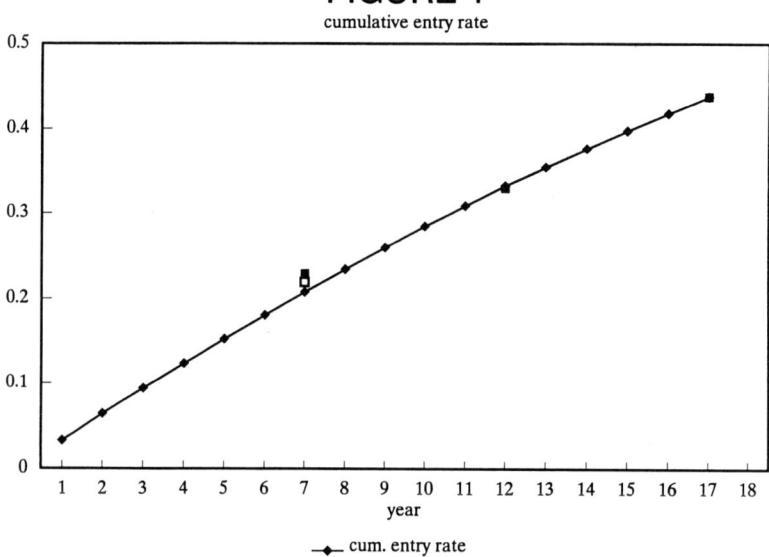

FIGURE 2
rate of entry

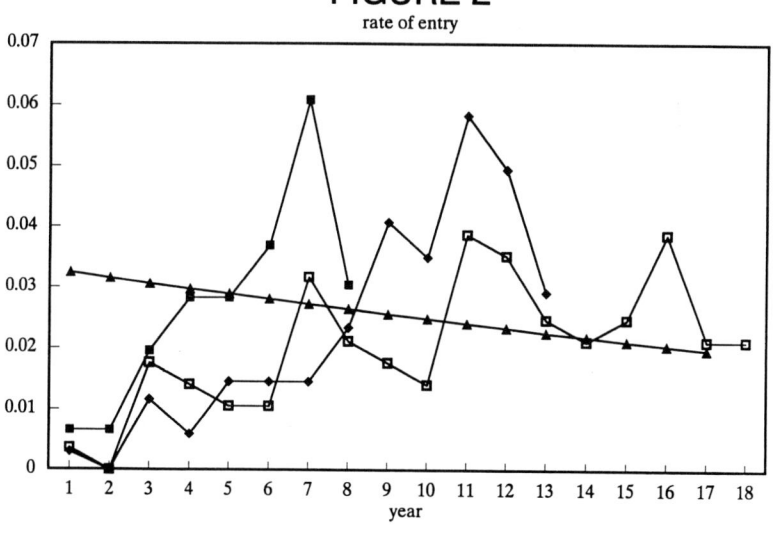

→ rate(1980)   → rate(1975)   → rate(1970)

III. STABILITY TESTS

These schedules simulate the behavior of a given imaginary cohort of engineers. These are their answers to the questionnaire as if they had been interviewed each year for 17 consecutive years. Using these constructed schedules and the observed frequency of entrepreneurial activities for the three cohorts, we will test for the stability of the different cohorts in our sample.

The intuition of the test is relatively straightforward. If the three cohorts behave as a single stable cohort, then the firm creation process among Quebec's engineers will be said to be stable over time. The test is done by simply comparing the predicted rates from our schedules after 7, 12 and 17 years with the observed rate of firm creation for the three cohorts. If the predicted values are consistent with the actual numbers, it will suggest that the behavior of the three cohorts is stable over time. On the other hand, if the actual value, let us suppose for the 1980 cohort, is above the predicted value, it will suggest that engineers from the younger cohort are more entrepreneurial than engineers from the older cohorts.

Figure 1 graphs the simulated cumulative entry schedule from Table IV. The squares in the graph each identify the observed cumulative rate of firm creation for each of the three cohorts. Clearly, the pattern of entrepreneurship appears to be stable over the period 1970-1987. The only small discrepancy is for the engineers from the 1980 cohort whose cumulative entry rate of 24% is above the schedule cumulative entry rate of 21%. This difference represents an observed constant average annual rate of firm creation of 3.75% as compared to 3.25% as predicted by our schedule.

Another way of looking at the same phenomenon is to compare the predicted rate of entry from Table IV with the actual number of firms created every year as a ratio of the total number of engineers in each cohort. See Figure 2. This particular comparison is not perfectly accurate since, among other things, the observed rates tend to underestimate the rates of real gross firm creation, especially in the earlier age of the cohorts. This is because, as noted above, the entrepreneurs who had previous entrepreneurial experience did not report the year in which they created their first enterprise.

The curves of this graph clearly show that the rates of firm creation are, in spite of very wide annual fluctuations, in line with our predictions. An interesting way of examining the graph is to hide the bottom part which is below the predicted schedule, and to only look at the upper portion of the figure. This way, the relative behavior of each cohort appears to be stable.

Figure 3 graphs the simulated reentry rates derived from the schedule presented in Table V. Again, the three squares on the graph identify the actual rate of reentry for the three cohorts. This time, the predicted pattern of firm reentry appears to be inconsistent with the observed behavior of the 1980 cohort. For this cohort, the rate of reentry is almost 2%, whereas the predicted rate of reentry for the constructed stable cohort is a mere 0.6% after 7 years of existence. The number of entrepreneurs of the 1980 cohort who had more than one entrepreneurial experience (we will call them recidivists) is 9, whereas it would have been 2 or 3 had their behavior been consistent with the behavior of the members of the older cohort.

The result is interesting for two reasons. First, it allows us to attribute most of the slight instability of the 1980 cohort detected in Figure 1 to the behavior of its recidivists. As Figure 1 shows, the cumulative rate of firm creation for the 1980 cohort, illustrated by an empty square in Figure 1, assuming that the rate of reentry is stable, is consistent with that of the other generations. In other words, we calculated the rate of entry of the engineers of the 1980 cohort assuming that the number of recidivists was 2 rather than 9. It turns out that, in this hypothetical case, the observed cumulative rate of entry would have been 22% rather than 24%. That would make the annual rate or yield of firm creation drop to *3.4%* rather than 3.75% making it almost identical to the simulated rate of 3.25%.

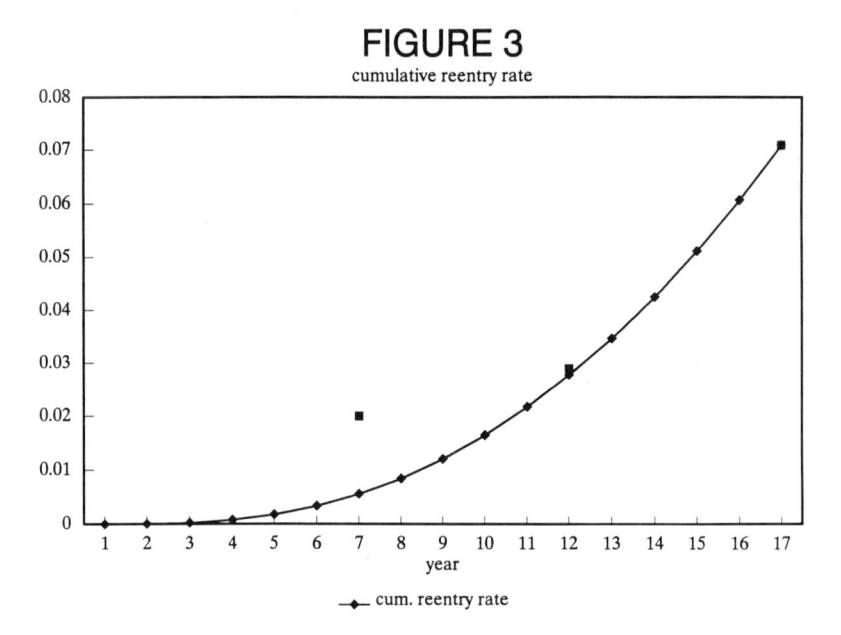

FIGURE 3
cumulative reentry rate

─◆─ cum. reentry rate

This result is also interesting because it could denote a change in society's negative attitude toward failure and those who fail. It appears that the entrepreneurs of the 1980 cohort have been better able to cope with failure, since they are more inclined than entrepreneurs from older generations to try again when they have failed. This mutation in mentality which acts as a safety net for those who fail is encouraging since, as the results suggest, most of the "productivity" gain in entrepreneurial activity over the last two decades has come from the behavior of the 1980 recidivists. This result corroborates the results of Lamont (1972); and Collins and Moore (1970), who observed that many successful entrepreneurs have gone through several start-ups, many of which failed, prior to creating a successful enterprise.

Moreover, as Vesper (1980) suggests, one learns from one's mistakes. Therefore, the entrepreneurial experience of those who failed is greater than the experience of those who have yet to try. This in turn suggests that there is a tremendous potential gain in encouraging people to try again, and that it is a terrible waste to inhibit the natural inclination of young individuals especially if, as it is likely, individuals who engaged early in entrepreneurial activities are the most entrepreneurial.

Our results contrast with those presented in a recent paper by Blais (1987) who used the same data set. In his paper he claims that "entrepreneurship among Quebec engineers is clearly on the upswing" (p.8). One reason Blais has reached this conclusion is that he failed to take into account the phenomenon of exit, the fact that some entrepreneurs had created more than one firm and that the pool of engineers was declining over time as individuals became entrepreneurs. These omissions clearly led him to overestimate the propensity of younger cohorts to create firms.

However, our results could have been anticipated by some, given the magnitude of real interest rates during the eighties. Table VI shows the relationship between the rate of new firm incorporation and the real interest rates in the U.S. since World War II.

TABLE VI

Period	1950-59	1960-69	1970-79	1980-87
Real i.r.	0.5	2	0	5
Entry rt	0.60	0.28	0.55	0.22

The numbers in Table VI speak for themselves: In the sixties and the eighties, during periods of relatively tight credit, the growth rate of firm incorporation has been considerably lower than in the fifties and the seventies when the real interest rate was almost zero.[12] Therefore, the stability of entrepreneurship over the 1970-87 period

---

[12] The new firms series was taken from Dun & Bradstreet. The series admittedly suffers from many flaws and its use has been criticized by some authors. See Evans (1987).

might even be somewhat of a surprise: Despite high real interest rates, engineers from the 1980 cohort have created, controlling for time, as many firms as their 1975 and 1970 counterparts. This may in fact signal that, ceteris paribus (i.e. had every thing else been the same), there has been an increase in the desire to engage in entrepreneurial activities in the eighties.

On the other hand, these results could mask other potential shifts in the nature of entrepreneurial activities that may have taken place over the last twenty years. In addition to cyclical changes, structural changes and several other factors might have affected the investment decisions of entrepreneurs. We address this issue in the next section.

IV. STABILITY WITHIN SECTORS AND SPECIALTIES

An interesting question is whether, in spite of global entrepreneurial stability, the nature of entrepreneurial activities has changed over the years. This could be suspected for four reasons which we have labelled below as hypotheses 1,2,3 and 4:

H1: As real interest rates increase, entrepreneurs are expected to shy away from ventures which require large initial investments. This hypothesis is termed the cyclical hypothesis.

H2: As the economy becomes more and more service oriented, entrepreneurs should be expected to create new firms in that sector and less firms in the manufacturing sector. This is the structural hypothesis.

H3: Because younger entrepreneurs are more likely to be cash constrained than older entrepreneurs, the former are expected to invest relatively less in sectors which require large initial investments, especially in sectors where business acquisitions are as frequent as business creations. This is the liquidity constraint hypothesis.

H4: Younger entrepreneurs are more likely to create firms in sectors that are closely related to their area of graduation. This is the training hypothesis.

The cyclical and structural hypotheses are both related to shifts attributable to the evolution of the economy and can be considered as exogenous factors to the firm creation process. On the other hand, the liquidity constraint and training hypotheses are more closely related to shifts attributable to changes in the nature of individuals characteristics over the life cycle of their career; these factors are endogenous to the firm creation process.

Three of the four hypotheses point in the same direction: toward more service, real estate and commercial firms, and toward less industrial and construction firms over the time period of our sample. This is because, on average, service, real estate and commercial firms require less capital investment than industrial and construction firms (H3), Canadian interest rates (H1) were rising between 1970 and 1987, as shown on Figure 4, and because the Canadian economy has become more of a service and less of an industrial or manufacturing economy over the past two decades (H2).

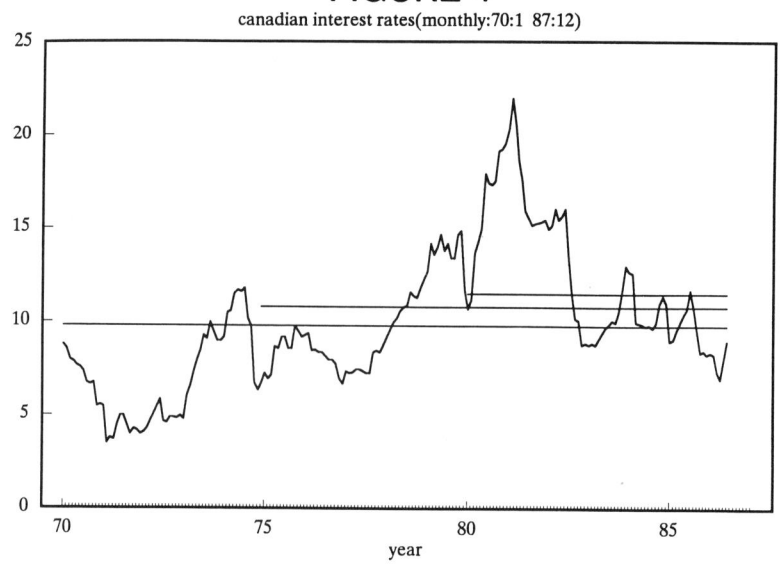

FIGURE 4
canadian interest rates(monthly:70:1 87:12)

Expectations from the training hypothesis (H4) are more ambiguous: While service (especially consulting[13]) firms can often be closely related to the skills acquired at University, the creation of real estate and commercial firms will often (especially for retail sales) require more expertise: A good knowledge of the market, a good network of contacts as suggested by Birley (1985), and an understanding of basic marketing concepts which graduating engineers are unlikely to have developed (except those holding an MBA). The creation of construction and industrial firms will also often require a substantial amount of practical experience which will mostly be very limited shortly after graduation. It may also require above average managerial skills.

We therefore expect the rate of entrepreneurship in the service sector to be higher in the eighties than in the seventies. We expect the opposite result for industrial and for construction firms. In the commercial and real estate sectors, we expect more stability, as H1, H2 and H3 suggest an increase in the pattern of firm creation in these sectors, while H4 points in the opposite direction.

It is important to note, before proceeding, that the results might be slightly biased because we do not know in which sectors recidivists created their first firms. If the training hypothesis (H4) is true, recidivists are more likely to have created service firms on their first attempt, since they are more likely to have created their first firm at a younger age than the average entrepreneur. As recidivists represent a larger proportion of entrepreneurs among older cohorts than younger cohorts (7% for the 1970 cohort versus 2% for the 1980 cohort), this could, for older cohorts, underestimate the rate of firm creation in services and overestimate the rate of firm creation in manufacturing and construction.[14]

The results are presented in the next six figures. Most are consistent with our expectations. There is, however, a big surprise in the industrial sector. In that sector, the 1980 cohort is clearly ahead of the other two cohorts, and the 1975 cohort is also clearly ahead of the 1970 cohort: The cumulative rates of firm creation for the 1970, 1975 and 1980 cohorts respectively are 2.8% after 17 years, 3.8% after 12 years, and 3.7% after 7 years (Figure 6).

As expected, there have been increasing trends in the rate of firm creation in the commercial sector (Figure 5), the service sector (Figure 7) and in real estate (Figure 9). Note, however that the rate of firm creation in the commercial sector appears as usual to be unstable: it fell during the seventies to pick up very strongly

---

[13]Over 60% of entrepreneurs involved in consulting did it in their specialty of graduation.

[14]To account for this, we estimated the number of recidivists, among the 120 from the 1970 cohorts and the 10 recidivists from the 1975 cohort, who might have created a firm in the service, based on the behavior of preceding cohorts. We showed that changes in the results were marginal. Therefore, we present our result without this correction.

in the eighties. In construction (Figure 8) and in other sectors[15] (Figure 10), there has been a recent decline in entrepreneurial activities, after a period of resurgence in the earlier years of the sample.

One may be surprised that the rate of business creation in the industrial sector does not increase with experience. Based on Lamont's (1972) results, we hypothesized that more experienced engineers would have created more industrial firms. However, our results suggest that experienced engineers create fewer firms in the industrial sector. An explanation may lie in the career progression of engineers. Previous research by Dofny (1970) has indicated that engineers are likely to follow one of two traditional career paths: They either become associates, or professional administrators in firms that are operating in traditional fields of engineering.

Our results suggest that there might exist a third alternative career path for engineers. Individuals may decide to opt out of the two traditional career patterns and use their experience as engineers to gain status by creating firms in other sectors (for example in real estate rather than in the industrial sector). This may be because they failed at becoming partners or administrators, or because their skills become obsolete. The results parallel those of Shapero (1972) who found that technical entrepreneurs create their firms around the age of 35. At that age, engineers are still relatively up to date regarding the new developments in the industry. This would explain why older engineers create fewer firms in the industrial sector.

Another explanation for this phenomenon is the recognition by universities in the early seventies of the importance of a better foundation for industrial engineering departments and their consequent creation of industrial engineering departments.[16] Our findings suggest that the creation of industrial engineering as a field of its own has had a great impact on firm creation.

Finally, we compared rates of entrepreneurship within areas of engineering. (The results are not presented in the paper). We found that entrepreneurship was on the rise for individuals who graduated in electrical or industrial engineering. On the other hand, the trends were down for mechanical and civil engineers who recently graduated, although they had been up at least until 1975. For the latter group, assuming that a large part of construction firms are created by civil engineers, these results are consistent with the results found above for the construction sector.

---

[15] The category "others" regroup social services, farming and a plethora of other firms.

[16] At l'Ecole Polytechnique, the department of industrial engineering was created in 1971. Before that, the department of mechanical engineering offered industrial engineering as an option.

FIGURE 5
industrial

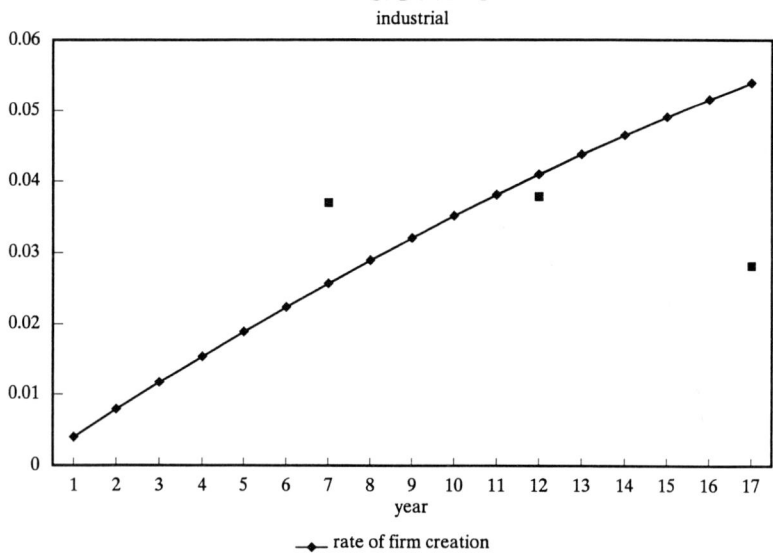

— rate of firm creation

FIGURE 6
service

— rate of firm creation

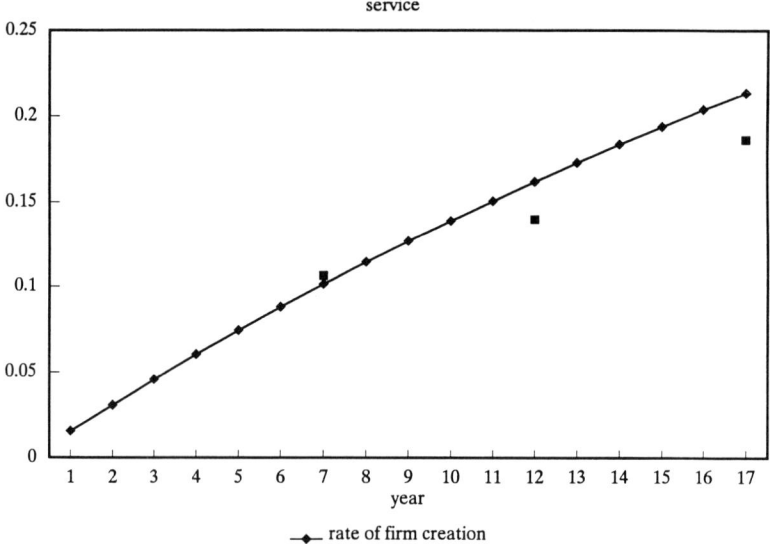

FIGURE 7
construction

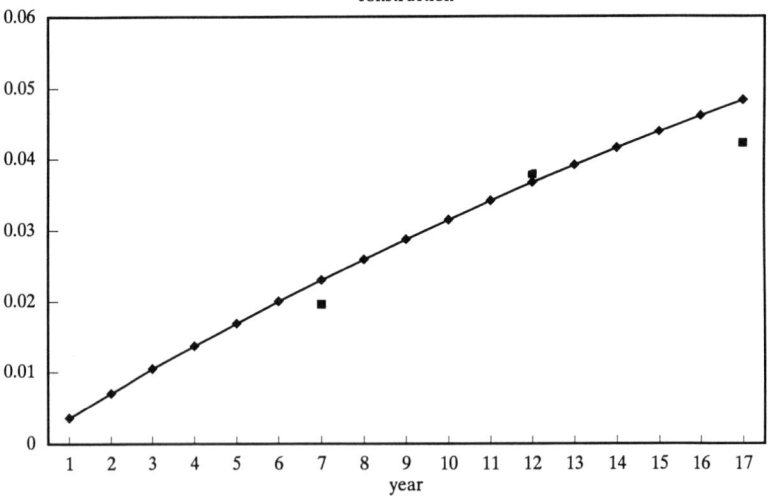

— rate of firm creation

Business Creations by Quebec's Engineers 383

FIGURE 8
commercial

rate of firm creation

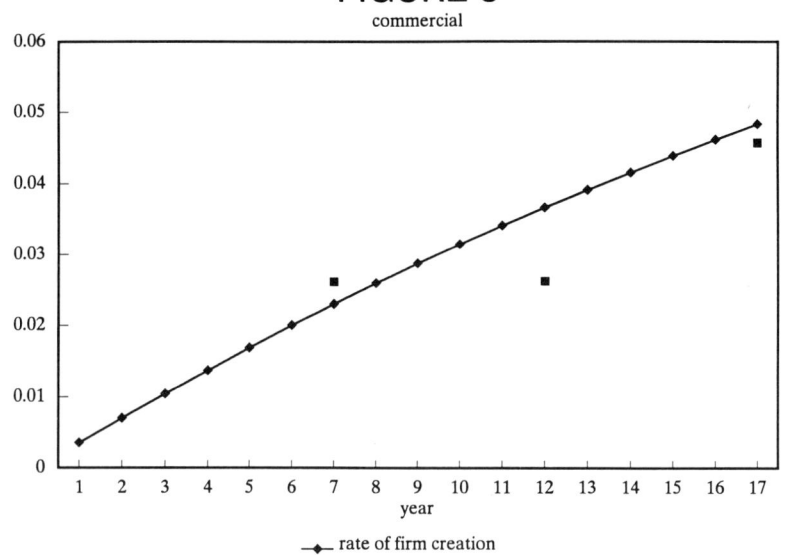

FIGURE 9
real estate

rate of firm creation

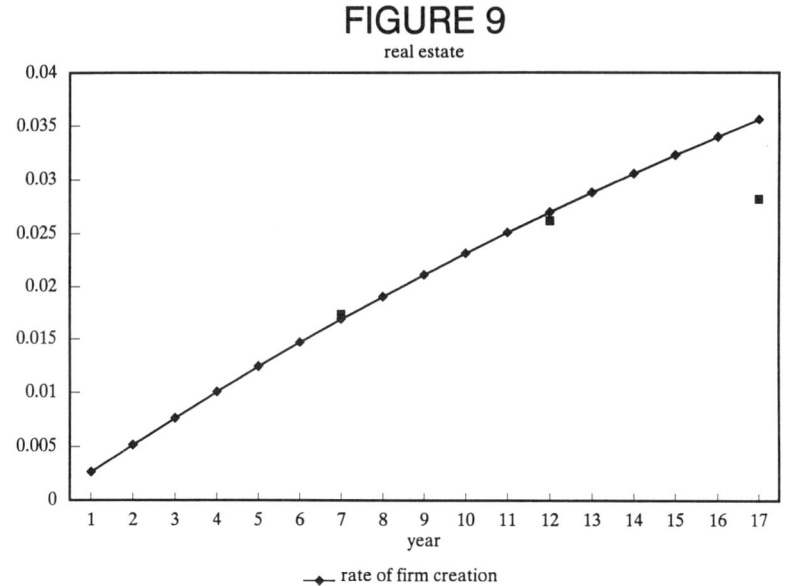

FIGURE 10
others

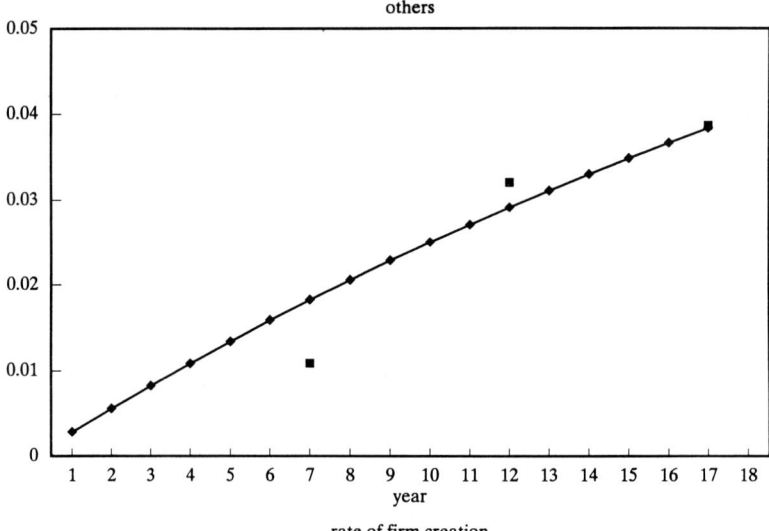

rate of firm creation

V. CONCLUSION

We have shown in this paper that the rate of entrepreneurship among Quebec's engineers over the 1970-87 period has been very stable. We have done so by carefully modelling the dynamic entry and exit behavior of entrepreneurs. Our result contrasts with most of the recent literature in indicating that the creation of businesses in a society is a pattern characterized by continuity and stability: It is not a phenomenon that will appear in a specific decade and then fade out.

We have also shown that most of the slight and recent increase in entrepreneurial activity can be attributed to the behavior of recidivists, that is to the entrepreneurs who had previous entrepreneurial experience. We offered a potential explanation for this encouraging result.

Examining the rates of entrepreneurship within sectors of the economy, we found the rate of entrepreneurship to be relatively stable, except in the industrial sector. In that sector, younger engineers are clearly ahead of the engineers from the older cohorts in the process of firm creation. We proposed two potential explanations for this phenomenon. First, many engineering schools in the early seventies set up departments of industrial engineering which appear to have been successful at encouraging entrepreneurship in the industrial sector. Second, older engineers may choose careers outside of the industrial sector as their skills become obsolete and their interests expand.

Finally, the results support the hypothesis, suggested by Toulouse (1990) that business creation is a dialectic interchange between individuals and society: when interest rates are high, entrepreneurs move into sectors where initial investments are low and when the structure of the economy moves in the direction of services, entrepreneurs create more service firms. We cannot prove which is first, but the relationship seems to stand.

APPENDIX 1

We used the following loop to calculate both probabilities. All values were initially set to zero, except for "year" which was initially set to "one" and the average rate of firm creation (the yield) was fixed at 3.25%.

PROGRAM

year = 1
yield = 0.0325

while (year < 18)
    entry rate(year) = yield * [1- cumulative entry rate(year) - cumulative exit rate(year) * yield]
    cumulative entry rate(year) = cumulative entry rate(year) + entry rate(year)
    year = year + 1

APPENDIX 2

The cumulative probability (CP) of reentry is calculated by summing the probability (P) of reentry at every period:

P(reentry in the first year) = O

P(reentry in the second year) =   P(entry in the first year)
          * CP(exit after one year)
          * P(entry in the second year)

P(reentry in the third year) =   P(entry in the first year)
          * CP(exit after two years)
          * P(entry in the third year)
          * [1-CP(reentry after two years)]

          + P(entry in the second year)
          * CP(exit after one year)
          * P(entry in the third year)

P(reentry in the fourth year) =   P(entry in the first year)
          * CP(exit after three years)
          * P(entry in the forth year)
          * [1-CP(reentry after three years)]

          + P(entry in the second year)
          * CP(exit after two year)
          * P(entry in the forth year)
          * [1-CP(reentry after two years)] --

          + P(entry in the third year)
          * CP(exit after one year)
          * P(entry in the forth year)

P(reentry in the nth year) = ...

We used the following loop to calculate both probabilities.
PROGRAM
year = 1
yield = 0325
while (year < 18)
reentry rate (year) = reemtry rate (year) + yield^2* cumulative exot rate (year
          *[1 - cumulative reentry rate (year)]
cumulative reentry rate (year) = cumulative reentry rate (year) + reentry rate (year)year
= year + 1

BIBLIOGRAPHY

ALTMAN, E. Corporate Bankruptcy in America, Lexington, Heath Lexington Books, 1971.

ALTMAN, E. Corporate Financial Distress, New York, Wiley-Interscience.

BALDWIN, J.R.; GORECKI, P.K. Firm Entry and Exit in the Canadian Manufacturing Sector», Statistics Canada - Analytical Studies Branch, no. 23, Fall 1989.

BIRCH, D.L. Job Creation in America, New York, The Free Press, 1985, 244 pages.

BIRLEY, S. The role of networks in the entrepreneurial process in J. Hornaday, B. Shils, J. Timmons and K. Vesper, Frontiers of Entrepreneurship Research, 1985, Wellesley, Mass., Babson Center of Entrepreneurial Studies, pp. 325-338.

BLAIS, R.A. «Entrepreneurship Among Quebec Engineers)., Transactions of the 2nd Canadian Conference on Entrepreneurial Studies, Kingston (Ontario), November 1987.

COLLINS, O.; MOORE, D. The Organization Maker, New York, Appleton-Century-Crafts, 1970.

DUNNE, T.; ROBERTS, M.; SAMUELSON, L. Patterns of Firm Entry and Exit in U.S. Manufacturing Industries., Rand Journal of Economics, 1988.

DUNNE, T.; ROBERTS, M.; SAMUELSON, L. The Growth and Failure of U.S. Manufacturing Plants, The Quarterly Journal of Economics, vol. CIV, Issue 4, November 1989, p. 671-698.

DOFNY, J. Les Ingénieurs Canadiens-Français et Canadiens-Anglais à Montréal", Documents de la Commission Royale d'Enquête sur le Bilinguisme et le Biculturalisme, no.6, Ottawa, 1970.

EVANS, D.S. Tests of Alternatives Theories of Firm Growth., Journal of Political Economy, vol. 95, no. 4, 1987, p. 657-674

FRANK, M.Z. An Intertemporal Model of Industrial Exit, Quarterly Journal of Economics, vol. 103, May 1988, p.333.

LAMONT, L. What Entrepreneurs Learn from Experience, Journal of Small Business, Summer 1972, pp. 3641.

PIORE, M.J. The Changing Role of Small Business in the U.S. Economy, MIT mimeo, May 1986.

REYNOLDS P.; FILLER, B. «New Firm Survival Analysis of a Panel's Fourth year in Brockhaus R. et al., Frontiers of Entrepreneurship, Wellesley, Babson College, 1989, pp. 159-172.

ROBERTS, E. Influence Upon Performances of New Technical Enterprises. in A. Cooper and J. Komives, Technical Entrepreneurship: A Symposium. Milwaukee, The Center for Venture Management, 1972, pp. 126-149.

SHAPERO A.; GIGLIERANO, J. Exits and Entries: A Study in Yellow Pages Journalism, in K. Vesper, Frontiers of Entrepreneurship Research, Wellesley Babson College, 1980, pp. 113-141.

SHAPERO, A., "The Process of Technical Company Formation in a Local Area," in Cooper, A. and Komives, Technical Entrepreneurship: A Symposium. Milwaukee, The Center for Venture Management, 1972.

TOULOUSE, J.-M. L'Entrepreneurship au Québec, Fides, Montréal, 1979.

TOULOUSE, J.-M. "L'Entrepreneurship Québécois: Nouveauté ou Continuité? in F. Dumont La Société Québécoise Après 30 Ans de Changements. Institut Québécois de Recherche sur la Culture, 1990.

VESPER, K. New Ventures Strategies, Englewood Cliffs, N.J., Prentice Hall, 1990.